An Advocate Persuades

An Advocate Persuades

SECOND EDITION

Joan M. Rocklin
Robert B. Rocklin
Christine Coughlin
Sandy Patrick

CAROLINA ACADEMIC PRESS
Durham, North Carolina

LIBRARY OF CONGRESS CATALOGING-IN-PUBLICATION DATA

Names: Rocklin, Joan Malmud, author. | Rocklin, Robert B., author. |
Coughlin, Christine Nero, author. | Patrick, Sandy, author.
Title: An advocate persuades / Joan Malmud Rocklin, Robert B.
    Rocklin, Christine Coughlin, Sandy Patrick.
Description: Second edition. | Durham, North Carolina : Carolina
    Academic Press, LLC, 2022. | Includes index.
Identifiers: LCCN 2022017813 (print) | LCCN 2022017814 (ebook) |
    ISBN 9781531019105 (paperback) | ISBN 9781531019112 (ebook)
Subjects: LCSH: Trial practice--United States. | Communication in
    law--United States. | Forensic oratory. | Persuasion (Psychology)
Classification: LCC KF8915 .M338 2022 (print) |
    LCC KF8915 (ebook) | DDC 347.73/5--dc23/eng/20220831
LC record available at https://lccn.loc.gov/2022017813
LC ebook record available at https://lccn.loc.gov/2022017814

Carolina Academic Press
700 Kent Street
Durham, NC 27701
(919) 489-7486
www.cap-press.com

Printed in the United States of America

Dedication

To our son, Sam, who we welcomed to our family as we wrote this book, and to Sol Rocklin, to whom we said goodbye.
RBR & JMR

To Jim and Henry: Although decades have passed and miles have widened since our bus stop days, our friendship, and my deep respect for you both, remains constant in my heart.
CNC

To my mom, Linda Copous, who taught me to love books, and to my lifelong mentor, Amy Blake Hearn, who inspired me to write one.
SCP

Contents

Appendices

Acknowledgments

This book would not exist without all those who read *A Lawyer Writes* and encouraged us to write a second book, one focused on the advocate. So, we must begin by thanking every professor who has adopted *A Lawyer Writes* and encouraged us to write again. The three of us who wrote *A Lawyer Writes* want to welcome Bob Rocklin, who joined us for this second journey and contributed his experience as an advocate and writer and his ever-present sense of humor to the task.

We depended on many others as we wrote. Our legal writing colleagues read initial drafts and provided us with invaluable feedback. Particular thanks go to Susan Bay (Marquette), Liz Frost (Oregon), Alison Julien (Marquette), Megan McAlpin (Oregon), Judith Miller (Lewis & Clark), and Suzanne Rowe (Oregon), for their willingness to contribute their time and energy to improve the quality, scope, and organization of this book.

Other colleagues provided us with thoughtful comments and enduring support. A hearty thank you goes to Lewis & Clark colleagues Steve Johansen, Daryl Wilson, Toni Berres-Paul, Bill Chin, Anne Villella, Judith Miller, Aliza Kaplan, and Hadley Van Vactor Kroll; to Wake Forest colleagues Jarrod Atchison, Maureen Eggert, Tracey Coan, Miki Felsenburg, Steve Garland, Barb Lentz, Hal Lloyd, Catherine Irwin-Smiler, Sally Irvin, Elizabeth Johnson, Chris Knott, Ruth Morton, Abigail Perdue, and Vanessa Zboreak; and to our friend, colleague, and expert legal writer, Lora Keenan.

The University of Oregon School of Law, Lewis & Clark School of Law, and Wake Forest School of Law also provided financial support for this work through summer research and writing grants. We also thank the Deans and Associate Deans who encourage our scholarship.

The examples within the book play a critical role in helping students see how to create an effective work product. We thank our colleagues — practicing lawyers and legal writing professors — who provided us with materials and examples: Laura Anderson, Luellen Curry (Wake Forest), Sue Grebeldinger (Wake Forest), Laura Graham (Wake Forest), John Korzen (Wake Forest), Leslie Oster (formerly, Northwestern), Terri Pollman (UNLV), Linda Rogers (Wake Forest), Jordan Silk, and Anne Villella (Lewis & Clark).

Research assistants helped us develop material and review drafts. Kamay LaFalaise, Christine Meier, Stephen Pritchard, and Ashley Sadler researched and prepared materials that assisted in ideas that developed into Chapter 1, *The Nature of Persuasion*. Rachel Tricket and Michael Goetz conducted the research that became Chapter 2, *The Ethical, Professional Advocate*. Jaime Garcia, David Giffin, and Shirley Smircic researched, developed materials, and reviewed drafts that became Chapter 3, *The Litigation Process*, and Chapter 13, *Editing and Polishing Your Persuasive Brief*.

Other students who read early drafts also provided valuable feedback. Noah Gordon, Corbett Hodson, Garrett Leatham, Kathryn Napier, and Shirley Smircic provided insightful ideas and candid suggestions as we revised each chapter. Lauren Boyd, Beth Ford, Corbrett Hodson, and David Mintz edited later drafts. We hope we have not introduced too many typographical errors since their review.

Our work, without question, draws upon the research and scholarship of respected professors and authors in our field. Again we find ourselves standing on the shoulders of giants. Michael Smith, Ruth Anne Robbins, Brian Foley, Kathy Stanchi, Ellie Margolis, Mary Beth Beazley, Linda Edwards, Ken Chestek, and Steve Johansen are but a few of the people whose words and works influenced this text. We continue to marvel at the depth and breadth of ideas offered by members of our national legal writing community. Undoubtedly, many of those ideas contributed to this book in some way. Although we have attempted to acknowledge everyone whose work contributed to this book, if we have missed someone, please forgive our unintentional error.

Several judges have substantially contributed to our understanding of persuasive writing and oral argument. Among others, we would like to acknowledge Senior Oregon Court of Appeals Judge David Schuman, Senior Oregon Supreme Court Justice Virginia Linder, Oregon Supreme Court Justice Jack Landau, and Federal Magistrate Judge John Acosta.

Once again, great thanks go to our families who sacrificed their time for this project, either by reading chapters or by carving out time for us to write and edit. In particular, Tom Malmud and Rick Coughlin read drafts and, drawing upon their experience as lawyers and readers, helped us improve our work. Others in our families adjusted their schedules, postponed events, stayed with babysitters, or just made their own suppers so that we could have more time to write, edit, or have a conference call.

Finally, we would like to thank Carolina Academic Press and the wonderful people who work there. The folks at CAP are truly our publishing family — they guided us, encouraged us, and helped us maneuver every bumpy road. Special thanks must go to Linda Lacy, our editor, and Tim Colton, the most patient typesetting expert around, for all that they did in getting this book to press. We could not have done this work without you.

Acknowledgments for the Second Edition

The only person who is educated is the one who has learned how to learn and change.

—Dr. Carl Rogers, psychologist

Just as we hope our students are always learning and open to change, we are always learning and open to change. This second edition is the result of our learning from students, colleagues, scholars in many fields, and practicing lawyers and judges.

We particularly wish to thank Matthew Blakely, Brad Doering, Nathan Dunn, Zoe Garrett, Calesta Groff, Gianni Jaramillo, Jessica Mason, and Radhika Shah, who provided research support for the second edition. Hannah Harding re-read the entire first edition and recommended edits to incorporate into the second edition.

We are also always grateful for the feedback we receive from our readers—students, professors, lawyers, and judges. We would like to thank Jennifer Babcock, Gareth Ford, Jessica Macauley, Judith Miller, Susie Salmon, Jonathan Siegel, Judge Steven Powers, and Eric Voigt, whose suggestions helped us improve both the form and substance of this second edition.

As always, thank you to Carolina Academic Press—Scott Sipe, Linda Lacy, Steve Oliva, Jessica Curtis, Rachael Meier, and Ryland Bowman—for your trust and support.

Introduction

Lawyers, in representing their clients, often ask a court to act. A lawyer might ask the court to set bail, exclude certain evidence at trial, order that one party compensate another party, or review a legal decision from a lower court. When asking the court to do something, the underlying question is this: How do you persuade a court to act in a way that benefits your client?

This book answers that question. It explains how to marshal law and facts in the way that will most likely persuade a court that the outcome you seek is justified. In other words, it teaches you how to advocate for your client, in writing and orally.

Before reading on, always remember this: Persuasive writing is not so very different from objective writing. Objective writing seeks to persuade a colleague that your legal analysis is correct. To achieve that end, your arguments must be well organized, make a clear point, and be supported by the law and facts. In addition, your colleague will be more receptive to your arguments if your arguments are presented in a polished, professional-looking document. So, too, with persuasive writing. When writing to a court, your arguments must also be well organized, make a clear point, and be supported by the law and facts. Moreover, a judge, like any other lawyer, will be more receptive to your arguments if they are polished and comply with the court's rules. Thus, when writing as an advocate, you will rely on all the skills you learned when writing objectively.

Accordingly, this book builds on your existing ability to objectively analyze a client's legal question. Here, you will learn about the subtle shift from objective analysis to persuasive argument. For example, persuasive writing usually takes the form of a brief or motion, rather than an objective memorandum of law. The briefs and motions are also directed at a different audience—judges and their law clerks. Writing for this different audience will require you to present both law and facts in a slightly different way, highlighting your strong points and explaining why weaknesses, ultimately, do not undermine your argument.

To help you make the shift from objective analysis to persuasive argument, this book begins by providing some background. In the initial chapters, this book explains what makes an argument persuasive, describes the ethical and professional responsibilities of an advocate, provides an overview of the litigation process, and introduces you to trial motions and appellate briefs.

The book then walks you through the steps necessary to build a trial motion or appellate brief and to expertly revise and polish your work. The last chapter explains how to prepare for and present oral arguments before trial and appellate courts.

Finally, the appendices provide advice if you are competing in a moot court competition and additional examples of trial motions and appellate briefs. Through these chapters, *An Advocate Persuades* provides a step-by-step guide to producing arguments that can persuade a court to act in your client's favor.

An Advocate Persuades

Part I

Introduction to Advocacy

An "advocate" is someone whose role it is to support or defend another—another person, another cause, or another idea. To be an effective advocate requires an understanding of which persuasive efforts are most likely to succeed and the limits you are required, as a member of the legal profession, to place on those efforts. The chapters that follow explore those ideas.

Chapter 1, *The Nature of Persuasion*, explores the parts of a persuasive argument. Understanding *why* an argument is persuasive makes it that much easier to build such an argument.

Chapter 2, *The Ethical, Professional Advocate*, explores the limits on your advocacy. As a lawyer you have professional obligations to be, among other things, truthful and fair. As you begin to build and explore arguments, you must take care to stay well within the boundaries of your professional obligations.

Together, the ideas in these chapters form the foundation for your work as an advocate.

Chapter 1

The Nature of Persuasion

Persuasion has been defined in various ways, but for our purposes, to persuade is to prevail on a person or persons to do something or to believe something.[1] For example, a lawyer may persuade a judge to issue a discovery order—that is, to prevail on the judge to do something. Similarly, as part of a brief, a lawyer might persuade an appellate court that the law should be interpreted or applied in a certain way.

To persuade a judge or a panel of judges, the advocate must transfer the view of the universe in the advocate's head into the head of the judge or judges before whom the advocate is appearing. Only then—when the court perceives the universe as the advocate does—will the court be moved to act in the advocate's favor.

I. Principles of Persuasion

To bring the court around to your view of the universe, your argument must take into account the three parts of persuasion: the source of the message, the content of the message, and the audience that receives the message. By understanding those three components of persuasion, and by putting each to use, you can determine how best to persuade a court. This chapter explains how the source of a message, the content of a message, and the audience hearing the message each play a part in whether a message—such as your legal argument—will be persuasive.

---

1. *See, e.g., Persuade, The American Heritage Dictionary of the English Language* https://www.ahdictionary.com/word/search.html?q=persuade (last visited Aug. 1, 2021) (defining "persuade" as "to cause (someone) to accept a point of view or to undertake a course of action by means of argument, reasoning, or entreaty").

Source, content, and audience are not, however, the only ways to think about persuasion. The field of classical rhetoric recognizes three modes of persuasion: *ethos*, *logos*, and *pathos*. *Ethos* is an appeal based on the credibility and trustworthiness of the material and the author. *Logos* is an appeal to the logic and reasoning of the listener. *Pathos* is an appeal to the emotion or passion of the listener. To effectively persuade, you will use all three principles in varying degrees depending upon your audience and the purpose of the communication.

This chapter explains the relationship between the ideas of source, content, and audience on the one hand and *ethos*, *logos*, and *pathos* on the other. It concludes by examining how those different modes of persuasion can be used in combination to persuade judges.

What Is Classical Rhetoric?

Originating in Greece around 450 B.C., classical rhetoric involved the comprehensive and systematic study of the art of persuading through written and verbal expression. In fact, Aristotle — one of the first and best known of the classical rhetoricians — defined rhetoric as the power "of discovering in the particular case what are the available means of persuasion."

Michael R. Smith, *Advanced Legal Writing: Theories and Strategies in Persuasive Writing* 11 (3d ed. 2012) (footnotes omitted).

A. Source and *Ethos*

As mentioned above, the source of a message plays an important role in persuasion. In persuasive legal writing and oral argument, *you* are the source of the message. Thus, you must ask yourself, what about *you* will enhance, or detract from, the persuasive force of your message? The short answer is this: your credibility.

"Credibility" is the "quality, capability, or power to elicit belief."[2] That is to say, whether the source of a message persuades depends on whether that source is believable. In classical rhetoric, *ethos* refers to one's character or credibility. Classical rhetoric recognizes that a speaker with a credible character is more likely to persuade.

A number of factors influence the audience's perception of the source's credibility. In some instances, you may be able to immediately influence your audience's perception of your credibility, perhaps based on the pro-

---

2. *Credibility*, *The American Heritage Dictionary of the English Language*, *supra* note 1.

fessional look of your work or by your status as a lawyer in the community. In other instances, you must wait and allow time and experience to develop your credibility before your audience. Whether or not you can take immediate action to increase your credibility, you should be aware of all the factors that will affect it.

The first factor that influences the audience's perception of the source is the source's status or position. Imagine, for example, that you are a judge. On the cover of the brief you are reading, you notice the name of the attorney who wrote the brief and the attorney's bar number. The bar number shows that the attorney is newly admitted to the bar. You then turn to an opposing brief. That brief, you observe, was written by a noted constitutional scholar.

Without doing any research, which source are you likely to find more credible? The constitutional scholar, you might agree, will have greater initial credibility. That brief will, at the outset, be more persuasive—simply because of the scholar's status as a scholar.

Although you may not be able to change your status or position overnight, you can do other things as you interact with the court that will enhance your credibility. In classical rhetoric, the three components of *ethos* are character, intelligence, and good will. By demonstrating each of those three components, a source uses *ethos* to create credibility.[3]

For example, you can employ *ethos* by demonstrating your good character. As an advocate, you establish your good character when you are consistently honest, candid, and trustworthy in all professional interactions. You must always explain the law accurately, which requires you to acknowledge any weaknesses in the facts or law that may support the other party's argument. You should also pay attention to details. Submit documents that are grammatically correct, are properly cited, and conform to court rules. Those details establish your reliability in small things and will lead the court to assume that you are also reliable in the larger issues:

> If a reader believes that a writer is, to use Aristotle's word, a rascal, that is, if a reader believes that a writer is not above lying, cheating, deceiving, or misleading, then the reader will view the writer's arguments with skepticism and doubt. Conversely, if a reader believes that a writer possesses good character—or at

> **Ethos**
>
> In classical rhetoric, the three components of ethos are character, intelligence, and goodwill. By demonstrating each component part, a source uses *ethos* to create credibility.

---

3. Michael R. Smith, *Advanced Legal Writing: Theories and Strategies in Persuasive Writing* 127 (3d ed. 2013). Smith's book gives an in-depth discussion of these three components with examples, and this chapter draws heavily from his excellent work.

***Ethos*— Establishing Credibility**

Amicus curiae (friend of the court) briefs in the United States Supreme Court must include a statement of the *amicus*'s interest in the case. In that section, most *amici* use *ethos* to establish their credibility. Consider, for example, this excerpt from a brief filed by the American Bar Association (ABA). In it, the ABA uses the breadth of its membership to establish its credibility:

> The ABA is the leading association of legal professionals and one of the largest voluntary professional membership organizations in the United States. Its membership comprises nearly 400,000 attorneys in all fifty states, the District of Columbia, and the U.S. territories, and includes attorneys in private firms, corporations, non-profit organizations, and government agencies. Membership also includes judges, legislators, law professors, law students, and non-lawyer associates in related fields.
> Since its founding in 1878,…

Brief of Amicus Curiae American Bar Association In Support of Petitioners in *Obergefell v. Hodges*, 576 U.S. 644 (2015).

As a judge, aren't you likely to say to yourself, "Gee, these folks must know what they're talking about"?

least if the reader has no reason to question the writer's character—then the reader will be more receptive to the writer's arguments and assertions.[4]

Thus, to persuade, begin by establishing and maintaining your good character.

In addition to developing a reputation as a trustworthy lawyer, you can also influence the court's perception of your credibility by demonstrating your intelligence. You can demonstrate your intelligence to the court by showing a comprehensive knowledge of the governing law and the facts of your case.[5] Such comprehensive knowledge will lead the court to believe you and to have confidence in your work product.

Finally, you can establish your credibility by showing "good will" toward others.[6] Attorneys show good will toward others in how they refer to parties, opposing counsel, the judges, or the jury. A respectful tone toward all players when writing or speaking to a court establishes your good will toward others involved in the litigation. A condescending, insensitive, or overly passionate tone can negate good will and leave the judge less favorably disposed toward you and your arguments.

To maximize your credibility through the use of *ethos*, you will want to ask yourself the following questions:

---

4. *Id.*
5. *Id.* at 155.
6. *Id.* at 144.

- Am I consistently professional, honest, and ethical in all my professional dealings?
- Do the arguments and authorities I assert accurately present the law and facts, while still representing the interests of my client?
- Does this document or oral argument reflect my competence and professionalism as a lawyer?
- Is the argument that I am presenting respectful of all parties involved in the litigation?

The Pitfalls of Being Perceived as a "Rascal"

An advocate's inaccurate statements in a brief can cause judges to become skeptical of the source of the message:

JUSTICE SOTOMAYOR: I—I have a real problem with whatever you're reading, because I'm going to have to go back to that article. I am substantially disturbed that in your brief you made factual statements that were not supported by the cited…sources and in fact directly contradicted.

I'm going to give you just three small examples among many I found. So nothing you say or read to me am I going to believe, frankly, until I see…with my own eyes the context, okay?

Oral Argument in *Glossip v. Gross*, 576 U.S. 863 (2015).

B. Content and *Logos*

Not surprisingly, *what* the source says to the audience strongly influences whether the audience will be persuaded. The content of the message obviously matters. In written advocacy before a court, the content of the message is delivered through a brief, a motion, or a memorandum in support of a motion. In oral advocacy, the oral argument delivers the content. No matter the vehicle, the content of your message should be crafted to persuade.

In crafting your message, you may try this approach: (1) Decide where you want the court to go, that is, what result you seek; (2) give the court a reason to want to go there; and (3) provide the court with a valid means of getting there.[7]

---

7. Bradley G. Clary, Sharon Reich Paulsen, & Michael J. Vanselow, *Advocacy on Appeal* 4 (3d ed. 2008); *see also* Bradley G. Clary, *Primer on the Analysis and Presentation of Legal Argument* 45 (1992) ("You have to know where you are going before you can persuade someone else to go there with you.").

To be persuasive, that content—the result you want and the means to go there—must be structured logically. The court must be able to see the relationship between the result you seek and the law and facts that support that result—and the court must want to reach the result you seek because it believes that result is the correct one.[8]

This idea brings us to the idea of *logos*. *Logos* is an appeal to logic. And logic, it has been said, is "the lifeblood of American law."[9] At its core, *logos* provides the substance of your legal argument in a clear, organized structure. In a sense, *logos* is the message's content, exclusive of the audience or the source.[10] Thus, regardless of the source and their credibility, regardless of the audience, a message must always be rationally and logically presented to be persuasive.

As a lawyer, you will invoke *logos*—that is, you will appeal to the court's logic—if you use an expected organizational structure. You likely already know the particular structures that lawyers use to present their arguments. Lawyers begin an argument by stating the issue the argument addresses or the conclusion the argument will reach. Lawyers then explain the relevant law, apply that law to the facts of the client's case, and conclude. "IRAC," "CREAC," "CRRPAP," and other organizational structures you may have learned are the mechanisms by which attorneys create rational, organized arguments—using *logos* to persuade. Because these structures play such an important role in persuading, Chapter 7, *Organizing Persuasive Arguments*, is devoted to reminding you of the logical structures attorneys use in their written work, and it provides examples so that you can see how logical, organized structures can be used for persuasive effect.

In addition to structuring your arguments in a logical way, you can also enhance the logic of your argument by emphasizing those aspects of your argument that are strongest and explaining why any weaknesses ultimately should not dissuade the court from reaching the result you seek. Chapters 5 and 6, *Developing Persuasive Arguments* and *Refining Persuasive Arguments*, explain how to craft such a message. Chapter 4, *Themes for Persuasive Arguments*, addresses how to use themes to tie the content of your message together.

---

8. Making the court want to reach a certain result includes appealing to the court's emotions through the use of *pathos*, discussed below.

9. Ruggero Aldisert, Stephen Clowney, & Jeremy D. Peterson, *Logic for Law Students: How to Think Like a Lawyer*, 69 U. Pitt. L. Rev. 1, 1 (2007). This article is both informative and witty—a great read for law students and attorneys.

10. Carole C. Berry, *Effective Appellate Advocacy: Brief Writing and Oral Argument* 49 (5th ed. 2017).

Thus, when assessing the persuasiveness of your message content, ask yourself the following questions:

- Did I organize each argument in a logical manner?
- Is each argument rational and logical?
- Is each argument supported by relevant law and facts?
- Did I eliminate extraneous arguments and include only those arguments that are strong and directly relevant for the judge to decide the case?
- Did I clearly set out and deal with any weaknesses in my client's facts or relevant law?

C. Audience and *Pathos*

The final consideration in any attempt to persuade is the audience. Who is your target audience? What use will that person or those people make of your argument? What kinds of messages might the audience be predisposed to accept? How should you craft your argument in light of your responses to those questions? To be sure, many messages are directed at diverse audiences with different goals. Most advertising, for example, is directed at a diverse audience whose members will make different uses of the message. So, while you might pay attention to that slick car commercial because you are in the market for a car, your classmate may pay attention because he wants to know what band is on the soundtrack. Advertisers have to consider a diverse audience with myriad interests when they craft their persuasive messages.

Your job as a legal advocate is, in a sense, easier. Your goal is to persuade a judge or a panel of judges; that's a fairly narrow audience. That audience will use the information you convey for only one purpose: to decide. Knowing that you have a judge audience whose goal is to decide a legal question will help you craft a more persuasive document or oral argument. At bottom, your message should be aimed at helping that audience do its job: issue a decision.

Moreover, because judges have the same goal, they share several predispositions. One predisposition that all judges are likely to share is the predisposition, discussed above, for a logically structured argument. Judges are educated, intelligent, law-trained decision makers. They have gone through the same educational system as the advocates and will thus be predisposed to "think like a lawyer." Use of *logos*—logical argument—will resonate with them.

Another predisposition that judges are likely to share is for an advocate to get to the point quickly. Judges are busy people. Federal appellate court judges read filings in approximately 1,200 cases each year. If each appellate judge were to read just the opening, opposing, and reply brief, the average judge would read 42 million words each year—and that word count does not include the pages of record, trial transcripts, and other materials appellate judges must also read.[11] Because your reader is busy, write efficiently. Tell the court what decision you seek and provide the necessary law and facts to support that decision. Include only the most important arguments rather than presenting every possible argument.

Other preferences are likely to be more specific to the court in which you are appearing or the particular judge who will be hearing the case. As an advocate, you should learn as much about your audience as possible. Although you know that your audience is law-trained, intelligent, and tasked with making a decision, there is more you can learn about the court. Is this a court that handles only Social Security matters, or is it a court that handles everything from dog bite disputes to intellectual property issues? Put differently, knowing whether your audience is composed of specialists or generalists may help you decide the amount of detail you provide. For example, if you are arguing to a specialized court or to a particular judge who you know has experience in the area, you may be able to omit background information about the law that governs the case. Conversely, if you are appearing before a generalist or a panel of generalists, you will need to begin your complex corporate income tax argument with some fundamental tax concepts.

On a more individual level, think about whether anything about the particular judge or judges before whom you are appearing will make that judge or panel of judges more or less receptive to your legal argument. If, for example, the judge before whom you are appearing has rejected your position in the past based on a certain theory, you should consider a different theory. If you are presenting a statutory construction argument, evaluate whether the judge will be more likely to rely on legislative history to interpret the statute or simply to stick with the plain language.

Personal characteristics of a judge may also be relevant to how you go about persuading. Is the judge before whom you are appearing particularly conservative or liberal, "tough on crime" or pro-defendant, sympathetic to corporate interests or sympathetic to interests of the individual person or community? Knowing that kind of information, like more general information about the court and about the court's legal preferences, will increase your ability to persuade.

Finally, remember that judges are human. That fact brings us to the third classical rhetorical device, *pathos*. *Pathos* involves persuading by appealing to the audience's emotions. Although subtle, *pathos* exerts its influence by appealing to your legal reader's emotion.

---

11. Elizabeth Olson, *Judges Push Brevity in Briefs, and Get a Torrent of Arguments*, N.Y. Times, Oct. 3, 2016, https://www.nytimes.com/2016/10/04/business/dealbook /judges-push-brevity-in-briefs-and-get-a-torrent-of-arguments.html.

The effective use of emotion involves creating a response in the audience that makes the audience want to do things your way. It means the audience not only believes at an intellectual level that you are right, but feels it at a gut level and wants to do something about it.[12]

Pathos is a powerful mode of persuasion because most people, especially legally-trained people who are taught to focus on *logos*, underestimate it. Watch, for example, any political or product advertisement. Which emotion was the advertisement designed to evoke? The political advertisement was probably designed to produce fear if the opposing party is elected and a sense of well-being based on the election of the proposed candidate. The product advertisement probably focused on happiness, love, and success based on the preferred product choice. All of these emotional appeals can be powerful and sometimes unconscious influences on your decision-making process.

With respect to your legal argument, you can use *pathos* to create a "commanding narrative"[13] that can move a judge in a variety of ways. You can use emotion to help the judge understand what motivated the parties to act or react in a particular way; emotion can help the judge understand why the outcome you seek is just or fair; and it can help the judge sympathize with your client's position.

Although most judges are trained to check their emotions—law is, after all, a *logos*-based discipline—judges are still human. They too feel anger, fear of loss, guilt, sadness, and happiness. Importantly, they want to do the right thing. Subtly invoking emotions can powerfully influence rational judgment and a judge's decision. Reminding the court, for example, that your seemingly unsympathetic client is not just a criminal "defendant," but is also a human with typical human frailties invokes *pathos*. As mentioned above, your message's content should, among other things, make a judge *want* to reach the conclusion you seek. *Pathos* is the means to do that.

Emotional appeals can be tricky, however, and should be done in an understated manner. The best way to make an emotional appeal without sounding emotional is to allow the facts to speak for themselves and to provide little to no commentary. For example, when Chief Justice John Roberts (then, attorney John Roberts) wanted to show the vital role a mine played in a remote Alaskan community, he did not say, "The Red Dog Mine is vital to the economy." Rather, he said this:

Operating 365 days a year, 24 hours a day, the Red Dog Mine is the largest private employer in the Northwest Arctic Borough,

---

12. Louis J. Sirico, Jr., & Nancy L. Schultz, *Persuasive Legal Writing* 12 (4th ed. 2015).

13. Steven D. Stark, *Writing to Win: The Legal Writer* 110 (2d ed. 2012).

> an area roughly the size of the State of Indiana with a population of about 7,000. The vast majority of the area's residents are Inupiat Eskimos whose ancestors have inhabited the region for thousands of years. The region offers only limited year-round employment opportunities, particularly in the private sector.... Prior to the mine's opening, the average wage in the borough was well below the state average; a year after its opening, the borough's average exceeded that of the State.[14]

In other words, Justice Roberts allowed the facts to speak for themselves so that the Justices who read his brief could feel the importance of the mine to the community. Without making any overtly emotional appeal, his phrasing creates a commanding narrative that helps the legal reader connect to that litigant's side of the story.

As you consider your audience, ask yourself the following questions:

- Did I structure my arguments in a way that makes the judge feel good about ruling in my client's favor?
- Did I create and explain rules, and acknowledge unfavorable rules, from my client's perspective in a manner that advances my client's argument?
- Have I effectively addressed any weaknesses in my client's facts or authority?
- Have I made my client come across as likable?
- Does my brief or document (or my oral argument) evoke the intended emotion from my audience?

II. Using the Principles Together

When writing to a court and in oral argument, you will use all of the above principles in varying degrees depending on your audience and the purpose of the legal document or argument. *Logos*—the structure of your message—is the most basic mode of persuasion attorneys use, but *logos* is intertwined with other aspects of persuasion: the substantive content of your message; your credibility as the source of the message; and the judge's predisposition to agreeing with your message. Understanding these different aspects of persuasion and how you will use them in your arguments will enhance the persuasiveness of your document or oral argument.

Different sections of your document may rely more heavily on one mode of persuasion than another. For example, you are more likely to

---

14. From Brief for Petitioner at 9, *Alaska, Dept. of Envtl. Conservation v. U.S. E.P.A.*, 540 U.S. 461 (2004) (No. 02-658), 2003 WL 2010655; *see also* Ross Guberman, *Five Ways to Write Like John Roberts*, http://www.legalwritingpro.com/articles/john -roberts/ (last visited June 7, 2021).

employ *pathos* in your statement of facts (see Chapter 10, *Statement of Facts and of the Case*), where *how* you present the facts can have a significant impact on how the court feels about your client. Your argument section likely will be more *logos*-intensive, but you should nonetheless consider how *pathos* may play into your argument. Finally, *ethos* should permeate every part of every document you prepare, from the cover to the last page; you always want the court to perceive you as a reliable, believable, and credible source.

Different types of cases and the court in which you are appearing also will affect how you use the rhetorical devices introduced above and how considerations of source, content, and audience play out. For example, there may be less room for the use of *pathos* in a technical statutory construction problem before a supreme court. But skillful use of *pathos* is indispensable if you represent a parent in a termination of parental rights case, a defendant in a criminal case, or an injured plaintiff in a tort case—especially when you are addressing a trial court.

Consciously considering how the audience will perceive you, the message you want to convey, and the needs of your audience is vital to producing a persuasive document or oral argument. Similarly, crafting your message by creating just the right mix of *ethos*, *logos*, and *pathos* will allow you to transfer your view of the case and your desired outcome into the head of the judge to whom you are presenting your argument.

As you read the rest of this book, keep in mind considerations of source, message content, and audience. Think about how the rhetorical devices of *ethos*, *logos*, and *pathos* can be used together to persuade your judge audience. Finally, always be mindful of the purpose of your argument: to make the court want to rule in your client's favor and to give the court everything it needs to do so.

Practice Points

- In any attempt to persuade, you should consider the source, the message content, and the audience. Then, craft your message accordingly.
- Always use *ethos* to enhance your credibility and make your message more persuasive.
- Use *logos* to present a well-organized, logical, and coherent argument.
- Use *pathos* to involve your audience emotionally in your message.
- Use the three rhetorical devices together to best persuade your audience.

Chapter 2

The Ethical, Professional Advocate

The majority of this book focuses on *how* to present arguments to a court; this chapter, by contrast, focuses on *who* you present to the court. In other words, this chapter focuses on you—the source of the message. Every interaction you have as an attorney, whether that interaction is with the court, opposing counsel, or a client, gives you the opportunity to demonstrate—and others the opportunity to observe—what kind of lawyer you have chosen to be. Have you chosen to be fair? Truthful? Respectful? Aggressive? Evasive? Sloppy? Your goal should be to always act as an ethical, professional, and credible lawyer.

In an adversarial setting, it is easy to get caught up in the fight and to become lax about acting ethically and professionally. This chapter serves as a gentle reminder not to leave your ethics and professionalism at the door when you transition to situations that require persuasive, rather than objective, writing.

I. Why Act Ethically and Professionally?

As you learned in the last chapter, *The Nature of Persuasion*, one reason to act ethically and professionally is because your credibility as an advocate affects the persuasiveness of your argument. A court will be more receptive to your argument if it perceives you, the source of that message, as credible. For example, if you tell the court, "Your Honor, the evidence will show that the police officers continued to question my client even after my client unequivocally invoked her right to counsel," the court must be able to assume that you have diligently investigated the facts and that you are representing those facts accurately. Although you might prevail the first, or even the second, time that you inaccurately represent the facts or the law to the court, your luck will eventually run out. When it does, you will have tarnished your credibility. Moreover, in the extreme case, it will become impossible to persuade a court of anything because you will have been suspended from practice or disbarred for unethical conduct. Thus, if your goal is to persuade courts on behalf of your clients, become an unfailingly credible resource for the court.

You should, however, keep in mind one other important reason for acting ethically and professionally: It is the right thing to do. Members of the public who seek out an attorney are vulnerable. They have an important matter they are unable to resolve. To resolve that matter, they need to enter the legal system—a system whose procedures can seem confusing and inaccessible. Ethical and professional rules protect those members of the public and the integrity of the court system. The rules ensure fairness amongst the parties before the court. Acting in an ethical and professional way—even when doing so is not required by a rule— protects us and our profession. We must face ourselves in the mirror every day, and we must interact with other lawyers nearly every day. Those everyday interactions are more satisfying and vastly easier when we act ethically and professionally.

"Ethics" and "Professionalism"

The two terms we use throughout this chapter are broad. "Ethics" at its broadest means "[a] set of principles of right conduct." *The American Heritage Dictionary of the English Language* 630 (3d ed. 1992). "Professionalism" often refers to the standards of people practicing an occupation when that occupation requires significant training and study. *See id.* at 1446 (defining "professionalism" and "professional").

Those terms can be narrowed to "professional ethics," "legal ethics," or "rules of professional conduct." Generally, those more narrow terms refer to required standards that govern a lawyer's conduct. An attorney who fails to follow those governing standards risks a disciplinary action or disbarment.

This chapter uses the broader terms—ethics and professionalism—to encourage you to think broadly about the set of principles or standards you will adhere to in your practice.

II. Some Guiding Principles

Although specific rules govern the conduct of an advocate, a few general principles will make those specific rules much easier to follow.

Here, we present a few general principles before we turn to the specific rules that govern a lawyer's conduct.

A. A "Zealous Advocate" Is Not a "Zealot"

First, understand what it means to be a "zealous" advocate. You will hear the word "zealous" bandied about a lot in the context of representing clients. Lawyers sometimes use the obligation to represent clients zealously as a justification for unethical, unprofessional, aggressive, or inappropriate behavior. Those lawyers, however, misunderstand the term.

The concept of "zeal" as a professional ethic was first introduced in 1908 when the Canons of Professional Ethics explained that a lawyer owes his client "warm zeal in the maintenance and defense of [the client's] rights."[1] But even then, the Canons took care to remind lawyers that "[t]he office of attorney does not permit, much less does it demand... violation of law or any manner of fraud or chicane. He must obey his own conscience and not that of his client."[2] By 1980, the professional code emphasized that being a zealous advocate does not change a lawyer's duty to "treat with consideration all persons involved in the legal process and to avoid the infliction of needless harm."[3]

Nevertheless, concerns arose that attorneys misunderstood what it means to "represent a client zealously." Thus, in the most recent revision, the concept of "zeal" has been replaced by the requirements of diligence and promptness.[4] The commentary to today's rules discusses the idea of "zeal in advocacy." That commentary explains that, "[a] lawyer is not bound... to press for every advantage that might be realized for a client" and "the lawyer's duty to act with reasonable diligence does not require the use of offensive tactics or preclude the treating of all persons in the legal process with courtesy and respect."[5] As one court put it, "[t]o be vigorous... does not mean to be disruptively argumentative; to be aggressive is not a license to ignore the rules of evidence and decorum; and to be zealous is not to be uncivil."[6]

Thus, "zeal" does not mean you should become a "zealot."[7] The first term means "enthusiastic diligence"; the second means "fanatic." Do not

---

1. ABA Canons of Prof'l Ethics Canon 15 (1908).

2. *Id.*

3. Model Code of Prof'l Responsibility EC 7-10 (1980).

4. Annotated Rules of Prof'l Conduct 43 (1992) ("Rule 1.3 substitutes reasonable diligence and promptness for zeal; the comment [explaining Rule 1.3 does], however,... requir[es] zeal in advocacy upon the client's behalf.").

5. Annotated Model Rules of Prof'l Conduct R. 1.3 cmt. (2007).

6. *In re Williams*, 414 N.W.2d 394, 397 (Minn. 1987).

7. *See* G.C. Hazard, Jr., & W.W. Holdes, *The Law of Lawyering* 70 (2d ed. 1990); *see also* Michael D. Murray & Christy H. DeSanctis, *Advanced Legal Writing and Oral Advocacy: Trials, Appeals, and Moot Courts* 3 (2d ed. 2014) (commenting that attorneys misunderstood the term "zeal" to mean "fanatically" or "cravenly").

confuse the two. Although others will cry "zealous advocacy" to justify boorish behavior, you know better.

Who's in Charge Here?

As you can see from the discussion about the word "zealous," the rules governing professional conduct have changed over time. Those changes can sometimes be confusing, in particular, because those changes involve a variety of "rules," "codes," and "canons." In an effort to help you sort through the different "rules," "codes," and "canons," here is a brief explanation of the rules governing the professional conduct of lawyers.

To begin, individual states adopt the rules that govern the conduct of lawyers practicing within that state. Thus, every state has its own unique set of rules governing the professional conduct of its practicing lawyers.

The American Bar Association (ABA) has, however, exerted enormous influence on the rules that each state has adopted. Since 1908, the ABA has published a set of model rules of professional conduct. As "model" rules, the ABA's rules are merely a recommended set of rules and have no binding authority. However, because most states have, to one degree or another, adopted the ABA's model rules, the ABA's rules provide a fairly good gauge for the rules that states have adopted. Over time, the ABA's model rules have changed. So that the change in names does not confuse you, here's a short history of the model rules of professional conduct.

1908 ABA adopts the Canons of Professional Ethics.

1969 ABA adopts the Model Code of Professional Conduct.

1983 ABA adopts the Model Rules of Professional Conduct.

Each new set of rules replaced the preceding set of rules. Thus, today, the ABA's recommended rules are the Model Rules of Professional Conduct. However, as mentioned above, each state is free to adopt the ABA's revisions or not.

B. Face the Facts

In your life as a lawyer, you will undoubtedly encounter facts that are inconvenient and law that is unfavorable. When you encounter an inconvenient fact or unfavorable law, you should say to yourself, "It is what it is." Face the facts. Acknowledge the law. And then explain why, despite the one or the other, your client should still prevail. If the particular facts or relevant law preclude you from arguing that your client still wins, then you must admit that conclusion. Talk to your client about the available options and, if necessary, settle or withdraw your complaint or appeal.

The alternative—ignoring inconvenient facts or unfavorable law— will ultimately do more harm than good. For example, if you avoid the undesirable facts or law, you will lose the opportunity to present them in the light that will best serve your client. Worse, if the problematic facts or law prevent you from arguing that your client should still prevail, then you will have pursued a frivolous argument, wasting your client's money and exposing yourself to sanctions. Either way, when those bad facts or contrary law come to light—and they will—your credibility will be tarnished and possibly damaged beyond repair. Thus, although skirting some facts or a part of the law may seem like a good idea in the short term, the damage to you and to your client is simply not worth it. Instead, accept "it is what it is," and take the opportunity to couch the problematic facts and law in a way that minimizes their impact.

C. "Winning" Is a Relative Term

Finally, as an advocate, you should think carefully about what it means to "win." In adversarial settings, people talk a lot about winning and losing. Trials often are conceived as battles or, if really long and drawn-out, as wars. On appeal, people win or lose, as if appeals are sporting events in which one team is a winner and the other a loser. Lawyers refer to counsel representing other parties as their opponents, and they often revel in beating them.

Although that kind of shorthand for adversarial proceedings is common and sometimes useful, try to view proceedings as something other than a to-the-death battle. Doing so helps to avoid some of the ethical and professional pitfalls that befall those who become too caught up in the battle. Avoid seeing adversarial settings as wars in which all opponents are to be mercilessly crushed, and you may also avoid the temptations to take unethical or unprofessional shortcuts.

What does it mean to win? Winning in an adversarial setting may be defined as achieving the best possible outcome for your client in light of the existing facts and law and consistent with acting professionally and ethically.

An example involving an inmate's appeal and an assistant attorney general will illustrate the point. Along the way, you will also see how an attorney can accept that "it is what it is" and still act as a zealous advocate. In that case, an inmate brought a tort action against the prison. The inmate lost and—acting *pro se*—appealed the decision arguing that the trial court judge had erroneously granted summary judgment in favor of the state. An assistant attorney general was assigned to the case to represent the state government. Upon reviewing the facts and the law, the assistant attorney general determined that the inmate was correct: The trial court had, in fact, erroneously granted judgment in favor of the state. Although a non-frivolous argument could have been made that the appellate court should uphold the trial court's judgment, it had little chance of succeeding. Worse, if the appellate court rejected the inmate's argument, there was a chance that the appellate court would announce a rule that would be detrimental to the state in the many other tort actions filed by prison inmates.

The assistant attorney general decided that the best outcome would be achieved by conceding that the trial court had erred but suggesting a rule that would benefit the state in the long run.[8] The court adopted the state's proposed rule. Although the appellate court held in favor of the inmate, the state "won" the appeal in the sense that it achieved the best possible outcome given the facts and the law.

Winning is not always about winning the case. If you carefully and objectively assess the facts and law, and make the best of what you have, you are less likely to push the boundaries of professionalism to achieve an illusory victory.

III. Specific Rules an Advocate Should Know

Although the general principles above will point you in the right direction most of the time, you can also turn to the rules of professional conduct. Each state's bar adopts rules of professional conduct that apply to members of that bar, which you can find by going to your state bar's website.[9] In most states, though, the rules of professional conduct generally follow the American Bar Association's Model Rules of Professional Conduct. Based on those model rules, here are some guidelines about how to conduct yourself as an ethical, professional advocate.

RULE	DO	DON'T
1.1	**Be competent**, which includes • Investigating the law and facts sufficiently to determine whether your client has grounds for a claim. • Submitting briefs that are organized, thoroughly researched, and supported by legal authority.	**Demonstrate incompetence by** • Failing to educate yourself about claims or arguments that your client might assert or about facts that might support those claims or arguments. • Submitting briefs that are so disorganized or unsupported by legal authority that the court is "called upon to supply the legal research and organization to flesh out a party's arguments." *Smith v. Eaton*, 910 F.2d 1469, 1471 (7th Cir. 1990)

---

8. *See Canell v. Oregon*, 58 P.3d 847 (Or. Ct. App. 2002) (adopting state's proposed rule).

9. You can find a link to the various states' rules on the American Bar Association's website: http://www.americanbar.org/groups/professional_responsibility/resources/links_of_interest.html#States.

RULE	DO	DON'T
1.3	**Be diligent**. "Diligence" is an earnest, persistent effort to accomplish the task at hand, in this case, representing your client.	Allow an ever-expanding workload (or other personal events in your life) to cause you to **neglect** a client's case.
1.3	**Be prompt** in communicating with your client and attending to your client's matter.	**Procrastinate** such that you needlessly raise your client's anxiety; undermine your client's confidence in you; or, worst of all, adversely affect your client's legal position.
1.4	**Communicate regularly with your client**, both to consult about the means of achieving your client's objectives and to keep the client informed about the status of the case.	Avoid returning phone calls, letters, or e-mails.
1.6	**Maintain confidences**. Except under limited circumstances designated in the model rules or under the law, you cannot reveal any information relating to the representation of your client.	Gossip, tell tales, or post information about your clients, especially in a manner that would allow someone to identify your client.
3.1	**Assert an argument only if it can be supported by both the law and facts.** If winning your argument would require the court to overturn existing case law or a statute, your argument must recognize that.	**Assert a frivolous argument**. A lawyer makes a frivolous argument when it is wholly unsupported by either the law or the facts of the case. Although an attorney can argue that the law should be extended to new areas or that a previous decision should be overruled, such an argument should acknowledge that it is attempting to extend or overrule current law.
3.3	**Acknowledge contrary authority from the governing jurisdiction.** Doing so is not only ethical, but is good advocacy.	**Ignore contrary authority in the governing jurisdiction.** If you find yourself thinking, "maybe the court and opposing counsel won't find this case," you're asking for trouble.
3.3	**Correct a false statement of law or fact.** You may, at some time, inadvertently state the law or a fact incorrectly, or the law may change while your client's case is being considered. In either situation, you must alert the court.	**Knowingly make a false statement of law or fact to the court.** Never stretch your reading of the law or the facts such that you are misrepresenting one or the other.
3.4	**Follow court rules.**	Fail to research and, thereby, fail to become familiar with a court's rules.
3.4	**Be fair to the opposing party and counsel.**	**Be unreasonable by** • Making frivolous discovery requests. • Failing to respond to, or delaying a response to, a reasonable discovery request. • Raising a fact or issue at trial when you believe that the fact or issue is irrelevant or inadmissible.

RULE	DO	DON'T
3.5	**Avoid improper communications** with the court, counsel, or others.	**Communicate ex parte** with the judge or jury, unless permitted or required to do so by law. "Ex parte" means the communication occurs without the other party (or counsel for the other party) being present.

If the above basic principles and specific guidelines prove insufficient, and you find yourself confronting a decision about which you are uncertain, imagine that whatever you are about to do will "go viral." In other words, imagine that anyone with an Internet connection—that is, everyone—knows about the decision you just made. Do you still feel comfortable? If you have to spend much time and effort deciding whether a proposed course of action is ethical or professionally appropriate, you probably shouldn't do it.

Finally, remember that being a decent person will go a long way toward being an ethical lawyer. As one professor of legal ethics explained, "Being an ethical lawyer is not much different from being an ethical doctor or mail carrier or gas station attendant. You should treat others as you want them to treat you. Be honest and fair. Show respect and compassion. Keep your promises."[10] A good lawyer can competently and vigorously represent a client and, at the same time, be a decent person.

Practice Points

- An effective advocate is one whom the court can rely on. Adhering to the rules of professional conduct will enhance your credibility before the court and, therefore, your effectiveness as an advocate.

- Accept the limits of the law and the facts. Advocate for your client, but do so within the limits of the law and facts.

- Be familiar with the rules of professional conduct that govern in your jurisdiction.

- At all times, "[b]e honest and fair. Show respect and compassion. Keep your promises."[11]

---

10. Patrick J. Schiltz, *On Being a Happy, Healthy, and Ethical Member of an Unhappy, Unhealthy, and Unethical Profession*, 52 Vand. L. Rev. 871, 909 (1999).
11. *Id.*

Part II

Developing Persuasive Arguments

When lawyers ask a court to do something—halt an action, reverse a decision, award damages—they must explain why the court should take a desired action. Part II discusses how to develop arguments that are most likely to persuade a court.

As explained in the introduction to this book, good persuasive writing builds on standard principles for good legal writing. Thus, often, the chapters in this part will remind you of those techniques that all legal writers should use—whether the document will be submitted to a court or not. For example, attorneys use the same organizational structures to develop persuasive arguments that they use when writing objectively. Chapter 3, *Organizing Persuasive Arguments*, explains those structures and, importantly, provides examples so that you can see how the same structures you deployed to write objectively will also support a persuasive argument. So, look closely at the text and the examples to see how the same basic principles that you used when writing objectively can be used to persuade a court.

In addition, the chapters in this part will explore those techniques that will shift your argument so that the court can see the law and the facts from your client's perspective. For example, Chapter 4, *Themes for Persuasive Arguments*, will discuss how to deploy themes to create a cohesive narrative for your client's story. Chapter 5, *Drafting Persuasive Arguments*, will explain how to write a rule broadly or narrowly, how to draft case illustrations so that the case illustrations best support your argument, and how to address arguments that opposing counsel might raise. Chapter 6, *Refining Persuasive Arguments*, will provide tips to help your argument pop from the page. Finally, Chapter 7, *Editing Persuasive Arguments*, will help you to polish your arguments before submitting them to a court.

Chapter 3

Organizing Persuasive Arguments

The previous chapters have provided you with the background necessary for the writing process. In the previous chapters you have learned about the nature of persuasion, and the ethics and professionalism required of an advocate (Chapters 1 and 2). Now, we turn to the heart of the matter: the arguments you will present to a court. After researching the law and understanding the facts of your client's case, you are likely to begin the drafting process.

The drafting process begins by thinking about how to organize the various claims and arguments you intend to present to the court. This chapter addresses how to organize those claims and arguments.

This chapter is broken down into several sections. The first section, § 3.1, addresses how to organize multiple claims and multiple arguments. Parties to litigation often raise multiple claims, and a single claim is often addressed with multiple arguments. Thus, § 3.1, *Organizing Claims and Arguments*, will be applicable to almost any argument you make. The sections that follow address how to organize particular legal arguments. Some arguments depend more on analogical arguments, some on rule-based arguments, and others on a factor analysis. Of course, some briefs rely on all three. The remaining sections of this chapter — § 3.2 through § 3.5 — explain how to organize your legal arguments whether those arguments depend on analogical arguments, rule-based arguments, a factor analysis, or some combination.

As you read this chapter and the individual sections within it, you will likely notice two guiding principles emerge: First, no matter what your argument, use a traditional structure. Lawyers — and, therefore, judges—share certain ingrained expectations about how information will be presented. If your writing conforms to those expectations, your arguments will be easier for the judge to follow and to absorb. The more your writing deviates from those expectations, the more likely the judge will struggle to follow your argument. The sections that follow describe traditional organizational structures.

Second, whenever possible, help your reader see your organization by explicitly stating how the argument ahead is organized. As an advocate, you want to carry your reader along with your argument. A judge, surprised by new information, will have to stop, go back, and figure out how it all fits together. You have just lost the judge. To avoid losing the judge along the way, be explicit about your organization.

Finally, as you read the material that follows, you may notice that the information is already familiar to you. The organizational structures you use when writing to a court are by and large the same organizational structures you use when writing an objective, interoffice memo. The purpose of this chapter is to show how those very same organizational structures can be used to present a persuasive argument.

Organizing Claims and Arguments

The first step in developing the argument section of a brief is to de-termine the order in which you will present the claims you are raising and the order of the arguments within each claim. In addition, you will want to make that order and the reason for that order clear to the court. When the court can easily follow the order of your arguments, you make it easier for the court to understand and absorb your arguments. Thus, in addition to explaining how to order your claims and arguments, this section of the book also addresses how to make that organization clear to the court.

I. Organizing Multiple Claims

A "claim" is an assertion of a right that, if proved, entitles a party to relief. Usually, litigation involves multiple claims.

At trial, if a party fails to raise all the claims arising from a single event, that party can be barred from raising that claim later. Thus, most litigation includes multiple claims. For example, an employment dispute might raise claims of breach of contract and a variety of tort claims such as intentional infliction of emotional distress, discrimination based on gender, and invasion of privacy. Usually, the different claims are governed by different law.

If you represent the responding party, you will likely respond to the claims, arguing that they are unsupported by the law or facts, and you may also have defenses to the claims. You may argue that the court lacks jurisdiction, which would be a defense to the entire claim, or you might argue that the statute of limitations has run on a particular claim. Defenses, like the initial claims, often are each governed by different law.

In this section, to keep the discussion simple, we will use the word "claim" broadly, to identify any dispositive legal issue. Whether you are the moving party, the responding party, or arguing an appeal, you will likely have to decide the order in which to address each claim or defense.

What is a "claim"?

A "claim" is an assertion of a right. Usually, litigation involves multiple claims arising from a single event. For example, an employment dispute might raise claims of breach of contract and discrimination.

In the legal world, the word "claim" is often used to refer to a plaintiff's claims listed in a complaint. Lawyers use other words to refer to other assertions of right. For example, a "defense" identifies a defendant's assertion that a plaintiff's claim is unfounded. On appeal, lawyers raise "issues" or advance "arguments" that identify trial court errors.

To keep the discussion about organizing your writing simple, this book uses the word "claims" to discuss any legal issue a lawyer raises to assert a client's right.

A. Order Your Claims

With respect to ordering claims, the default rule is simple: Address your strongest claim first. First impressions count, and you want the court's first impression to be that your arguments are strong.

That rule—that you should state your strongest claim first—is sometimes forgotten when you are writing a responding motion or brief. In that case, your opponent has set out a series of claims and chosen how to order those claims. You may be inclined to simply follow the structure established by your opponent's opening motion or brief. Do not fall into that trap! Instead, run your own race. Think about the claims *you* want to present and determine the order that will be most effective. Then, present your claims in that order.

Of course, every rule has its exception. Sometimes logic requires that one claim be addressed before others. For example, procedural issues— such as the court's jurisdiction or a statute of limitations—must be presented before the substantive claims are presented because the court cannot address the substantive issues until the procedural issues are resolved. In that situation, present the procedural issue first.

B. Tell the Reader the Order of Your Claims

As discussed above, you want to make your organizational scheme easy for the court to see and follow. You can do that by alerting the court to the order in which you are addressing the claims or defenses.

In fact, any time one unit of analysis breaks down into smaller units of analysis, you should alert your reader to that analytical fork in the road. In a persuasive document, the argument section is the largest analytical unit. That argument section often addresses several claims. When the argument section—the largest analytical unit—breaks down into individual claims—smaller analytical units—you must alert the court to that analytical divide.

A roadmap sentence will do the job. A "roadmap sentence" (or sentences) is any sentence (or group of sentences) that explains the number of smaller units that lie ahead. For example, the roadmap sentences in Example 3.1-A identify the claims that will be addressed within the argument section. In that example, the roadmap sentences are conclusions. Using conclusions to identify the issues is a persuasive tactic because it begins the process of shaping the court's thinking about the outcome of the case. Example 3.1-B illustrates a one-sentence roadmap.

Example 3.1-A • Two sentences create a roadmap for an argument section

---

ARGUMENT

Defendants John Ashcroft, in his official capacity as United States Attorney General, and Asa Hutchinson, in his official capacity as Administrator of the Drug Enforcement Agency, hereby oppose Plaintiffs' motion for a preliminary injunction. That injunction would prohibit the Attorney General from enforcing the Controlled Substances Act, 21 U.S.C. §§ 801–971, against doctors who prescribe federally controlled substances to help patients commit suicide. As explained below, the State of Oregon, the principal plaintiff in this case, lacks standing to seek an injunction against the enforcement of federal law against private parties and should therefore be dismissed from the case. Moreover, Plaintiffs cannot sustain their burden of showing both a likelihood of success on the merits and irreparable injury absent a preliminary injunction.

The last two sentences (shaded) provide a roadmap by identifying the two claims that will be addressed in the argument section.

Notice that those two sentences are stated as conclusions. Reread those last two sentences imagining that they were written instead as "the first issue is whether" and "the second issue is whether." Which formulation is more persuasive?

I. The State of Oregon lacks standing to seek an injunction; thus, the complaint must be dismissed.

The State of Oregon lacks standing to enjoin the Federal Government from enforcing federal law against private parties . . . .

Example 3.1-B • One sentence creates a roadmap for the argument section

---

ARGUMENT

The first sentence (shaded) provides a roadmap.

The text before the colon would, by itself, also be a roadmap sentence. However, the writer likely thought the sentence would be more powerful if the reasons were explained.

The plaintiff's complaint should be dismissed for two reasons: The complaint fails to state a claim, and the statute of limitations has run.

I. Plaintiff's complaint should be dismissed because Plaintiff's complaint fails to state a claim on which relief can be granted.

Plaintiff's complaint should be dismissed because Plaintiff has failed to allege conduct that is "extreme and outrageous," a necessary element of the tort.

II. Organizing Multiple Legal Arguments Within a Single Claim

After determining the order in which you will address each claim or defense, you will have to determine how to organize their constituent parts. Each claim or defense is usually governed by rules that can be broken down into elements or factors. Thus, your next organizational task is to determine the order in which to address those constituent elements or factors and to describe that organizational choice to the court.

A. Order the Arguments Within a Claim

The typical organizational structure you are likely to choose depends on whether your claim is composed of elements or factors. Below, we discuss each in turn.

1. Elements

An "element" is a condition that *must* be proved for a party to succeed in its claim. For example, to establish a claim of negligence, the plaintiff typically must prove five elements: a duty, a breach of that duty, factual causation, proximate (or legal) causation, and harm. Usually, the elements are recited in that order. Because the elements are usually recited in that way, your default assumption should be to present them in that order.

Although you will usually present your arguments in their commonly recited order, you should consider whether another order is better. If, for example, you are counsel to a defendant accused of negligence and your research tells you that your strongest argument is that the plaintiff cannot prove harm, you might start there.

Remember, though, that if you present your arguments in an order different from the order in which the elements appear in the governing rule, you will want to explain the different order to the judge in the roadmap section of that claim, as explained below in Part II.B, *Use a Roadmap Section to Tell the Reader the Order of Your Arguments.*

2. Steps

A "step" is also an element; a step, however, is an element that must be addressed within a particular sequence. That is, when a claim is composed of steps, courts have established a particular order in which the elements are to be addressed.

One common area in which you will see arguments structured around steps is in any argument involving employment discrimination or retaliation. Often, to prove that she has been discriminated against, a plaintiff will have to, first, prove a *prima facie* case of discrimination. That is, the plaintiff will have to introduce evidence that she was discriminated against because of some protected characteristic (such as race or gender) or because of some protected action (such as whistle-blowing). In the next step, the employer must come forward with some legitimate, nondiscriminatory reason for taking the action about which the plaintiff is complaining. Finally, and in the step necessary for the plaintiff to win, she must prove that the ostensibly legitimate reason provided by the defendant is "mere pretext."

When a claim is composed of steps, the organization is easy: Follow the sequence the court has established.

3. Factors

In contrast to an element or step, a "factor" is a condition that is weighed to determine an outcome. When an argument is dependent on factors, no one factor must be present for a party to win. Rather, to reach a conclusion, the decision-maker will assess the strength of each factor and the degree to which each factor weighs in favor of or against a particular conclusion.

For example, to determine whether a party entered into a prenuptial agreement voluntarily, a court may consider a variety of factors including when the agreement was signed, whether the parties had adequate opportunity to consult with a lawyer, the relative sophistication of the parties, and whether the assets of each party were sufficiently disclosed.[1]

---

1. *In re Rudder*, 217 P.3d 183, 194 (Or. Ct. App. 2009).

No one factor is determinative of the outcome. Rather, all the relevant facts are considered, and the decision-maker determines whether the agreement was entered into voluntarily based on the relative weight of the different factors.

When an analysis depends on factors, you are likely to find that the organization is less obvious. Because factors are weighed against one another to reach a conclusion, factors are connected in a way that elements are not. This connection among factors creates organizational challenges. Ultimately, you will have to choose between addressing all the factors in a single argument or addressing each factor in its own argument. Section 3.5, *Structuring Factor Analyses*, discusses in more detail these different organizational patterns and how to choose between them. For now, understand that a factor analysis can be addressed as either one legal argument, which addresses all the factors in combination, or as multiple legal arguments, in which each argument addresses just one factor.

If you address a factor analysis with multiple legal arguments, then you must decide which factor to address first. The advice for ordering a multi-factor analysis is the same as for ordering a multi-element analysis. As a default, address the factors in the same order in which they are explained in the governing rule. If, however, one factor is a particularly dominant factor that is likely to swing the analysis in your client's favor, you will likely want to address that factor first.

Again, if your arguments occur in an order different from the order explained in the governing rule, take a moment to explain the different order to the court in the roadmap section to that claim, as explained below.

B. Use a Roadmap Section to Tell the Reader the Order of Your Arguments

> **A Roadmap Section Is Not an Argument**
>
> A roadmap section tells your reader what arguments you will be making later in the motion or brief and the order in which you will be making them. The introduction does not provide the necessary legal and factual foundation to actually make the arguments.

Once you have chosen the order in which you will present the elements or factors within a claim, you must explain that order to the court by providing a roadmap section. A "roadmap section" is a more extensive form of roadmapping that differs from the roadmap sentences described above. A roadmap section is used when the smaller units of analysis share some governing law. Figure 3.1-C illustrates when you might use a roadmap section as opposed to roadmap sentences.

A roadmap section is always necessary at the beginning of a claim that is composed of more than one element or when a factor analysis addresses the factors one-by-one. A typical roadmap section to a claim includes up to five parts.

- The conclusion about the claim
- The governing rule for the claim, which identifies the constituent elements, steps, or factors, and any sub-rules

- A statement identifying any of the smaller elements or factors that
  will *not* be addressed in a full legal argument and an explanation
  of why
- A roadmap of the remaining elements or factors that will be
  addressed with full legal arguments
- A conclusion regarding what you will show about each element or
  factor for the claim as a whole

Each part is designed to give the court a look at the landscape ahead so
that it can better follow your arguments.

Although a roadmap section has up to five parts, you do not always
need all five parts. The remainder of this section briefly explains the parts
and describes when you are more or less likely to employ them.

Figure 3.1-C · Roadmap sections and roadmap sentences

Roadmap sentences vs. roadmap sections

Roadmap sections and roadmap sentences have similar functions. Both alert your reader that a larger analytical unit breaks down into smaller analytical units. Whether you use one or the other depends on the circumstances.

You use a roadmap section whenever the smaller units of analysis share some governing law. Thus, any time an argument breaks down into one or more elements or factors, you will need a roadmap section.

By contrast, you use a roadmap sentence to explain any idea that has different parts. For example, you could use a roadmap sentence to alert the reader to the number of claims in an argument. Those claims are distinct ideas, but share no governing law. Similarly, you could use a roadmap sentence to alert the reader to a court's analysis that has several parts.

---

1. Conclusion

A roadmap section begins with a conclusion for two reasons. First, a conclusion tells the court where you are headed with the series of arguments that follow, and it provides one more opportunity to remind the court of what you hope will be its ultimate conclusion. Thus, the roadmap section provides both an organizational and a persuasive opportunity. Despite the importance of an initial conclusion, some attorneys choose not to include a conclusion at the outset because it may repeat an immediately preceding point heading.

Repeating an initial conclusion in the point heading and at the outset of your argument can, however, be effective. A court may want to read just the point headings, or the court may choose to skip the point headings and read just the text. Because you do not know which way a judge will read your argument, it's best to include a conclusion at the outset even if it asserts the same idea that is in the point heading. Why lose an opportunity to help organize and persuade the court? To avoid having the same sentence verbatim, you may choose to repeat the conclusion with slightly different phrasing.

2. Governing rule

After stating the conclusion, you will usually state the governing rule. The governing rule identifies the law that will govern the claim. The governing rule can have several parts.

a. Identifies elements, steps, or factors governing the substantive claim

First, the governing rule always identifies the elements, steps, or factors that comprise the substantive legal claim. Because the governing rule identifies all the elements, steps, or factors in that claim, the governing rule provides a roadmap of the possible arguments ahead.

b. Identifies sub-rules that explain how the governing rule works

Next, the governing rule should also describe any additional rules that explain how the governing rule works. Those additional rules, or sub-rules, can explain the policy goals that animate the governing rule, whether courts typically construe the governing rule broadly or narrowly, or whether one factor is weighed more heavily than others, to name a few possibilities.

Example 3.1-D shows how one might explain a governing rule in which the lawyer wants to explain both the elements that comprise the governing rule and sub-rules explaining how that rule works. In Example 3.1-D, the first lines of shaded text explain the elements of the governing rule. The next lines of shaded text provide sub-rules that explain how courts tend to construe the governing rule. The sub-rules explain that courts have historically construed the statute "liberally…in favor of extending benefits." Together, the explanation of the elements of the statute and the sub-rule explain the "governing rule."

Example 3.1-D · Roadmap section includes additional explanation about the governing rule

---

The Workers' Compensation Board improperly denied workers' compensation benefits to Mr. Mark Floyd, and its decision should be reversed. Under California law, a person injured during an off-duty recreational activity is entitled to workers' compensation if the activity was a reasonable expectancy of employment. Cal. Lab. Code Ann. § 3600(a)(9) (West 2011). An activity is a reasonable expectancy of employment if (1) the employee subjectively believed he was required to participate in the activity and (2) the employee's belief was objectively reasonable. *Meyer v. Workers' Comp. Appeals Bd.*, 204 Cal. Rptr. 74, 76 (Ct. App. 1984). In assessing whether an activity is a reasonable expectancy of employment, California courts liberally construe the statute in favor of extending benefits. Cal. Lab. Code Ann. § 3202 (West 2003).

Governing rule explained.

Additional information about how courts interpret governing rule.

In this case, Mark Floyd subjectively believed he was required to participate in the paddleball game and his belief was objectively reasonable. He is therefore entitled to workers' compensation benefits.

The tricky part in explaining the governing rule is determining whether you need to provide any sub-rules. The decision to include a sub-rule depends on whether the sub-rule addresses the governing rule as a whole or whether the proposed sub-rule addresses just one part of the governing rule. In Example 3.1-D, the sub-rule explains that a California statute is liberally construed. That rule is relevant to all the elements of the governing rule. By contrast, it would not be appropriate, in the introductory roadmap, to provide a rule explaining how a court determines whether a subjective belief is reasonable because that rule applies to only the second element. More specific rules that focus on just one element (step or factor) should be explained later, in the argument that addresses that one element (step or factor).

When you include sub-rules that explain how the governing rule works, you have a choice about the order in which to describe the governing rule. You may begin the explanation of the governing rule by describing its constituent elements, steps, or factors. Doing so is, perhaps, the most typical way to begin explaining the governing rule.

Sometimes, however, you may want to shape your explanation of the governing rule by first explaining some aspect of how the governing rule works. In Example, 3.1-E the writer emphasizes the policy animating the governing rule by describing that policy first.

Example 3.1-E · A governing rule that begins with the rule's underlying policy

Conclusion ⟶ Allegheny University's motion for summary judgment must be denied because Allegheny University is violating Title IX. Summary judgment may be granted only when no material fact is in dispute and the moving party is entitled to judgment as a matter of law. Fed. R. Civ. P. 56(a).

The writer begins the description of the governing rule by explaining the legislature's goals when enacting the statute.

Congress enacted Title IX to remedy discrimination against women, a group historically underrepresented in intercollegiate athletics. *Cohen v. Brown Univ.*, 991 F.2d 888, 894 (1st Cir. 1993). In enacting Title IX Congress sought to ensure that women were afforded "opportunities to enjoy the thrill of victory [and] the agony of defeat…." *Neal v. Bd. of Trs.*, 198 F.3d 763, 773 (9th Cir. 1999).

After explaining the policy that animates the statute, the writer explains what the statute and its regulations require.

⟶ Under Title IX, "[n]o person in the United States shall, on the basis of sex, be…subjected to discrimination under any education program or activity receiving Federal financial assistance…." 20 U. S.C. § 1681(a). Under the regulations interpreting Title IX, a university violates Title IX if it fails to "provide equal athletic opportunity for members of both sexes." 34 C.F.R. § 106.41(c) (2020).

c. Identifies procedural governing rules

Finally, a complete governing rule may include both a substantive component and a procedural component. The substantive component of a governing rule is the explanation of the elements, steps, or factors comprising the legal claim and any sub-rules. Those parts were described above.

The procedural aspect addresses any particular rules the court must address given the procedural posture of the case. For example, if the court is addressing a motion for summary judgment, you will need to explain both the elements of the claim and the standard for summary judgment. Both the substantive and procedural rules govern the legal claim and are, therefore, part of your governing rule. Example 3.1-F shows the same introductory roadmap section as in Example 3.1-E, but

Example 3.1-F also includes rules that address the procedural posture of the case.

Example 3.1-F • A governing rule that includes both procedural and substantive law

Allegheny University's motion for summary judgment must be denied ◄— Conclusion
because Allegheny University is violating Title IX. Summary judgment may be
granted only when no material fact is in dispute and the moving party is ◄— Governing procedural rules
entitled to judgment as a matter of law. Fed. R. Civ. P. 56(a).   describe the standard for
                                                                       granting a motion for summary
    Title IX, for its part, requires that "[n]o person in the United States shall,   judgment.
on the basis of sex, be…subjected to discrimination under any education
program or activity receiving Federal financial assistance…." 20 U. S.C. §   The writer explains the
1681(a). In enacting this statute, Congress sought to eliminate discrimination ◄— governing substantive rules in
against women in intercollegiate athletics. *Cohen v. Brown Univ.*, 991 F.2d 888,   the second and third
                                                                        paragraphs.
894 (1st Cir. 1993). More specifically, Congress sought to ensure that women
were afforded "opportunities to enjoy the thrill of victory [and] the agony of
defeat…." *Neal v. Bd. of Trs.*, 198 F.3d 763, 773 (9th Cir. 1999).
    Under the regulations interpreting Title IX, a university violates Title IX if it
fails to "provide equal athletic opportunity for members of both sexes." 34
C.F.R. § 106.41(c) (2020)….

3. Disposing of uncontested elements or factors

When reading the governing rule, a judge will instinctively break that rule down into its elements, steps, or factors. The judge will then expect that each element, step, or factor will be addressed with a full legal argument. If you are not going to meet that expectation, alert the judge. An element, step, or factor named in the governing rule will not warrant a full legal argument if that element is clearly met or not disputed, or if the factor clearly weighs in favor of one party. When you are the moving party and an element is clearly met or a factor clearly weighs in your favor, you may want to quickly establish the element or the factor[2] in the roadmap section and then move on, as in Example 3.1-G.

---

2. When an element is clearly met or a factor clearly favors your client, you may decide to establish that element or factor in the roadmap section and then move on. However, for persuasive effect you may decide to nevertheless address the factor or element in a separate legal argument. Doing so may emphasize the strength of your case. Especially with factors, you may want to create a separate argument for each factor. Because factors are weighed against each other and courts may consider the strength of each factor, you may want to take the opportunity to elaborate on the extent to which the factor weighs in your client's favor.

Example 3.1-G • Roadmap section disposes of elements that are clearly met

Rabbi Davis cannot be compelled to testify. Under New York law, a "minister of any religion," is prohibited from disclosing a "confidence made to him in his professional character as a spiritual advisor," if the privilege has not been waived. N.Y.C.P.L.R. § 4505 (McKinney 2007). The statute is construed liberally to encourage people to feel comfortable in talking with their ministers. *In re Fuhrer*, 419 N.Y.S.2d 426, 430 (N.Y. Sup. Ct. 1979). In this case, the defendant, Ms. Schlomberger, has not waived her privilege. Moreover, as explained in his affidavit, Rabbi Davis is an ordained rabbi, and the senior rabbi at Beth El Israel Synagogue. Rabbi Davis thus qualifies as a "minister of any religion." Thus, the only questions before this court are (1) whether the conversation between Rabbi Davis and the defendant was confidential and (2) whether Rabbi Davis was acting in his professional character as a spiritual advisor. As explained below, all the evidence shows that the conversation was confidential and that, during that conversation, Rabbi Davis was acting in his capacity as a minister. Thus, Rabbi Davis cannot be compelled to testify against Ms. Schlomberger.

Here, the moving party disposes of two elements — "waiver" and "minister of any religion" — because both are clearly met and there will be no dispute about them.

The moving party then maps the remaining argument.

In addition, an element, step, or factor does not warrant a full legal argument when you must concede the element or factor or the moving party has already conceded that element or factor. Conceding a part of an argument is, of course, a delicate task. You do not want to strengthen the opposing party's position by emphasizing weaknesses in your own position. Thus, when you must concede an element or factor, sometimes the best route is to simply focus the court's attention on what is at issue, rather than discussing what is not at issue, as in Example 3.1-H.

Example 3.1-H • Roadmap section focuses on disputed elements only

Mr. McCabe is entitled to an order of dismissal because the evidence, viewed in the light most favorable to the State, is not legally sufficient to prove that Mr. McCabe is guilty of burglary in the first degree. To establish burglary in the first degree, the state must prove that the defendant "knowingly enter[ed] or remain[ed] unlawfully in a dwelling with intent to commit a crime therein," and as is relevant to this case, "when, in effecting entry or while in the dwelling or in immediate flight therefrom, he...[was] armed with explosives or a deadly weapon..." N.Y. Penal Law § 140.30(1) (McKinney 2010).

As explained more fully below, the evidence is not legally sufficient to show that Mr. McCabe "knowingly entered or remained unlawfully" in Ms. McCabe's home or that he "intend[ed] to commit a crime" either when entering or remaining in her home. Ms. McCabe had previously provided Mr. McCabe with a key to her home and, as he had often done before, while waiting for Ms. McCabe to return home, Mr. McCabe ate some of the food in the home, while waiting for Ms. McCabe to return home. These facts are insufficient to prove burglary in the first degree.

By failing to contest two elements — whether the house was a dwelling and whether he was armed — the defendant has conceded those elements.

Alternatively, you may decide to more explicitly concede a factor or element as in Example 3.1-I.

Example 3.1-I · Roadmap section disposes of a set of factors that the party must concede and then focuses on the factors in dispute

Competitive cheer, as it is structured at Central State University of Utah, is not a sport for purposes of Title IX compliance. To determine whether an athletic opportunity constitutes a sport, the Office of Civil Rights examines the activity's program structure and administration, and then the activity's competitive opportunities. In balancing these factors, the Office of Civil Rights has urged that more weight be given to an activity's competitive opportunities. In *Beidiger v. Quinnipiac*, the only case yet to consider whether cheer is a sport, the court followed this approach giving particular weight to the availability of competitive opportunities, noting that the quality of competition is "highly important, if not essential, to the varsity experience." 728 F. Supp. 2d 62, 100 (D. Conn. 2010). In this case, the parties agree ⟵ that the program structure and administration of competitive cheer at Central State are sufficient. However, Central State cannot show that the competitive opportunities are sufficient to provide its program with the competition "essential to the varsity experience." For that reason, competitive cheer cannot currently be considered a sport for purposes of assessing a university's compliance with Title IX.

Plaintiff concedes that Central State's program and administration of competitive cheer is sufficient to comply with Title IX requirements for determining which activities constitute an athletic opportunity.

After disposing of factors that must be conceded, plaintiff maps the arguments that remain.

By contrast, if the opposing party concedes an element, step, or factor, you may take a moment to emphasize that point, as in Example 3.1-J.

Example 3.1-J · Roadmap section notes that the opposing party has conceded factors and then addresses factors in dispute

Competitive cheer at Central State University of Utah is a sport for purposes of Title IX compliance. The Office of Civil Rights assesses six factors to determine whether an activity is a sport. The first three factors assess the program's structure and administration. The remaining three factors assess the activity's competitive opportunities. These factors were developed to allow a university to expand its athletic program by including sports "not yet recognized by governing athletic organizations" such as the NCAA. Each activity is assessed on a case-by-case basis.

Plaintiff concedes the first three factors. First, Plaintiff concedes that Central State provides its cheer team with an operating budget, support services, and coaching staff equivalent to that of other established teams. Second, Plaintiff concedes that Central State recruits competitive cheerleaders and provides them athletic scholarships consistent with established varsity athletes. Third, Plaintiff concedes that Central State provides its cheer team with practice opportunities equivalent to opportunities provided to its established teams.

Introduction emphasizes that the plaintiff has conceded that a series of factors weigh in favor of the defendant.

Because an analysis of the remaining three factors shows that Central State's competitive cheer team also has sufficient competitive opportunities, competitive cheer at Central State should be deemed a sport for purposes of Title IX compliance.

Finally, if all the elements or factors in the governing rule need to be supported by a legal argument, you will not dispose of any component of the governing rule.

4. Mapping the remaining arguments

Next, you will want to consider whether you need to map the remaining arguments. You will need to map the remaining arguments under two circumstances.

First, you will need to map the remaining arguments if you have disposed of an element or factor. For example, if an element or factor is clearly met and therefore unlikely to be contested (as in Example 3.1-G) or if one of the parties has conceded the element or factor (as in Example 3.1-I), then you will want to set out which elements or factors remain. Mapping the remaining arguments helps to reorient the court because a judge may have difficulty remembering which elements or factors remain in play. Providing a roadmap will allow a judge to keep reading rather than going back to the governing rule to figure out what remains.

Second, you will need to map the remaining arguments if you have changed the order of the arguments from the order in which they were presented in the governing rule. As this chapter explained earlier, if one element or factor presents a particularly strong argument for your client, you may want to argue that element or factor first. If so, you will want to make sure that the judge is prepared to read the arguments in a different order from the one the governing rule established, as in Example 3.1-K.

If either of those two circumstances exist, then you will map the remaining arguments. When you "map" the remaining arguments, you are simply using "roadmap sentences," described above in Part I.B, to explain the order of the remaining arguments.

Example 3.1-K · Map the remaining arguments

Serving raw fish and meats to diners is an ultra-hazardous activity, and Bellisimo Food Corporation must be held strictly liable for the damages that resulted from that activity. Under Illinois law, the court, not a jury, determines whether an activity is ultra-hazardous. *See Miller v. Civil Constructors, Inc.*, 651 N.E.2d 239, 244 (Ill. App. Ct. 1995). In its determination, the court must analyze six factors to determine whether an activity is ultra-hazardous:

1. The existence of a high degree of risk of some harm to the person, land, or chattels of others;

2. The likelihood that the resulting harm will be great;
3. The inability to eliminate the risk by exercise of reasonable care;
4. The extent to which the activity is not a matter of common usage;
5. The inappropriateness of the activity to the place where it is carried on; and
6. The extent to which the activity's value to the community is outweighed by its dangerousness.

Id.

Of the above factors, Illinois courts give the third factor—the inability to eliminate risk by exercise of reasonable care—the most weight. Id. All six factors weigh in favor of finding that serving raw fish and meats is an ultra-hazardous activity. However, because the third factor is weighted most heavily, the analysis begins there.

> The introduction alerts the court that the argument will address the third factor first and explains why.

If, however, you have not disposed of any part of the governing rule and if you will address each part of the governing rule in the same order in which it was identified in the governing rule, then the governing rule will itself act as a roadmap and there is no need to create a second roadmap.

5. Final conclusion

Finally, in a persuasive argument, your roadmap section should include a final conclusion about what you will prove about the remaining elements or factors, or about what you will prove about the claim as a whole. Doing so will remind the court of the direction you are headed and the conclusion you want the court to reach.

6. Order of the parts

Typically, your introductory roadmap will follow the order described above:

- Conclusion
- Governing rule
- Dispose of aspects in the governing rule that won't be addressed in the argument section
- Map the remaining arguments
- Conclude again

Following that order is always a good place to start.

Sometimes, however, you may need to vary the order of the parts. For example, you may need to vary the order of the parts as your governing rule becomes more complex. When the governing rules become more complex, you may want to dispose of certain aspects of the governing rule as you are explaining the governing rule rather than waiting until you have finished explaining the governing law. In Example 3.1-L, the writer walks the court through the procedural and substantive law that governs a Title IX claim. The substantive law includes rules derived from statutes and regulations. Because the explanation of the governing rule is lengthy (it spans five paragraphs), the writer disposes of some aspects of the governing rule as soon as that aspect is explained rather than waiting until the lengthy explanation of the governing rule is over.

Example 3.1-L • A more complex governing rule in which the writer disposes aspects of the rule along the way

Conclusion ⟶

Here, the writer disposes of one-half of the standard for a motion for summary judgment by ⟶ acknowledging no issue of material fact exists.

Defendant Allegheny University's motion for summary judgment must be denied because Allegheny University is violating Title IX. Summary judgment may be granted only when no material fact is in dispute and the moving party is entitled to judgment as a matter of law. In this case, no material fact is in dispute; however, Allegheny University is not entitled to judgment as a matter of law because the undisputed facts establish that Allegheny University discriminates against its female athletes in violation of Title IX.

Congress enacted Title IX to remedy discrimination against women, who have been historically underrepresented in intercollegiate athletics. *Cohen v. Brown Univ.*, 991 F.2d 888, 894 (1st Cir. 1993). In enacting Title IX Congress sought to ensure that women were afforded "opportunities to enjoy the thrill of victory [and] the agony of defeat…." *Neal v. Bd. of Trs.*, 198 F.3d 763, 773 (9th Cir. 1999).

Here, the writer disposes of the issue of whether the defendant is "an educational program…receiving federal financial assistance." ⟶

Title IX requires that "[n]o person in the United States shall, on the basis of sex, be…subjected to discrimination under any education program or activity receiving Federal financial assistance…." 20 U. S.C. § 1681(a). As an accredited university that receives federal funds, Allegheny University must comply with Title IX.

Here, the writer disposes of nine of ten factors, explaining that in the type of case now before the court, courts typically examine only the first of the ten ⟶ enumerated factors.

Under the regulations interpreting Title IX, a university violates Title IX if the university fails to "provide equal athletic opportunity for both sexes." 34 C.F.R. § 106.41(c) (2021). To determine whether a university provides "equal athletic opportunities," courts may consider up to ten factors. *Id*. However, when the issue before the court is whether the number of athletic opportunities (as opposed to the quality of those athletic opportunities) are equal, federal courts usually consider only the first of the ten factors. *Mansourian v. Regents of the University of Cal.*, 602 F.3d 957, 964-65 (9th Cir. 2010). The first factor states that universities provide unequal athletic opportunities if "the selection of sports and levels of competition [do not] effectively accommodate the interests and abilities of members of both sexes." 34 C.F.R. § 106.41(C)(1).

Finally, the writer implicitly disposes of one of the three tests used to determine whether a university "effectively ⟶ accommodates the interests and abilities of its students" on the ground that defendants never raised the third test in defense of its actions.

A university effectively accommodates the interests and abilities of its students only if satisfies at least one of three tests. Intercollegiate Athletics: Sex Discrimination, 44 Fed. Reg. 71,413, 71,418 (Dec. 11, 1979). At trial, Allegheny argued that it complied with Title IX under both of the first two tests. Under the first test, a university shows that it "effectively accommodates" the interest and abilities of both sexes if it can show that "participation opportunities for male and female students are provided in numbers substantially proportionate to their respective enrollments." *Id.* Under the second test, a university shows that it "effectively accommodates" the interest and abilities of both sexes if it can show "a history and continuing practice of program expansion [that] is demonstrably responsive to the developing interests and abilities of members of the [underrepresented] sex." *Id.*

Allegheny University meets neither of these two tests. The university is not offering substantially proportionate athletic opportunities, and it cannot prove a history and continuing practice of program expansion. Thus, Allegheny is violating Title IX and is not entitled to judgment as a matter of law. ◄——————

> The writer concludes the introductory roadmap by mapping the remaining two arguments and stating the ultimate conclusion the court should reach.

Sometimes you may also want to end your roadmap section with the map of what is to come rather than by stating the ultimate conclusion you would like the court to reach. You are likely to want to end your introductory roadmap section with a map of what is to come when you address the arguments in an order other than the order explained in the governing rule. In Example 3.1-M, the ultimate conclusion is stated in the second-to-last sentence while the map of what is to come is in the final sentence.

Example 3.1-M • An introduction in which mapping the arguments to come is the last step

Serving raw fish and meats to diners is an ultra-hazardous activity, and Bellisimo Food Corporation must be held strictly liable for the damages that resulted from that activity. Under Illinois law, the court, not a jury, determines whether an activity is ultra-hazardous. *See Miller v. Civil Constructors, Inc.*, 651 N.E.2d 239, 244 (Ill. App. Ct. 1995). In its determination, the court must analyze six factors to determine whether an activity is ultra-hazardous:

1. The existence of a high degree of risk of some harm to the person, land, or chattels of others;
2. The likelihood that the resulting harm will be great;
3. The inability to eliminate the risk by exercise of reasonable care;
4. The extent to which the activity is not a matter of common usage;
5. The inappropriateness of the activity to the place where it is carried on; and
6. The extent to which the activity's value to the community is outweighed by its dangerousness.

Id.

Of the above factors, Illinois courts give the third factor — the inability to eliminate risk by exercise of reasonable care — the most weight. *Id.* All six factors weigh in favor of finding that serving raw fish and meats is an ultra-hazardous activity. However, because the third factor is weighted most heavily, the analysis begins there.

> The writer returns to the ultimate conclusion.

> The writer maps the order of the arguments.

III. Introducing Sub-Arguments

Just as a roadmap section explains the order in which you will address the arguments within a claim, you will sometimes need a roadmap section to explain the order in which you will address sub-arguments. Whenever an element or step within a claim breaks down into two or more smaller elements or factors, you will need a roadmap section to alert the court to the structure ahead. Figure 3.1-C, above, illustrates where you would place a second roadmap section in the event that one element splits into two smaller elements or factors.

The potential parts of a roadmap section mid-claim are the same as those for a roadmap section at the outset of the claim: A conclusion (to that element), the governing rule (for that element), dispose of any sub-elements that will not be addressed, and state the conclusion for the element. Figure 3.1-C, above, illustrates an argument with a roadmap section in the middle of a single claim, as does Example 3.1-N.

Example 3.1-N · A roadmap section mid-claim

B. Mr. Floyd's subjective belief that he was expected to play paddleball with his supervisor was objectively reasonable.

Mark Floyd reasonably believed that he was expected to participate in the paddleball game with his supervisor. To determine whether an employee's subjective belief is objectively reasonable, California courts usually weigh three factors: (1) whether the employer was involved in the activity, (2) whether the employer benefited from the activity, and (3) whether the employer pressured the employee to participate. *Meyer v. Workers' Comp. Appeals Bd.*, 204 Cal. Rptr. 74, 76 (Ct. App. 1984). In this case, Fitness Functions was involved with the paddleball game; Fitness Functions benefited from the game; and, given the circumstances, Mr. Floyd felt pressured to join the game.

IV. Organizing a Single Legal Argument

Once you have introduced a single claim and identified the elements or factors that make up that claim, you must then structure the individual arguments that address each element or factor. The parts of a single legal argument and their order are no different when writing a persuasive brief to a court than when writing an objective memorandum. That single legal argument is made up of four parts:

- A conclusion
- An explanation of the law
- An application of the law
- A final conclusion

You may have learned this argument structure by using a mnemonic such as IRAC, CREAC, CREXAC, or CRRPAP. All of those mnemonics describe the same structure, albeit with different vocabulary, as illustrated in Table 3.1-O. Example 3.1-P illustrates that structure in a very short motion to dismiss.

Table 3.1-O · One legal argument; various mnemonics

	IRAC	**CREAC**	**CREXAC**	**CRRPAP**
Conclusion	Issue	**C**onclusion	**C**onclusion	**C**onclusion
Explain the law	**R**ule	**R**ule	**R**ule	**R**ule
		Explanation	**Ex**planation	**R**ule **P**roof
Apply the law	**A**pplication	**A**pplication	**A**pplication	**A**pplication
Conclusion	**C**onclusion	**C**onclusion	**C**onclusion	**P**rediction

Example 3.1-P · A single legal argument

This case is moot and should, therefore, be dismissed. A case is moot if ◄— Conclusion
there is no justiciable controversy. *State v. Hauskins,* 281 P.3d 669, 672 (Or. Ct.
App. 2012). A justiciable controversy exists only when the interests of the
parties to the action are adverse and the court's decision in the matter will have ⎤— Explanation of the law
some practical effect on the rights of the parties to the controversy. *McIntire v.*
Forbes, 909 P.2d 846, 850-51 (Or. 1996) (internal quotation marks omitted).

This case is moot because Ms. Peterson has already received that which
she sought—the return of her two dogs, Peaches and Tango, which were
previously seized by a Klamath County animal control officer. The attached ⎤— Application of the law
agreement, which Ms. Peterson signed, demonstrates that Ms. Peterson's dogs,
Peaches and Tango, have been returned and are once again residing in the
Peterson household. Because the appellant has received that which she sought,
the parties no longer have any interests that are adverse and any ruling by the
Court would have no practical effect. The case should be dismissed as moot. ◄— Final conclusion

Judges, like other attorneys, will expect to see legal arguments structured in this same way. Accordingly, you will reduce confusion and make your arguments easier for a judge to absorb if you, too, structure each legal argument in this way: conclusion, explanation of the law, application of the law to facts, and conclusion.

Developing the arguments within your brief is a multi-step process. The first step is to simply determine a framework within which your arguments will sit. This section of Chapter 3, *Organizing Claims and Arguments*, provides guidance so that you can develop a framework appropriate for the claims or defenses you will present. It also provides guidance so that you can make your organizational choices known to the court.

After you order your claims or defenses and order the individual legal arguments that make up the claim, the next step is to begin developing the individual legal arguments within each claim. Sections 3.2 through 3.5 address how to structure each legal argument, whether that argument is based on analogical or rule-based reasoning.

Practice Points

- Use a traditional structure to organize your arguments.
- Provide a roadmap at the outset of the argument section if your argument section addresses more than one claim.
- For each claim, make your organizational structure clear:
  - Create a roadmap section for each claim.
  - Divide the claim in a way that is appropriate for its component pieces, whether those component pieces are elements or factors.
  - Structure each argument so that it has a conclusion, an explanation of the law, an application of the law, and a final conclusion — in that order.

Structuring Analogical Arguments

Analogical reasoning is the hallmark of "thinking like a lawyer." An analogical argument asserts that a client's case raises the same legal issue as a prior case and is factually similar to that case. It then asserts that, because of the factual similarity, the same legal outcome is warranted in a client's case. Alternatively, an analogical argument can assert that a client's case is factually distinct and, because of the distinction, the prior case should not direct the outcome in the client's case. Either way, the heart of an analogical argument is a factual comparison to a prior case. Once the comparison is established, the legal outcome follows.

A persuasive analogical argument follows the same structure as an objective analogical argument. That structure is outlined in Table 3.2-A, and Example 3.2-B allows you to see that structure in action.

Table 3.2-A • An analogical argument's typical structure

Basic Framework	Analogical argument
Conclusion	• Conclusion
Explain the law	• Explain rules relevant to the element or factor being examined. • Explain factually similar prior cases that address the same legal issue. Your description should focus on the facts, holding, and rationale that led the court to reach its conclusion about the element or factor being examined.

Apply the law	• Compare the prior case to client's case.
	  ◦ If the prior case and your client's case are similar
	    ▪ Establish the factual similarity, and
	    ▪ Establish the legal outcome that results from the similarity.
	  ◦ If the prior case and your client's case are distinguishable
	    ▪ Establish factual distinction, and
	    ▪ Explain that, therefore, the precedent is inapplicable and an alternative conclusion is warranted.

Conclusion	• Conclusion

Example 3.2-B · An analogical argument

Conclusion

The explanation of the law begins here.

   The trial court correctly concluded that Ms. Moran did not voluntarily execute the premarital agreement. A wife voluntarily executes a premarital agreement only if she signs the agreement without being coerced, intimidated, or unduly pressured. *In re Rudder*, 217 P.3d 183, 193 (Or. Ct. App. 2009). In addition, she must have "some modicum" of knowledge of the terms of the agreement and the property affected. *Id.* at 194. To determine whether the wife

The rules explain, among other things, the factors that the court must consider.

entered the agreement voluntarily and had the appropriate degree of knowledge, courts look at a variety of factors: (1) the timing of the agreement in relation to the wedding, (2) whether the assets were sufficiently disclosed, (3) the relative sophistication of the parties, and (4) whether the complaining party had adequate opportunity to consult with independent counsel. *Id.*

The case illustrations—*In re Rudder* and *Coward*—address all the factors that the court considered and then explain how the court weighed those factors to reach its conclusion.

   A wife does not enter a premarital agreement voluntarily if the agreement is provided one day before the wedding, the agreement does not disclose assets, the wife is unsophisticated, and an attorney is not present. *Id.* at 194-95. In the *Rudder* case, the husband, an electrician, and the wife, a cosmetologist who had owned a beauty salon, discussed in general terms a pre-marital agreement a few weeks before the wedding. *Id.* at 194. The husband's attorney drafted the

Persuasive case illustrations have the same parts as objective case illustrations. Notice that the writer begins each case illustration with a hook (shaded), explaining the point the court should learn from the prior case. The writer then explains the trigger facts, the court's reasoning about those facts, and the court's holding.

agreement, which the wife first saw the day before leaving for the wedding. Although she had asked that her attorney be present when she signed the agreement, her attorney was not. Her husband urged her, "[g]o ahead and just sign it. The wedding is on." *Id.* After reading through the agreement, which did not list all the husband's assets or their value, the wife signed the agreement. *Id.* On these facts, the court determined that the circumstances created a coercive environment. *Id.* In discussing the wife's relative business sophistication, the court of appeals agreed with the trial court that "although...[the] wife had some experience in business matters, that experience was limited and she was relatively unsophisticated in financial matters." *Id.* at 195. Therefore, the wife did not enter into the agreement voluntarily. *Id.*

   By contrast, an experienced businesswoman who has an opportunity to know her husband's assets and is provided with an agreement more than two weeks in advance, can enter into the premarital agreement voluntarily. *In re Coward*, 582 P.2d 834, 835 (Or. Ct. App. 1978). In the *Coward* case, the couple signed the pre-marital agreement seventeen days before the wedding. *Id.* At that time, the husband's attorney advised the wife to seek independent counsel. *Id.* The wife, who had worked as a bookkeeper and assisted her husband with his financial affairs, declined to speak with an attorney and signed the agreement. *Id.* The court concluded that the wife had had sufficient opportunity to consult with an attorney, was an experienced businesswoman, and was aware of her husband's property. *Id.* Accordingly, the court held that the wife voluntarily signed the pre-marital agreement. *Id.* at 836. Although the 1978 *Coward* case was decided before the 1987 enactment of Oregon Revised Statutes § 108.725, the legislature intended § 108.725 to codify existing case law; therefore the *Coward case* still stands as an example of "voluntariness." *See Rudder*, 217 P.3d at 192.

Ms. Moran did not enter into her premarital agreement voluntarily. She is an unsophisticated businesswoman who had limited time before the wedding to review the document. Moreover, the agreement did not disclose her future husband's assets, and she was unable to consult with an attorney.

These facts are similar to the facts in *Rudder*, in which the court found the agreement was not signed voluntarily. First, <u>in both cases the agreement was signed within days of the wedding.</u> In *Rudder*, it was one day before the wedding, and in this case, it was five days. Although Ms. Moran had a few more days to consider the agreement, the time span created pressure. In *Rudder*, the pressure was evidenced by the husband's urging the wife, "[g]o ahead and just sign it. The wedding is on." In this case, Ms. Moran stated that, "she didn't want to wait to find an attorney, not with so many people traveling so far." Thus, in this case, as in *Rudder*, the shortened time span created pressure and did not leave adequate time to consult with an attorney. Moreover, <u>like the wife in *Rudder*, Ms. Moran is not a sophisticated businesswoman</u>. As an office manager she has the approximate business experience of a cosmetologist who owned a beauty salon, and the *Rudder* court decided that the business-owner was not a sophisticated business person. In addition, Ms. Moran, like the wife in *Rudder*, <u>was not told the value of her husband's assets</u>. Finally, although Ms. Moran was advised to speak with an attorney, that one fact should not outweigh the other facts that are similar to the facts in *Rudder*. Those facts show a pressured environment in which Ms. Moran did not have sufficient time to fully assess the agreement. For these reasons, this Court should reach the same conclusion that the *Rudder* court did: The agreement was not entered into voluntarily.

Defendant's reliance on *Coward* is misplaced. The wife in *Coward* had previously reviewed her husband's finances; thus, she understood the value of her husband's assets. In this case, no evidence indicates that Ms. Moran was aware of the value of her husband's assets. Her lack of knowledge of her husband's assets, the lack of evidence that her job as an office manager would allow her to assess the value of his assets, and the compressed time span of only five days in which to decide whether to sign the agreement support the trial court's conclusion that she signed in an coercive environment. She, therefore, did not sign voluntarily.

The application begins here.

Note the careful fact-to-fact comparison. For each comparison, the writer first asserts what is similar. (The overt statement of similarity is underlined.) The writer then describes the specific facts that prove that similarity exists.

*The writer is also careful to use parallel structure when describing similar facts to bring out the similarities between the client's case and the *Rudder* case.*

Finally, the last sentence explains how these similarities lead to a particular conclusion.

These are all the same devices used to create an effective objective analogical argument.

Addressing a counter-argument

Final conclusion

As you can see, the same structure that effectively develops an objective analogical argument also effectively develops a persuasive analogical argument.[1]

An analogical argument is often the strongest argument you can develop because an analogical argument relies on stare decisis. "Stare decisis" is the principle that a court should reach the same conclusion as a prior court when presented with the same legal issue and the same facts

---

1. Should you want to review in more detail how to construct an effective analogical argument, review section 8.2 in *A Lawyer Writes*. *See* Christine Coughlin, Joan Malmud Rocklin & Sandy Patrick, *A Lawyer Writes: A Practical Guide to Legal Analysis* 147–61 (3d ed. 2018).

as presented in the prior case. This principle will almost always persuade a court to follow its own precedent.

Although an analogical argument is a powerful tool, sometimes you do not need all the strength of an analogical argument and sometimes you have no similar prior case to rely on. In those circumstances, as §7.3 explains in greater detail, a rule-based argument is appropriate.

Practice Points

- A persuasive analogical argument uses the same structures as an effective objective analogical argument.

  ◦ A persuasive analogical argument states a conclusion about the element, step, or factor at issue.

  ◦ It explains both the rules and case illustrations relevant to that element, step, or factor.

  ◦ The application establishes how the facts of the client's case are similar to (or distinguishable from) the facts of a prior case and explains how that similarity or distinction leads to a particular conclusion.

  ◦ It repeats the initial conclusion at the end of the argument as a way to sum up and emphasize the conclusion.

Section 3.3

Structuring Rule-Based Arguments

I.   A Simple Rule-Based Argument
II. Statutory Construction Arguments
III. Policy Arguments
IV. Syllogisms

In addition to relying on analogical arguments, attorneys also rely on rule-based arguments. In a rule-based argument, an attorney asserts that a conclusion is warranted by comparing the facts of a client's case directly against a legal standard (i.e., the rule). Such an argument follows the structure in Table 3.3-A.

Table 3.3-A • A rule-based argument's typical structure

Basic Framework	Rule-based argument
Conclusion	• Conclusion
Explain the law	• Explain the rules relevant to the element or factor being examined.
Apply the law	• Apply the rules to the facts of your client's case.
Conclusion (if necessary)	• Conclusion

I. A Simple Rule-Based Argument

A very simple rule-based argument might look like the argument in Example 3.3-B. In the example, notice how key language from the rule is repeated in the application. That juxtaposition of key concepts from the rule against facts from the client's case is the technique that makes a rule-based argument persuasive.

Example 3.3-B • An effective rule-based argument uses the language of the rule in the application

---

The rule is explained here. Its key concepts are highlighted.

This case is moot and should, therefore, be dismissed. A case is moot if there is no justiciable controversy. *State v. Hauskins,* 281 P.3d 669, 672 (Or. Ct. App. 2012). A justiciable controversy exists only when the interests of the parties to the action are adverse and the court's decision in the matter will have some practical effect on the rights of the parties to the controversy. *McIntire v. Forbes*, 909 P.2d 846, 850-51 (Or. 1996) (internal quotation marks omitted).

The application begins here. Notice how the key concepts are repeated and aligned with the facts.

This case is moot because Ms. Peterson has already received that which she sought—the return of her two dogs, Peaches and Tango, which were previously seized by a Klamath County animal control officer. The attached agreement, which Ms. Peterson signed, demonstrates that Ms. Peterson's dogs, Peaches and Tango, have been returned and are once again residing in the Peterson household. Because the appellant has received that which she

Final conclusion

sought, the parties no longer have any interests that are adverse and any ruling by the Court would have no practical effect. The case should be dismissed as moot.

Example 3.3-C • A rule-based argument that does not use the language of the rule in the application is less effective

---

The rule is explained here. Its key concepts are highlighted.

This case is moot and should, therefore, be dismissed. A case is moot if there is no justiciable controversy. *State v. Hauskins,* 281 P.3d 669, 672 (Or. Ct. App. 2012). A justiciable controversy exists when the interests of the parties to the action are adverse and the court's decision in the matter will have some practical effect on the rights of the parties to the controversy. *McIntire v. Forbes*, 909 P.2d 846, 850-51 (Or. 1996) (internal quotation marks omitted).

The application begins here. Notice how the key concepts are not repeated.

Ms. Peterson has already received that which she sought. The only relief Ms. Peterson sought was the return of her two dogs, Peaches and Tango, which were previously seized by a Klamath County animal control officer. The attached agreement, which Ms. Peterson signed, demonstrates that Ms. Peterson's dogs, Peaches and Tango, have been returned and are once again residing in the Peterson household. Because the appellant has received that which she sought, no ruling by the Court is necessary, and the case should be dismissed as moot.

Repeating key language from the rule in the application, as in Example 3.3-B, allows the court to easily see how the facts of the case align with the rule and lead to the desired outcome. In Example 3.3-C, however, counsel did not rely on the language of the rule in the analysis. Do you see how Example 3.3-C is less compelling because the application does not re-integrate key language from the rule?

An attorney relies on a rule-based argument in one of several situations. Sometimes a sufficiently similar prior case does not exist. In that case, the attorney has no choice but to develop a rule-based argument.

Attorneys will also develop a rule-based argument when the legal issue is simple and unlikely to be contested. In that case, the attorney does not need the firepower of an analogical argument, and a rule-based argument will usually establish the point much more efficiently than an analogical argument. Why waste your time and the court's time comparing detailed facts, when the point can be made effectively and much more quickly?

Finally, in some cases, the facts of your particular case are not relevant or necessary to the resolution of the legal issue in dispute. For example, in a statutory construction argument, the specific facts of a client's case are not central to the argument because the question revolves around the meaning of the statutory language and the legislature's intent when it enacted the statute. In such a case, a method of argument in which the facts are central would be inapt.

Table 3.3-A, above, illustrates a very simple rule-based argument. However, rule-based arguments are also used to present more complex arguments. In particular, statutory construction arguments and policy-based arguments are, at their heart, rule-based arguments. Although more complex, the persuasiveness of those arguments also depends on showing the court how key concepts from a legal standard line up against other evidence. Let's look.

II. Statutory Construction Arguments

In a statutory construction argument, the parties are asking a court to determine the meaning of particular words in a statute.[1]

As mentioned above, a statutory construction argument is a more complex rule-based argument. In a simple rule-based argument the rule and its meaning are known. Thus, the court's—and the advocate's— only task is to apply that rule to the facts. In a statutory construction argument the rule is a statute, and that statute is susceptible to more than one interpretation. Your task is two-fold. First, you must argue to the court what the legislature intended the statute to mean when the legislature enacted the statute. Then, you must apply that clarified rule to the facts of your case. Both steps involve rule-based reasoning. Let's look at each step more closely.

The first step—arguing how a rule should be understood—constitutes the bulk of a statutory construction argument. In this first step, you must help the court determine the legislature's intent when it enacted the statute.

---

1. Although this section refers to "statutory" construction, the concepts it discusses apply similarly to construing administrative rules, ordinances, and constitutional provisions.

Because courts are repeatedly asked to construe the meaning of a statute, most jurisdictions have developed a particular methodology to determine the legislature's intent. Although the steps vary somewhat from jurisdiction to jurisdiction, most courts use the same tools. First, the court will analyze the plain meaning of the text. Next, the court will analyze the text in context—that is, the court will analyze the text in light of the larger statutory scheme. Finally, the court will consider other evidence of the legislature's intent when enacting the statute, such as statements made at committee hearings or during floor debates.[2]

At each of these steps, a court might use a "canon of construction" to assess the meaning of a statute. A canon of construction is simply a traditional way that words, a sentence, or a paragraph are to be understood. Table 3.3-D provides some common canons of construction that courts use.

Table 3.3-D · Textual canons of construction[3]

1. **Canon regarding the plain meaning rule**
   - "If language is plain and unambiguous it must be given effect."

2. **Canons regarding specific words**
   - "May" is permissive; "shall" is "mandatory."
   - "And" is conjunctive; "or" is "disjunctive."
     - Example: "fruits, seeds, nuts, vegetables, honey, sheep, cattle, pigs, *and* poultry." A person must produce all of these things to come under the statute. Change "and" to "or," and a person would have to produce only one of them.

3. **Canons regarding ambiguous modifiers**
   - "A modifier or exception applies only to the last antecedent in a phrase or list."
     - Example: "Employees shall be paid base wages, environmental hazard pay, and overtime <u>as determined by the lead agency to be consistent with private sector practices</u>." Under this canon, the underlined phrase modifies only "overtime," the last antecedent; if, however, a comma had followed the word "overtime" the underlined phrase would have modified all three kinds of compensation listed.

4. **Canons regarding lists of things**
   - **Noscitur a sociis:** Interpret an ambiguous word in a list by the company it keeps, that is, in light of the surrounding words.
     - Example: "pigs, cattle, sheep, and poultry." Does "poultry" include exotic birds?

---

2. For a more complete discussion of statutory construction arguments, *see* Christine Coughlin, Joan Malmud Rocklin & Sandy Patrick, *A Lawyer Writes: A Practical Guide to Legal Analysis* 193–209 (3d ed. 2018).

3. These examples of canons have been frequently used over the years. The original source of the examples is unknown.

- **Ejusdem generis:** General, catch-all phrases at the end of a list are construed to mean the same kind or type as the rest of the list. If "motor vehicle" is defined as a "car, truck, or any other self-propelled vehicle not designed for running on rails," does it include an airplane? A motorized scooter?
- **Expressio unius, exclusion alterius:** The enumeration of specific things implies the exclusion of all others. If the word is not in, then it is meant to be out.
  - Example: "rain, sleet, and hail" excludes snow.

5. **In pari materia:** Statutes with the same subject or purpose should be read together to effectuate that purpose.
   - Example: A statute setting out the punishment for kidnapping should be read in conjunction with a statute setting out sentencing guidelines for felonies.

A statutory construction argument is, essentially, a series of nested rule-based arguments. Example 3.3-E provides a statutory construction argument.[4] It highlights some of the key rules and shows how those key rules are then applied to the statutory text and other evidence before the court.

Example 3.3-E · A statutory construction argument

ARGUMENT

The indictment against Mr. Hidalgo must be dismissed because Arizona's anti-human smuggling statute was never meant to be used to prosecute individuals who were smuggled. Under Arizona's anti-human smuggling statute, it is "unlawful for a person to intentionally engage in the smuggling of human beings for profit or commercial purpose." Ariz. Rev. Stat. Ann. § 13-2319 (2010). In human smuggling, there are only two "person[s]" involved: the smuggler (also known as the "coyote") and his human cargo. The question before this Court is whether the person to be prosecuted under this statute is only the smuggler or whether the person to be prosecuted also includes the human cargo.

To answer that question, this Court must construe the word "person." When construing the text of a statute, Arizona courts must ascertain the legislature's intent when it enacted the statute and give effect to that intent. *Wyatt v. Wehmueller,* 806 P.2d 870, 872 (Ariz. 1991). To do so, Arizona courts begin their analysis with the plain text of the statute. *State v. Christian,* 66 P.3d 1241, 1243 (Ariz. 2003). The plain text of the statute is the "best and most reliable" indication of a statute's meaning. *Id.* If the court finds the plain text of § 13-2319 ambiguous, the court may next look to the text in context, the legislative history of the statute, and the historical context of the statute. *Id.*

This paragraph is the roadmap section for the statutory construction argument. The roadmap section explains that the governing rules for this analysis are Arizona's rules of statutory construction. The arguments that follow each address one step in Arizona's rules of statutory construction.

---

4. A special thanks goes to Professor Anne Villella at Lewis & Clark School of Law who developed this issue and to Alexis Curry who drafted an earlier version of this example. This example is based on prior Arizona law and may not reflect recent changes to the statute.

In this case, the text in context, its legislative history, and the historical context surrounding enactment of the statute all establish that the legislature never intended the prosecution of the human cargo. Accordingly, Mr. Hidalgo should not be prosecuted under § 13-2319, and the charges should be dismissed.

A. The plain text of Arizona Revised Statute § 13-2319(a) limits the scope of the statute to "persons" in the business of smuggling human beings.

The plain language argument is the first rule-based argument. It includes several other embedded rule-based arguments.

The first paragraph begins with a conclusion to the plain language analysis. It then explains the rules with respect to how the court should interpret the plain language of the text.

The shading below allows you to see how this rule is applied in the context of Arizona's anti-smuggling statute.

The plain text of § 13-2319(a) limits application of the statute to the smuggler, and not his human cargo. When analyzing the plain text of a statute, Arizona courts must give "each word, phrase, clause and sentence…its natural, obvious, and ordinary meaning" such that no other part of the statute is rendered "void, inert, redundant or trivial." *Arpaio v. Steinle III*, 35 P.3d 114, 116 (Ariz. Ct. App. 2001); *Stein v. Sonus, USA, Inc.*, 150 P.3d 773, 776 (Ariz. Ct. App. 2007). When a word is undefined by the statute, Arizona courts turn to any established and widely used dictionary to determine the natural and obvious meaning of a term. *Helvetica Servicing, Inc. v. Pasquan*, 277 P.3d 198, 205 (Ariz. Ct. App. 2012).

The most natural and obvious meaning of a "person…smuggling…for profit or commercial purpose" limits this statute to the prosecution of smugglers, not the smuggler's human cargo. Where smuggling is concerned, as explained above, a "person" is either the smuggler or his cargo. Neither "profit" nor "commercial purpose" is defined by statute, but both limit the "person" who can be prosecuted to the smuggler, and not the individual migrant.

This next rule-based argument is embedded within the plain language argument.

Again, it begins with a conclusion (in the sentence that begins "First, ..."). It then explains the relevant rules, which are underlined.

You can see how key aspects of the rule are repeated, here, in the application.

First, the ordinary meaning of the phrase "for profit" limits the person who can be prosecuted to those in the business of smuggling. "Profit" is widely understood as "net income…from the conduct of business." *Webster's Third New International Dictionary* 1811 (2002); *see also The American Heritage Dictionary* 989 (5th ed. 2009) (defining profit as "financial gain from a… business activity"). Therefore, a "person" who smuggles "for profit" is one who seeks a "net income" from the "business" of smuggling. Only the coyote is seeking income from the smuggling. And only the coyote — not the individual migrant — is in the business of smuggling. Thus, the phrase "for profit" limits the "person" who can be prosecuted to the smuggler, and not the individual migrant.

This next argument is the second ruled-based argument embedded within the plain language argument.

Again, it begins with a conclusion (in the sentence that begins "Next,…."). It then explains the relevant rules, which are underlined.

You can see how key aspects of the rule are repeated in the application.

Next, the ordinary meaning of the phrase "for…commercial purpose" similarly limits the person who can be prosecuted. "Commercial" means "of or relating to 'commerce.'" *Webster's Third New International Dictionary* at 594. "Commerce" refers to "an exchange of goods…especially on a large scale between different countries." *Id.* The human cargo hopes to be smuggled once. By contrast, the coyote is involved in the exchange of goods on a large scale. Again, the statutory text shows that the Arizona legislature chose to impose criminal sanctions on the person who repeatedly profits from a smuggling operation, not the human cargo.

To read the statute as imposing criminal liability on individual migrants would, effectively, render the phrases "for profit" and for "commercial purpose" void and inert. As explained above, the individual migrant is not seeking to profit or engage in the activity commercially. Thus, to extend the reach of the statute to permit the prosecution of individual migrants would be to ignore the words "for profit" and "commercial purpose," which limit the "person" to be prosecuted under the statute. Such a reading would contravene the legislature's intent.

Thus, the plain meaning of the statutory section demonstrates that human cargo falls outside the intended scope of § 13-2319(a). Accordingly, this Court should dismiss Count I of the indictment against Mr. Hidalgo.

> The plain language argument ends here with the application of the rule (shaded) and a final conclusion.

If this Court nevertheless concludes that the meaning of the word is ambiguous, this Court may also look at the text in context and the statute's legislative history. Both examinations lead to the same conclusion: The Arizona legislature did not intend to subject individual migrants to criminal prosecution.

B. The text of § 13-2319(a) read in context also demonstrates a legislative intent to make § 13-2319(a) a tool for prosecuting organized crime, not individual migrant activity.

> The text-in-context argument addresses the second step in Arizona's method of statutory construction.

The text in context — specifically the heading of § 13-2319(a) — also evidences a legislative intent to criminalize organized crime, not individual migrant activity. When examining the text in context, the court may consider the headings of the statute to aid the interpretation of the statute and to ascertain legislative intent. *State v. Hauser*, 105 P.3d 1158, 1161 (Ariz. 2005). Chapter 23 of the Arizona Criminal Code is entitled "Organized Crime, Fraud and Terrorism." Ariz. Rev. Stat. Ann. § 12-2301 (2005). This heading shows that when enacting § 13-2319, the legislature intended to target organized crime, fraud, or terrorism, and not individual migrant activity.

> Conclusion
>
> Rules
>
> Application and conclusion

C. The legislative history of § 13-2319(a) also demonstrates a legislative intent to target organized crime, not individual migrant activity.

The legislative history of § 13-2319 also shows that the legislature was focused on criminalizing the conduct of the smuggling organization and not the conduct of the individual migrant. When the bill that became § 13-2319 was first drafted, it focused exclusively on criminalizing human trafficking. Ariz. Fact Sheet, S.B. 1372, 2005 Reg. Sess. (2005). Thus, the legislative history focuses on human trafficking. *Id.* In discussing human trafficking, the legislature distinguished between the "traffickers" who received "illicit profits" and those who were trafficked. *Id.* Accordingly, the bill subjects traffickers to prosecution and incarceration, while those who are trafficked may, under the statute, receive restitution. *Id.* Thus, the statute from its inception distinguished between those who organize the movement of others and those who were moved and treated those two groups differently. *See id.* The Judiciary Committee then added to the bill the provision that also criminalizes "smuggling for profit or commercial purpose." *Id.* Given that the statute had consistently distinguished between those organizing the movement of others and those who were moved, the most consistent understanding of the text that criminalizes "smuggling for profit or commercial purpose" is that it, too, distinguishes between those who organize the movement of others and those

> The legislative history argument addresses the next step in Arizona's method of statutory construction.
>
> The description of what the legislature intended when it enacted the statute acts as the rules that are then applied.
>
> The application integrates the key idea from the explanation of what the legislature was thinking when enacting the law.
>
> Conclusion

who are moved. Accordingly, the legislative history suggests that the legislature contemplated criminalizing the conduct of only the smuggler, not the person who was smuggled.

D. Finally, the historical context of § 13-2319(a) also demonstrates a legislative intent to target organized crime, not individual migrant activity.

The historical background to § 13-2319 also supports the interpretation that the legislature intended to target organized crime, and not human cargo. In 2005, the year § 13-2319 was passed in Arizona, the United States Government Accountability Office reported to Congress that "[p]eople smuggling is a huge and highly profitable business worldwide, involving billions of dollars annually." Colleen DiSanto, *Alien Smuggling Along the Arizona-Mexico Border*, 43 Ariz. Att'y, Jan. 2007, at 29. At that time, the "volume and sophistication" of human smuggling rings had increased dramatically, and

Arizona, which shares a border with Mexico, was already feeling the great weight of human smuggling by trafficking organizations. *Id.* The same year § 13-2319 was enacted, Arizona declared a state of emergency due to the severe financial burden from jailing thousands of indiviudals crossing the border without appropriate documents. *Id.* at 32. This historical background makes it unlikely that the Arizona legislature intended individual migrant activity to be treated as a class four felony because it would increase jail time for smuggled migrants. A more natural interpretation of § 13-2319, given this historical background, is that the statute is intended to target the members of the trafficking organizations who were responsible for the severe financial burdens placed on the State of Arizona.

In sum, the text, the text in context, its legislative history, and the historical context surrounding enactment of the statute of § 13-2319 all support the interpretation that people in the business of human smuggling, not their human cargo, are the intended target of the statute. Accordingly, Mr. Hidalgo should not be prosecuted under § 13-2319 because he was merely the commodity from which other criminal organizations profit. The statute does not extend to cover Mr. Hidalgo's conduct, and the Court should dismiss the indictment against him.

What makes a statutory construction argument more complex is that it usually involves a series of rule-based arguments, and often some of those rule-based arguments are nested within other rule-based arguments.

Figure 3.3-F provides a graphic representation of the arguments in Example 3.3-E above. That figure should help you see how the larger statutory construction argument is actually composed of a series of rule-based arguments, some of which are nested. Then, Examples 3.3-G and 3.3-H extract individual rule-based arguments from the larger argument in Example 3.3-E so that you can look at them individually.

Example 3.3-G shows excerpts from the "plain language argument," highlighting the aspects that make it a rule-based argument. Example

Figure 3.3-F • A statutory construction argument graphically represented as a series of rule-based arguments

ARGUMENT

Introduction

Governing rule: Arizona courts construe statutes by looking at plain text. If still ambiguous, courts will look at the text in context, the legislative history, and the historical context of the statute.

Plain Text

Conclusion
About the plain text

Explain the law
Determined by natural and obvious meaning of words. Construe text so that no words made void or inert. Use dictionary to determine meaning.

Apply the law

Thus, imposing criminal liability would render the phrases "for profit" and "commercial purpose" void and inert.

Conclusion
About the plain text

Text in Context

Conclusion
About the text in context

Explain the law
By explaining the rule that says courts can consider headings.

Apply the law
Examine heading in this case.

Conclusion
About the text in context

Legislative History

Conclusion
About the legislative history

Explain the law
The legislative history suggests that the legislature distinguished between those doing the moving and those who were moved.

Apply the law
Apply that same distinction to smuggling.

Conclusion
About the legislative history

Historical Context

Conclusion
About the historical context

Explain the historical context
Arizona was experiencing a crisis with respect to prison space and unable to accommodate current prison population.

Apply the historical context
Unlikely to pass a law that would, at the same time, substantially increase the need for prison space.

Conclusion
About the historical context

Ordinary meaning "for profit"

Conclusion about ordinary meaning of "for profit."

Explain the law by providing dictionary definition.

Apply the law by applying dictionary definition to this case.

Conclusion about ordinary meaning of "for profit."

Ordinary meaning "commercial purpose"

Conclusion about ordinary meaning of "commercial purpose."

Explain the law by providing dictionary definition.

Apply the law by applying dictionary definition to this case.

Conclusion about ordinary meaning of "commercial purpose."

3.3-H is a set of smaller arguments nested within the plain language argument, which is also a rule-based argument.

Example 3.3-G • A statutory construction argument as a rule-based argument

---

Conclusion about the plain text

Explain the law: Explain how courts analyze the plain meaning of a statutory text.

The plain text of § 13-2319(a) limits application of the statute to the smuggler, and not his human cargo. When analyzing the plain text of a statute, Arizona courts must give "each word, phrase, clause and sentence…its natural, obvious, and ordinary meaning" such that no other part of the statute is rendered "void, inert, redundant or trivial." *Arpaio v. Steinle III*, 35 P.3d 114, 116 (Ariz. Ct. App. 2001); *Stein v. Sonus, USA, Inc.*, 150 P.3d 773, 776 (Ariz. Ct. App. 2007). When a word is undefined by the statute, Arizona courts turn to any established and widely used dictionary to determine the natural and obvious meaning of a term. *Helvetica Servicing, Inc. v. Pasquan*, 277 P.3d 198, 205 (Ariz. Ct. App. 2012).

Apply the law: Each of these paragraphs applies the law regarding how to analyze the plain text to specific words in the statute.

The most natural and obvious meaning of a "person…smuggling…for profit or commercial purpose" limits this statute to the prosecution of smugglers, not the smuggler's human cargo….

To read the statute as imposing criminal liability on individual migrants would, effectively, render the phrases "for profit" and for "commercial purpose" void and inert….

Conclusion about the plain text

Thus, the plain meaning of the statutory section demonstrates that human cargo falls outside the intended scope of § 13-2319(a). Accordingly, this Court should dismiss Count I of the indictment against Mr. Hidalgo….

Example 3.3-H • A statutory construction argument as a rule-based argument

---

Conclusion about the ordinary meaning of "for profit"

Explain the rule: dictionary definition

Application of the dictionary definition to the statute

Conclusion about the ordinary meaning of "for profit"

First, the ordinary meaning of the phrase "for profit" limits the person who can be prosecuted to those in the business of smuggling. "Profit" is widely understood as "net income…from the conduct of business." *Webster's Third New International Dictionary* 1811 (2002); *see also The American Heritage Dictionary* 989 (5th ed. 2009) (defining profit as "financial gain from a…business activity"). Therefore, a "person" who smuggles "for profit" is one who seeks a "net income" from the "business" of smuggling. Only the coyote is seeking income from the smuggling. And only the coyote, not the individual migrant, is in the business of smuggling. Thus, the phrase "for profit" limits the "person" who can be prosecuted to the smuggler, and not the individual migrant.

Table 3.3-I compares the structure of a simple rule-based argument against the more complex structure of a statutory construction argument. As you can see, most of your work occurs in explaining the law. That is because you and opposing counsel are actually arguing about how the law should be understood.

Table 3.3-I • Comparing the structure of a simple and complex rule-based argument

Basic Framework	A simple rule-based argument	A statutory construction argument
Conclusion	Conclusion	Conclusion

Explain the law	Explain the rules	**Explain the statutory language (as you understand it).**
		
		Explain the jurisdiction's methodology for construing a statute.
		
		Rule-based argument 1 (plain meaning)
		  Conclusion about the plain meaning of the statute's text
		  Rules regarding the plain meaning
		
		    Nested rule-based argument 1A
		      Conclusion about the meaning of a particular word or phrase
		      Rules that allow you to reach that conclusion
		      Application of those rules
		      Conclusion
		
		    Nested rule-based argument 1B
		      Conclusion about the meaning of a particular word or phrase
		      Rules that allow you to reach that conclusion
		      Application of those rules
		      Conclusion
		
		  Application of plain meaning rules to the text of the statute
		  Conclusion about the plain meaning
		
		Rule-based argument 2 (text in context)
		  Conclusion about the text within its context
		  Rules regarding how to construe the text of the statute within its context
		  Application of those rules to the text and surrounding provisions
		  Conclusion about the text in context
		
		Rule-based argument 3 (legislative history)
		  Conclusion about the legislature's intent as drawn from legislative record
		  Any **rules** about how legislative record should be read, including quotes from the legislative history that establish the legislature's intent
		  Application of those rules to the legislative record.
		  Conclusion about the legislature's intent as drawn from the legislative record
		
		Conclusion stating how the statute should be understood

Apply the law	Apply the rule to the facts of your client's case	**Apply the statute as you have proposed that it should be understood to the facts of your client's case.**
Conclusion (if necessary)	Conclusion	Conclusion

In reviewing Table 3.3-I, keep in mind several points. First, the table above offers an example of a statutory construction argument. As mentioned above, different jurisdictions have different methods for construing statutes. Any statutory construction argument you develop must follow the analytical method of that jurisdiction. As a result, make sure you research what types of statutory construction arguments are used in your jurisdiction. For example, in Example 3.3-E, the statutory construction argument addresses the historical background of the statute because Arizona courts will consider that aspect. Table 3.3-I does not show that step because many statutory construction arguments do not include historical background. Similarly, the number of nested arguments will vary from argument to argument.

Second, notice that all of the "action" in a statutory construction argument occurs in the explanation of the law. That is because in a statutory construction argument, you will need to make a series of rule-based arguments simply to establish your position about how the statute should be construed. Once you have finished arguing how the statutory language should be understood, you have one final rule-based argument to make. That final rule-based argument is applying the statute—as you believe it should be understood—to the facts of your client's case.

Finally, remember that when developing a statutory construction argument you will use all the same skills that you use when developing a rule-based argument: state the rule; then apply that rule to the evidence before the court, whether that evidence is the text of the statute, the surrounding text, or the legislative record.

III. Policy Arguments

Policy arguments also rely on rule-based reasoning. A "policy" is a means of achieving a "broader moral, philosophical, or social goal[]" behind a law."[5] A policy argument asserts that a particular outcome is warranted because such an outcome would be consistent with a particular goal that is beneficial to society. In a policy argument, a lawyer asserts that a favorable decision by the court will lead to positive moral, philosophical, or social outcomes while the opposite decision will generate negative moral, philosophical, or social ramifications. A policy argument may have the flavor of, "If you don't agree with our argument, it will be the end of the world as we know it."

In Example 3.3-J, the lawyer representing the state argues that a police search should be upheld, in part, because doing so protects police officer

---

5. Coughlin, Rocklin & Patrick, *supra* note 2, at 185–92.

safety. (In that example, the social goal is police officer safety.) The policy is to allow "considerable latitude" in searches of criminal suspects to protect the officers' safety. That policy is applied to potential outcomes in the case. If the court upholds the search, so the argument goes, police officer safety will be protected. If the court does not uphold the search, police officer safety will be at risk.

Example 3.3-J • A policy argument considers whether certain social goods will be achieved in light of the court's decision

---

Finally, the officer's search was appropriate because it occurred within the "considerable latitude" given to police officers when their safety is at stake. This Court has observed in the officer safety context that an officer's judgment in the field should not be "second-guessed":

> [I]t is not our function to uncharitably second-guess an officer's judgment. A police officer in the field frequently must make life-or-death decisions in a matter of seconds. There may be little or no time in which to weigh the magnitude of a potential safety risk against the intrusiveness of protective measures. An officer must be allowed considerable latitude to take safety precautions in such situations.

State v. Bates, 747 P.2d 991, 994 (Or. 1987).

That admonition recognizes that, because police work is inherently dangerous, an officer engaged in otherwise lawful activity should not have to choose between continuing to engage in that activity and placing his or her life at risk. Giving weight to those concerns, a reviewing court's "inquiry therefore is limited to whether the precautions taken were reasonable under the circumstances as they reasonably appeared at the time that the decision was made." *Id.*

As the Court of Appeals correctly explained, the admonition not to "second-guess" an officer's judgment is a "method of analysis, not an apologia." *State v. Miglavs*, 63 P.3d 1202, 1209 (Or. Ct. App. 2003). As such, it must be followed, not merely recited.

Here, the precaution the officers took was reasonable under the circumstances as they reasonably appeared at the time. The defendants were known to associate with a gang whose members regularly carry weapons. The officers engaged in a pat down to protect themselves against those possible weapons. Even if the question was a close one — which it is not — this Court should err on the side of giving the officers latitude in the situation and should conclude that the trial court properly denied Defendant's motion to suppress evidence discovered during the pat-down search.

Margin annotations:

Conclusion

The explanation of the law begins here.

In a policy argument, the explanation of the law explains the public good that is at stake.

A public policy argument is stronger when the explanation of the policy cites to a case or other authority that recognizes that public good.

The application of the rule to the facts of this case begins here.

Note how the application relies on the same language used to explain the policy. Doing so helps the court see how the sought after conclusion is consistent with the public good described above.

Table 3.3-K compares the structure of a policy-based argument with a rule-based argument so that you can see the similarity between the two.

Table 3.3-K · Comparing the structure of a simple rule-based argument and a policy-based argument

Basic framework	A simple rule-based argument	A policy-based argument
Conclusion	• Conclusion	• Conclusion
Explain the law	• Explain the rule(s)	• Explain the policy that is at stake.
Apply the law	• Address whether the standard articulated in the rule is met in light of the facts of the case.	• Address whether the moral, social, or philosophical good articulated in the policy will be achieved if the court reaches the conclusion you seek.
Conclusion	• Conclusion	• Conclusion

IV. Syllogisms

Although rule-based arguments are, in theory, simple, in practice they can be difficult to execute. For that reason, here is an alternative way of thinking about rule-based arguments: the syllogism. A "syllogism" is an argument structure in which a conclusion is derived from two other premises. Those two premises are (1) the major premise and (2) the minor premise. The "major premise" is usually a broad statement of general applicability. The "minor premise" is a more particular statement that is related to the major premise. The "conclusion" should follow logically from the major and minor premises.[6]

Although the syllogism provides a different way of thinking about rule-based arguments, the syllogism should result in the same kind of structure. If rule-based arguments seem hard to grasp and a different or additional explanation would be helpful, then you might want to think in terms of syllogisms.

Example 3.3-L is a classic syllogism and illustrates the major premise, minor premise, and conclusion drawn from them.

Example 3.3-L · A classic syllogism

Major premise:	All humans are mortal.
Minor premise:	All Greeks are humans.
Conclusion:	All Greeks are mortal.

---

6. James A. Gardner, *Legal Argument: The Structure and Language of Effective Advocacy* 4 (2d ed. LexisNexis 2007).

Rule-based arguments are syllogisms.[7] In a rule-based argument, the rule is the major premise. For lawyers, a rule is an assertion of general applicability. When cited to a binding authority, that rule has a force that is difficult to controvert. The "minor premise" is the evidence from your case against which the standard is applied. A minor premise is most effective when it presents evidence that is also difficult to controvert. The conclusion results from the application of the undisputed major premise (the rule) to the undisputed minor premise (facts or other evidence in the case).

Let's look back at two rule-based arguments, provided here in Examples 3.3-M and 3.3-N, to see how they fall within the structure of a syllogism.

Example 3.3-M • A rule-based argument as a syllogism

This case is moot and should, therefore, be dismissed. A case is moot if there is no justiciable controversy. *State v. Hauskins*, 281 P.3d 669, 672 (Or. Ct. App. 2012). A justiciable controversy exists when the interests of the parties to the action are adverse and the court's decision in the matter will have some practical effect on the rights of the parties to the controversy. *McIntire v. Forbes*, 909 P.2d 846, 850-51 (Or. 1996) (internal quotation marks omitted).

Major premise is shaded.

This case is moot because Ms. Peterson has already received that which she sought. The only relief Ms. Peterson sought was the return of her two dogs, Peaches and Tango, which were previously seized by a Klamath County animal control officer. The attached agreement, which Ms. Peterson signed, demonstrates that Ms. Peterson's dogs, Peaches and Tango, have been returned and are once again residing in the Peterson household. Because the appellant has received that which she sought, the parties no longer have any interests that are adverse and any ruling by the Court would have no practical effect. The case should be dismissed as moot.

Minor premise is underlined.

Final conclusion. For purposes of effective writing, the conclusion is repeated.

Example 3.3-N • A rule-based argument as a syllogism

First, the ordinary meaning of the phrase "for profit" limits the person who can be prosecuted to those in the business of smuggling. "Profit" is widely understood as "net income…from the conduct of business." *Webster's Third New International Dictionary* 1811 (2002); *see also The American Heritage Dictionary* 989 (5th ed. 2009) (defining profit as "financial gain from a… business activity"). Therefore, a "person" who smuggles "for profit" is one who seeks a "net income" from the "business" of smuggling. Only the coyote is seeking income from the smuggling. And only the coyote—not the individual

Major premise (shaded) is established.

Minor premise is underlined.

---

7. Analogical arguments can also be understood more or less in terms of syllogisms. *See id.* at 7-9. The syllogistic structure is usually more helpful when constructing rule-based arguments than it is when constructing analogical arguments. Thus, this discussion about syllogisms is limited to rule-based arguments.

Final conclusion. For purposes of effective writing, the conclusion is repeated.

<u>migrant—is in the business of smuggling.</u> Thus, the phrase "for profit" limits the "person" who can be prosecuted to the smuggler, and not the individual migrant.

Thinking about your arguments as a syllogism can also help strengthen your arguments. Once you determine your major and minor premise, you can examine each, asking how that premise might be attacked. Asking that question can help you shore up your argument before you present it to the court. Moreover, you can subject opposing counsel's argument to that same scrutiny and determine where its weaknesses might lurk.

Practice Points

- A persuasive rule-based argument uses the same structure as an objective rule-based argument.

    - A persuasive rule-based argument states a conclusion about the element, step, or factor at issue.

    - It explains the rule relevant to that element, step, or factor.

    - The application juxtaposes the key concepts from the rule against the facts from the client's case. Juxtaposing the key concepts from the rule against the facts is the technique that makes a rule-based argument persuasive.

    - A persuasive rule-based argument repeats the initial conclusion at the end of the argument as a way to sum up and emphasize the conclusion.

- A statutory construction argument follows that same pattern; however, the explanation of the law becomes an argument about what the statutory text means. The argument about what the statutory text means—is developed through a series of rule-based arguments.

- A policy argument follows the same structure as a simple rule-based argument. The "rule" is an assertion about what would be good for society, and the application shows that the outcome your client seeks is consistent with that societal good.

- A syllogism is another way to think about a rule-based argument. Examining your rule-based arguments as a syllogism is another way to test the logic of your argument.

Using Rule-Based and Analogical Arguments Together

In the preceding sections, rule-based arguments and analogical arguments were discussed separately; however, rule-based and analogical arguments can be used together to create a single legal argument. Usually, when using them in combination, you will first rely on the rule-based argument and then shore up that argument with one or more analogies to prior cases.

The advantage of using the two different kinds of argument in combination is that you get the benefits of both. The rule-based argument allows you to focus on the broader legal principles and tell a cohesive story about how the court should apply the law to your client's case. The analogies that follow add strength to that story by showing that previous courts have come to the same conclusion that you want the current court to reach.

Example 3.4-A provides an example of an argument that uses rule-based and analogical reasoning.

Example 3.4-A • An argument that relies on both rule-based and analogical reasoning[1]

Officers Brown and Cockerham had a reasonable suspicion that justified a protective frisk of the defendant. Whether a suspicion is reasonable depends on the inferences drawn from the particular circumstances confronting the officer viewed in light of the officer's experience. *See State v. Ehly*, 854 P.2d 421, 430 (Or. 1993) (citing *Terry v. Ohio*, 392 U.S. 1, 21-22, 27-30 (1968)). An "intuitive sixth sense" or "instinct" cannot "form the entire basis for 'reasonable suspicion.'" *State v. Valdez*, 561 P.2d 1006, 1010-11 (Or. 1977). Rather, an officer must be able to point to specific and articulable facts that give rise to a reasonable inference that the person might pose an immediate threat. *See Ehly*, 854 P.2d at 430. An officer need not show that the threat was "more likely than not." Or. Rev. Stat. 131.005(11) (defining "probable cause"). An officer must simply have a rea-

The shaded text shows the key ideas from the rules, which will later be applied to the facts.

---

1. This example (also seen in Examples 5-M, 5-S, 5-U, and 7-J) is adapted from arguments presented in *State v. Miglavs*, 63 P.3d 1202 (Or. App. 2003). Some descriptions of supporting case law have been altered for educational purposes.

sonable belief that a circumstance may exist or that a particular event might occur. *See State v. Stanley*, 935 P.2d 1202, 1204 (Or. 1997). In other words, for a protective frisk to be justified, an officer must only show that the particular circumstances gave rise to a reasonable belief that the defendant might pose an immediate threat.

To establish a reasonable belief that the defendant might pose an immediate threat, officers may rely on their knowledge that the defendant associates with a known dangerous person or that the person is connected with an activity that involves weapons. For example, in *Ehly*, this Court determined that officers had reasonable suspicion to conduct a protective search. *Ehly*, 854 P.2d at 432. In that case, officers knew that the defendant was a drug user and that "many people who use illegal narcotics possess guns." *Id.* at 430. Moreover, the officers also knew that defendant was "running" with a person who carried weapons. *Id.* Because the defendant was rummaging through a gym bag with his hands concealed and did not respond to the officer's suggestion to dump out the contents of the bag, this Court concluded that it was reasonable for one of the officers to dump the contents of the bag out on the motel room bed. *Id.*

Officers must, however, rely on more than the defendant's "looks" when that "look" does not reasonably connect the defendant to a criminal or threatening activity. For example, in *Valdez*, this court held that police officers lacked reasonable suspicion to stop a person who was dressed in a blue leisure suit, wore shiny black shoes, and looked "real sharp." *Valdez*, 561 P.2d at 1010. Although the police officers thought the defendant looked like a "typical pusher," the court disagreed, stating that "[n]eedle scars on forearms may legitimately speak of possible criminal activity in drugs, but shined shoes, sharp clothes, and staring at a police officer do not say much." *Id.* at 1010–11. Similarly, in *Bates*, this court held that the officers had not established reasonable suspicion when all that the officers could point to was that the defendant had long hair and a beard, was wearing a leather jacket, and looked suspicious. *State v. Bates*, 747 P.2d 991, 994 (Or. 1987).

Officers Brown and Cockerham can point to specific, articulable facts that gave rise to a reasonable suspicion that the defendants posed an immediate threat. First, the officers knew that the defendant was associated with the 18th Street Gang. Defendant was wearing a shirt with the phrase "18th Street" printed on it, and his companion had a tattoo under his eye, which is a tattoo that is associated with membership in the 18th Street Gang. In addition, both men had shaved heads and were wearing baggy gang-style clothes. Thus, the officers knew that the defendant was associated with the 18th Street Gang.

Second, the officers knew that members of the 18th Street Gang were dangerous, often carrying concealed weapons. In fact, one of the officers had encountered a gang member in the parking lot of the same apartment complex who, on a pat-down search, was found to have a weapon concealed in the waistband of his pants under a baggy shirt. Another officer had personally removed weapons from several 18th Street Gang members in that same neighborhood. Indeed, he had found a gun on a gang member "just previously to this incident." Thus, the officers knew that members of the 18th Street Gang

---

*Sidebar notes:*

A case illustration of *State v. Ehly* establishes the rule that the writer wishes to rely on later and will provide the basis for an analogical comparison.

The writer provides case illustrations of *Valdez* and *Bates* as a defensive move. These are cases the defense is likely to rely on; thus, the writer must show how these cases are distinguishable.

The rule-based argument begins here and continues into the next paragraph. Do you see how the writer re-integrates key ideas from the rule into the analysis of the facts? In that way, the writer shows how the law, when applied to the facts, establishes a particular outcome.

carried weapons and posed a danger to the officers, and they knew that the defendant was associated with that gang and its activities.

Based on these facts, the officers had reason to believe that the defendant might pose an immediate threat. In fact, the officers relied on the same kinds of facts that established reasonable suspicion in *Ehly*. Just as the officer in *Ehly* relied on the defendant's drug activity, an activity that often involves weapons and therefore poses a danger to others, the officers in this case relied on the defendant's gang membership, an activity that often involves weapons and also poses a danger to others. Moreover, just as the officers in *Ehly* relied on the defendant's association with a person who was known to carry weapons, the officers in this case relied on the defendant's association with a group of people — the 18th Street Gang — who were known to carry weapons. Finally, just as the officers in *Ehly* were concerned for their safety because the defendant was rummaging through a bag (a place where a gun could be concealed) and they could not see his hands, the officers in this case were concerned because the defendant's waistband was concealed and was a place where a handgun could be concealed. Thus, the officers in this case relied on the same kinds of facts as did the officers in *Ehly* and, accordingly, had reasonable suspicion to pat down the defendant.

The writer then analogizes to *Ehly*. The analogy asserts that because the facts described above established reasonable suspicion in that case, similar facts should establish reasonable suspicion here.

For these same reasons, the officers relied on far more than simply the defendant's "looks." In *Valdez* and in *Bates*, the "look" that the officers relied on — a blue leisure suit and shiny black shoes in *Valdez* and long hair, a beard, and a leather jacket in *Bates* — could not be particularly associated with a weapons-related activity or with a particular group of people who regularly carry weapons. By contrast, here, the "look" at issue established a reasonable suspicion of gang activity and membership in the 18th Street Gang. Both the association with gang activity generally and the association with a particular gang known to carry weapons are specific, articulable facts that raise a reasonable suspicion that the defendant might pose an immediate threat.

Here, the writer distinguishes *Valdez* and *Bates*.

Practice Points

- Lawyers sometimes combine a rule-based and an analogical argument.

- Such an argument allows the writer, in the rule-based argument, to tell a story about how the law applies to the facts and, in the analogical argument, to show that the conclusions are supported by precedent.

- When using both a rule-based and analogical argument, the more general rule-based argument should precede the more specific analogical argument.

Structuring Factor Analyses

As mentioned in section § 3.1, *Organizing Claims and Arguments*, organizing a factor analysis presents particular organizational challenges. That is because, in a factor analysis, the court reaches its conclusion by weighing the factors against each other. The presence or absence of any one factor is not determinative; rather, the court will consider the degree to which the factors weigh in favor of one conclusion as compared to the degree to which the factors weigh in favor of the opposite conclusion. Because factors are weighed against one another, the relationships among factors are different from the relationships among elements.

When an analysis depends on factors, the organizational structure may not be obvious. The connection among factors creates organizational challenges. Ultimately, you will have to choose between addressing all the factors in a single argument or addressing each factor in its own argument.[1] This section describes both possibilities and explains how to choose between the two.

I. Factors Analyzed as a Single Legal Argument

The first way you might organize a factor analysis is to address all the factors and how they should be weighed in one legal argument. Schematically, such an organization would look like Figure 3.5-A.

---

1. Occasionally, attorneys will group related factors together. Such a case presents a third organizational choice. To keep the discussion simple, this section focuses on the two most common organizational structures.

Figure 3.5-A · A factor analysis organized into one legal argument

---

Conclusion about the factor analysis

Explain the Law about the factor analysis

- <u>Rules</u> will name the factors the court will consider and describe any general principles about those factors.

- <u>Case illustrations</u> will show how courts have previously weighed *all* the relevant factors to reach a conclusion.

Apply the Law to the Facts

- <u>Rule-based arguments</u> will step through each factor, examining the degree to which each factor is present.

- <u>Analogical arguments</u> will compare the degree to which each factor is present in this case as compared to a prior case to reach a conclusion about whether the current case is like or not like a prior case. Because you will be comparing a group of factors in a prior case to a group of factors in a current case, the comparison will likely be complex, and you will have to work hard so that you don't lose your reader.

Conclusion about the factor analysis

If you choose to organize your factor analysis in one legal argument, the most challenging aspect will likely be writing case comparisons. If you use one legal argument to address all factors, then your comparison will have to address *all* the factors that the court considered in the prior case and compare the relevant facts for each factor to the analogous facts in your client's case. Thus, the case comparison will be complex, and you will have to take care so that the court does not lose track of your argument.[2]

In Example 3.5-B you can see how you might organize a factor analysis in one legal argument. Pay particular attention to how the lawyer carefully walks the court though the comparison of the current case to a prior case.

---

2. *A Lawyer Writes*, pages 150 through 159, provides many useful techniques to help a reader through a difficult case comparison. Christine Coughlin, Joan Malmud Rocklin & Sandy Patrick, *A Lawyer Writes: A Practical Guide to Legal Analysis* 150–59 (3d ed. 2018).

Example 3.5-B • A factor analysis organized into one legal argument

The trial court correctly concluded that Ms. Moran did not voluntarily execute the pre-marital agreement. A wife voluntarily executes a pre-marital agreement only if she signs the agreement without being coerced, intimidated, or unduly pressured. *In re Rudder*, 217 P.3d 183, 193 (Or. Ct. App. 2009). In addition, she must have "some modicum" of knowledge of the terms of the agreement and the property affected. *Id.* To determine whether the wife entered the agreement voluntarily and had an appropriate degree of knowledge, courts look at a variety of factors: (1) the timing of the agreement in relation to the wedding, (2) whether the assets were sufficiently disclosed, (3) the relative sophistication of the parties, and (4) whether the complaining party had adequate opportunity to consult with independent counsel. *Id.* at 194.

A wife does not enter a pre-marital agreement voluntarily if the agreement is provided one day before the wedding, the agreement does not disclose assets, the wife is unsophisticated, and an attorney is not present. *Id.* at 194-95. In *Rudder*, the husband, an electrician, and the wife, a cosmetologist who had owned a beauty salon, discussed in general terms a pre-marital agreement a few weeks before the wedding. *Id.* at 194. The husband's attorney drafted the agreement, which the wife first saw the day before leaving for the wedding. Although she had asked that her attorney be present when she signed the agreement, her attorney was not. Her husband urged her, "[g]o ahead and just sign it. The wedding is on." *Id.* After reading through the agreement, which did not list all the husband's assets or their value, the wife signed the agreement. *Id.* On these facts, the court determined that the circumstances created a coercive environment. *Id.* In discussing the wife's relative business sophistication, the Court of Appeals agreed with the trial court that "although…[the] wife had some experience in business matters, that experience was limited and she was relatively unsophisticated in financial matters." *Id.* at 195. Therefore, the wife did not enter into the agreement voluntarily. *Id.*

By contrast, an experienced businesswoman who has an opportunity to know her husband's assets and is provided with an agreement more than two weeks in advance can enter into the premarital agreement voluntarily. *In re Coward*, 582 P.2d 834, 835 (Or. Ct. App. 1978). In that case, the couple signed the pre-marital agreement seventeen days before the wedding. *Id.* At that time, the husband's attorney advised the wife to seek independent counsel. *Id.* The wife, who had worked as a bookkeeper and assisted her husband with his financial affairs, declined to speak with an attorney and signed the agreement. *Id.* The court concluded that the wife had been given sufficient opportunity to consult with an attorney, was an experienced businesswoman, and was aware of her husband's property. *Id.* Accordingly, the court held that the wife voluntarily signed the pre-marital agreement. *Id.* at 836. Although the 1978 *Coward* case was decided before the 1987 enactment of Or. Rev. Stat. § 108.725, the legislature intended § 108.725 to codify existing case law; therefore the *Coward case* still stands as an example of "voluntariness." *See Rudder*, 217 P.3d at 192.

Conclusion

The explanation of the law begins here.

The rules explain, among other things, the factors that the court must consider.

The case illustrations — *In re Rudder* and *In re Coward* — address all the factors that the court considered and then explain how the court weighed those factors to reach its conclusion.

The application begins here.

Here, Ms. Moran did not enter into her premarital agreement voluntarily. She is an unsophisticated businesswoman who had limited time before the wedding to review the document. Moreover, the agreement did not disclose her future husband's assets, and she was unable to consult with an attorney.

These facts are similar to the facts in *Rudder*, in which the court found the agreement was not signed voluntarily. First, in both cases the agreement was signed within days of the wedding. In *Rudder,* it was one day before the wedding, and in this case, it was five days. Although Ms. Moran had a few more days to consider the agreement, the time span created pressure. In *Rudder*, the pressure was evidenced by the husband's urging the wife, "[g]o ahead and sign it. The wedding is on." In this case, Ms. Moran stated that, "she didn't want to wait to find an attorney, not with so many people traveling so far." Thus, in this case, as in *Rudder*, the shortened time span created pressure and did not leave adequate time to consult with an attorney. Moreover, like the wife in *Rudder,* Ms. Moran is not a sophisticated businesswoman. As an office manager she has the approximate business experience of a cosmetologist who owned a beauty salon, and the *Rudder* court decided that the business-owner was not a sophisticated business person. In addition, Ms. Moran, like the wife in *Rudder*, was not told the value of her husband's assets. Finally, although Ms. Moran was advised to speak with an attorney, that one fact should not outweigh the other facts that are similar to the facts in *Rudder*. Those facts show a pressured environment in which Ms. Moran did not have sufficient time to fully assess the agreement. For these reasons, this Court should reach the same conclusion that the *Rudder* court did: The agreement was not entered into voluntarily.

In the application, you can see the lawyer carefully walk through each factor that was important to the prior court and compare the relevant facts from the prior case to the facts in Ms. Moran's case.

Defendant's reliance on *Coward* is misplaced. In *Coward*, the wife had previously reviewed her husband's finances; thus, she understood the value of her husband's assets. In this case, there is no evidence that Ms. Moran was aware of the value of her husband's assets. Her lack of knowledge of her husband's assets, the lack of evidence that her job as an office manager would give her sufficient experience to assess the value of his assets, and the compressed time span of only five days she had in which to make a decision support the trial court's conclusion that she signed in an coercive environment. Ms. Moran did not sign voluntarily.

Final conclusion

II. Factors Analyzed in Multiple, Distinct Legal Arguments

Although a factor analysis can be organized in one legal argument, sometimes the better choice is to break out the individual factors and create one legal argument for each factor, as in Figure 3.5-C.

Example 3.5-C · A factor analysis organized by factor

Roadmap to Factor Analysis

Factor 1

State a **conclusion** about the degree to which factor 1 weighs in favor of the desired outcome.

Explain the law about factor 1.

- Rules will focus on only those rules relevant to factor one.

- Case illustrations will be limited to a prior court's analysis of factor 1. The case illustrations may be difficult to write because you will have to pick out the facts and reasoning that the court relied on to reach a conclusion about factor 1. All facts and reasoning related to other factors should be eliminated.

Apply the law of factor 1.

- Rule-based arguments will compare the facts relevant to factor 1 to the rules above.

- Analogical arguments will compare the facts of this case to those of a prior case, but only with respect to factor 1.

State a **conclusion** about the degree to which factor 1 weighs in favor of the desired outcome.

Factor 2

State a **conclusion** about the degree to which factor 2 weighs in favor of the desired outcome.

Explain the law about factor 2.

- Rules will focus on only those rules relevant to factor two.

- Case illustrations will be limited to a prior court's analysis of factor 2. The case illustrations may be difficult to write because you will have to pick out the facts and reasoning that the court relied on to reach a conclusion about factor 2. All facts and reasoning related to other factors should be eliminated.

Apply the law of factor 2.

- Rule-based arguments will compare the facts relevant to factor 2 to the rules above.

- Analogical arguments will compare the facts of this case to those of a prior case, but only with respect to factor 2.

State a **conclusion** about the degree to which factor 2 weighs in favor of the desired outcome.

Factor 3

State a **conclusion** about the degree to which factor 3 weighs in favor of the desired outcome.

Explain the law about factor 3.

- Rules will focus on only those rules relevant to factor three.

- Case illustrations will be limited to a prior court's analysis of factor 3. The case illustrations may be difficult to write because you will have to pick out the facts and reasoning that the court relied on to reach a conclusion about factor 3. All facts and reasoning related to other factors should be eliminated.

Apply the law of factor 3.

- Rule-based arguments will compare the facts relevant to factor 3 to the rules above.

- Analogical arguments will compare the facts of this case to those of a prior case, but only with respect to factor 3.

State a **conclusion** about the degree to which factor 3 weighs in favor of the desired outcome.

Weigh conclusions to reach final conclusion

If you choose this second structure, illustrated in Figure 3.5-C, in which each factor is addressed in a separate legal argument, you will likely face two challenges.

First, your case illustrations will have to be carefully drafted because each case illustration will focus on only one factor. In their opinions, courts sometimes carefully delineate their determination about each factor, but sometimes they do not. Thus, you will have to review the relevant prior decisions and extract the court's analysis about each individual factor. Depending on how explicitly it analyzed individual factors, this step could be very easy to do or very difficult.

The other challenge in presenting a factor analysis with separate arguments for each factor is determining the conclusion that you can reach about a single factor. Remember that a factor analysis depends on assessing the weight of each factor and then weighing all the factors against each other. Thus, when you are finished analyzing a factor, the only conclusion you can reach is whether that factor weighs in favor of a particular outcome. Factors are not "satisfied" or "met." Rather, they weigh—perhaps strongly or not so strongly—in favor of or against an outcome. So, you will need to structure your conclusion about each factor carefully.

Finally, if you use a separate legal argument to analyze each factor, you will have an additional step. After analyzing each factor, you will need a final paragraph that weighs all the factors against each other. This paragraph will not be structured as a typical legal argument because there should be no additional law to explain. Rather, you will take the conclusions that you reached with respect to each individual factor and explain how those conclusions weigh in favor of your client's desired outcome.

In Example 3.5-D you can see how you might organize a factor analysis by creating one legal argument for each factor. Look at the conclusions that the lawyer reaches with respect to each factor, and then take a look at the last paragraph, which brings together the conclusions for each factor to reach an overall conclusion.

Example 3.5-D · A factor analysis organized into one legal argument for each factor[3]

B. Mr. Floyd's subjective belief that he was expected to play paddleball with his supervisor was objectively reasonable.

The introduction describes the factors that must be analyzed.

Mark Floyd reasonably believed that he was expected to participate in the paddleball game with his supervisor. To determine whether an employee reasonably believed he was required to participate in an activity, California courts usually weigh three factors: (1) whether the employer was involved in the activ-

---

3. Professor Leslie Oster of Northwestern University School of Law first developed this hypothetical fact pattern.

ity, (2) whether the employer benefited from the activity, and (3) whether the employer pressured the employee to participate. *Meyer v. Workers' Comp. Appeals Bd.*, 204 Cal. Rptr. 74, 76 (Ct. App. 1984). In this case, an analysis of all three factors shows that Mr. Floyd reasonably believed that he was required to play paddleball as part of his job.

1. Fitness Functions was involved in the paddleball game.

Fitness Functions was involved in the paddleball game because it provided all the resources necessary for employees to play the game. When an employer subsidizes the activity, courts have routinely found the employer to be involved in the activity. *See, e.g. Ezzy v. Workers' Comp. Appeals Bd.*, 194 Cal. Rptr. 90, 95 (Ct. App. 1983); *Meyer*, 204 Cal. Rptr. at 77. For example, in *Ezzy*, the court held that an employer was involved with an after-hours softball game when the employer had subsidized the game. 194 Cal. Rptr. at 95. There, a part-time law clerk was injured after joining members of the law firm in an after-hours softball game. *Id.* The law firm paid for all equipment, t-shirts, refreshments, and an awards banquet. *Id.*

> Conclusion about factor 1 — whether Fitness Function was "involved." The explanation of the law for factor 1 begins immediately after the conclusion.

Only when the employer has not contributed any resources to the activity will courts find minimal involvement under this factor. *See, e.g. Meyer*, 204 Cal. Rptr. at 77. For example, in *Meyer*, the court held that the employer was only "minimally involved" in a weekend rafting trip. *Id.* The court explained that although a supervisor had invited other employees to go rafting and stay at his house on a river, no evidence showed that the employer had subsidized the trip. *Id.*

Whether an activity occurs on an employer's property does not affect whether an employer was involved. *See e.g. Todd v. Workers' Comp. Appeals Bd.*, 243 Cal. Rptr. 925, 927 (Ct. App. 1988). As the *Todd* court explained, "the statute does not differentiate between recreational activities on and off the employer's premises." *Id.* at 927.

In this case, Fitness Functions was involved because it provided all the resources necessary for the game to occur. In fact, Fitness Functions provided more resources than the employer in *Ezzy*, which was determined to be involved. In *Ezzy*, the employer provided equipment and t-shirts and hosted a banquet. Similarly, here, Fitness Functions allowed Ms. Randolph to purchase paddleball equipment with money from her expense account. In addition, Fitness Functions paid for and installed the paddleball court. In *Ezzy*, although the employer held a banquet, the employer did not actually build a softball field. By building the paddleball court and providing the equipment, Fitness Functions was "involved" with the activity.

> The law is then applied.

For these same reasons, Fitness Functions's involvement goes beyond the involvement in *Meyer*, where a supervisor invited employees to go rafting together, but the employer provided no other resources. Although Ms. Randolph similarly invited the employee, Mark Floyd, to play, Fitness Functions provided additional resources to facilitate the paddle ball games, whereas the employer in *Meyer* provided none. Because Mr. Floyd can show employer involvement greater than in both *Meyer* and *Ezzy*, Fitness Functions was involved in the paddleball game.

2. Fitness Functions also benefited from the paddleball game.

Fitness Functions also benefited from Ms. Randolph's paddleball games because they were a means to generate camaraderie. One benefit an employer may derive from employee participation in a recreational activity is improved "cooperation, spirit, morale, and camaraderie." *Ezzy*, 194 Cal. Rptr. at 95. To determine whether an activity builds employee camaraderie, California courts have looked at (1) the employer's intention to create a spirit of camaraderie, (2) the activity's regularity, and (3) the number of employees involved. *See id.* For example, in *Ezzy*, the court concluded that there was substantial employer benefit from an employee's participation in a law firm softball team. In that case, a partner testified that the games were "good for office spirit." *Id.* at 92. The games were played according to a schedule, and the office also had a schedule of practices. *Id.* Partners, other members of the firm, and some secretaries played, and all firm employees received a team t-shirt and were invited to a final banquet. *Id.* at 91. By contrast, in *Meyer*, the court held that the benefit to an employer from a "last minute get together" of a "few salesman" and their wives was "speculative and remote." *Meyer*, 204 Cal. Rptr. at 77.

The law is then applied.

In this case, Fitness Functions benefited from the paddleball game through improved office camaraderie. Mr. Floyd's case is like *Ezzy*. First, the employers in both cases intended to create a spirit of camaraderie through employee participation. In *Ezzy*, a partner stated the games were "good for office spirit." Similarly, in Mr. Floyd's case, Ms. Randolph stated that she played paddleball regularly with employees because "[i]t's a great way to get to know my employees" and she thought "people work better together when they're also friends and know each other in ways other than work." Second, in both cases the activity was played regularly. In *Ezzy*, the softball games and practices followed a schedule. In Mr. Floyd's case, although there was no schedule, Ms. Randolph acknowledged that she played regularly and estimated that she plays with other employees between two and three times a week. Finally, in both cases, a wide array of employees were involved. In *Ezzy*, the team included members of the firm as well as secretaries. In Mr. Floyd's case, Ms. Randolph stated she plays with "people who report to [her,]" "people above [her,]" and "people in other departments." Because his supervisor expected a benefit from employee participation and because the games were played regularly with numerous employees, Fitness Functions, like the law firm in *Ezzy*, benefited from employee participation in the paddleball game.

A final conclusion about factor 1

For these same reasons, the paddleball game is distinct from the last minute get together of a few salesmen in *Meyers*. Accordingly, Fitness Functions benefited from the paddleball games, and this factor weighs in favor of finding that his subjective belief was objectively reasonable.

3. Mr. Floyd can show he was pressured to play paddleball.

Mark Floyd was also pressured to play paddleball with Ms. Randolph....

* * *

Thus, this factor also weighs in favor of concluding that Mr. Floyd's subjective belief was reasonable.

4. Weighing all three factors, Mr. Floyd's belief that he was expected to play paddleball was objectively reasonable.

Based on the above facts, Mr. Floyd's subjective belief that he was expected to play paddleball with his supervisor was objectively reasonable. Fitness Functions was involved with the game by providing the court and equipment necessary to play. Fitness Functions also benefited from employee participation in the paddleball game because it provided Ms. Randolph an opportunity to build relationships with her employees in a manner with which she was comfortable. Finally, given Mr. Floyd's status as a probationary employee, his recent employment reviews, and the advice of the human resources officer that playing paddleball would help his relationship with Ms. Randolph, Ms. Randolph's invitation to play created pressure. Thus, all the relevant factors tend to show that Mr. Floyd reasonably believed he was expected to play, and the decision of the Workers' Compensation Board of Appeals should be reversed.

After all the factors are analyzed individually, the factors are weighed together to reach a final conclusion.

Moreover, this Court has repeatedly stated that California worker's compensation laws are to be construed liberally to benefit the employee. For all of these reasons, Mr. Floyd should be compensated for the injuries he sustained in the course of his work for Fitness Functions.

III. Choosing an Organizational Structure for a Factor Analysis

When you are faced with a factor analysis, choosing whether to structure the analysis as a single legal argument or multiple legal arguments is often a difficult decision. In fact, you may begin to write under one structure only to find that, actually, the other structure may work better.

At first your decision may be largely influenced by how the courts have analyzed the factors in the past. If the prior decisions tend to focus on the ultimate outcome and leave individual factors unexplained, it may be very difficult for you to pull apart the analysis and explain the law one factor at a time. In that situation, you may decide to explain the law as the courts have—analyzing all the facts relevant to all the factors in a single legal argument.

Sometimes, however, the courts have analyzed the factors individually, or (even if they haven't) you can pull apart the court's analysis and address the factors individually. In those cases, you have a choice: You can analyze all the facts relating to each factor in one legal argument or you can create individual arguments for each factor. After addressing each factor individually, a final paragraph at the end will weigh the factors together.

Whenever you have the choice of how to present a factor analysis—and as you gain more experience it is more and more likely that you will have that choice—you should consider what will be most persuasive to the court. Sometimes, if you have a series of factors, all of which you can argue weigh in your favor, it can be persuasive to have a series of shorter arguments, each of which ends, "This factor, too, weighs in favor of finding for my client." The repetition of factor after factor weighing in your client's favor has a persuasive effect. On the other hand, if you analyze all the factors in a single argument, you have other persuasive opportunities. When analyzing all the factors in a single argument, you will have more facts to work with in one place. The greater range of facts may afford you with more choices about how to order the facts, thus allowing you greater opportunity to arrange the facts in the most favorable light.

Practice Points

- A persuasive factors analysis uses the same structure as an objective factors analysis. It is usually structured in one of two ways.

  ◦ The factors can be analyzed as a group in a single legal argument.

  ◦ Each factor can be analyzed separately, and at the end of the argument, a final paragraph will weigh the factors to reach a conclusion.

- The structure you choose will depend on the way in which prior courts have analyzed the factors and what will be most persuasive in your client's case.

Chapter 4

Themes for Persuasive Arguments

Developing a persuasive argument depends on telling a cohesive story about the law, the facts, and the conclusion that the court should adopt. Developing a theme is one way in which attorneys create a cohesive, compelling narrative for the court.[1] This chapter explains what a theme is, the purpose of having a theme, how to develop a theme, and how to integrate that theme into your argument.

I. Themes and How They Function

A "theme" is some unifying idea that quickly and simply explains why the court should rule in your client's favor. A brief to the court — whether at the trial level or on appeal—will usually address multiple claims. Each of those claims is, in turn, supported by a series of distinct legal arguments. A theme links the sometimes complex and detailed arguments in those claims in a way that justifies the end that your client seeks.

---

1. Although many people use "theory of the case" and "theme" interchangeably, they are a bit different. The theory of the case is your comprehensive plan for convincing the judge or the jury to rule in your client's favor. You develop your theory of the case when preparing for trial. *See* John Korzen, *Make Your Argument: Succeeding in Moot Court and Mock Trial* 153 (2010); Thomas A. Mauet, *Trials: Strategy, Skills, and the New Powers of Persuasion* 8 (2d ed. 2009) ("[T]he theory of the case…is simply each party's version of what really happened."). Your theme is a quick and simple explanation or summation of the case's overarching theory.

One well-known theme comes from the trial of the legendary football star and actor O.J. Simpson: "If it [the glove] doesn't fit, you must acquit." That single, catchy sentence explained the crux of O.J. Simpson's argument. Simpson was accused of killing his estranged wife and a local restaurant server at her home. Part of the evidence against him included a bloody glove found on Simpson's estate, and a matching glove found at the crime scene. In a surprising move, prosecutors had Simpson try on the exhibit during trial, but the glove did not fit. From that event, the defense latched on to a winning theme of the case, and Simpson was later acquitted of murder.

More often, themes are not nearly as catchy as the one presented to the jury in the O.J. Simpson trial. In fact, a catchy theme that might work for a jury could undermine your credibility with a judge.[2] Thus, in developing a theme for your argument, be careful not to undermine your credibility by choosing a theme that is too simplistic or that sacrifices substance for flash.

The theme in a brief should be grounded in the law, but it can also bring in compelling facts. Your purpose is to provide the court with a pithy synopsis that explains the law and why your client should prevail in light of the law. Example 4-A is an excerpt from the plaintiffs' brief in the landmark case of *Obergefell v. Hodges*.[3] In that case, the Supreme Court was asked whether the Fourteenth Amendment requires a state to recognize a marriage between two people of the same sex when their marriage was performed and licensed in another state. Read Example 4-A, and ask yourself, "What is plaintiff's theme?"

Example 4-A · An appellate brief excerpt that reflects a theme

Petitioners married seeking a cherished status that protects families throughout life, from cradle to grave. But Ohio refuses to respect the dignity and status conferred on Petitioners' marriages by other states. From the start of the marriage to the birth of children to the death of one spouse and beyond, Ohio erases the legal relationships of Petitioners' families. Ohio treats these spouses as legal strangers to one another and recognizes only one member of each couple as the legal parent to their children. Ohio even cruelly refuses to recognize Petitioners' marriages on death certificates when one spouse dies. Through its marriage recognition bans, Ohio strikes out at a class of individuals whose intimate, personal relationships have been afforded a solemn and special status by other states — men and women who love and marry a person of the same sex.[4]

---

2. *See* Korzen, *supra* note 1, at 40–43.

3. *Obergefell v. Hodges*, 576 U.S. 644 (2015).

4. Brief for Petitioner Obergefell at 3, *Obergefell v. Hodges*, 576 U.S. 644 (2015) (No. 14-556), 2015 WL 1776076.

The *Obergefell* plaintiffs' theme seems to be this: By refusing to recognize out-of-state same-sex marriages, Ohio erases legal and deeply meaningful personal relationships. Because Ohio does recognize out-of-state opposite-sex marriages, Ohio unlawfully and cruelly discriminates against same-sex couples. Attorneys articulated the theme early in the plaintiff's brief, allowing these ideas to serve as the cornerstone for the whole argument. Plaintiffs' counsel could return to the theme throughout the brief, thereby anchoring each argument to that theme. The justices could also return to it when reading the brief and considering the arguments.

II. Developing a Theme

Developing a theme is not always easy. For one, it must be a concise statement of why your client wins. If a theme gets too complex, you'll lose your reader. So, you will have to choose among many ideas and focus on the one or two ideas that are central to your case.

Also, a theme is enhanced if it has some emotional resonance for your reader. Like everyone else, lawyers and judges can be moved by appeals to a social good or a value that is at stake. A social good or value could be an appeal to basic fairness or for a just outcome. Thus, when developing your theme, you might ask yourself a few questions like what social good or value is at stake? And, what facts in this case illuminate the social good or value that is at stake? Then, formulate a theme around that social good or value at stake and the relevant supporting facts.

Judges—being judges—will also be moved by appeals to basic legal doctrine, the policies or goals behind the substantive laws, and legal procedures. Thus, when looking to develop a theme, you might also look to the substantive law, the procedural legal standard, or a policy underlying the law.

After considering these sources for your theme, hone your theme to its essentials so that it will be compelling and concise.

The following section provides examples of themes derived from these various sources. You may notice, however, that although one of these sources may predominate, a theme may draw upon more than one source at a time.

A. Based on a Social Good or Value

As mentioned above, themes can emphasize that a decision will promote (or undermine) a social good or value, such as fairness, justice, individual autonomy, individual responsibility for damages caused, or the public's health, safety, or welfare. Themes can also emphasize core values about our legal or political system, such as efficiency in the administration of justice, separation of powers between branches, or the appropriate allocation of authority between states and the federal government.[5]

In the *Obergefell* case, mentioned above, the theme relied heavily on core values about family and marriage, and questioned the fairness of the Ohio statute. The plaintiffs in *Obergefell* could have simply argued that a statute that treats same-sex and opposite-sex couples differently was discriminatory. But that purely legal theme would have been less compelling than the one presented. Instead, the *Obergefell* argument reminded the reader of what was at stake: whether plaintiffs' family life would be erased by the State.

Advocates in the *Bush v. Gore* litigation also developed themes focused on core values. In that case, however, the themes invoked core values about our political and legal system. In *Bush v. Gore*, the candidates for President of the United States disputed which candidate had earned Florida's electoral votes in the 2000 general election. Before the United States Supreme Court, the legal questions were whether the Florida Supreme Court's decision was consistent with certain federal statutes and the United States Constitution. Although the legal questions focused on the intersection of federal and state laws and the Florida Supreme Court's interpretation of those laws, the parties developed themes that focused on what was at stake in the litigation. As illustrated in Table 4-B, George W. Bush argued that, if the Florida Supreme Court's decision stood, the rule of law would be ignored and "electoral chaos" would ensue. By contrast, and as illustrated in Table 4-C, Albert Gore focused on the "legitimacy of public power" and "respecting the intent of the electorate."[6]

---

5. Ellie Margolis, *Teaching Students to Make Effective Policy Arguments in Appellate Briefs*, 9 Perspectives 73, 75 (Winter 2001).

6. Table 4-B is based on Brief for Petitioner, *Bush v. Gore*, 531 U.S. 98 (2000) (No. 00-949). Table 4-C is based on Brief of Respondent Albert Gore, Jr., *Bush v. Gore*, 531 U.S. 98 (2000) (No. 00-949) (emphasis in the original).

Table 4-B · Developing a theme focused on a social value at stake

The case	After a close general election in 2000, the Florida Supreme Court ordered a statewide manual recount of all votes. Petitioner argued that ordering such a recount violated federal law. Specifically, the petitioner argued that ordering a statewide recount violated the U.S. Constitution's guarantee to equal protection because each county had different recount procedures and, therefore, votes might be counted differently in different counties. In addition, the petitioner argued that in ordering the recount, the Florida Supreme Court established procedures that differed from those legislatively authorized, and in so doing the Florida Supreme Court inappropriately exercised legislative power.	
Theme	"This case is the quintessential illustration of what will inevitably occur in a close election where the rules for tabulating ballots and resolving controversies are thrown aside after the election and replaced with judicially created *ad hoc* and *post hoc* remedies…. The Florida Supreme Court has not only violated the Constitution and federal law, it has created a regime virtually guaranteed to incite controversy, suspicion, and lack of confidence not only in the process but in the result that such a process would produce."	Petitioner's theme suggests that the decision of the Florida Supreme Court to order manual recounts violates the rule of law and, if upheld, will undermine confidence in federal elections and in the government.
Technique	Petitioner returns to this theme throughout the brief. A few examples are provided below. **Statement of the case:** "The thirty-three days since the election have been characterized by widespread turmoil resulting from selective, arbitrary, changing, and standardless manual recounts." **Argument:** "The decision below therefore ushers in a regime that cannot possibly be supported by any reasonable reading of the contest statute or any other provision of the Florida Election Code. The authority to count votes, entrusted by the Legislature to county officials subject to limited judicial review, has now been seized by the state judiciary…." **Argument:** "The Florida Supreme Court's decision is a recipe for electoral chaos. The court below has not only condoned a regime of arbitrary, selective and standardless manual recounts, but it has created a new series of unequal after-the-fact standards. This unfair, new process cannot be squared with the Constitution."	

Table 4-C · Developing a theme focused on a social value at stake

The case	Same case as in Table 4-B, above. Respondent argues that the Florida Supreme Court has properly exercised judicial review of Florida election law.
Theme	"This case raises the most fundamental questions about the legitimacy of political power in our democracy. In this case, the Court will decide whether the Electors for President of the United States, and thus the President of the United States himself, will be chosen by ascertaining the actual outcome of the popular vote in Florida in the election of November 7, 2000, or whether the President will instead be chosen without counting all the ballots lawfully cast in that state."
Technique	**Introduction:** "The question is whether this Court may properly override Florida's own state-law process for determining the rightful winner of its electoral votes in this Presidential election. Such intervention would run an impermissible risk of tainting the result of the election in Florida — and thereby the nation. For this Court has long championed the fundamental right of all who are qualified to cast their votes 'and to have their votes counted.'"
	Argument: The Florida Supreme Court's order does nothing more than place the voters whose votes were not tabulated by the machine on the same footing as those whose votes were so tabulated. In the end, all voters are treated equally: Ballots that reflect their intent are counted.
	Argument: "[P]etitioners would have the Court abruptly end the counting altogether and *toss out lawfully cast ballots that have been, and are now being, counted.* That is an absurd and unprecedented response…, and one that surely is not required by the U.S. Constitution."
	Argument: "The only due process right even arguably implicated by this case is the right of voters to have their ballots counted…."

To create a theme, the respondent steps back from technical arguments about whether the Florida Supreme Court's order is consistent with federal law to remind the court that the value at stake is respect for the intent of the voters.

B. Based on Substantive Law and Its Underlying Policy

Themes may also arise out of the substantive law and the policies, or reasons, behind that law. Take, for example, the case *Oregon v. Ashcroft*.[7] In that case, the State of Oregon passed a statute that permitted physician-assisted suicide. The U.S. Attorney General then issued an interpretive regulation that would allow the federal government to revoke the license of any physician who dispensed a controlled substance sufficient for a

---

7. 192 F. Supp. 2d 1077 (D. Or. 2002), *aff'd*, 368 F.3d 1118 (9th Cir. 2004), *aff'd*, *Gonzales v. Oregon*, 543 U.S. 1145 (2005).

person to commit suicide under the state statute. If that interpretive regulation went into effect, it would prevent all physician-assisted suicides in Oregon. Thus, the State of Oregon sought to enjoin the United States Attorney General from enforcing his interpretive regulation

Table 4-D shows how the U.S. Attorney General might approach the argument for a motion to dismiss, and Table 4-E shows how the State of Oregon might approach its brief in response.[8] As you can see, the U.S. Attorney General can emphasize his statutory authority to regulate controlled substances, and the State of Oregon can emphasize a state's authority to regulate medical practice. Note that, although both perspectives are valid, they emphasize different laws and the reasons for those laws.

Table 4-D · Developing a theme for a motion to dismiss based on the substantive law

The case	The State of Oregon passed a statute that permitted physician-assisted suicide. Citing his authority under the Controlled Substances Act, the U.S. Attorney General issued an interpretive regulation that would allow the U.S. Attorney General to revoke the licenses of physicians who prescribed drugs sufficient for an individual to commit suicide under the state statute. Among other things, the interpretive regulation stated that, "assisting suicide is not a 'legitimate medical purpose' within the meaning of [the Controlled Substances Act and its regulations]." 66 Fed. Reg. 56,607-02 (Nov. 9, 2001). The state and several private parties filed a complaint that sought to enjoin the Attorney General from enforcing that interpretive regulation. You are an Assistant U.S. Attorney seeking to dismiss that complaint.
Legal standard	Under the Controlled Substances Act, "[a] prescription for a controlled substance…must be issued for a legitimate medical purpose." 21 C.F.R. §1306.04 (2015). The Attorney General has the authority to promulgate "rules and regulations…relating to the registration and…distribution and dispensing of controlled substances." *Id.* §801.
Theme	The Controlled Substances Act permits the distribution of controlled substances for only a "legitimate medical purpose" and assisted suicide is not a "legitimate medical purpose."
Technique	In the brief, emphasize the everyday and historical understanding of "medicine" as "healing" and that Congress delegated to the Attorney General authority to regulate controlled substances. In this case, the U.S. Attorney General properly used that authority.

8. Tables 4-D and 4-E are based on Brief for Appellants, 368 F.3d 1118 (9th Cir. 2004) (No. 02-35587), 2002 WL 32290869, and Appellee's Brief of the State of Oregon, 368 F.3d 1118 (9th Cir. 2004) (No. 02-35587), 2002 WL 32290871, respectively.

Table 4-E · Developing a theme for a motion to dismiss based on the substantive law

The case	Same scenario as in Table 4-D, but you are an Assistant Attorney General for the State of Oregon, and you are arguing against the motion to dismiss and in favor of an injunction.
Legal standard	The clear statement doctrine: When "Congress intends to alter the 'usual constitutional balance between the States and Federal Government,' it must make its intention to do so 'unmistakably clear in the language of the statute.'" *Will v. Mich. Dept. of State Police*, 491 U.S. 58, 65 (1989) (quoting *Atascadero State Hosp. v. Scanlon*, 473 U.S. 234, 242 (1985)). Historically, states have retained the authority to regulate the practice of medicine.
Theme	The U.S. Attorney General's interpretive regulation is an unwarranted federal intrusion into the sovereign interests of Oregon, the medical practice of its physicians, and end-of-life decisions.
Technique	In the motion, emphasize the state's historical right to regulate medical practice and that, in enacting the Controlled Substances Act, Congress meant to regulate drug trafficking, not medical practice. Thus, the U.S. Attorney General overreached his authority under the Controlled Substances Act.

C. Based on Procedural Law

Finally, judges examine legal issues within their procedural posture. For that reason, your theme can be based on the legal standard for the issue before the court. For example, if you are opposing a motion for summary judgment, you will likely build a theme around the standard for denying a motion for summary judgment, as in Table 4-F. If you want to overturn a jury verdict, you would build a theme around that standard, as in Table 4-G. Both themes emphasize the applicable procedural standard.

Table 4-F · Developing a theme to oppose a motion for summary judgment based on the procedural law

The case	You want to argue that summary judgment should not be granted.
Legal standard	Summary judgment may be granted only if "there is no genuine dispute as to any material fact and the movant is entitled to judgment as a matter of law." Fed. R. Civ. P. 56(a).
Theme	There *is* a "material issue of fact" and, therefore, summary judgment is inappropriate.
Technique	As frequently as possible (1) state that a genuine issue of fact exists and that the fact is material, and (2) prove the dispute by pointing to contradictory factual assertions and prove that the factual dispute is material by explaining the relationship between the fact and the legal standard. Thus, the summary judgment standard becomes the touchstone to which you will return because it governs how the court will decide the issue.

Table 4-G · Developing a theme to overturn a jury verdict

The case	You want to argue that the court should overturn a jury's verdict.
Legal standard	A judgment of acquittal must be entered for any offense for which the evidence is insufficient to sustain a conviction. Fed. R. Crim. P. 29. Evidence must be viewed in the light most favorable to the winning party. *United States v. Augustine*, 663 F.3d 367, 373 (8th Cir. 2011).
Theme	Even considering the evidence in the light most favorable to the winning party, the evidence does not support the verdict.
Technique	In the conclusion for every element, and as frequently as otherwise possible, (1) state that the evidence does not support the element, and (2) prove the evidence does not support the element by bringing forward all the evidence put forward by the winning party and explaining why it cannot support the element. Thus, the standard for a judgment of acquittal becomes the touchstone to which you will return.

D. Based on Undisputed Law, Facts, or Values

Whatever the inspiration for your theme may be, remember that it must be consistent with the law and facts relevant to the argument. In fact, to the extent that you can incorporate facts or legal concepts that are not in dispute, your theme is more likely to be accepted.

For example, the *Obergefell* plaintiffs identified undisputed facts that would lead to a tremendous loss. No one could dispute that, if the plaintiffs in *Obergefell* lost and the Ohio statute remained in place, partners in same-sex marriages would no longer be recognized as spouses, and at least one partner would no longer be recognized as a legal parent to the children. Those facts were both compelling and indisputable.

Undisputed legal standards supported the themes described in Tables 4-F and 4-G. No one can dispute the standard for summary judgment or overturning a jury verdict. Similarly, in Tables 4-D and 4-E the themes were based on undisputed substantive law—the Controlled Substances Act and the clear statement doctrine, respectively.

Your theme may also rely on an undisputed core value. The themes in Tables 4-B and 4-C rely on core values that everyone would agree are "good" values—the importance of following the rule of law and that, in an election, every vote should count. In each case, the theme is founded on a law or principle that is not in dispute.

III. When to Develop a Theme

Attorneys develop their themes at different times. Many attorneys begin to think about a theme as part of their theory of the case at the beginning. It develops as they get to know their client and research the facts and law surrounding the case. Many times, though, a theme does not fully emerge until they have researched the law and developed their arguments. At that point, the attorney has a full grasp of the law and facts. Also, at that point, the attorney can take a step back to reflect on the argument and develop a cohesive theme consistent with the theory of the case.

Do not worry too much if a theme is not immediately evident. Often when you begin working on an argument, you will not know what the theme will be. As you continue to write and think about a case, the key legal or moral principle will likely reveal itself. You may not see a theme early on, but one may emerge after you have started organizing your arguments or developing the strengths and weaknesses of your case. As you wrestle with your case's legal and factual minutiae, if you find yourself saying, "What's *really* going on here is…," you have likely found your theme. Once a theme has emerged—be it a legal standard or something "catchier"—you can go back and make sure you have integrated the theme into the structure of your legal argument.

Practice Points

- Develop a theme that is consistent with both the law and your facts and reminds the court why you win.

- Lawyers often develop themes from examining the procedural legal standard, a policy underlying the substantive law, or a social value that is at stake.

- When developing a theme, remember that the court is more likely to accept your theme to the extent that you can incorporate facts or concepts that are not in dispute.

- Continue to develop and refine your theme as you write.

Chapter 5

Drafting Persuasive Arguments

As you saw in the last chapter, attorneys use the same structures to organize their writing whether they are writing objectively or persuasively. This chapter focuses on what does change when you write persuasively. Although you will use the same structures, the content of your arguments will shift. In all instances, the purpose of that shift is to make it easier for the court to rule in favor of your client.

That shift to persuasion is subtle. When advocating for a particular outcome, neither the law nor the facts suddenly change. As discussed in Chapter 2, *The Ethical, Professional Advocate*, "it is what it is," and you must work within the confines of the law and the facts. Moreover, if you stretch the law or facts too far, you are likely to undermine every effort at persuasion because the court will no longer trust you.

Although you must accept the law and facts as they are, you can present both so that they more readily allow the court to reach the outcome you seek. This chapter, *Developing Persuasive Arguments*, and the next chapter, Chapter 6, *Refining Persuasive Arguments*, provide you with techniques to do just that. This chapter focuses on developing the substance of a persuasive legal argument, while the next chapter addresses how to fine-tune that substance.

In developing the substance of a persuasive argument, this chapter looks at each component part of a legal argument—the conclusion, the explanation of the law, the application, and the final conclusion—and addresses how each can be developed to present your client's case in the most persuasive way and make it easier for a court to find in your client's favor.

I. Begin with Your Conclusion

A persuasive legal argument should begin with a conclusion. That conclusion should state the decision you believe the court should reach regarding the element or factor at issue.

Stating your conclusion at the outset of your argument has at least two persuasive functions. First, stating your conclusion tells the judge where you are going and, therefore, helps the judge follow your argument. An argument that is easier to follow is more likely to be absorbed and accepted. In addition, stating your conclusion at the outset is likely to provide repetition about a key point. You may also state your conclusion in a point heading and at the end of your argument. That repetition helps your main idea stick in the judge's head.

Occasionally, you may choose to omit the initial conclusion and begin an argument with a statement of the issue before the court. For example, if your introduction and a point heading already state the conclusion, stating it again may seem overly repetitive. When in doubt, though, state your conclusion about the element or factor in dispute and take advantage of its persuasive effect.

II. Explain the Law Persuasively

Although you will likely begin with a conclusion, and the conclusion is your first persuasive step, the real work begins with explaining the law. Many attorneys think that explaining the law is the easy part. You simply look up the law and write down what you find. If, however, you think that the real work of developing arguments begins when the law is *applied* to the current case, you will lose significant persuasive opportunities. In particular, you will lose the opportunity to present the law in a way that is most favorable to your client. You will also lose the opportunity to prime the court so that it is receptive to the analysis that will follow. Thus, do not wait. Begin persuading as soon as you begin explaining.

The next two sections address how to present rules and case illustrations persuasively. Although the two sections explain rules and case illustrations separately, keep in mind that when your argument includes both rules and case illustrations, the two must work together.

A. Rules

You can use several techniques to present legal rules in a persuasive light. First, you can present existing rules so that they state the law from your client's perspective. Second, you can develop new rules that will advance your argument. Finally, you can address unfavorable rules in a way that minimizes their negative impact.

1. Explain existing rules from your client's perspective

When explaining the rule, you can do more than merely cut and paste the rules as you found them. As you set out a rule, think about how you can emphasize those parts of the rule that are most helpful to your position. Although no set formula dictates how to do that, here are a few techniques to get you thinking.

First, you should consider whether to state a rule positively or negatively. If you are arguing that a standard is met, then frame the rule so that it explains when the required standard is met. By contrast, if you are arguing that a standard is not met, then frame the rule so that it explains when the standard is not met.

Take, for example, the rule for summary judgment. If you represent the moving party and argue that the court should grant summary judgment on your client's behalf, you should emphasize when summary judgment *must* be granted. By contrast, if you represent the non-moving party, you will want to emphasize when summary judgment should *not* be granted. Table 5-A shows the rule for summary judgment and how opposing counsel might present that same rule in two different ways. Note that the rule is the same under either version; what has changed is how the rule is presented.

Table 5-A · Explaining the summary judgment standard consistently with your client's position by stating when the standard is met or not met

The rule as written	"The court shall grant summary judgment if the movant shows that there is no genuine dispute as to any material fact and the movant is entitled to judgment as a matter of law." Fed. R. Civ. P. 56(a).
The moving party	Summary judgment must be granted if there is no issue of material fact and the moving party is entitled to judgment as a matter of law. Fed. R. Civ. P. 56(a).
The non-moving party	Summary judgment may not be granted if there is an issue of material fact. Fed. R. Civ. P. 56(a).

What "must" a court do?

When using the auxiliary verb "must," choose your subject carefully. Although lawyers often state what "must" happen under the law, a judge may be put off if you assert what the court "must" do. Thus, explain what "must" happen under the law, but urge the court to do what it "should."

You can use the same technique with more substantive rules. If you are alleging discrimination, explain when discrimination takes place. If you are defending against a charge of discrimination, explain when a party does not discriminate under the law, as in Table 5-B.

Table 5-B • Explaining a substantive rule consistently with your client's position by stating the rule positively or negatively

The rule as written	"A recipient which operates or sponsors interscholastic…athletics shall provide equal athletic opportunity for members of both sexes. In determining whether equal op-portunities are available the Director will consider, among other factors: (1) Whether the selection of sports and levels of competition effectively accommodate the inter-ests and abilities of members of both sexes…." 34 C.F.R. 106.41(c)(1).
Plaintiff	A university discriminates against its female students if it fails to effectively accom-modate the interests and abilities of its female students. 34 C.F.R. 106.41(c)(1); *Roberts v. Colo. St. Bd. of Agric.*, 998 F.2d 824, 828 (10th Cir. 1993).
Defendant	A university complies with Title IX if it effectively accommodates the interests and abilities of its female students. 34 C.F.R. 106.41(c) (1); *Roberts v. Colo. St. Bd. of Agric.*, 998 F.2d 824, 828 (10th Cir. 1993).

Second, your explanation of the rule can emphasize the breadth or the narrowness of a standard. Compare the explanations of the standard for granting summary judgment in Table 5-C. Notice how the non-moving party uses the word "only" to suggest that summary judgment should be granted in limited circumstances.

Table 5-C • Explaining the summary judgment standard consistently with your client's position by emphasizing the narrowness of a standard

The rule as written	"The court shall grant summary judgment if the movant shows that there is no gen-uine dispute as to any material fact and the movant is entitled to judgment as a mat-ter of law." Fed. R. Civ. P. 56(a).
The non-moving party	Summary judgment may be granted **only** if there is no issue of material fact and the moving party is entitled to judgment as a matter of law. Fed. R. Civ. P. 56(a).

You can also present substantive rules more broadly or more narrowly by describing the rule more abstractly or a more concretely.

Imagine, for example, that you are a defense attorney, and you want to establish that a police officer illegally stopped your client. The police officer had demanded that your client establish her name and residency. Since your client did not have a driver's license, your client handed over a library card as proof of identity and residency. You must first prove that your client was stopped.

You consider the possible ways that the law regarding stops can be framed. Your options include those listed in Figure 5-D. You, as a defense attorney, might want to emphasize a broader rule—that a person is stopped whenever a citizen believes that the citizen's liberty has been constrained and that belief is reasonable. By contrast, the prosecutor might emphasize a narrower rule—that a stop occurs when a police officer takes possession of a driver's license, not a library card.

Figure 5-D · Rules describing when a citizen is stopped

- A police officer stops a citizen if the citizen's liberty is constrained.
- A police officer stops a citizen if the citizen believes the citizen's liberty has been restrained and that belief is objectively reasonable.
- A police officer stops a citizen if the police officer requests and takes possession of an individual's driver's license.

Broad

Narrow

By considering rules on a scale from broad to narrow, you can consider different ways you might explain the law, and you can begin to consider the position opposing counsel might take.

Developing persuasive rules using an abstraction ladder[1]

To generate ideas about how to persuasively craft your legal argument, you can think about the law in terms of a "ladder of abstraction."[2]

Imagine a ladder with multiple rungs. On the higher rungs are abstract principles and rules, with the broadest or most abstract rule on the top. More concrete rules are found on the lower-level rungs, with the bottom rung being the rule that is the most fact specific. When framing a rule, the ladder can help you determine how broadly or narrowly you might frame that rule. If all rules stay on the highest rungs of the ladder, you may be talking only about broad concepts. If your rules stay on the ladder's bottom rung, then you may be talking about extremely narrow rules that are case-specific and not easily applied to future situations.

The ladder-image below takes rules from property law and illustrates how you can think of rules more broadly (on the higher rungs of the ladder) or more narrowly (on the lower rungs of the ladder).

Thinking about rules as existing along a ladder of abstraction can help you consider different ways you might frame a rule. Then, as an advocate, you can choose the formulation that will explain the law accurately and advance your client's case.

---

1. We thank Professor Judith Miller for encouraging us to include this topic.

2. Katherine Simmons Yagerman, *Clear Thinking for Students of Legal Writing*, 4 Second Draft 9, 9-10 (2004) (borrowing from S.I. Hayakawa, *Language in Thought and Action* (4th ed. 1988)). Samuel Ichiye Hayakawa is credited for creating the ladder of abstraction concept in 1939.

Ladder of Abstraction

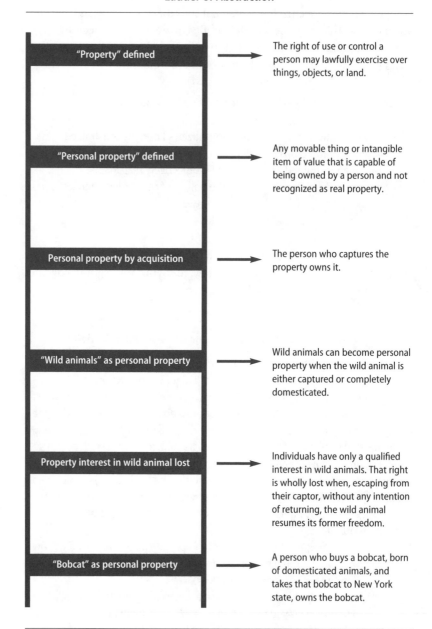

Most general principle of property law.

"Property" defined — The right of use or control a person may lawfully exercise over things, objects, or land.

"Personal property" defined — Any movable thing or intangible item of value that is capable of being owned by a person and not recognized as real property.

Personal property by acquisition — The person who captures the property owns it.

"Wild animals" as personal property — Wild animals can become personal property when the wild animal is either captured or completely domesticated.

Property interest in wild animal lost — Individuals have only a qualified interest in wild animals. That right is wholly lost when, escaping from their captor, without any intention of returning, the wild animal resumes its former freedom.

The narrowest rule is fact-specific to a particular case.

"Bobcat" as personal property — A person who buys a bobcat, born of domesticated animals, and takes that bobcat to New York state, owns the bobcat.

Finally, consider the order in which you present the rules. Usually, attorneys begin by explaining the most broadly relevant rule and then discussing more specific aspects of the rule. The judge will be confused if you begin with specific parts of a rule and then present the rule more broadly.

Sometimes, however, you might have some opportunity to choose which rules to present first. Consider, for example, how two different parties might present the rules regarding whether a defendant's encounter with a police officer was "mere conversation" or was a "stop" that needs to be justified by reasonable suspicion. The defendant would like to argue that the encounter was a stop and, therefore, had to be justified by reasonable suspicion. The defendant would likely begin by discussing what constitutes a stop, as in Example 5-E. By contrast, the state would likely begin by describing what constitutes "mere conversation" because the state wants to focus the court's attention on that legal standard, as in Example 5-F. Notice that both parties ultimately describe the same law, but the order in which they describe the relevant rules differs because they wish to emphasize different aspects of the law.

Example 5-E • Defendant's explanation of the rules emphasizes when an encounter is a stop

When a police officer stops a citizen, evidence gathered during the course of that stop is not admissible against that citizen unless the stop was justified by reasonable suspicion. *State v. Spenst*, 662 P.2d 5, 6 (Or. Ct. App. 1983). A police officer "stops" a citizen if that person's liberty is restrained, by physical force or a show of authority, by a peace officer lawfully present in any place. Or. Rev. Stat. § 131.605(6); *State v. Warner*, 901 P.2d 940, 942 (Or. Ct. App. 1995). More generally, a person's liberty may be restrained if an individual believes his liberty has been restrained and that belief is objectively reasonable. *Warner*, 901 P.2d at 942. To determine whether a person reasonably believes his liberty was restrained, a court will consider the totality of the circumstances. *State v. Wenger*, 922 P.2d 1248, 1251 (Or. Ct. App. 1996). Only if, under the totality of the circumstances, a person could not reasonably believe his liberty was restrained, is the encounter "mere conversation." *See, e.g., State v. Smith*, 698 P.2d 973, 975 (Or. Ct. App. 1985).

The defendant, who wants to focus on when a "stop" occurs, begins his explanation of the law by discussing the requirements for a valid stop. A reader's attention wanes over time. Thus, ideas at the outset receive more focused attention, and it advances your argument to explain first those ideas that you want to emphasize.

Example 5-F • The state's explanation of the rules emphasizes when an encounter is mere conversation

Under Oregon law, citizens can have different encounters with police officers. When an encounter is "mere conversation," evidence an officer acquires during the encounter is admissible against the defendant. *State v. Shelton*, 796 P.2d 390, 392 (Or. Ct. App. 1990).

An encounter is "mere conversation" if, under the totality of the circumstances, a person could not reasonably believe his liberty is being restrained. *See, e.g., State v. Smith*, 698 P.2d 973, 975 (Or Ct. App. 1985). By contrast, if a person reasonably believes his liberty is being restrained, he is "stopped." Or. Rev. Stat. §

The state, by contrast, wants to focus on when an interaction with a law enforcement agent is "mere conversation." Thus, the state begins its explanation with that idea, giving more emphasis to the idea that some encounters are only "conversation" and not stops.

131.605(6); *State v. Warner*, 901 P.2d 940, 942 (Or. Ct. App. 1995). Any evidence obtained during that stop is admissible only if the stop was justified by reasonable suspicion. *State v. Spenst*, 662 P.2d 5, 6 (Or. Ct. App. 1983).

To determine whether an encounter is "mere conversation" or a "stop," the court considers the totality of the circumstances. *State v. Wenger*, 922 P.2d 1248, 1251 (Or. Ct. App. 1996).

---

2. Develop rules that advance your client's argument

Presenting rules consistently with your client's perspective may involve developing rules that will advance your analysis. You might think of the law as settled and believe that you should not "create" new law. Although reasonable, that kind of thinking will limit your usefulness to your client. Within the settled law—and usually within the settled case law—there exist patterns of judicial or legislative thinking. Before they are articulated, those patterns are sometimes called "implicit rules." As an advocate, one of the ways you can help your client is to make those implicit rules explicit. By making implicit rules explicit, you will provide the court with a way to reach a conclusion that is consistent with the currently existing law. And courts want their decisions to be consistent with the existing law.

Of course, all sorts of patterns exist in the law and only some are relevant and helpful. To make sure that you are drawing out relevant and helpful patterns, you need to (1) formulate a possible rule and then (2) evaluate that rule. To formulate a possible rule, you must first identify a pattern in the cases that seems to explain why courts reach their conclusions and, second, craft a rule from the pattern that encompasses both the prior cases and your client's case. Crafting the rule may require you to explain the rule more broadly or more narrowly.

After you have formulated a possible rule, then you must evaluate the rule to make sure that it is wise to use. To evaluate the rule, ask yourself these two questions:

- Is my proposed rule consistent with all the other law that governs this issue?
- If so, does my proposed rule make common sense?

These two questions are important because, if your proposed rule is not consistent with other applicable authorities, then you are not providing the court with an easy way to rule in your favor. Moreover, and perhaps not surprisingly, judges prefer rules that make sense.

Let's look at how you might develop a rule that advances your client's position. Take, for example, the case in which two police officers conducted a safety frisk and found an unregistered, concealed gun. The officers have stated that the reason they conducted the safety frisk was that the defendants were wearing clothing that suggested they were members of a gang. The officers knew that members of this gang often carried weapons and, therefore, they conducted the safety frisk.

Now imagine you are the prosecutor, and you wish to argue that the officers' safety frisk was justified. You begin by reviewing the cases. You read a variety of cases, two of which are excerpted in Table 5-G.

You then begin to formulate a possible rule. From the cases, you notice two things. First, in past cases in which safety frisks were permitted, the defendant had been with a dangerous person. That's a problem for you. In the current case, no known gang member was actually present when the officers arrived. So, a rule that "a safety frisk can be supported if the defendant is *with* a dangerous person at the time of the stop" would not be helpful to your position. You will have to explain the pattern in slightly broader terms. For example, you could argue that officers are permitted to conduct safety frisks if the defendant "associates with" someone dangerous. That explanation of the law accurately reflects past decisions, but it does so in a way that supports your client's position.

Second, you notice that in past cases, police officers presented evidence that the stop related to an activity that involved weapons. Arguably, the protective search in this case was related to an activity that involved weapons. In this case, the officers conducted a safety frisk because they believed the defendants were associated with a gang. Being a member of a gang is an activity that often involves weapons.

Table 5-G · Formulating an explicit rule from implicit rules in case law

Case	Holding	Facts
State v. Stanley	Safety frisk upheld	The defendant was suspected of robbing a bank. The officers testified that those who commit robberies often carry weapons. The defendant was with a man who, during the course of the stop, acted aggressively by grabbing the officer's hand.
State v. Ehly	Safety frisk upheld	The defendant was known to be a drug user, and officers testified that drug users often possess guns. The officer had just seen another man leave the motel where the officers were currently confronting defendant. The man who had just left was known to use guns and was friends with the defendant. Finally, the defendant's hands were concealed.
Proposed rule	To establish a reasonable suspicion for a protective search, officers may rely on their knowledge that the defendant associates with a known dangerous person or that the person is connected with an activity that involves weapons.	

You have now developed a proposed rule: "To establish a reasonable suspicion for a protective search, officers may rely on their knowledge that the defendant associates with a known dangerous person or that the person is connected with an activity that involves weapons."

Now, you need to evaluate the rule. First, you must make sure that no other case rejects the very rule you are proposing. In addition, you would want to consider whether your proposed rule is consistent with the other rules, case law, and policies that govern this area of the law. For example, you know that an officer must have reasonable suspicion for a frisk and that reasonable suspicion must be supported by "clearly articulable facts." Is this an example of a clearly articulable fact, and not a hunch? Arguably, it is. Officers can explain the facts that lead them to believe that the defendants were associated with a dangerous group. Thus, this proposed rule is consistent with at least one other rule.

If your proposed rule is consistent with existing law, you will want to ask yourself the final question. Does your proposed rule make sense? Answering that question requires some knowledge about this area of the law and some imagination. You want to imagine other situations in which the court might be faced with someone "associated with" a dangerous person. Would a frisk still be justified in those circumstances? Suppose the defendant and someone known to carry a gun were on the same basketball team and were, therefore, wearing the same uniform. The defendant would be "associated with" a dangerous person. Would a frisk be warranted in that case? Of course not. But that case can be distinguished because the association is not one that involves the danger. By considering other scenarios the court might face in the future, you can determine whether the proposed rule is likely to appeal to a court.

Once you have formulated and then evaluated the rule, you can finally include it in your explanation of the law, as in Example 5-H.

Example 5-H · Developing a favorable rule from case law

The proposed rule is stated in the first sentence. The case illustrations that follow prove that case law supports the proposed rule.

To establish a reasonable suspicion for a protective search, officers may rely on their knowledge that the defendant associates with a known dangerous person or that the person is connected with an activity that involves weapons. For example, in *Ehly*, this Court determined that officers had reasonable suspicion to conduct a protective search. *Ehly*, 854 P.2d at 431. In that case, officers knew that the defendant was a drug user and that "many people who use illegal narcotics possess guns." *Id.* at 430. Moreover, the officers also knew that defendant was "running" with a person who carried weapons. *Id.* Because the defendant was rummaging through a gym bag with his hands concealed and did not respond to the officer's suggestion to dump out the contents of the bag, this Court concluded that it was reasonable for one of the officers to dump the contents of the bag onto the motel room bed. *Id.; see also Stanley*, 935 P.2d at 1204 (finding reasonable suspicion because the defendant was suspected of robbing a bank; officers knew that those engaged in a possible robbery may carry weapons; and the defendant associated with a man who, during the course of the stop, acted aggressively by grabbing the officer's hand).

Notice that in Example 5-H the statement of the rule is followed by case illustrations. When making an implicit rule explicit, be sure to provide the court with all the information it will need to see the same pattern in the law that you do. For that reason, when making an implicit rule explicit, state the rule, and then provide case illustrations that will prove your understanding of the law is accurate.

Of course, opposing counsel is likely to follow the same steps and, if at all possible, explain the preceding case law in a way that will be helpful to his client. As explained below, one technique attorneys use in formulating a favorable rule is to state the rule more broadly or more narrowly.

In this case, the prosecutor has described the law more broadly to provide maximum opportunity for the court to uphold the stop. By contrast, defendant's counsel will propose a narrower rule that would restrict an officer's right to stop and frisk a citizen. Defendant's counsel will argue that a police officer can consider a defendant's association with another person as a basis for a frisk only if the other person was present or recently present.

Thus, in the same case, the lawyers may very well explain the prior case law more broadly or more narrowly, as suggested in Table 5-I. Doing so is good advocacy.

Table 5-I · Prior case law explained more broadly or more narrowly

Case	Holding	Facts
State v. Stanley	Safety frisk upheld	The defendant was suspected of robbing a bank. The officers testified that those who commit robberies often carry weapons. The defendant was with a man who, during the course of the stop, acted aggressively by grabbing the officer's hand.
State v. Ehly	Safety frisk upheld	The defendant was known to be a drug user, and officers testified that drug users often possess guns. The officer had just seen another man leave the motel where the officers were currently confronting defendant. The man who had just left was known to use guns and was friends with the defendant. Finally, the defendant's hands were concealed.
Prosecutor's proposed rule	To establish a reasonable suspicion for a protective search, officers may rely on their knowledge that the defendant associates with a known dangerous person or that the person is connected with an activity that involves weapons.	
Defendant's narrower rule	A police officer may not conduct a safety frisk merely because a person has a relationship with someone who is known to be dangerous. Such a relationship, by itself, does not provide a sufficient connection to a dangerous activity such that it would support a protective search.	

Developing rules from patterns in case law is as much art as it is science. To help you get a better feel for it, look at another example.

Imagine that, now, your clients are a four-year-old child and her parents. While riding her bicycle, the four-year-old struck an elderly pedestrian who later died. The estate of the elderly pedestrian sued the four-year-old and her parents.[3] You would like to argue that, as a matter of law, a four-year-old cannot be held liable for negligence. Unfortunately, the case law is not entirely clear on that point. Some prior cases hold that four-year-olds, as a matter of law, cannot be held liable for negligence. Other cases, however, hold that four-year-olds can be held liable for negligence and that a jury should decide whether a particular four-year-old was negligent. Of course, you do not want the case to go to the jury; you want it dismissed. How can you shape your description of the law to provide the court with an easy way to dismiss the case?

Reviewing the cases, as illustrated in Table 5-J, you might see that some cases were dismissed when the court held that the child could not, as a matter of law, be negligent. In those cases, the child was under the parent's supervision. Thus, you begin to consider a rule that says, "A four-year-old child under the supervision of a parent cannot, as a matter of law, be held liable for negligence."

Table 5-J • Formulating a rule from implicit patterns in case law

Case	Holding	Facts
Ehrlich v. Marra	4-year-old not liable as a matter of law	Child of 4 years and 10 months "under direction of mother" was crossing the street when hit by car.
Romanchuk v. County of Westchester	4-year-old not liable as a matter of law	Child of 4 years and 11 months "under the direct supervision and control of the father" was sledding when accident occurred.
Boyd v. Trent	4-year-old not liable as a matter of law	Child of 4 years had climbed to front seat where mother permitted her to stay. Child distracted mother, and a car accident resulted.
Camardo v. New York State Railways	Question for the jury	Child of 4 years and 10 months walking home from school, unaccompanied by adult, when accident occurred.
Defendant's proposed rule	A four-year-old child under the supervision of her parents cannot, as a matter of law, be held liable for negligence.	

---

3. Based on *Menagh v. Breitman*, Index No. 107856/09 (NY S. Ct. N.Y. Co. 2010).

Again, before deciding to rely on that rule, you would have to check every case to make sure no court allowed a negligence claim against a four-year-old when a parent was present at the time of the accident. If there were such a case, you would either need to abandon the proposed rule or acknowledge the case as an outlier that is inconsistent with the majority of decisions.

Finally, you would need to ask yourself whether this proposed rule makes sense. Arguably, it does. When a parent is present, the parent is in charge and making decisions. Under those circumstances, you could argue, the child should not be liable for injuries.

Thus, you might explain the law as in Example 5-K.

Example 5-K · Including a favorable rule from case law in your explanation of the law

---

With respect to claims of negligence brought against infants, this Court has consistently held that a four-year-old child, who is under the supervision of an adult, is incapable of negligence. *Ehrlich v. Marra*, 300 N.Y.S.2d 81, 82 (N.Y. App. Div. 1940); *Romanchuk v. County of Westchester*, 337 N.Y.S.2d 926, 927 (N.Y. App. Div. 1972); *Boyd v. Trent*, 746 N.Y.S.2d 191, 193 (N.Y. App. Div. 2002). For example, in *Ehrlich v. Marra*, this Court held that a child of four years and ten months could not be found guilty of contributory negligence. 300 N.Y.S.2d at 82. In that case, the child had been crossing the street "at the direction and under the supervision of his mother" when he was struck by a car. *Id.*

Similarly, in *Romanchuk v. County of Westchester,* this Court held that a child "then several days short of his fifth birthday...must be deemed, as a matter of law, to have been free of contributory negligence" in a sledding accident. 337 N.Y.S.2d at 927. In that case, the court noted that the child was "under the direct supervision and control of the father" when the father placed the child on a sled and the child then coasted down a slope by himself. *See id.*

Most recently, in *Boyd v. Trent*, this Court again held that a four-year-old could not be held liable for negligence. 746 N.Y.S.2d at 193. In that case, the parent was also present. *Id.* The four-year-old had extricated herself from her car seat and made her way to the front of the car where her mother, who was driving, permitted her to remain. *Id.* Soon thereafter, the mother failed to negotiate a turn and collided with another car. This Court held that the four-year-old was "incapable of being held liable for negligence." *Id.*

The proposed rule is stated in the first sentence. The case illustrations that follow prove that case law supports the proposed rule.

Again, opposing counsel is likely to review the same prior case law and recommend a different rule. Although the defendant's lawyer will argue for a strict rule, that four-year-olds under the supervision of an adult can never be found to be negligent, plaintiff's counsel is likely to look at the same case law and derive a more permissive rule. Plaintiff's counsel is likely to emphasize those instances when a jury is allowed to consider whether a four-year-old is negligent and may propose this rule: "With respect to four-year-olds no bright-line rule exists; rather, a jury is permitted to determine whether a four-year-old was negligent."

In each case, the lawyer is doing her job: providing a way for the court to rule in favor of that lawyer's client. Some people find this process uncomfortable. To some, it seems odd that lawyers can look at the same law and argue that the law should be understood in two very different ways. That, however, is how the law develops. Opposing counsel look at the prior case law and advocate different, but reasonable, ways for the court to understand that prior case law. The court may choose one of the proposed rules to follow, or the court may see the law in yet another way and modify the rules proposed by counsel when issuing its decision. As an advocate, your role is to explain one reasonable interpretation of the existing law.

3. Acknowledge unfavorable rules in a favorable way

The theme of this chapter (and this book) is that as an advocate your job is to provide a way for the court to rule in your client's favor. To do so, you sometimes must acknowledge unfavorable, relevant law and show the court why the outcome you seek is still appropriate. In fact, consider your explanation of unfavorable law to be an opportunity to explain why, despite anything opposing counsel might say, you still win. And, in addition to being a way to produce the most persuasive argument, acknowledging unfavorable rules is your ethical duty.[4]

Take for example the scenario in which you are a prosecutor trying to uphold a frisk based in part on the officer's observation that the defendant was wearing clothes that associated the defendant with a gang. (The scenario is described above in the text accompanying Tables 5-G and 5-I.) The unfavorable rule for your position is that an officer cannot base reasonable suspicion for a frisk on the suspect's appearance. In your case, the officers had, arguably, done just that. They had conducted a safety frisk based on the clothes the defendants were wearing. By acknowledging that rule in your explanation of the law, you will begin the process of disposing of opposing counsel's argument. In particular, by acknowledging that the rule exists, you are implicitly saying, "I know about that rule. I'm not scared of it. And it does not preclude the outcome I seek."

Example 5-L demonstrates how you might draft an explanation of the law that also addresses unfavorable law. You might state, as in Example 5-L, that an officer cannot conduct a safety frisk based on a defendant's looks *if* those looks do not reasonably connect the defendant to a dangerous activity. Framed that way, you have created an opportunity to argue that

---

4. Model R. of Prof'l Conduct R. 3.3(a)(2) ("A lawyer shall not knowingly... fail to disclose to the tribunal legal authority in the controlling jurisdiction known to the lawyer to be directly adverse to the position of the client and not disclosed by opposing counsel.").

the safety frisk was justified because, in this case, the clothes were reasonably connected to a dangerous activity.

Example 5-L • An explanation of law that acknowledges unfavorable law

Officers Brown and Cockerham had a reasonable suspicion that justified a protective frisk of the defendant. Whether a suspicion is reasonable depends on the inferences drawn from the particular circumstances confronting the officer viewed in light of the officer's experience. *See State v. Ehly*, 854 P.2d 421, 430 (Or. 1993) (citing *Terry v. Ohio*, 392 U.S. 1, 21-22, 27–30 (1968)). An "intuitive sixth sense" or "instinct" cannot "form the entire basis for 'reasonable suspicion.'" *State v. Valdez*, 561 P.2d 1006, 1010-11 (Or. 1977). Rather, an officer must be able to point to specific and articulable facts that give rise to a reasonable inference that the person might pose an immediate threat. *See Ehly*, 854 P.2d at 430. An officer need not show that the threat was "more likely than not." *See* Or. Rev. Stat. 131.005(11) (defining "probable cause"). An officer must simply have a reasonable belief that a circumstance may exist or that a particular event might occur. *See State v. Stanley*, 935 P.2d 1202, 1204 (Or. 1997). In other words, for a protective frisk to be justified, an officer must show only that the particular circumstances gave rise to a reasonable belief that the defendant might pose an immediate threat.

> The explanation of the law begins here. It describes general principles about which both parties would agree.

To establish a reasonable belief that the defendant might pose an immediate threat, officers may rely on their knowledge that the defendant associates with a known dangerous person or that the person is connected with an activity that involves weapons. For example, in *Ehly*, this Court determined that officers had reasonable suspicion to conduct a protective search. *Ehly*, 854 P.2d at 431. In that case, officers knew that the defendant was a drug user and that "many people who use illegal narcotics possess guns." *Id.* at 430. Moreover, the officers also knew that defendant was "running" with a person who carried weapons. *Id.* Because the defendant was rummaging through a gym bag with his hands concealed and did not respond to the officer's suggestion to dump out the contents of the bag, this Court concluded that it was reasonable for one of the officers to dump the contents of the bag onto the motel room bed. *Id.*

> Here, the explanation of law asserts a rule that the State wants to rely on later — that officers can take into account dangerous activities or dangerous people that the defendant is associated with.

Officers must, however, rely on more than the defendant's "looks" when that "look" does not reasonably connect the defendant to a criminal or a dangerous activity. For example, in *Valdez*, this court held that police officers lacked reasonable suspicion to stop a person who was dressed in a blue leisure suit, wore shiny black shoes, and looked "real sharp." *Valdez*, 561 P.2d at 1010. Although the police officers thought the defendant looked like a "typical pusher," the court disagreed, stating that "[n]eedle scars on forearms may legitimately speak of possible criminal activity in drugs, but shined shoes, sharp clothes, and staring at a police officer do not say much." *Id.* at 1010–11. Similarly, in *Bates*, this court held that the officers had not established reasonable suspicion when all that the officers could point to was that the defendant had long hair and a beard, was wearing a leather jacket, and looked suspicious. *State v. Bates*, 747 P.2d 991, 994 (Or. 1987).

> The explanation of the law acknowledges an unfavorable rule — that officers cannot rely on the way defendants look.

Do not wait for your opponent to explain the unfavorable rule or, worse, for the court to find the unfavorable rule on its own. If you know that a rule is relevant and implicated by the facts of the case, your client will be best served if you present that law couched in your client's favor. Never ignore unfavorable law and hope the court will not notice it. The court will notice. And then both your client and your reputation will suffer.

B. Case Illustrations

In addition to presenting rules in the most persuasive way, you will also want to present case illustrations of those rules in the most persuasive way.[5]

1. Highlight helpful facts

Just as you want to shape rules so that the rules reflect your perspective, you also want to shape your explanation of the cases that illustrate those rules. With respect to cases, your argument will ultimately rely on comparing the facts of a prior case to the facts of your client's case. You will usually argue either that your client's case is like the prior case and the same outcome is warranted, or you will argue that your client's case is distinguishable from the prior case and, therefore, the prior case is not precedent for the current case.

To support that ultimate argument, you will want to carefully draft the case illustrations you provide in your explanation of the law. In particular, you will want your case illustration to highlight those facts in the prior court's analysis that will support your argument. Drafting a case illustration to support your argument is a straightforward task when the facts that you want to highlight were clearly central to the court's analysis.

Sometimes, however, you want to base your argument on a factual similarity or distinction that was not obviously central to the prior court's analysis (i.e., the fact is mentioned in the statement of the facts, but the court does not mention it when analyzing the particular legal issue). In that case, you need a process for determining whether the factual comparison or distinction you would like to draw is a good one. That process is very similar to the process for determining whether a proposed rule is a good one. With respect to factual comparisons, you need to determine the comparison you would like to make and then evaluate that comparison. Evaluating the comparison requires you to ask the same questions as with proposed rules:

- Is the proposed similarity or distinction consistent with all other relevant law?

---

5. Note that some legal arguments will have no case illustrations, e.g., rule-based arguments.

- Does the proposed similarity or distinction make sense?

Consider again the case of the four-year-old bicyclist who ran into an elderly pedestrian. Imagine, this time, that you represent the estate of the elderly woman who was struck by the four-year-old cyclist. Your client, the estate of the elderly woman, would like to sue the four-year-old (and her parents) for negligence. Many cases say that the question of negligence goes to the jury. One case, however, holds differently. The court in *Romanchuk* held that a four-year-old child who had been involved in a sledding accident could *not*, as a matter of law, be held liable for contributory negligence.

In reviewing the *Romanchuk* case, you notice that the sledding accident took place in an area designated for sledding. You question whether that fact could be the basis of distinguishing the *Romanchuk* case. After all, in your client's case, the four-year-old was not in a designated bicycling area; rather, the child was on a city street. Thus, you have identified a possible distinction.

Now you must evaluate that distinction. Is the fact that the accident in the *Romanchuk* case occurred in a designated sledding area a reasonable basis on which to distinguish the case? To answer that question, you would first need to review all the other prior cases to determine whether there is a case in which the court held that a child who injured another person in a designated play area could not be held liable for negligence.

Assuming you find no such cases, you will need to ask yourself whether that distinction is a reasonable one on which the court could distinguish the case. Arguably, it is. When a child is in a designated play area, the child is paying less attention and should not be held liable for an injury that occurs in an area designated for that purpose. By contrast, in an area not designated for that purpose, a child may be held more accountable.

Assuming that the distinction makes sense, then you simply need to craft a case illustration that highlights the fact that, later, will form the basis of your case comparison, as seen in Example 5-M.

Example 5-M • Plaintiff highlights facts that will support a helpful distinction

---

In the *Romanchuk* case, the child was sledding in a park designated for that activity when the child was struck by a parks department vehicle. *Romanchuk v. Westchester Ct.*, 337 N.Y.S.2d 926, 926 (N.Y. App. Div. 1972). The key fact in that case was not the child's age or the parent's supervision. Rather, the key fact was that the child was sledding "in an area of the park where such activities were permitted." *Id.* Thus, the jury could reach only one conclusion, that whoever was sledding in that area, regardless of age or parental supervision, was not contributorily negligent. *See id.*

For the plaintiff, the key fact is that the child was sledding in an area designated for sledding. Note how that fact is emphasized in the topic sentence and again in the second textual sentence.

Developing persuasive case illustrations using a ladder of abstraction

The goal of a case illustration is to show how a rule functioned in a prior case. Examining a case's holdings, facts, and analyses using a ladder of abstraction can also help you generate ideas about how to present a prior case or even a series of cases.

As explained before, a ladder of abstraction is a way to organize and sort through ideas. On an abstraction ladder, more abstract ideas are placed on higher rungs, with the most abstract idea placed on the highest rung. More concrete ideas are on the lower rung, with the bottom rung reserved for the most specific idea. A prior case has a variety of parts. Most typically, those parts include the facts of the prior case, the court's holding about the legal issue, and any reasoning that connects the facts to the holding. Each of those parts can be placed on a ladder of abstraction. That is, the holding and analysis can be stated more or less broadly, and the facts of the prior case can be set out in more or less detail.

To see how using a ladder of abstraction can help you generate ideas about how to shape a prior case, consider again the case in which an elderly woman is struck by a four-year-old cyclist. The legal issue is whether a four-year-old-child can be sued for negligence or whether a four-year-old child is immune from such a claim due to the child's age. You represent the elderly woman who was struck by the four-year-old cyclist. The child was in a bicycle lane, and the child's father was several car lengths behind the child.

You have found a case, *Carmado v. New York State Railway*, in which a New York court allowed a four-year-old to be sued for negligence. In that case, a four- year-old child was allowed to walk home from school under the supervision of the child's sister. On the day of the accident, the child did not wait for his sister, and he was walking home by himself. After getting caught up in a game with some friends, the four-year-old ran out into the street and caused an accident. The court allowed the child (and the child's parents) to be sued for negligence explaining that "the law does not arbitrarily fix an age at which the duty to exercise some care begins."

You want to use the *Carmado* case to argue that the four-year-old cyclist can be sued for negligence. A ladder of abstraction can help you think about how you might describe the holding from *Carmado* in a variety of different ways. You can then consider which of those descriptions will explain the law in a way that will best support your client's argument.

Carmado v. N.Y. State Railway	Your client's case	
		At the top of the ladder of abstraction, the *Carmado* holding is stated most broadly.
A jury should be permitted to consider a child's negligence	A jury should be permitted to consider the child's negligence	This formulation states that a four-year-old can always be sued for negligence, which is not consistent with other cases that have not allowed a jury to consider a four-year-old's negligence. So, ultimately, you would likely reject this formulation of the holding.
A jury should be permitted to consider a child's negligence when conflicting inferences may be drawn as to the child's ability to avoid danger.	A jury should be permitted to consider the child's negligence because children vary in their capacity to appreciate and avoid danger.	This rung states the holding from *Carmado* more narrowly by indicating that a negligence case against a four-year-old can move forward to a jury only sometimes.
A jury should be permitted to consider a child's negligence when the child is old enough to engage in activities without adult supervision.	A jury should be permitted to consider the child's negligence because the child was without meaningful adult supervision at the time of the accident.	Here, the holding more specifically delineates when a negligence case against a four-year-old can move forward, which depends on a child's maturity level.
A jury appropriately considers a child's negligence when a child can walk home without adult supervision.	In this case, a jury should be permitted to consider the child's negligence because the child was mature enough to ride her bike several car lengths ahead of her parent—a position from which she was no longer under adult supervision.	This holding is the most narrow holding. It defines the maturity level of a child that is required for a case to move forward to a jury.

Because determining which facts to focus on can sometimes be challenging, consider one more example. In this example, you will see how following the steps described above might help you avoid making an unpersuasive argument.

Imagine that you are prosecuting a defendant for unlawful possession of a controlled substance. Police officers found the drugs when they stopped a car that looked like a stolen car. The officer checked the defendant's identification and registration and quickly discovered that the car belonged to the defendant and was not stolen. At the same time, the officers also checked the companion's identity. That check took longer because the companion lacked identification. So as not to make the whole stop a complete waste of time, the officer also asked the defendant whether any drugs were in the car. The defendant said that there were. The officer found the drugs in a subsequent search. All told, the stop lasted twenty minutes. The defendant will argue that the evidence should be suppressed because the stop was too long. Of course, as the prosecutor, you would like both the defendant's admission and the drugs found in the car to be admitted into evidence.

During your research, you find a case, the *Wolfe* case, which has remarkably similar facts. You particularly like the court's analysis, which is provided in Example 5-N.

Example 5-N • An excerpt from a prior case: which facts to focus on?

In *Wolfe*, the stop lasted twenty-seven minutes, and the court held that the stop lasted for a reasonable period of time.

You want to argue that twenty minutes is also a reasonable period of time for a stop.

Can you rely on *Wolfe* for that argument?

"An officer may detain an individual only for the time reasonably necessary to accomplish the purpose of the stop. [Officer] Truedson testified that he detained defendant and his companion for approximately 27 minutes in order to question them about their activities in the neighborhood, check their identity and fill out a field contact report documenting the stop. He testified that, normally, if an individual has identification, he would spend ten minutes per individual to verify identity, check his record and fill out a field identification card. In this case, it took him longer, however, because defendant's companion did not have any identification. We hold that the stop did not extend for longer than reasonably necessary to accomplish the purposes of the stop."

—*State v. Wolfe*, 763 P.2d 154, 156 (Or. App. 1988).

You consider making the argument that because the twenty-seven-minute stop in *Wolfe* was appropriate, a twenty-minute stop must also be appropriate.

Such a comparison would be unpersuasive. As discussed above, you need to make sure that the comparison you rely on is consistent with other authority. In this case, the rule cited by the court in *Wolfe* is that the stop must be no longer than the time "reasonably necessary to accomplish the purpose of the stop." Thus, whether a stop is reasonable is tied to the purpose of the stop, not just how long the stop lasts. By focusing on the twenty-seven minutes as a bright-line rule, your analysis

would be in conflict with the governing statute, which requires only reasonableness as compared to the purpose of the stop.

Looking again at the court's analysis, you might realize that the court
did not say that ten minutes was always reasonable (that was the police
officer's testimony). That fact was not actually important to the court's
analysis. The important fact was that twenty-seven minutes was reasonable
when the defendant's companion had no identification because the
purpose of the stop was to "question them about their activities in the
neighborhood [and] check their identity."

Thus, before explaining prior case law, take a moment to think about
which facts will be most useful to your ultimate analysis. If those facts
were not central to the prior court's analysis, take another moment to
consider whether emphasizing those facts—and, therefore, suggesting
that those facts were important in the prior case—would be consistent
with the surrounding law. If so, go ahead and shape your explanation of
the law so that it advances your client's case.

2. Create hooks for your case illustrations

A "hook" is a sentence that introduces a case illustration. It states the
specific legal point the case represents. In doing so, a hook focuses the
judge's attention and explains why the judge should bother reading about
the case.

If you have developed an implicit rule, that rule can be used as a hook
to introduce those cases that support the proposed rule. In the examples
above that illustrated how to draw out an implicit rule, the final text uses
the implicit rule as the hook to those case illustrations. Examples 5-O and
5-P, below, reproduce excerpts of those examples and point out the hooks.

Notice that the hooks for the case illustrations explain exactly what the
attorney wants the court to learn from those cases. In that way, the hooks
help to shape how the courts will think about the governing case law.

**Example 5-O · A hook for a series of case illustrations shapes the court's
thinking about those cases**

With respect to claims of negligence brought against infants, this Court has
consistently held that a four-year-old infant, who is under the supervision of an
adult, is incapable of negligence. *Ehrlich v. Marra*, 300 N.Y.S.2d 81, 82 (N.Y. App.
Div. 1940); *Romanchuk v. County of Westchester*, 337 N.Y.S.2d 926, 927 (N.Y. App.
Div. 1972); *Boyd v. Trent*, 746 N.Y.S.2d 191, 193 (N.Y. App. Div. 2002). For
example, in *Ehrlich v. Marra*, this Court held that a child of 4 years and 10
months could not be found guilty of contributory negligence. In that case, the
child had been crossing the street "at the direction and under the supervision
of his mother" when he was struck by a car. 300 N.Y.S.2d at 82. Similarly, in
Romanchuk v. Westchester County, this Court held that a child "then several days
short of his fifth birthday…must be deemed, as a matter of law, to have been
free of contributory negligence" in a sledding accident. 337 N.Y.S.2d at 927. In

A thoughtfully explained rule
acts as a hook for a series of case
illustrations. The hook shapes
how the court should think
about the cases that follow.

that case, the court noted that the child was "under the direct supervision and control of the father" when the father placed the child on a sled and the child then coasted down a slope by himself. *See id.*

Example 5-P • Hooks for case illustrations tell the court the rule it should follow

---

This hook, like the hook in Example 5-O, explains an implicit rule and guides the court to think about the case illustration that follows in a particular way.

To establish a reasonable belief that the defendant might pose an immediate threat, officers may rely on their knowledge that the defendant associates with a known dangerous person or that the person is connected with an activity that involves weapons. For example, in *Ehly*, this Court determined that officers had reasonable suspicion to conduct a protective search. 854 P.2d at 432. In that case, officers knew that the defendant was a drug user and that "many people who use illegal narcotics possess guns." *Id.* at 430. Moreover, the officers also knew that the defendant was "running" with a person who carried weapons. *Id.* Because the defendant was rummaging through a gym bag with his hands concealed and did not respond to the officer's suggestion to dump out the contents of the bag, this Court concluded that it was reasonable for one of the officers to dump the contents of the bag onto the motel room bed. *Id.*

This hook allows the prosecutor to frame a rule that is important to the defendant's argument. The hook frames the rule in a way that will be helpful later. In Example 5-R, below, you can see how this explanation of the *Valdez* case later helps the writer to distinguish the *Valdez* case.

Officers must, however, rely on more than the defendant's "looks" when that "look" does not reasonably connect the defendant to a criminal or a dangerous activity. For example, in *Valdez*, this court held that police officers lacked reasonable suspicion to stop a person who was dressed in a blue leisure suit, wore shiny black shoes, and looked "real sharp." 561 P.2d at 1010. Although the police officers thought the defendant looked like a "typical pusher," the court disagreed, stating that "[n]eedle scars on forearms may legitimately speak of possible criminal activity in drugs, but shined shoes, sharp clothes, and staring at a police officer do not say much." *Id.* at 1010–11.

To see how powerful a hook can be, consider alternative, less persuasive hooks. The hook in Example 5-Q still states a point that the court should draw from reading the case illustration that follows. However, by focusing on the holding rather than on the legal principle, the hook does less to advance the client's argument.

Example 5-Q • A case illustration with no hook

Less carefully crafted hooks, not surprisingly, do less to advance your argument before the court.

Many cases have held that a four-year-old cannot be found guilty of contributory negligence. *Ehrlich v. Marra*, 300 N.Y.S.2d 81, 82 (N.Y. App. Div. 1940); *Romanchuk v. County of Westchester*, 337 N.Y.S.2d 926, 927 (N.Y. App. Div. 1972); *Boyd v. Trent*, 746 N.Y.S.2d 191, 193 (N.Y. App. Div. 2002).For example, in *Ehrlich v. Marra*, this Court held that a child of 4 years and 10 months could not be found guilty of contributory negligence. In that case, the child had been crossing the street "at the direction and under the supervision of his mother" when he was struck by a car. 300 N.Y.S.2d at 82. Similarly, in *Romanchuk v. Westchester County*, this Court held that a child "then several days short of his fifth birthday .

..must be deemed, as a matter of law, to have been free of contributory negligence" in a sledding accident. 337 N.Y.S.2d at 927. In that case, the court noted that the child was "under the direct supervision and control of the father" when the father placed the child on a sled and the child then coasted down a slope by himself. *See id.* . . . .

Other cases have held that a four-year-old can be found guilty of contributory negligence. . . .

---

3. Acknowledge unfavorable cases in a favorable way

Just as you should never ignore an unfavorable rule, never ignore an unfavorable case hoping opposing counsel and the court will not notice it. Ignoring relevant precedent is unethical. Besides, the chances are too great that the judge or opposing counsel will find the case.

Instead, take the opportunity to describe that authority on your terms. Doing so provides you with the advantage of being the first to shape the court's understanding of the law. For example, if you plan to distinguish a prior case from your client's case, describe the prior case and highlight those facts that distinguish it from your client's case. If you plan on disposing of a case by arguing that the law is trending away from the analysis in the prior decision, your explanation of law should highlight that trend. Again, your explanation of the law should provide the foundation for the argument you will make.

Finally, addressing unfavorable law will also improve your credibility with the court. If you voluntarily come forward and address unfavorable law the court will begin to think of you as a trustworthy advocate who will fully address all the issues the court must confront. As explained in Chapter 1, *The Nature of Persuasion*, a trustworthy lawyer is a more persuasive lawyer.

III. Apply Your Persuasive Explanation of the Law to the Facts

Now that you have explained the relevant law, you must apply that law to your client's case to explain why the outcome you seek is justified under the law. Applying the law requires two steps: First, you must apply the law as you have asserted it should be applied. Second, you must explain why an opposing analysis is incorrect.

A. Developing Your Application

Explaining how the court should apply the law to your client's facts should be fairly straightforward. The hard work is actually writing an explanation of the law that is specifically crafted to support your application. Remember that the explanation of the law and the application should reflect each other. If you explain the law so that it supports your ultimate argument, all you need to do now is show how that same set of rules and case law apply to your client's case.

The key to matching your application to your explanation is to use the same language in both sections of your argument. In Example 5-R, you can see how re-using the language from the explanation of the law in the application allows the writer to show how her argument is supported by the law.

Example 5-R • An effective application re-uses the language used in the explanation of the law.

Officers Brown and Cockerham had a reasonable suspicion that justified a protective frisk of the defendant. Whether a suspicion is reasonable depends on the inferences drawn from the particular circumstances confronting the officer viewed in light of the officer's experience. *See State v. Ehly*, 854 P.2d 421, 430 (Or. 1993) (citing *Terry v. Ohio*, 392 U.S. 1, 21–22, 27–30 (1968)). An "intuitive sixth sense" or "instinct" cannot "form the entire basis for 'reasonable suspicion.'" *State v. Valdez*, 561 P.2d 1006, 1010-11 (Or. 1977). Rather, an officer must be able to point to specific and articulable facts that give rise to a reasonable inference that the person might pose an immediate threat. *See Ehly*, 854 P.2d at 430. An officer need not show that the threat was "more likely than not." *See* Or. Rev. Stat. 131.005(11) (defining "probable cause"). An officer must simply have a reasonable belief that a circumstance may exist or that a particular event might occur. *See State v. Stanley,* 935 P.2d 1202, 1204 (Or. 1997). In other words, for a protective frisk to be justified, an officer must show only that the particular circumstances gave rise to a reasonable belief that the defendant might pose an immediate threat.

To establish a reasonable belief that the defendant might pose an immediate threat, officers may rely on their knowledge that the defendant associates with a known dangerous person or that the person is connected with an activity that involves weapons. For example, in *Ehly*, this Court determined that officers had reasonable suspicion to conduct a protective search. *Ehly*, 854 P.2d at 431. In that case, officers knew that the defendant was a drug user and that "many people who use illegal narcotics possess guns." *Id.* at 430. Moreover, the officers also knew that defendant was "running" with a person who carried weapons. *Id.* Because the defendant was rummaging through a gym bag with his hands concealed and did not respond to the officer's suggestion to dump out the contents of the bag, this Court concluded that it was reasonable for one of the officers to dump the contents of the bag onto the motel room bed. *Id.*

Officers must, however, rely on more than the defendant's "looks" when that "look" does not reasonably connect the defendant to a criminal or a dangerous activity. For example, in *Valdez*, this court held that police officers lacked reasonable suspicion to stop a person who was dressed in a blue leisure suit, wore shiny black shoes, and looked "real sharp." *Valdez*, 561 P.2d at 1010. Although the police officers thought the defendant looked like a "typical pusher," the court disagreed, stating that "[n]eedle scars on forearms may legitimately speak of possible criminal activity in drugs, but shined shoes, sharp clothes, and staring at a police officer do not say much." *Id.* at 1010–11. Similarly, in *Bates*, this court held that the officers had not established reasonable suspicion when all that the officers could point to was that the defendant had long hair and a beard, was wearing a leather jacket, and looked suspicious. *State v. Bates*, 747 P.2d 991, 994 (Or. 1987).

Officers Brown and Cockerham can point to specific, articulable facts that gave rise to a reasonable suspicion that the defendants posed an immediate threat. First, the officers knew that the defendant was associated with the 18th Street Gang. Defendant was wearing a shirt with the phrase "18th Street" printed on it, and his companion had a tattoo under his eye, which is a tattoo that is associated with membership in the 18th Street Gang. In addition, both men had shaved heads and were wearing baggy gang-style clothes. Thus, the officers knew that the defendant was associated with the 18th Street Gang.

Second, the officers knew that members of the 18th Street Gang were dangerous, often carrying concealed weapons. In fact, one of the officers had encountered a gang member in the parking lot of the same apartment complex who, on a pat-down search, was found to have a weapon concealed in the waistband of his pants under a baggy shirt. Another officer had personally removed weapons from several 18th Street Gang members in that same neighborhood. Indeed, he had found a gun on a gang member "just previously to this incident." Thus, the officers knew that members of the 18th Street Gang carried weapons and posed a danger to the officer, and they knew that the defendant was associated with that gang and its activities.

Based on these facts, the officers had reason to believe that the defendant might pose an immediate threat. In fact, the officers relied on the same kinds of facts that established reasonable suspicion in *Ehly*. Just as the officer in *Ehly* relied on the defendant's drug activity, an activity that often involves weapons and therefore poses a danger to others, the officers in this case relied on the defendant's gang membership, an activity that often involves weapons and also poses a danger to others. Moreover, just as the officers in *Ehly* relied on the defendant's association with a person who was known to carry weapons, the officers in this case relied on the defendant's association with a group of people—the 18th Street Gang—who were known to carry weapons. Finally, just as the officers in *Ehly* were concerned for their safety because the defendant was rummaging through a bag (a place where a gun could be concealed) and they could not see his hands, the officers in this case were concerned because the defendant's waistband was hidden and was a place where a handgun could be concealed. Thus, the officers in this case relied on the same kinds of facts as did the officers in *Ehly* and, accordingly, had reasonable suspicion to pat down the defendant.

The shaded text echoes the key language used in the explanation of the law.

For these same reasons, the officers relied on far more than simply the defendant's "looks." In *Valdez* and in *Bates*, the "look" that the officers relied on—a blue leisure suit and shiny black shoes in *Valdez* and long hair, a beard, and a leather jacket in *Bates*—could not be particularly associated with a weapons-related activity or with a particular group of people who regularly carry weapons. By contrast, here, the "look" at issue established a reasonable suspicion of gang activity and membership in the 18th Street Gang. Both the association with gang activity generally and the association with a particular gang known to carry weapons are specific, articulable facts that raise a reasonable suspicion that the defendant might pose an immediate threat.

Remember, though, as you write, you refine your thinking. As a result, you will need to return to your explanation of the law after you draft your application to ensure that the words you use in your explanation of the law and your application are consistent. Doing so will make it easy for the court to see how the law that you have explained supports the arguments that you are making.

B. Responding to Your Opponent's Analysis

The aspect of persuasive writing that is most different from objective writing is addressing weaknesses that give rise to an opposing analysis. You must address those weaknesses without emphasizing them—a balancing act that is not always easy to accomplish. Thus, this section addresses *how* to address the weaknesses and then *where* to address the weaknesses.

With respect to how to address weaknesses, the key is to address the weakness from your client's perspective and not from your opponent's perspective.

Often when we think about a weakness in a case, we think about how our opponent will exploit a certain facet of the law or a certain fact. Thus, we tend to think about weaknesses from our opponent's perspective. As a result, a common impulse is to first explain a weakness from our opponent's perspective and then explain why that perspective is incorrect. To the extent possible, avoid that first step—explaining the weakness from your opponent's perspective. Instead, skip right to the second step—explaining the weakness from your perspective. Compare Examples 5-S and 5-T.

Example 5-S is less effective because in that example the plaintiff's attorney first explains the defendant's argument. In doing so, the attorney inadvertently emphasizes the defendant's argument—in essence, making defendant's argument for him. You should not help your opponent in that way.

Example 5-S • Less effective approach: highlighting your opponent's argument

---

Defendant carves out an exception for four-year-olds who are supervised by an adult. Defendant has pointed to three cases, *Ehrlich, Trent,* and *Romanchuk.* In those cases, the courts have held that, as a matter of law, the four-year-old could not be held liable for negligence. *Ehrlich v.* Marra, 300 N.Y.S.2d 81, 82 (N.Y. App. Div. 1940); *Boyd v. Trent*, 746 N.Y.S.2d 191, 193 (N.Y. App. Div. 2002); *Romanchuk v. Westchester Cnty.,* 337 N.Y.S.2d 926, 927 (N.Y. App. Div. 1972). In each of those cases, a parent was present when the alleged negligent act took place. *Ehrlich*, 300 N.Y.S.2d at 82 (parent present when child crossed street and was struck by car); *Boyd*, 746 N.Y.S.2d at 193 (parent present when child extricated herself from her car seat, moved to the front seat, and contributed to a car accident); *Romanchuk*, 337 N.Y.S.2d. at 928-928 (parent present when child went sledding and hit another at the bottom of the slope). On that basis, Defendant concludes that when a parent is present and supervising a child, the child cannot be found guilty of negligence as a matter of law.

> Plaintiff addresses a weakness by first explaining that weakness.

Although each of those cases did conclude as a matter of law that a four-year-old could not be held liable for negligence, such a conclusion is a minority conclusion. The majority of courts that have considered the issue have concluded that a four-year-old can be held liable for negligence. *See e.g., Sun Jeong Koo v. St. Bernard*, 392 N.Y.S.2d 815, 816 (Sup. Ct. Queens Cnty. 1977) (considering *Ehrlich* but rejecting a bright-line rule in negligence case against a child of 4 years and 10 months); *Searles v. Dardani*, 347 N.Y.S.2d 662, 665 (Sup. Ct. Albany Cnty. 1973) (considering *Ehrlich*, but concluding that jury should decide whether a child of four and a half years was negligent); *Republic Ins. Co. v. Michel*, 885 F. Supp. 426, 433 (E.D.N.Y. 1995) (considering *Ehrlich*, but concluding that a four-and-a-half year old could be liable for negligence).

> After explaining the weakness, counsel turns to her counter-argument.

Thus, the bright-line rule first expressed in *Ehrlich,* and then followed in *Trent* and *Romanchuk* represents a minority view. The majority view in this jurisdiction is that a jury is permitted to decide whether a four-year-old is liable for negligence.

The fix for an argument that begins with your opponent's position is easy: Just skip over your description of the opposing position. In Example 5-T, you can see how plaintiff's counsel can re-write the argument so that the defendant's argument is not emphasized and just go straight to explaining how the plaintiff sees things.

Example 5-T • More effective: present the argument from your perspective only

---

The majority view in this jurisdiction is that a four-year-old can be held liable for negligence. *See, e.g., Sun Jeong Koo v. St. Bernard*, 392 N.Y.S.2d 815, 816 (Sup. Ct. Queens Cnty. 1977); *Searles v. Dardani*, 347 N.Y.S.2d 662, 665 (Sup. Ct. Albany Cnty. 1973); *Republic Ins. Co. v. Michel*, 885 F. Supp. 426, 433

> Here, plaintiff's counsel has removed his explanation of opponent's argument and moves directly to explaining why defendant's explanation of the law is incorrect.

(E.D.N.Y. Feb 23, 1995). Any attempt to carve out an exception for four-year-olds who are supervised by an adult is unsupported by the weight of authority. In asserting that novel rule, the defendant relies on *Romanchuk, Ehrlich,* and *Trent.* Although each of those cases did conclude as a matter of law that a four-year-old could not be held liable for negligence, the courts that have considered the issue since then have rejected the bright-line rule relied on in those cases and concluded that a four-year-old can be held liable for negligence. *See e.g., Sun Jeong Koo,* 392 N.Y.S.2d at 816 (considering *Ehrlich,* but rejecting a bright-line rule in negligence case against a child of four years and 10 months); *Searles,* 347 N.Y.S.2d at 665 (considering *Ehrlich,* but concluding that a jury should decide whether a child of four-and-a-half years was negligent); *Republic Ins. Co.,* 885 F. Supp. at 433 (considering *Ehrlich,* but concluding that a four-and-a-half year old could be liable for negligence). No court has considered, let alone followed, *Trent* or *Romanchuk.* Thus, the bright-line rule first expressed in *Ehrlich,* and then followed in *Trent* and *Romanchuk* represents a minority view. This court should conclude — as all recent courts have concluded — that a jury can determine whether a four-year-old was negligent.

Admittedly, when drafting an argument, you may find it easier to first draft your opponent's argument and then respond to it, as in Example 5-S. Doing so may help you clarify your opponent's argument and write a more effective response. But that is your *draft.* In the final product, eliminate as much of your opponent's argument as possible so that the court reads about the issue only from your client's perspective.

With respect to *where* to address a weakness, you will ordinarily respond to a counter-analysis after you have presented your primary analysis. The judge will expect to see your argument first, so when you apply the law, first explain your analysis before explaining why an alternative analysis is unwarranted.[6]

IV. End with a Final Conclusion

End each legal argument by stating the conclusion you want the court to reach about the element or factor being examined, as in Example 5-U. The last sentences of your argument are in positions of emphasis, so clearly and concisely state the idea you want the court to walk away with. Be sure to make your conclusion explicit.

---

6. Some weaknesses are less significant and do not need to be addressed with a full counter-analysis. Less significant weaknesses can be addressed with a dependent clause, as discussed in Chapter 6, *Refining Persuasive Arguments.*

Example 5-U · A final conclusion

…Both the association with gang activity generally and the association with a particular gang known to carry weapons are specific, articulable facts that raise a reasonable suspicion that the defendant might pose an immediate threat. For these reasons, the police officers properly stopped the defendant and conducted a safety-frisk. The unregistered weapon the officers found during that frisk is admissible.

Practice Points

- Explain rules from your client's perspective. For example, you can explain when a standard is met or an outcome must occur if that description is favorable to your client. If you are on the opposite side, you can explain when a standard is not met or an outcome may not occur.

- Consider whether past cases yield a rule that will help your client's argument. If such a rule exists, test that rule to make sure it is consistent with all prior law and makes sense in the real world. If it does, explain that rule to the court.

- Acknowledge unfavorable rules, but demonstrate that, despite that rule, the outcome your client seeks is still the most reasonable outcome.

- Use a hook to introduce case illustrations and explain to the court what rule it should draw from a prior case.

- Acknowledge unfavorable cases; then, distinguish them.

Chapter 6

Refining Persuasive Arguments

After you have developed the substance of your arguments, you will then want to review your arguments to ensure that each part is presented as persuasively as possible. To present arguments as persuasively as possible, attorneys use a variety of writing techniques. These techniques emphasize why the outcome their client seeks is a correct and preferable outcome compared to the one opposing counsel seeks. These techniques, while helpful, are not magical. They will not cause you to prevail if the law and facts are not on your side. If, however, you have an argument that could win, these techniques make it easier for the court to see why your argument should win.

I. Core Concepts

Before turning to specific writing techniques, this chapter focuses on a few core concepts. If you understand these core concepts, you will find it easier to adjust the specific writing techniques to the particular argument you are drafting.

A. Assert Your Point. Then, Provide Details.

To write persuasively, you must be clear about the point you wish to make. A judge must first know what you are arguing for before the judge can decide whether to agree with you.

Lawyers, though, sometimes get distracted. Legal arguments are chock full of details—details about rules, about prior cases, about the client's case. Lawyers sometimes get so absorbed in the detail that they forget to tell the judge the point of all those details. Those lawyers will lose the judge in the details.

Instead, explain your point before providing supporting details. Explain why the details are important. Doing so will help focus the judge's attention and make it easier for the judge to work through the details.

In fact, to effectively communicate your argument you will need to repeatedly assert your point. You will need to assert your large, overarching point—that is, the ultimate legal conclusion you want the court to adopt. But you will also need to clearly assert those smaller points that support your larger argument. Lawyers assert their point —and explain the purpose of the details that follow—in numerous places. For example,

- A **point heading** asserts the conclusion the judge should reach after reading the more detailed arguments in that section.

- A **conclusion** at the outset of a legal argument explains the conclusion the judge should reach after reading the more detailed explanation and application of the law.

- A **thesis sentence** at the beginning of a paragraph explains the point the judge should take away after reading the details explained within the paragraph.

- A **hook** at the beginning of a case illustration explains the legal principle a court should derive after having read the particulars of a prior case.

Asserting your point before providing details has numerous benefits. It tells the judge what is to come. When you tell your reader what is to come, your reader feels more comfortable because she will have context for the argument. Your reader—the judge—is no longer stumbling in the dark wondering in which direction to head. Feeling comfortable and oriented, your reader is better able to absorb the argument.

Second, when you tell the judge where you are going and then actually go there, you gain the judge's trust. The judge knows you will do what you have promised to do. A judge who trusts you is one who is more likely to accept the information you provide.

Finally, explaining your point in advance of the detail shapes the way the judge will absorb the details. If you explain your point in advance, the judge will read the details trying to match the details to the point you have said you are going to make. By first stating your point, you give the judge a framework on which to hang the details. As the judge matches details to your stated point, those details will come together in the way you and your client see those details. Of course, a judge reads critically and may have other ideas than the one explained. Still, the judge will at least be encouraged to consider seeing the details in the way you and your client see them. Thus, by clearly stating your point before the supporting details, you begin the process of shaping how the judge will view the upcoming information.

Too many writers do not recognize when a mass of detail is in need of a clearly stated point. If you are one of those writers, you will leave the judge struggling in the dark and looking for direction; you will lose an opportunity to gain the judge's trust; and you will have missed an opportunity to shape those details in the way you want the judge to see it. Worst of all, without your guidance, the judge may reach an entirely different conclusion than the one you wanted.

Accordingly, this chapter highlights locations within your argument that are likely in need of a sentence that explains the point of all the detail to follow.

B. Use Location to Your Advantage

One of the best ways to emphasize your point is to put your point where the judge is most likely to see and process it. When reading text, most readers' eyes—including judges' eyes—tend to fall and rest on a few positions of emphasis. Thus, many of the techniques below are based on the idea that you should put information where a judge is most likely to see it and absorb it. In particular, review your point headings, the first sentence of each paragraph, and the last sentence of each paragraph. Those are locations where the judges' eyes will rest. Take advantage of that fact and use those locations for the information you want to emphasize. Similarly, use those locations where the judges' eyes are less likely to rest to disclose information that is less helpful to you. Thus, disclose unhelpful information in the middle of a paragraph and in the middle of sentences, where that information will receive less emphasis.

C. Be Explicit

The last core concept is to "be explicit." In other words, consider talking directly to the judge and state what you are up to. Judges appreciate candor, and being explicit helps gain their trust.

For example, if you are about to launch into a five-page detailed discussion of the relevant case law, tell the judge what you are about to do and why, as in Example 6-A. By giving such an explanation, the judge knows to settle in and expect a lot of facts. The judge will also appreciate being told why the factual minutiae is worth reading.

Example 6-A · Be explicit

The discussion of the cases that follows is necessarily fact-intensive because the standard this Court must apply is a "totality of the circumstances" standard.

Similarly, tell the court when you will address matters out of the normal order, as in Example 6-B. By doing so, you have told the court that it should expect something different and that you are doing something different to benefit the court.

Example 6-B · Be explicit

Although normally a court will consider the merits of a legal argument first, this brief begins with a discussion of harmless error because the case is most efficiently resolved on that basis.

In short, be explicit about where your argument is going and why—especially if you are about to do something unexpected or particularly difficult to absorb. By explicitly stating what you are doing, you help the judge follow your argument and you enhance your credibility with the court.

With these core concepts in mind, let's turn to specific writing techniques.

II. Persuasion Through Point Headings

One of the first locations where a judge's eyes will rest will be on your point headings. Moreover, a judge is likely to return to your point headings if the judge needs an overview of your argument or is searching for particular information. Thus, construct your point headings so that they emphasize the main points you want the court to accept.

To create persuasive point headings in your argument, follow these five guidelines. First, in your argument section, create assertive point headings that tell the judge the conclusion you want the court to reach and the reasons the court should reach that conclusion. Second, create point headings that work together and provide an outline of your argument. Third, keep your point headings short. Fourth, use point headings to divide the argument into readable chunks. Finally, create polished point headings in a traditional format so that they make your brief look professional and credible.

A. Create Assertive Point Headings

An assertive point heading has up to two parts:

1. The action you want the court to take or the conclusion you want the court to adopt, and

2. The primary reason the court should take that action or adopt that conclusion.

Of the point headings you will craft, you will need to think most carefully about the main point headings designated by Roman numerals. Those point headings designate a new claim. They should, therefore, assert the procedural action that you want the court to take with respect to that claim. Compare Example 6-C with 6-D. Example 6-C is the more effective opening point heading because it tells the court the procedural action it should take.

Example 6-C • A main point heading that asserts the procedural action the court should take

---

I. Plaintiffs' complaint should be dismissed because the ADEA does not permit disparate impact claims.

Example 6-D • A main point heading that does not assert the procedural action the court should take

---

I. The ADEA does not permit disparate impact claims.

Although as a general rule you should use point headings to assert the legal conclusions that you want the court to adopt, occasionally you may opt for descriptive point headings. Descriptive point headings are appropriate—not surprisingly—when the purpose of a section is to describe rather than to assert a legal argument, as in Example 6-E. (Descriptive point headings are also appropriate in statements of fact, but that idea will be addressed in more detail in Chapter 10, *Statements of Fact and of the Case*.)

Example 6-E · A descriptive point heading

I. Oregon's method of statutory construction

B. Coordinate Your Point Headings

Because more than one element or factor will be argued within each claim, attorneys use sub-headings to alert the reader to each new element, factor, or part of an argument. These sub-headings, together with the main point heading, should be coordinated so that, together, they provide an overview of the arguments that support the claim. In longer motions and in all appellate briefs, you will see the point headings and sub-headings gathered together in a table of contents. Gathering the point headings and sub-headings in a table of contents not only helps the court find particular parts of your argument, it also allows the court to see the overarching structure of your argument. Example 6-F illustrates how a main point heading and its sub-headings can provide an overview of your argument.

Example 6-F · Example of a main point heading and supporting sub-headings

---

I. Plaintiffs' complaint should be dismissed because the ADEA does not permit disparate impact claims.

    A. The text of the ADEA precludes disparate impact claims.

        1. Section 4(a) of the ADEA, which prohibits discrimination "because of age," prohibits only intentional discrimination.

        2. Section 4(f) of the ADEA, which permits employers to consider "reasonable factors other than age," precludes a discrimination claim based on the impact of an employment decision.

    B. The legislative history confirms that disparate impact claims are not cognizable under the ADEA.

C. Use Short Point Headings

In drafting point headings, your goal should be for the reader to be able to look down and quickly absorb the point heading's conclusion. Thus, pay attention to the length of the heading. A point heading that is too long will be difficult to absorb. How long is too long? No definitive answer exists, but here are some guidelines.

First, a point heading that sits on a single line is easiest to absorb. If your point heading is more than three lines, the point heading may be perceived as a forbidding block of text and your reader is less likely to wade through it. Thus, keep your point heading short.

Second, use multiple point headings if you have a complex idea that cannot be expressed in a single line. You will not always be able to draft a precise point heading that sits on a single line. You may need more than one line—or maybe several lines—to fashion a complete and accurate point heading. If a point heading is becoming too long for the reader to absorb its meaning, consider stating the conclusion you want the court to reach in one point heading and the reasons for that conclusion in sub-headings as in Example 6-F, above.

Finally, consider whether the point heading *needs* both the conclusion and the reasons for that conclusion. Sometimes, you may want to sacrifice completeness for conciseness. You will notice that in Example 6-F not all the point headings state the conclusion counsel wants the court to adopt and the reason the court should adopt that conclusion.

Different practitioners have different ideas about when a point heading becomes too long and the importance of including both your conclusion and the primary reason the court should adopt that conclusion. If you are working with a more senior attorney, follow the senior attorney's preference; likewise, if you are writing to a judge who you know prefers a particular style, follow that judge's preference.

Generally, most judges and attorneys prefer short point headings. We recommend aiming for one to two lines and not going beyond three lines. Your goal is to keep the point headings short, but choose words that convey as much substance as possible.

D. Divide the Text into Readable Chunks

When drafting point headings, one question that sometimes comes up is how frequently to insert a point heading. As a general rule, you should have a point heading before each dispositive issue. If those issues break down such that you have a single legal argument for each element or factor, you should include a point heading for each argument that addresses a single element or factor. Whether to sub-divide an argument addressing a single element or factor further depends on how long the legal argument is. Point headings should break text into readable chunks, both to give your reader a break and to help your reader return to your argument and find specific information. However, do not include so many point headings that the text becomes choppy.

E. Use a Professional, Easy-to-Read Format

Point headings can also help provide a professional look to your argument if they are formatted effectively. Although attorneys vary in how they format their point headings, we recommend this format:

- **Numbering.** Each dispositive legal issue is given a Roman numeral. Sub-issues are identified with a capital letter, an Arabic number, a lower case letter, and then a lower-case Roman numeral.

- **Single space.** Each heading and sub-heading is single-spaced.

- **Punctuate properly.** If your point heading is a full sentence—and in your argument section usually all of your point headings will be full sentences that assert a conclusion—use proper punctuation, which includes a period at the end of the heading or sub-heading. If, as in Example 6-E, your heading is not a full sentence, it should not be punctuated.

- **Hanging indent.** If your point heading wraps to a second line, the first letter of the second line should appear under the first letter of the point heading. (This bulleted list uses hanging indent. The first letter of the second line appears under the first letter of the first line. The second line does not extend to the left under the bullet.)

- **Use bold.** Point headings should be in bold so that they stand out from the text and are easy to see. Italicized text tends to slow the reader down and, therefore, is less effective. Nonetheless, italicize if your workplace or court custom requires that you do so.

- **ALL CAPS?** TRADITIONAL POINT HEADINGS USE ALL CAPS FOR POINT HEADINGS OF DISPOSITIVE ISSUES. ALL CAPS ARE, HOWEVER, MORE DIFFICULT TO READ. SO, AVOID THEM IF YOU CAN. NONETHELESS, IF YOUR WORKPLACE OR COURT REQUIRES ALL CAPS FOR MAIN HEADINGS, THEN ADHERE TO THOSE GUIDELINES.

- **Initial Caps.** A Point Heading Using Initial Caps Capitalizes the First Letter of Most Words in the Point Headings. Typography Experts Now Recommend Against Using Initial Caps Because That Format Is More Difficult to Read and Tends to Slow the Reader Down. Thus, Capitalize Only the First Letter of the Heading and Any Proper Nouns.

- ***Do not combine typeface alterations.*** *Headings become especially hard to read when the writer combines two or more typeface alterations.*

The format described above will create point headings that are both professional-looking and easy-to-read. Example 6-G illustrates that format.

Example 6-G • Professional, easy-to-read point headings

I.   **Each dispositive point heading has a Roman numeral.**

    A. **An outline should not have an "A" without a "B" or a "1" without a "2."**

    B. **However, when your argument has only one dispositive point, you may have a "I" without a "II."**

        1. **Hanging indents make your point headings look polished.**

        2. **Create a hanging indent by positioning the first word of the second line under the first word of the first line.**

            a. **Experts in typography have recommended changes to traditional formats.**

                i.   **Avoid "all caps," which is difficult to read and slows the reader down.**

                ii. **Avoid italicized text, which is difficult to read and slows the reader down.**

            b. **Use bold instead, which will make the point heading pop from the page.**

    C. **Assertive point headings are complete sentences with final punctuation.**

Although we recommend the format described above and illustrated in Example 6-G, if you work in a very traditional office or jurisdiction, you may need to follow a more traditional format. The most traditionally formatted point headings will be formatted as in Example 6-H.

Example 6-H • Traditionally formatted point headings

I.   **EACH DISPOSITIVE POINT HEADING STILL HAS A ROMAN NUMERAL, BUT YOU WILL USE ALL CAPS AND THE TEXT MAY BE BOLDED AS WELL.**

    A. **The First Sub-Heading Will Use Initial Caps and May Be Bolded As Well.**

        1. **In the next sub-heading, the text is bolded, but, like any other sentence, only the first letter of the point heading is capitalized.**

        2. **Hanging indents still make your point headings look polished.**

      a. <u>The next sub-heading will, again, use ordinary capitalization,</u>
         <u>but the text will likely be underlined.</u>

         i. You can see a trend in the formatting.

         ii. Each sub-heading is formatted with less emphasis than the previous heading to reflect the smaller ideas contained in each sub-heading.

      b. <u>Again, never have an "A" without a "B"; however, when your</u> <u>argument has only one dispositive point, you may have a "I"</u> <u>without a "II."</u>

B. Assertive Point Headings are Complete Sentences With Final Punctuation.

III. Paragraph-Level Persuasion

The techniques for persuading at the paragraph level are straightforward and can be explained quickly.

A persuasive paragraph is one that is cohesive and coherent. A "cohesive" paragraph is a paragraph that focuses on a single idea. Cohesion requires that a paragraph's first sentence clearly state what the whole paragraph is about and that every sentence within the paragraph relate to that first sentence. A "coherent" paragraph is a paragraph in which the ideas flow logically, from one to the next. When a paragraph is cohesive and coherent, a judge is more likely to follow your logical path to the conclusion you wish the judge to reach. By contrast, when a paragraph lacks cohesion or coherence, a judge is more likely to stumble along, veer off your intended path, and arrive at a different conclusion.

Each part of your paragraph—the thesis, the sentences that comprise the body of the paragraph, and the final sentence of a paragraph—can be used to persuade. Although simple, these techniques are powerful. Their appropriate use will provide organization and direction to your reader and will be critical to the effective presentation of your argument.

A. The Thesis Sentence

Every single paragraph within your argument should begin with a thesis sentence. That's right: every single paragraph.

Thesis vs. Topic Sentences

A thesis sentence asserts a proposition that the paragraph's text will prove. By contrast, a topic sentence merely describes the kind of information that the paragraph includes. A topic sentence asserts no point that will be proved.

Lawyers prefer thesis sentences over topic sentences because paragraphs should be structured to make a point.

> ### Cohesion and Coherence
>
> A persuasive paragraph is both **cohesive** and **coherent**. A **cohesive** paragraph has a main idea established in the thesis sentence and every sentence within the paragraph supports that thesis. In a **coherent** paragraph, the ideas flow logically from one to the next.

A "thesis" is a proposition put forward for consideration—one that the speaker will prove. A "thesis sentence" is an assertion to be proved in the paragraph that follows. By first asserting the point you intend to prove, your reader will have an easier time absorbing the details within the paragraph. In the best motions and briefs, the thesis sentences for each paragraph form a skeletal outline of the argument you are presenting to the court.

Compare the paragraph in Example 6-I, which uses a thesis sentence, and the paragraph in Example 6-J, which does not. Notice how the thesis sentence in Example 6-I tells the court the conclusion it should reach after reading the paragraph. In doing so, the thesis sentence shapes the way the court absorbs the information provided in the paragraph.

Example 6-I · More effective approach: a thesis sentence that asserts the point the paragraph will prove

....An officer establishes reasonable suspicion to search a suspect if the officer can point to specific and articulable facts that give rise to a reasonable inference that the person might pose an immediate threat. *See State v. Ehly*, 854 P.2d 421, 430 (Or. 1993).

To establish a reasonable belief that the defendant might pose an immediate threat, officers may rely on their knowledge that the defendant associates with a known dangerous person or that the person is connected with an activity that involves weapons. For example, in *Ehly*, this Court determined that officers had reasonable suspicion to conduct a protective search. *Id.* at 432. In that case, officers knew that the defendant was a drug user and that "many people who use illegal narcotics possess guns." *Id.* at 430. Moreover, the officers also knew that defendant was "running" with a person who carried weapons. *Id.* Because the defendant was rummaging through a gym bag with his hands concealed and did not respond to the officer's suggestion to dump out the contents of the bag, this Court concluded that it was reasonable for one of the officers to dump the contents of the bag onto the motel room bed. *Id.* at 432.

With a strong thesis sentence, the judge knows the writer's primary assertion and what point the paragraph will prove. Here, the thesis sentence also acts as a hook for the case illustration.

Example 6-J • Less effective approach: a paragraph with no thesis sentence

The writer omits the thesis sentence and jumps directly into the facts of a case. By not providing a thesis sentence, the lawyer has lost an opportunity to focus the court's attention on the legal proposition that is important in that case.

....An officer establishes reasonable suspicion to search a suspect if the officer can point to specific and articulable facts that give rise to a reasonable inference that the person might pose an immediate threat. *See State v. Ehly*, 854 P.2d 421, 430 (Or. 1993).

→ In *Ehly*, this Court determined that officers had reasonable suspicion to conduct a protective search. *Id.* at 432. In that case, officers knew that the defendant was a drug user and that "many people who use illegal narcotics possess guns." *Id.* at 430. Moreover, the officers also knew that defendant was "running" with a person who carried weapons. *Id.* Because the defendant was rummaging through a gym bag with his hands concealed and did not respond to the officer's suggestion to dump out the contents of the bag, this Court concluded that it was reasonable for one of the officers to dump the contents of the bag out on the motel room bed. *Id.* at 432.

B. The Body of the Paragraph

Because the body of the paragraph contains your arguments and supporting evidence, it needs to be both cohesive and coherent. You can create a cohesive and coherent paragraph with a few techniques: creating "sentence chains" within the paragraph, using appropriate transitional words between sentences, and by following an expected order. These techniques will link the sentences of your paragraph—from the paragraph's first sentence to its last—so that your paragraph is cohesive and coherent. The middle of the paragraph is also where you can insert less favorable information so that the less favorable information is de-emphasized.

1. Sentence Chains

Writers use "sentence chains" as a technique to keep the reader focused on the actor, topic, or idea being discussed in that paragraph. You can create sentence chains in different ways.

One kind of sentence chain is a topic chain. Topic chains connect each sentence within a paragraph to the paragraph's topic by focusing on a specific actor, thing, or subject. In examples 6-K and 6-L below, notice the difference between the two versions of the paragraph. Which one has more cohesion? Why?

Example 6-K • A paragraph without a sentence chain

In this example, each sentence supports the topic sentence, although the subject of each sentence varies (as noted by the shaded sections).

Lem Kasaka graduated from the Wharton School of Business in 2010 and immediately began working for a start-up company, Pure, which sells high-end vitamin and food supplements, skin and haircare products, make-up, books on physical and mental wellness, and other products promoting a clean and healthy lifestyle. The company grew exponentially in value, reaching a net worth of $52 million in just nine years with Mr. Kasaka as CFO. He had been promoted from lead financial analyst in 2013. Securing capital and growing the business were Mr. Kasaka's initial job duties. By 2017, the company had a chain of fifteen stores spanning the West Coast with venues in Los Angeles, Santa Barbara, San Francisco, and Seattle, along with stores in Seoul, Tokyo, and London. Much of the company's success was driven by Mr. Kasaka's vision to brand the company as one promoting a pure Zen lifestyle that would inspire clean living and good physical and mental health.

Example 6-L · The same paragraph with a topic chain

Lem Kasaka is the Chief Financial Officer of Pure, and he was the guiding force behind the company's quick rise to international success. Mr. Kasaka graduated from Wharton School of Business in 2010, and he immediately became a partner in the fledgling start-up company. Under Mr. Kasaka's leadership, Pure went from a small store selling high-end beauty products and vitamins to an international company worth more than $52 million dollars in just nine years. Mr. Kasaka expanded the store's brand to one that promotes a clean Zen lifestyle supporting clean living and good physical and mental health. By 2017, Mr. Kasaka had grown the company from a single store in Los Angeles to an international brand with storefronts in major West Coast cities and across the world in Seoul, Tokyo, and London.

Here, the shaded portions show the technique of chaining sentences by using the same subject or topic. Which paragraph is more cohesive?

Notice how the topic chains in Example 6-L create paragraph cohesion because each sentence focuses on the same subject—Mr. Kasaka. By keeping the focus on one person, a reader can more easily see how the sentences connect to each other and support the paragraph's thesis. In contrast, the sentences in Example 6-K are harder to follow because the subject of each sentence changes—some topics are about Mr. Kasaka and others focus on the business or its success.

You can also create sentence chains by using "bridges" that connect sentences. "Bridges," sometimes called lexical chains or substantive transitions, take a key word or phrase from a preceding sentence and repeat that key word or phrase at the beginning of the very next sentence. The overlap from sentence to sentence allows the reader to track the progression of your ideas. Notice how a writer's use of bridging (or overlapping) language promotes coherence and cohesiveness in Example 6-M. Figure 6-N further illustrates how language choices can link ideas. By contrast, the lack of bridging language in Example 6-O makes it more difficult for the reader to follow the explanation of the law.

> **Cohesion and Coherence**
>
> A persuasive paragraph is both **cohesive** and **coherent**. A **cohesive** paragraph has a main idea established in the thesis sentence and every sentence within the paragraph supports that thesis. In a **coherent** paragraph, the ideas flow logically from one to the next.

Example 6-M • Bridging language creates a coherent explanation of rules

The shaded text highlights bridging language. Notice how each sentence begins with an idea expressed in the previous sentence.

A university complies with Title IX if it provides equal athletic opportunities to both sexes. 34 C.F.R. § 106.41(c) (2015). Whether equal athletic opportunities exist depends on an analysis of ten factors. *Id.* at 106.41(c)(1)-(10). However, an institution's failure to comply with the first factor is sufficient to constitute a violation of Title IX. *Mansourian v. Regents of U. of Cal.*, 602 F.3d 957, 965 (9th Cir. 2010).

The first factor requires an institution to "effectively accommodate" the interests of its students. An institution can effectively accommodate the interests of its students if it meets any one part of a three-part test. Under that test, an institution can comply with Title IX if it . . .

Figure 6-N • Use bridging language to link ideas

A university complies with Title IX if it provides equal athletic opportunities to both sexes. 34 C.F.R. § 106.41(c) (2015).

Whether equal athletic opportunities exist depends on an analysis of ten factors. Id. at 106.41(c)(1)–(10).

However, an institution's failure to comply with the first factor is sufficient to constitute a violation of Title IX. *Mansourian v. Regents of U. of Cal.*, 602 F.3d 957, 965 (9th Cir. 2010).

The first factor requires an institution to "effectively accommodate" the interest of its students.

An institution can effectively accommodate the interests of its students if it meets any one part of a three-part test.

Under that test, an institution can comply with Title IX if it....

**Example 6-O • The lack of "bridging language" makes the logic of a
paragraph more difficult to follow**

A university complies with Title IX if it provides equal athletic opportunities
to both sexes. 34 C.F.R. § 106.41(c) (2015). The conclusion rests on an analysis
of ten factors. *Id.* at 106.41(c)(1)-(10). However, an institution's failure to
comply with the first factor is sufficient to constitute a violation of Title IX.
Mansourian v. Regents of U. of Cal., 602 F.3d 957, 965 (9th Cir. 2010).

An institution can "effectively accommodate" the interests of its students if it
meets any one part of a three-part test. An institution can comply with Title IX if
it…

Notice how the connection
between ideas is more difficult
to follow without bridging
language.

Sentence chains are a powerful way to enhance the cohesion of your
paragraph and lead your reader from one idea to the next. At other times,
a good transitional word or phrase will do the trick.

2. Use the appropriate transitions

Appropriate transitions can also connect ideas and promote coherence.
Occasionally, a writer will add a transitional word, but the selected transitional word does not accurately describe the relationship between ideas.
Compare Examples 6-P and 6-Q. Can you see how the wrong transitional
word can disrupt the logical flow of your argument? Table 6-R will help
you select an appropriate transitional word if you are unsure which transitional word will best connect two ideas.

**Example 6-P • The correct transition allows your reader to understand
the relationship between ideas**

Plaintiffs can establish actual possession by showing that they used the
land as an owner would use that particular type of land. *Zambrotto v. Superior
Lumber Co.*, 4 P.3d 62, 65 (Or. Ct. App. 2000). Courts focus on the type of use for
which the land is suited and do not necessarily focus on the amount of activity.
Id. For example, in one past case plaintiffs established actual possession by
showing that they used the property in the same way they did their adjoining
land. *Davis v. Park*, 898 P.2d 804, 806-07 (Or. Ct. App. 1995). In another case,
plaintiffs proved actual possession by building a fence and planting vegetation.
Slak v. Porter, 875 P.2d 515, 518 (Or. Ct. App. 1994).

Example 6-Q • An incorrect transition confuses

"In addition" is not an appropriate transition because the sentence that follows does not add to the law. The sentence that follows provides an example of the rule just stated.

"By contrast" is also inappropriate because the sentence is another similar example of the rule that courts focus on the type of activity.

Plaintiffs can establish actual possession by showing that they used the land as an owner would use that particular type of land. *Zambrotto v. Superior Lumber Co.*, 4 P.3d 62, 65 (Or. Ct. App. 2000.) Courts focus on the type of use for which the land is suited and do not necessarily focus on the amount of activity. *Id.* In addition, in one past case plaintiffs showed that they used the disputed land as an owner would by showing that they used the property in the same way they did their adjoining land. *Davis v. Park*, 898 P.2d 804, 806-07 (Or. Ct. App. 1995). By contrast, plaintiffs in another case proved actual possession by building a fence and planting vegetation. *Slak v. Porter*, 875 P.2d 515, 518 (Or. Ct. App. 1994).

Table 6-R • Transitions[1]

Introduce	Add	Contrast	Sequence	Emphasize
First	Again	However	First, second,	Certainly
Initially	Moreover	Although	third…	Above all
To begin	Additionally	But	Initially	Indeed
The first reason	Similarly	Yet	Then	Especially
Primarily	Also	Unlike	Finally	Accordingly
In general	Likewise	In contrast	Before	Since
Alternatively	Further	Nevertheless	Next	Not only…
A further reason		Nonetheless	Last	but also
		Rather		
Connect	**Exemplify**	Despite	**Restate**	**Conclude**
Because	For example	Instead	That is	Finally
Thus	For instance	Still	In other words	As a result
As a result	To illustrate	On the other	More simply	Thus
Thereby	In particular	hand	As noted	Therefore
Therefore	Namely			In short
Hence	Specifically			Consequently

1. Excerpted from Laurel Oates, Anne Enquist, and Jeremy Francis, *The Legal Writing Handbook: Analysis, Research & Writing* 620-21 (8th ed. 2021), and supplemented by Bryan A. Garner, *Legal Writing in Plain English: A Text with Exercises* 86 (2d ed. 2013).

3. Order information in expected ways

Throughout this book, we have described logical orders that lawyers expect. Using an expected order can also create coherence. Information presented in a customary order will seem logical to your legal reader. This section emphasizes the customary order in which to present rules and case illustrations.[2]

With respect to rules, usually, your rules should be explained with the broadest concept first.[3] Rules are refined and explained in more detail as you move through a paragraph. Then, use a bridge to connect one rule to the next. Again, in Examples 6-M and 6-O, you can see the difference between an explanation of rules that uses bridging language and an explanation that does not.

For case illustrations, follow this standard order: Begin with a hook that explains the legal principle that the following case will illustrate. Next, explain the facts. Usually, chronological order is the best order for facts; although, you may occasionally prefer a topical organization.[4] Be sure to provide all the facts relevant to the court's decision before moving on. The final two steps are to state the court's holding and the court's reasoning (if the court provides reasoning beyond the relevant facts). Often, lawyers will end with the court's holding because it offers a nice summary, but you can end on either the court's holding or the court's reasoning, whichever most emphasizes the point you want to make.

Rules and case illustrations do not always form independent paragraphs, but when they do, the above organizational principles will help provide cohesion and logical coherence to your paragraph. Using sentence chaining techniques can further enhance coherence and cohesion.

---

2. Other logical orders that lawyers might expect to see in a paragraph are (1) the order described for a roadmap paragraph, explained in §3.1, *Organizing Claims and Arguments*; (2) the order described for an analogical argument, dicussed in §3.2, *Structuring Analogical Arguments*; and (3) the order in which a statutory construction argument is presented, described in §3.3, *Structuring Rule-Based Arguments*.

3. As explained in Chapter 5, *Drafting Persuasive Arguments*, part A.1, *Rules*, you may for persuasive reasons sometimes choose not to follow the common approach of explaining the more general rules first.

4. For more on chronological versus topical organizations, see Chapter 10, *Statements of Fact and of the Case*.

4. Place damaging information in the middle of a paragraph

The body of the paragraph can also be used to disclose information that is less favorable to your client, but that you are ethically bound to disclose. In the middle of the paragraph, you can frame the less favorable information in a more favorable light. Also, as discussed above, information in the middle—of a section, paragraph, or sentence—gets less attention.

Examples 6-S, 6-T, and 6-U show the difference between a paragraph that puts damaging information in the middle, beginning, or end of a paragraph. Which structure minimizes the damaging information the most?

Example 6-S · Damaging information buried in the middle of the paragraph

Here, the writer embeds the damaging information (the fact that Moore's blood alcohol level was far in excess of the permitted level of .08 percent) in the middle of the paragraph, a position that will de-emphasize that information.

The facts in this case, even when viewed most favorably for the plaintiff, failed to establish any "substantial evidence" of Moore's intoxication. Although Moore's blood alcohol level was .13, she did not demonstrate any outward signs of intoxication. Her speech was not slurred. She appeared to be in control of her body. She did not have the odor of alcohol. Because Moore exhibited none of these symptoms, Defendant Soto could not have known she was intoxicated.

Example 6-T · Damaging information at the beginning of the paragraph

Here, the damaging fact is at the beginning of the paragraph, a position that tends to highlight the information.

Although Moore's blood alcohol level was .13, she did not demonstrate any outward signs of intoxication. Her speech was not slurred. She appeared to be in control of her body. She did not have the odor of alcohol. Because Moore exhibited none of these symptoms, Defendant Soto could not have known she was intoxicated. Therefore the facts in this case, even when viewed most favorably for Plaintiff, failed to establish any "substantial evidence" of Moore's intoxication.

Example 6-U · Damaging information at the end of the paragraph

Here, the damaging fact is in the last sentence. Although the last sentence receives less attention than the first sentence, it still receives more attention than the middle of the paragraph.

The facts in this case, even when viewed most favorably for Plaintiff, failed to establish any "substantial evidence" of Moore's intoxication. She did not demonstrate any outward signs of intoxication. Her speech was not slurred. She appeared to be in control of her body. She did not have the odor of alcohol. Because Moore exhibited none of these symptoms that would support her blood alcohol level of .13, Defendant Soto could not have known she was intoxicated.

C. The Final Sentence

Finally, cohesion and coherence can be created by carefully crafting the final sentence of your paragraph. In the final sentence of your paragraph, consider returning to the point you asserted in your thesis sentence. Returning to your thesis closes the loop by establishing that you have now proved what your thesis sentence said you would prove. In addition, and as noted at the outset of this chapter, a reader's eyes tend to rest on (and the reader tends to absorb) the first and last sentences of a paragraph, so the last sentence is an ideal place to remind the reader of the conclusion you believe the reader should reach.

Look at Example 6-V. In that example, you can see how a final sentence repeating the paragraph's thesis helps drive home the point you want to make.

Example 6-V · Repeating assertion in the final sentence

Officer Ephgrave's interaction with defendant Adams was mere conversation, and not a stop because the defendant could not reasonably believe his liberty was ever restrained at any point during his encounter with Officer Ephgrave. Like the officer who asked for identification in *Gilmore*, here Officer Ephgrave wanted to learn if Adams was involved in the bank robbery. In addition, as in *Gilmore* where the officer only requested information but did not alter the defendant's course, Officer Ephgrave did not alter Adams's course or prevent him from leaving. Officer Ephgrave asked Adams if he was planning to leave, to which Adams responded that he was not. Further, Officer Ephgrave said he would move his car whenever Adams needed to leave. According to Officer Ephgrave, Adams said, "Oh, okay. No problem." Therefore, Officer Ephgrave did not prevent Adams from leaving nor did he alter Adams's course. Accordingly, Adams could not reasonably believe that his liberty was restrained; the statement was mere conversation.

The final sentence re-asserts the conclusion, thereby driving home the point of the paragraph.

Although having a final sentence that repeats the original thesis is helpful, occasionally such a sentence is overly repetitive or adds length unnecessarily. In those instances, omit it. For complex or detailed paragraphs, use the opportunity to hammer home your point by restating your thesis in the final sentence of a paragraph.

IV. Sentence-Level Persuasion

Just as paragraphs can be shaped to present your arguments more or less persuasively, individual sentences can be shaped to present information more or less persuasively.

A. Beginning, Middle, and End

The same locational guidelines that apply to paragraphs apply to sentences. Readers tend to absorb information at the beginning and end of sentences; readers pay less attention to information in the middle.

Compare Examples 6-W and 6-X. Can you see how the same information in different locations is emphasized differently? Thus, think carefully about where you locate information within a sentence.

Example 6-W • Damaging information at the beginning of the sentence

Here, the damaging information appears at the beginning of the sentence, which is a point of emphasis.

Even with a blood alcohol level of .13, Moore did not demonstrate outward signs of intoxication such as having slurred speech or smelling of alcohol.

Example 6-X • Damaging information in the middle of the sentence

Here, the negative information appears in the middle of the sentence, a place where it will receive less emphasis.

Moore did not demonstrate signs of intoxication consistent with a blood alcohol level of .13 because her speech was not slurred and she did not smell of alcohol.

B. Subjects and Verbs

Another focal point of a sentence is the subject and verb. Readers naturally want to know "who did what," and they will consciously or subconsciously seek out that information first. You can make it easier for the judge to find that information if you follow the steps below.

1. Place the subject and verb close together and at the beginning of the main clause

You will make the information in your sentences easier to absorb if you place the subject and verb of the sentence at the beginning of the main clause and if you place the subject and verb close together. Compare Examples 6-Y and 6-Z. In the first example, Example 6-Y, the subject and verb (shaded) are far apart. In the second example, Example 6-Z, they are close together. Can you see how, as a result, the sentence in the first example is more difficult to absorb?

Example 6-Y • Subject and verb far apart

The police officer, believing that it was suspicious that the defendant's vehicle sped up after the police officer began following it, pulled the defendant's vehicle over.

Example 6-Z · Subject and verb close together

The police believed that it was suspicious that the defendant's vehicle sped up after the police officer began following it. The police officer, therefore, pulled the defendant's vehicle over.

As Examples 6-Y and 6-Z indicate, often, when the subject and verb of a sentence are far apart, one way to fix the problem is to remove the information that separates the subject and verb and put it into its own sentence.

2. Prefer the active voice

As a general rule, you should write using the active voice.

The active voice is best understood in comparison to the passive voice.[5] In the active voice, the subject is the "be-er" or the "do-er" of the sentence. By contrast, in a sentence written in the passive voice the subject is neither a "be-er" nor a "do-er." Rather, the subject is acted on by another force.[6]

Example 6-aa is written in the active voice, while Examples 6-bb and 6-cc are written in the passive voice. In the first example, Example 6-aa, the supervisor is the subject of the sentence, and he is the "do-er" because he dismisses the plaintiff from his job. Because the subject is the "do-er," that sentence is in the active voice. By contrast, in the next two examples, Examples 6-bb and 6-cc, the plaintiff is the subject, but is not doing anything. Rather, something is happening to the plaintiff by the supervisor, in Example 6-bb, and by some unnamed source in Example 6-cc. Thus, those two sentences are written in the passive voice.

Example 6-aa · Active voice

The plaintiff's supervisor then dismissed the plaintiff from his job.

Example 6-bb · Passive voice

The plaintiff was then dismissed from his job by his supervisor.

Example 6-cc · Passive voice

The plaintiff was then dismissed from his job.

---

5. Remember that "passive voice" is different from "past tense." "Past tense" refers to *when* an action occurs. "Passive voice" refers to *who* did the action.

6. Capital Community College, *Guide to Grammar & Writing*, http://guidetogrammar.org/grammar/passive (last visited Aug. 4, 2021).

Although, usually, you should prefer to clearly name "who did what," there are times when you do not want to call attention to "who did what." For example, if you represent an automobile driver following an accident with a cyclist, you may want to de-emphasize the role of your client (the driver), by using the passive voice, as in Example 6-dd. Other times, your client may have done something appropriate but distasteful, such as fire an employee. Again, you might use the passive voice, as in Example 6-ee. In both of those cases, the passive voice puts the actor (your client) in the background and the action in the foreground.

Example 6-dd · Appropriate passive voice

The cyclist was hit in the intersection.

Example 6-ee · Appropriate passive voice

Ms. Jones was then fired.

Finally, you may have to use the passive voice when you do not know who did what. For example, you may need to refer to a report, but the record does not disclose who prepared the report. In that case, you may have no choice but to use the passive voice.

Although passive voice has its uses, remember that the active voice is usually easier for your reader to absorb and makes for more evocative and stronger writing, both of which help persuade. Thus, prefer the active voice.

Verb Choice Makes a Difference!

Word choice can affect both the reader's perception and memory. In a 1974 experiment, psychologists Elizabeth Loftus and John Palmer showed a film of an auto accident to study participants. Some participants were asked how fast they thought the cars were going when they "hit" each other. Other participants were asked, respectively, how fast the cars were going when they "smashed into" each other, "collided with" each other, "bumped into" each other, or "contacted" each other. The results were impressive: The average speed estimate by those who were asked how fast the cars were going when they "smashed into" each other was nearly ten miles per hour faster than the estimate by those who were asked how fast the cars were going when they "contacted" each other.

The Loftus and Palmer study demonstrates that your choice of wording can have a significant impact on the reader's perception of what happened.

3. Prefer evocative verbs

When selecting verbs, go for strong verbs that show action. In Example 6-dd, for instance, the sentence could be rewritten with active verbs for punch. Saying the driver collided, hit, bumped, or crashed into the cyclist elevates the impact and visual image in the sentence. Unless, of course, you represent the driver, in which case, less evocative verbs will serve your client better.

4. Avoid "it is" and "there are"

For all the reasons stated above, avoid the "it is" or "there is" structure in a sentence when the "it" and the "there" do not actually refer to a specific subject. We often use the phrases "it is" and "there are" when we speak, but that structure creates weak writing. Those phrases obscure the subject of the sentence by creating a false subject ("it" or "there"); they use a weak verb, "is" or "are"; and they often create a wordier sentence. Compare the sentences in Example 6-ff. Which version of each sentence is stronger?

Example 6-ff · Avoid "it is" and "there are"

Version 1: It is likely the defendant posted the information after her conversation with the seller.

Version 2: The defendant likely posted the information after her conversation with the seller.

Version 1: There are five factors that the court considers.

Version 2: The court considers five factors.

---

5. Use a noun instead of "it"

Another good rule of thumb is to eliminate the word "it" altogether, and use a noun instead. "It" can create confusion or ambiguity when the reader is not clear which noun "it" refers to. For example, look at this sentence: "The tractor-trailer hit the bridge, but it was not damaged." What was not damaged—the truck or the bridge? Be clear in your writing—replace "it" with a noun.

C. Dependent Clauses

Dependent clauses are a wonderful way to acknowledge less favorable information. A dependent clause is a group of words that have a subject and verb but cannot stand alone. In Example 6-gg the shaded text is a dependent clause. The important point about dependent clauses is that the actual subject and verb of the sentence are located elsewhere. As mentioned above, readers naturally look for the subject and verb of a sentence. Thus, the subject and verb of a sentence receive more attention. By putting information in a part of the sentence that is separate from the subject and verb, you will de-emphasize that information. Compare the two different versions of the sentence in Example 6-gg. Can you see how the emphasis shifts depending on which information is placed in the dependent clause? Choose the structure that works best for your argument.

Example 6-gg • The dependent clause receives less emphasis

Version 1: Although Moore's blood alcohol level was .13, she did not demonstrate any outward signs of intoxication.

Version 2: Although she did not demonstrate any outward signs of intoxication, Moore's blood alcohol level was .13.

Be careful, though, about putting a dependent clause in the first sentence of a paragraph. The first sentence of a paragraph is emphasized. Thus, you will undo your efforts to de-emphasize information if that information appears at the beginning of a paragraph.

D. Short Sentences

Short sentences add punch. Use them. Sparingly.

Example 6-hh • Too many short sentences

Officer Ephgrave pulled into the lot. He parked his car behind the defendant's car. The defendant yelled to move the car. Officer Ephgrave walked over to the defendant. He asked if the defendant was planning to leave. The defendant said, "No, I'm going to sit a little longer." Officer Ephgrave said no other parking slots were available. Ephgrave said he could move. The defendant said, "Oh, okay. No problem."

Although we love a punchy, short sentence, a short sentence has punch only when placed in contrast to longer sentences. Thus, if every sentence you use is short and punchy, the resulting read will be bumpy, like riding a bike over cobblestones, as in Example 6-hh. A short sentence has a stronger effect if interspersed among longer, flowing sentences. The short sentences in Examples 6-ii and 6-jj are much more effective.

Example 6-ii • Contrast a long sentence with a short punchy sentence[7]

By 2000, the investigation of the helicopter-conversion industry was winding down, with disappointing results for Wales and the U.S. Attorney's Office. Only one case remained.

Example 6-jj • Contrast a long sentence with a short punchy sentence

The firm, called Intrex Helicopters, which was based at Powell's home, was renovating a single helicopter for civilian use. Still, the stakes were substantial.

V. Persuasion through Quotations

When used appropriately, quotations can be used for persuasive effect. When used inappropriately, quotations disrupt your writing and clutter your prose.

To achieve persuasive effect and avoid quotation-clutter, you should, as a general rule, avoid quoting a text. Too often attorneys are not confident enough in their own analytical skills to explain what a court said or did and why. In motions and briefs written by those lawyers, you will see one quotation right after the next, with the tone, style, and word choice changing with each sentence. Such motions and briefs not only shout "Lazy!" and "This writer refuses to think!," they also are very difficult to read. As a state supreme court justice once stated, "Quotations are no substitute for analysis."[8] Instead, as a general rule, take the time to understand the law and explain it in a cohesive, straight-forward manner.

That said, when used thoughtfully, quotations can be persuasive.

A. Quote When Specific Words Matter

One good reason to quote text is because the specific wording matters to the legal argument. For example, attorneys will usually quote a governing statute so that the court knows the exact language of the statute. Similarly, if a witness's statement is important to the analysis, that statement should be quoted so that the reader knows what the witness actually said—as opposed to your characterization of what the

---

7. Jeffrey Toobin, *An Unsolved Killing*, The New Yorker, Aug. 6, 2007, at 43, 48. This example was brought to our attention by Ross Guberman, *Legal Writing Pro: Lessons from* The New Yorker, http://www.legalwritingpro.com/articles/D09-new -yorker.php (last visited Aug. 4, 2021).

8. Former Oregon Supreme Court Justice W. Michael Gillette to one of the authors.

witness said. Likewise, quote the contract when the contractual language is the subject of the dispute. On those occasions when the precise words matter, quoting text will emphasize the precision with which you are addressing the text and the care you are taking to accurately represent the facts.

B. Quote for Emphasis

Quotations are also effective when used to link your explanation of the law to your application. Sometimes a court will explain its reasoning in such an evocative way and in a way that so perfectly suits your client's case that you want to provide that quote in your explanation of the law. That's great. But if you provide that quote in only your explanation of the law, you are losing an opportunity. That quote will be most persuasive if you then repeat it in your application. By re-integrating that quote (or a key part of that quote) in your explanation of the law, you will be helping your reader to see how your analysis is exactly consistent with the analysis in prior case law. Table 6-kk provides an example.

Table 6-kk · Weaving a quotation into your analysis

Original quotation from *Richards v. Sandusky Community Schs.*, 102 F. Supp. 2d 753, 763 (E.D. Mich. 2000)	"The only evidence provided by plaintiff that would support a contention that she was 'about to report' defendants' alleged health and safety violations is the fact that plaintiff received the appropriate paperwork from OSHA. Plaintiff, however, admitted that she never completed the paperwork. (Richards Dep. at 63). This fact, by itself, falls drastically short of the clear and convincing proof required under the [Whistle-blowers' Protection Act]."
Quotation in the explanation of the law	In *Richards*, the court held that the plaintiff could not prove that she was "about to report" a violation. In that case, the plaintiff first reported a possible health violation internally to her employer. *See Richards v. Sandusky Community Schs.*, 102 F. Supp. 2d 753, 755, 763 n.14 (E.D. Mich. 2000). Then, she contacted OSHA and received the appropriate paperwork to file a complaint. *Id.* at 763 n.14. The plaintiff never completed the paperwork. *Id.* at 763. The *Richards* court held that this evidence was insufficient to prove that the plaintiff was "about to report" a violation. *Id.* In fact, the court held that the evidence fell "drastically short of the clear and convincing proof required." *Id.*
Quotation integrated into the application	Mr. Conway, like the plaintiff in *Richards*, reported the violation internally, to his supervisor, but he did nothing further. Although Mr. Conway went online and downloaded the necessary paperwork, this action is exactly like going to OSHA and receiving, but never filling out, the appropriate paperwork. As the *Richards* court explained, such action falls "drastically short of the clear and convincing proof required."

C. Avoid Block Quotes, but If You Must Use Them, Assert Your Point First

As a general rule, most careful writers would say, "Avoid block quotations." The reason: Most readers tend to skip over them because the dense text is difficult to read. Thus, if you must cite to a long portion of a case or some statutory material, try to integrate that text into your sentences, quoting only key sections or phrases of the source.

Sometimes, however, you cannot avoid a block quotation, such as when you need to cite to a statutory section in its entirety or when a large portion of a record needs to be presented in one block in your argument. When you cannot avoid the block quotation, explain the point of the quotation just before the quotation. By explaining the point of the quotation, your reader will be encouraged to read the quotation to see if, in fact, the quotation supports that point.

Examples 6-ll and 6-mm show how an explanatory sentence can make the advocate's point easier to understand. The quotation is from the legislative history to a statute that permits the revocation of a person's driver's license when that person has been convicted of driving under the influence of intoxicants "for a third time." In a brief, a state assistant attorney general wants to use the legislative history to argue that the statute should be construed so that the phrase "for a third time" is understood to permit a revocation when a person has been convicted of "three or more" DUIs. In Example 6-mm, notice how the sentence that precedes the block quote makes it easier to understand the point the assistant attorney general wants to make.

Example 6-ll · A block quotation without its point explained

When Representative Barker carried the bill on the House floor, he stated the following:

> Under the current law, someone convicted of driving under the influence of intoxicants does not permanently lose their driving privileges until after their fourth conviction. This means that after the initial DUI arrest, which often results in a diversion program, someone has to be convicted four more times to lose their privileges. As an Oregonian and the father of two daughters, I find this to be unacceptably tolerant towards such reckless behavior.

Example 6-mm · A block quotation with its point explained

When Representative Barker carried the bill onto the House floor, he stated that waiting until a fourth DUI conviction to revoke a driver's license was unacceptable:

> Under the current law, someone convicted of driving under the influence of intoxicants does not permanently lose their driving privileges until after their fourth conviction. This means that after the initial DUI arrest, which often results in a diversion program, someone has to be convicted four more times to lose their privileges. As an Oregonian and the father of two daughters, I find this to be unacceptably tolerant towards such reckless behavior.

In addition to providing an explanatory sentence before the quotation, consider also providing a sentence immediately after the quotation to sum up or further explain the point of the quotation. When a reader jumps over a block quote, the reader's eye often lands on the first text after the block quote. Thus, you can also emphasize your point by summarizing it in the text immediately after the block quote.

Because readers have difficulty extracting the point from a block of text, if you must use a block quote, help your reader: Explain the point the reader should have taken away had the reader actually read the block quote.

A Judge's Thoughts on Block Quotes

"Block quotes, by the way, are a must; they take up a lot of space but nobody reads them. Whenever I see a block quote I figure the lawyer had to go to the bathroom and forgot to turn off the merge/store function on his computer. Let's face it, if the block quote really had something useful in it, the lawyer would have given me a pithy paraphrase."

The Hon. Alex Kozinski
U.S. Court of Appeals, 9th Cir.
The Wrong Stuff,
1992 BYU L. Rev. 325, 329 (1992).

VI. Persuasion through Citations

The techniques discussed above will help you refine the substance of your argument. As a general rule, your argument should be made in the text, which the court will read, and not through citations, which many readers skip over. However, effective use of citations can bolster the argument that you make in the text.

A. Build Credibility Through Citations

As we explained in Chapter 2, *The Ethical, Professional Advocate*, you should always conduct yourself so that you are perceived as a professional and credible lawyer. Citations, though tedious, are one of those places where you can reinforce the idea that you are a professional, credible attorney. Simply do two things. First, many jurisdictions have local rules that establish how to cite in that jurisdiction. Follow those rules. Second, be accurate. Be certain that your citation is, in fact, directing the court to the proper authority and the proper page within that authority. No need to make the court's job more difficult by giving the judge a citation to nowhere.

In addition to conveying your credibility, citations can provide more substantive support for your argument, thus making it more persuasive.

B. Emphasize the Weight of Authority

Citations, first, emphasize the binding authority for your argument. As a general rule, attorneys choose cases from the same jurisdiction and from the highest court possible. The citation will then reveal that the case is binding on the courts below.

Sometimes, though, questions arise about which authority will best emphasize the binding nature of the authority. For example, when a legal proposition is frequently stated, you may wonder whether to cite the first case to have stated the proposition or a more recent case. Citing the earliest case highlights the point that the proposition has ancient roots, but may leave the reader wondering whether the proposition still holds true. Whether to cite the earliest case, the latest case, or a combination depends on the point you want to make in the text. For example, if your text emphasizes that a rule of law was first recognized decades ago, the appropriate citation is to the first case, as in Example 6-nn.

Example 6-nn • Citing to an early case to emphasize the historical roots of a doctrine

---

When determining the custody of a child, Minnesota has historically declared a preference for the natural parents of the child. *See State v. ex rel. Larson v. Halverson,* 127 Minn. 387, 389-89 (1914) (holding that a natural's parent's rights of custody and control are a "paramount" consideration).

By contrast, if you want to emphasize the applicability of a principle without particularly emphasizing its history, use a current case and the citation signal, "e.g.," as in Example 6-oo. The citation signal "e.g." means "for example" and is used to indicate that the cited case is just one of many cases that support a proposition.[9]

---

9. ALWD & Carolyn V. Williams, *ALWD Guide to Legal Citation* 370–72 (7th ed. 2021) (R. 35); *The Bluebook: A Uniform System of Citation* 4–5 (Columbia L. Rev. Ass'n et al. eds., 21st ed. 2020) (R. B1.2).

Example 6-oo • Citing to a current case to focus on current law

---

When determining the custody of a child, Minnesota prefers the child be placed with a natural parent. *See, e.g., Durkin v. Hinich*, 442 N.W.2d 148, 152–153 (Minn. 1989) ("[T]here is a presumption in custody determinations that a natural parent is fit to raise his or her own child.").

Finally, if you want to emphasize both the ancient roots of a proposition and that it is still good law, you can cite to both the first case and a recent application of the rule, as in Example 6-pp.

Example 6-pp • Citing to both an early and current case to emphasize continuity of policy

---

When determining the custody of a child, Minnesota has historically and to this day expressed its preference that a child be placed with the child's natural parents. *See State v. ex rel. Larson v. Halverson,* 127 Minn. 387, 389–89 (1914) (holding that a natural parent's rights of custody and control are a "paramount" consideration); *In re Custody of N.A.K.,* 649 N.W.2d 166, 175 (Minn. 2002) (concluding that upon the death of a custodial parent, custody will be awarded to the non-custodial parent unless that assumption is overcome by "extraordinary circumstances").

C. Show a Trend Through Citations

If you want to establish a trend in the law or argue that a majority of courts have reached a conclusion that you want the court to reach in your client's case, a string cite may be the simplest, most direct way of establishing that point. A string cite, when combined with parentheticals, can quickly establish a trend without having to describe the facts of each case in detail.

Take for example the case in which the estate of an elderly woman sued a four-year-old bicyclist and her parents after the four-year-old collided with the elderly woman. Counsel for the elderly woman wanted to establish that the majority of courts did allow for the possibility that a four-year-old could be negligent by using a string cite after describing the lead case. Thus, the attorney drafted the text in Example 6-qq in which the attorney asserts that the majority of courts allow for four-year-olds to be sued and then supports that assertion with a string cite.

Example 6-qq • Using string cites to show a trend in the law

The *Comardo* decision, which concludes that a jury must assess the culpability of a four-year-old, has been consistently followed since that case was decided in 1928. *See Chandler v. Keene*, 168 N.Y.S.2d 788, 791(N.Y. App. Div. 1957) (holding that a jury properly decided whether a child of four years and eleven months was contributorily negligent); *Weidenfeld v. Surface Transp. Corp. of N.Y.*, 55 N.Y.S.2d 780, 783 (N.Y. App. Div. 1945) (same regarding a four-year-old child); *Sun Jeong Koo v. St. Bernard*, 392 N.Y.S.2d 815, 816 (N.Y. Sup. Ct. 1977) (same regarding a child of four years and ten months); *Searles v. Dardani*, 347 N.Y.S.2d 662, 665 (N.Y. Sup. Ct. 1973) (same regarding a child of four and a half years); *Republic Ins. Co. v. Michel*, 885 F. Supp. 426, 433 (E.D.N.Y. 1995) (same regarding a child of four years and four and a half months); *Redmond v. City of New York*, 447 N.Y.S.2d 434, 434 (N.Y. 1981) (same regarding a child of four years and ten months).

As you can see, though, string cites can be difficult to read because they, essentially, create a long block of text, and readers tend to skip over long blocks of text. Moreover, a string cite is useful only if the point of law that you are discussing is in controversy. If your opponent is likely to agree that courts have adopted a particular point of law, then a string cite is simply a waste of space and of the court's time. Thus, use string cites sparingly.

If you wish to assert a point of law that is uncontroversial and is stated by a number of authorities, consider using the signal "e.g." rather than a string cite. When many cases state the same proposition and the opposing party is unlikely to dispute the proposition, you can simply choose one case that states the proposition and precede the citation with "e.g.," as in Example 6-rr. The abbreviation "e.g." tells the reader that the case you have chosen to cite is just one of several that state the same proposition.

Example 6-rr · Using "e.g." to present a common and undisputed proposition

---

When a district court grants an injunction based on its interpretation of a statute, this Court's review is de novo. *See, e.g., Edina Educ. Ass'n v. Bd. of Educ. of Indep. Sch. Dist. No. 273*, 562 N.W.2d 306, 311 (Minn. App. 1997) (reviewing de novo injunction based on interpretation of Data Practices Act).[10]

D. Use Explanatory Parentheticals Effectively

An explanatory parenthetical is a part of a citation that is used to help a reader understand the citation's significance.[11] When you assert a propo-

---

10. Adapted from *Williams v. Nat'l Football League*, 794 N.W.2d 391, 395 (Minn. Ct. App. 2011).

11. See the *ALWD Guide to Legal Citation, supra* note 9, at 385–89 (R. 37), or *The Bluebook: A Uniform System of Citation, supra* note 9, at 5–6 (R. B1.3), for details about how to incorporate explanatory parentheticals.

sition that depends on synthesizing the holdings from a series of cases, parentheticals can be an effective way to prove the asserted proposition without delving into the specific facts and holdings of each case you have reviewed. For example, parentheticals can be used to great effect to establish a trend in the law. Both Example 6-qq and Example 6-ss use parentheticals to show that a series of courts have reached the conclusion that the writer wants the court to reach in this case.

Example 6-ss • Parentheticals used to establish a trend[12]

Plaintiff's claim must fail because the First Amendment does not allow a citizen to avoid paying taxes because she objects to government policy. *Adams v. Comm'r*, 170 F.3d 173, 182 (3d Cir. 1999) ("Plaintiffs engaging in civil disobedience through tax protests must pay the penalties incurred as a result of engaging in such disobedience."); *United States v. Rowlee*, 899 F.2d 1275, 1279 (2d Cir. 1990) ("The consensus of this and every other circuit is that liability for a false or fraudulent return cannot be avoided by evoking the First Amendment[.]"); *Welch v. United States*, 750 F.2d 1101, 1108 (1st Cir. 1985) ("[N]oncompliance with the federal tax laws is conduct that is afforded no protection under the First Amendment[.]"); *United States v. Ness*, 652 F.2d 890, 892 (9th Cir. (1981) ("Tax violations are not a protected form of political dissent.").

Parentheticals should be used for less important ideas, not the primary points of your analysis. Great points can get lost in a mass of citations, and even the most engaged readers tend to skip over a string of citations with parentheticals. Thus, your argument must appear in the text and not in citations. To test whether you have used parentheticals effectively, read your motion or brief without the citations and their parentheticals to see whether you have also made your point within the text.

The techniques in this chapter, summarized in Table 6-tt, should help fine-tune your brief so that a court can see why your substantive arguments should win. Although these techniques cannot eradicate undesirable law or facts, they can help emphasize why the outcome your client seeks is a correct and preferable outcome to the one opposing counsel seeks.

---

12. Adapted from *Greene v. I.R.S.*, No. 1:08-CV-0280, 2008 WL 5378120, at *5 (N.D.N.Y. Dec. 23, 2008).

Table 6-tt · Persuasive Techniques Chart

Technique	What it does	Example of technique in action
Use a thesis sentence—one that directly tells the proposition you are advocating—to begin every paragraph in your document.	• Helps judge see the outline of points • Helps judge better absorb the ideas in the paragraph	Officer Ephgrave's interaction with the defendant was a mere conversation and not a stop because the defendant could not reasonably believe his liberty was restrained at any point during the encounter. [Remainder of paragraph follows]
Sandwich unfavorable law or facts in the middle of a paragraph.	• Embedding the material lessens the impact of the information, particularly when unfavorable material is sandwiched between favorable material	The facts in this case, even when viewed most favorably for the plaintiff, failed to establish any "substantial evidence" of Moore's intoxication. **Although Moore's blood alcohol level was .13**, she did not demonstrate any outward signs of intoxication. Her speech was not slurred. She appeared to be in control of her body. She did not have the odor of alcohol. Because Moore exhibited none of these symptoms, Defendant Soto could not have known she was intoxicated.
In a paragraph's last sentence, restate the point (or thesis) of that paragraph.	• Drives home point of paragraph, especially when a paragraph is long or more complex	Therefore, Officer Ephgrave did not prevent the defendant from leaving, nor did he alter the defendant's course. **Accordingly, the defendant could not reasonably believe that his liberty was restrained.**
Within a paragraph, use bridging language to connect rules or ideas.	• Increases coherence (the flow of logical ideas) and cohesion (the point a group of ideas together make) • Stating key words or phrases in one sentence then repeating them in the next sentence enhances a judge's ability to follow an idea	A university complies with Title IX if it provides **equal athletic opportunities** to both sexes. Whether **equal athletic opportunities** exist depends on an analysis of **ten factors**. However, an institution's failure to comply with **the first factor** is sufficient to constitute a violation of Title IX.
Within a paragraph, chain sentences to promote cohesion.	• Enhances cohesion and coherence • Can chain by using the same word or group of words • Can chain by focusing on the same topic	**Lem Kasaka** is the Chief Financial Officer of Pure, and he was the guiding force behind the company's quick rise to international success. **Mr. Kasaka** graduated with an MBA in 2010, and he immediately became a partner in the fledgling start-up company. Under **Mr. Kasaka's leadership**, the company went from a small store to an international company.

Chart continues on the next page

continued

Technique	What it does	Example of technique in action
Sandwich less-favorable law or facts within the middle of a sentence.	• The beginning or end of a sentence can be a point of emphasis; putting the less-favorable material in the end de-emphasizes it.	Ms. Moore did not demonstrate signs of intoxication **consistent with a blood alcohol level of .13** because her speech was not slurred, and she did not smell of alcohol.
Put less-favorable material in a dependent clause to lessen the material's impact.	• Acknowledges the material while de-emphasizing it • Avoid, though, using this technique at the beginning of a paragraph.	**Although Ms. Moore's blood alcohol level was .13,** she did not demonstrate any outward signs of intoxication.
Intersperse short sentences to add punch amidst a group of longer sentences.	• Helps vary pacing throughout a paragraph • Helps propel the reader through longer or complex material • Emphasizes a point or fact.	Although the respondent argues that two statutes support her claim, neither of the statutes supports her assertion that the statute of limitations should be extended. **Indeed, those statutes plainly assert the opposite.**
Keep subjects and verbs close together for maximum clarity.	• Strengthens sentence • Helps reader absorb information	The **police officer pulled over** the defendant's car, believing that it was suspicious that defendant's vehicle sped up after the officer began following him.
Try to use active voice more than passive voice.	• A sentence written in active voice shows who is doing the action. • Sentences that show who did the action and that use action verbs are typically clearer, shorter, and more vivid. • Use passive voice only when you want to intentionally de-emphasize who did the action or when you do not know who the actor was.	**Prefer:** The taxi driver **hit** the skateboarder in the intersection. **Not:** The skateboarder was hit in the intersection. (Unless you want to minimize the taxi driver's role.)

Technique	What it does	Example of technique in action
Avoid the "it is/there is" construction.	• This construction muddles the subject and verb. • Such construction often makes the sentence longer and wordier.	**Prefer:** The **court reviews** five factors. (5 words) **Not: There are** five factors that the court reviews. (8 words)
Replace the word "it" with a noun when possible.	• The word "it," while understandable when talking, can be confusing to a reader. • When possible, use the actual noun instead of the pronoun.	**Prefer:** The tractor-trailer hit the bridge, but **the bridge** was not damaged. **Not:** The tractor-trailer hit the bridge, but **it** was not damaged.
Use transitions appropriately to create context and to move the reader through the points.	• Transitions can act like signals for the reader, pointing to the direction the prose is going. • Transitions can connect thoughts, ideas, and arguments fluidly.	**First,** although the respondent purports to rely on two statutes to support her claim, neither of the statutes supports her assertion that the statute of limitations should be extended. **Instead,** those statutes flatly refute the respondent's argument.

Practice Points

- Effective writing techniques can help you more clearly explain why your client wins, but no writing technique can undo bad law or bad facts.

- Put information that you want the judge to retain in places where the judge is most likely to see it:
  - In point headings
  - In thesis sentences
  - In a sentence before a block quote

- Assert your point before providing detail so that you can focus the judge's attention on the point you wish to make.
  - State your conclusion before a new section in your brief.
  - Create a thesis sentence for each paragraph.
  - Create a hook for each case illustration.
  - Start your application with an assertion of what you will prove.
  - State the point of a block quotation as an introduction to the block quotation.

- Be explicit about what you are doing and why you are doing it so that a judge can more easily follow along.

- Create coherent paragraphs and clear sentences that are easy for an over-worked judge to absorb.

Chapter 7

Editing Persuasive Arguments

I.   Check Procedural and Local Rules
II. Edit Your Argument
     A. Editing for Substance
         1. Review point headings
         2. Review thesis sentences
         3. Review explanations of the law
         4. Review applications
         5. Confirm that you have addressed weaknesses from your client's perspective
     B. Editing for Style
         1. Flow
         2. Cohesion and coherence in each paragraph; clarity for every sentence
         3. Credibility
     C. Create and Customize Your Editing Checklist

To produce a persuasive legal argument, you must edit your work before submitting it to the court. Editing involves two steps: First, edit for substance. Editing for substance requires you to critically examine the structure and content of your work. When editing for substance, check whether each argument is complete, whether your arguments are arranged logically, and whether the law and facts are explained in a way that clearly supports your client's position.

After this first phase is complete, and your document is substantively and structurally sound, edit for style. When editing for style, look for and correct any snags, typos, or mistakes that might distract your reader from your message. In this phase, your first goal is to make your writing cohesive, coherent, and clear. You must also check your work for accuracy.

Not surprisingly, this two-part process takes time: Effective writers spend more than half their time editing their work product.[1] One reason this process takes so much time is because editing occurs in rounds. You cannot reread your argument once and call it quits. Rather, you must

> **Struggling with Persuasive Arguments?**
>
> Review Chapter 3, *Organizing Claims and Arguments*, which discusses how to organize and order different types of arguments.

---

1. *See* Anne M. Enquist, *Unlocking the Secrets of Highly Successful Law Students*, 82 St. Johns L. Rev. 609 (2007).

check your argument from a variety of angles to ensure that all the parts are working together to present the strongest argument possible. An overview of the editing process is provided in Table 7-A below. Each point listed in Table 7-A is discussed in greater detail below.

7-A · Overview of a process for editing your argument

- ❑ Check applicable procedural and local rules and ensure you adhere to them.
- ❑ Review your point headings and confirm that they outline your argument and integrate your theme.
- ❑ Evaluate your thesis sentences to ensure that each asserts a legal argument, that each matches the content of the paragraph, and that together they form a logical outline of your argument.
- ❑ Consider whether your explanations of the law—rules and case illustrations—are framed so that they are consistent with and support the outcome you seek.
- ❑ Review your applications of the law. Note whether they start and end with specific conclusions, whether they re-use key language from applicable rules, and key facts and reasoning from applicable cases.
- ❑ Ensure that you address weaknesses strategically from your client's perspective and use techniques that minimize weaknesses.
- ❑ Check that roadmap sections and sentences are placed wherever one legal concept breaks down into two or more legal concepts.
- ❑ Check each paragraph for cohesiveness and coherence; check each sentence for clarity.
- ❑ Proofread to find and correct errors.
- ❑ Check quotations and citations for accuracy in form and substance.

I. Check Your Procedural and Local Rules

Always begin the editing process by reviewing all applicable procedural and local rules that govern the document you will be submitting. Although you probably have read those rules at least once, you should now read them again.

Make sure that your document includes all required content and that your document conforms to the required format. Procedural and local rules may require you to abide by page limits or word counts, use certain fonts, file documents in a certain way, on a specific date, by a specific time of day, and attach affidavits, exhibits, or appendices in a certain manner.[2]

---

2. *See* Cheryl S. Bratt, *Doing Like the Locals Do: Using the Legal Writing Classroom to Teach Local Rule Practice*, 22 Persps.: Teaching Legal Res. & Writing 134 (2014).

Remember, courts can dismiss cases in their entirety or deny motions and briefs for failure to follow procedural and local rules, so always verify that any court filing complies with all applicable procedural and local rules.

II. Edit Your Argument

The argument section is the primary place where you will communicate your message to the court. In the subsections below, we describe guidelines for you to consider when editing your argument.

The first set of techniques, *Editing for Substance*, will help ensure that your argument is focused and that key supporting ideas are emphasized. The second set of techniques, *Editing for Style*, will help ensure that your argument is cohesive and coherent and that your credibility (or ethos) is maintained.

A. Editing for Substance

Editing for substance requires you to critically examine the organization and content of your work. You must check whether each argument is complete, whether your arguments are arranged logically, and whether you have presented the law and facts, so they effectively support your client's position. You can ensure that the organization of your work is sound by examining your (1) point headings and (2) thesis sentences. Checking the content of your work also requires you to take another look at your (3) explanations of the law, (4) applications, and (5) weaknesses in your argument.

1. Review your point headings

The first step is to review your point headings. To review your point headings, consider highlighting or otherwise pulling out your primary and subpoint headings to evaluate them both individually, and in connection with each other, as reflected in Example 7-B, below. This example, which has pulled out the point headings from the *Prakash v. Starr Publishing* briefs included in Appendix B, compares how the parties each used point headings to address a component of the overall relief sought for the claim. It further compares how sub-headings provide more detailed support for the primary points necessary to establish the claim.

Do you see how the point headings outline both parties' legal arguments to address their overall claims? Table 7-C, below, provides guidelines for you to consider as you edit your point headings.

Example 7-B • Point headings outline the components of your argument

Point headings from defendant's supporting memorandum	Point headings from plaintiffs' opposing memorandum
I. Plaintiff's claim for defamation should be dismissed based on any of the four reasons explained below.	I. Summary judgment is inappropriate because the record establishes sufficient evidence for a jury to find defamation *per se*.
A. Plaintiffs cannot establish the first element of a defamation claim — that the statement was defamatory.	A. The statements were defamatory.
B. Plaintiffs have suffered no general damages.	B. The evidence in the record allows a jury to find that the plaintiffs suffered great harm to their reputations.
C. Plaintiffs consented to the use of their names in connection with the 2022–2023 pocket parts.	C. Plaintiffs did not consent to defamation.
D. The statement that the 2022–2023 pocket part was "by Amit Prakash and Helen Vinocur" and "The Publishing Staff" was true or substantially true.	D. Defendant is not entitled to summary judgment on the supposed truth of the defamatory statements.

Table 7-C • Guidelines for editing point headings

❏ Pull out your point headings and examine them without the surrounding text.

❏ Do your point headings reflect (and are they consistent with) your overall theme?

- **Hint:** Because point headings are critical points of emphasis, consider reviewing Chapter 4, *Themes for Persuasive Arguments*, for additional guidance in developing and integrating a persuasive theme.

❏ Do your point headings provide a conclusion about the legal argument that follows along with the main reasons for that conclusion?

❏ Do your point headings divide your argument into readable chunks of material?

❏ Have you read through your point headings carefully to confirm that there are no spelling errors, or misplaced or missing words?

- **Remember:** Do not rely on spell check for point headings, particularly where point headings need to be in ALL CAPS.

❏ Are your point headings properly punctuated?

- **Hint:** Argumentative point headings are full sentences, so confirm that your point headings include the proper punctuation both within the sentence and at the end of the sentence.

> ### Thesis sentences at the beginning of a new section
> ### (a reminder)
>
> A thesis sentence at the beginning of a new section of your argument is likely to state the point of the section — not the point of the paragraph. You will likely have these kinds of thesis sentences at the beginning of a roadmap paragraph and at the beginning of your application.
>
> When you write a thesis sentence that states the point of a section, consider whether the second sentence of the paragraph should state the point of the paragraph. Especially at the beginning of your application, you will often want to state the overall conclusion of your application section and then state the paragraph's point in the paragraph's second sentence.

2. Review your thesis sentences

As discussed in Chapter 6, *Refining Persuasive Arguments*, one of the best techniques to improve the focus and persuasive effect of your document is to review the thesis sentences in your arguments. Your reader's eye will naturally rest on each thesis sentence, which is usually the first sentence of each paragraph. The information in that sentence is therefore the information your reader — the judge — is most likely to absorb.

Each thesis sentence in your argument sentence should support your argument and accurately reflect the content of the paragraph that follows. For these reasons, check your thesis sentences to ensure they (1) form a logical outline of your legal argument, (2) assert a conclusion you want the court to adopt, and (3) match the content of your paragraph.

First, your thesis sentences, taken together, should form a logical outline of your argument. To confirm that your thesis sentences do form a logical outline, go through the argument and highlight or pull your thesis sentences out of the document, as illustrated in Example 7-D, so that you can focus your attention on them.

Example 7-D · Read just your thesis sentences to determine whether they form a logical outline

- The indictment against Mr. Hidalgo must be dismissed because Arizona's anti-human smuggling statute was never meant to be used to prosecute individuals who were smuggled.

- To answer that question, this Court must construe the word "person."

- In this case, the text in context, its legislative history, and the historical context surrounding the enactment of the statute all establish that the legislature never intended the prosecution of the human cargo.

- The plain text of §13-2319(a) limits application of the statute to the smuggler, and not his human cargo.

- First, the ordinary meaning of the phrase "for…commercial purpose" similarly limits who can be prosecuted to those in the business of smuggling.

After ensuring that your thesis sentences logically outline your argument, evaluate whether each thesis sentence asserts a conclusion you want the court to adopt. If you find that a thesis sentence merely states a fact or principle that is true, consider revising the sentence; you have likely missed a prime opportunity to persuade the judge.

To illustrate the difference between a thesis sentence that asserts a conclusion you want the court to adopt and a thesis sentence that merely states a truth, compare the sentences in the two columns of Table 7-E. The statements in the left-hand column of Table 7-E assert conclusions that the lawyer wants the court to adopt. By contrast, the statements in the right-hand column assert statements that are true, but do not reflect a conclusion that the lawyer wants the court to adopt.

Table 7-E • Comparing thesis sentences that assert a legal argument with thesis sentences that assert a truth about a legal principle

Thesis sentences assert a legal argument	Thesis sentences assert a truth about a legal principle
• The plain text of § 13-2319(a) limits application of the statute to the smuggler, and not his human cargo.	• When analyzing the plain text of a statute, Arizona courts must give "each word, phrase, clause and sentence…its natural, obvious, and ordinary meaning." *Arpaio v. Steinle III*, 35 P.3d 114, 116 (Ariz. Ct. App. 2001).
• First, the ordinary meaning of the phrase "for profit" limits the person who can be prosecuted to those in the business of smuggling.	• "Profit" is widely understood as "net income…from the conduct of business." *Webster's Third New International Dictionary* 1811 (2002).

Can you see how the sentences in the right-hand column, which merely assert true statements, are not as compelling as the statements on the left that assert the proposition the writer wants the court to adopt?

Finally, check that your thesis sentences match the content of the paragraph that follows. If they do not match, adjust either the thesis sentence or the content (or both) until they match. This step works in conjunction with the previous two steps. Remember, if you adjust a thesis sentence so that it better outlines your argument or better asserts a point, then you may need to also adjust the content of the paragraph so that it supports your thesis sentence. Likewise, if you adjust a thesis sentence so that it better reflects the content of the paragraph, you'll need to confirm that any new material in your thesis sentence works together with other thesis sentences to build your overall argument. The questions in Table 7-F provide a starting point for reviewing thesis sentences.

Table 7-F · Guidelines for editing thesis sentences

- ❏ Do your thesis sentences, when read together, outline your legal argument?
- ❏ Do your thesis sentences assert the argument you want the court to adopt?
- ❏ Does each sentence within the paragraph support the thesis sentence?
  - **Hint:** If you cannot quite formulate a thesis sentence for a paragraph, ask yourself whether too many ideas are being forced into a single paragraph.

3. Review your explanations of the law

After reviewing your point headings and thesis sentences, review your explanations of the law to ensure that they have sufficient focus and emphasis. The guidelines in Table 7-G provide techniques for maximizing persuasiveness in your explanations of law. However, you may also want to review Chapter 3, *Organizing Persuasive Arguments*; Chapter 5, *Drafting Persuasive Arguments*; and Chapter 6, *Refining Persuasive Arguments*, which provide much more detail about developing persuasive arguments.

As you edit, remember this critical point: Frame rules in a manner that supports the outcome you seek. To illustrate this point, examine Table 7-G (originally seen as Table 5-B). This example shows how even the most straightforward rule can be drafted in different ways to support your client's argument.

Table 7-G · Explaining the summary judgment standard consistently with your position

The rule as written	"The court shall grant summary judgment if the movant shows that there is no genuine dispute as to any material fact and the movant is entitled to judgment as a matter of law." Fed. R. Civ. P. 56(a).
The moving party	Summary judgment must be granted if there is no issue of material fact and the moving party is entitled to judgment as a matter of law. Fed. R. Civ. P. 56(a).
The non-moving party	Summary judgment may not be granted if there is an issue of material fact. Fed. R. Civ. P. 56(a).

With respect to case illustrations, make sure that your description of a case is also consistent with your overall argument. Your case illustration should be fashioned so that it forecasts your upcoming application. Check also that your description of a prior case remains accurate. If accuracy and consistency with your argument are ever in conflict, accuracy wins. You will have to change your argument so that it is consistent with the law.

Take a moment to carefully re-read your explanations of the law and consider the guidelines set forth in Table 7-H.

Table 7-H · Guidelines for reviewing your explanations of the law

❑ Are rules framed to emphasize the outcome you seek?

❑ Are your case illustrations described in a way that is consistent with your overall argument?

❑ Does your case illustration focus on the facts, holding, and rationale that will later be relevant when you compare the prior case to your client's case?

❑ Is your case illustration accurate?

❑ When you illustrate a case, are the facts of the case presented in the past tense?

❑ Have you used authorities strategically to subtly rebut the other side's strongest points?

❑ If you have used parentheticals to illustrate cases, are they placed appropriately?

  • **Tip:** Usually parentheticals will fit either after the holding and reasoning of the main case you are discussing or following the comparison of your case to the prior case. Follow your instincts as to where the parenthetical will be most effective.

4. Review your application of the law

Your application of the law represents the heart of your legal argument and ties together the rules and any applicable case illustrations with the facts of your client's case. Because of the critical nature of the application section, consider reviewing the applicable sections in Chapter 3, *Organizing Persuasive Arguments*; Chapter 4, *Themes for Persuasive Arguments*; Chapter 5, *Drafting Persuasive Arguments*; and Chapter 6, *Refining Persuasive Arguments*. Table 7-I, below, provides guidelines for editing your application sections.

Table 7-I · Guidelines for editing the application

- ❑ Does each application section begin with a conclusion stating how the legal principle at issue should be decided?

- ❑ Consider which ideas are especially important to your application; return to your explanation of the law and highlight those ideas in your explanation of the law.

- ❑ Ensure key language in your explanation of the law and your application are consistent.

  - • **Remember:** Although some disciplines appreciate "elegant variation," lawyers do not, and using the same language to address the same legal concepts will add to your credibility.

- ❑ Where you apply a rule to the facts of your client's case, is the rule applied to concrete and specific facts?

- ❑ Where you compare a prior case to your client's case, did you establish the factual similarity and show how that factual similarity leads to a similar result?

- ❑ Where you distinguish a case from your client's case, did you establish the factual distinction and explain that, therefore, the precedent is inapplicable, and an alternative conclusion is warranted?

  - • **Hint:** Comparisons and distinctions may not line up quite as neatly as you would like. Don't "force them." But when reviewing your application, consider whether you have done the best with what you have to work with.

- ❑ Does your application repeat the initial conclusion at the end of the argument to sum up and emphasize the conclusion?

---

5. Confirm that you have addressed weaknesses from your client's perspective

When editing for substance, much of the editing involves looking for ways to emphasize the strengths of your arguments. However, you must also examine whether you have addressed weaknesses in your arguments.

Remember to explain any weaknesses from *your client's perspective*, rather than from the opposing party's perspective. If you find yourself explaining an argument that the opposing counsel will make, stop, and revise using the techniques explained in Chapter 5, *Drafting Persuasive Arguments*. Table 7-J provides a brief reminder of how to address a weakness from your perspective and not from the opposing party's perspective. After reading the two arguments in Table 7-J, compare the persuasive effect of addressing weaknesses from your client's perspective rather than the perspective of the opposing party.

> **Don't Forget Your Initial Concerns**
>
> Addressing weaknesses presents difficulties in some cases because, as we continue to research and write, we become more convinced of our own arguments. As a result, we sometimes lose sight of those issues that initially gave us pause. So, take a moment and think back to any issues that initially gave you pause and consider whether and how you addressed those potential weaknesses in your legal argument.

Table 7-J • Addressing Weaknesses from Your Client's Perspective

Addressing a Weakness from Opposing Counsel's Perspective	Addressing a Weakness from Your Client's Perspective
In this column, the writer describes in detail the opposing argument first. In doing so, the writer draws attention and provides airtime to the opponent's argument. The writer does not describe why opposing counsel's argument is less effective until the second paragraph.	In this column, see how the writer addresses the opposing argument but does so from her client's perspective by immediately explaining why the opposing argument fails without giving the opposing argument undue airtime. This method is far more persuasive (and concise).

Defendants argue that the officers impermissibly relied on the defendant's looks in their reason to conduct a protective search. Defendant compares this case to *Valdez* and *Bates*.

In this case, the officers relied on the t-shirt that defendant was wearing, his companion's tattoos, their baggy clothes, and their haircut to support their reason for a protective search. Defendant argues that these facts are similar to the facts in *Valdez*, in which the officer pointed to a "blue leisure suit and shiny black shoes" and similar to the long hair, beard, and leather jacket in *Valdez*. In both those cases, the courts held that the facts the officers presented were not sufficient to support a protective search.

This case is, however, different from *Valdez* and *Bates*. Here, the "look" at issue established a reasonable suspicion of gang activity and membership in the 18th Street Gang. The t-shirt defendant was wearing had the phrase "18th Street" printed on it. His companion's tattoo is one that's associated with the 18th Street Gang. Finally, the shaved heads and baggy clothes are typical of people who belong to that gang. Both the association with gang activity generally and the association with a particular gang known to carry weapons are specific, articulable facts that raise a reasonable suspicion that the defendant might pose an immediate threat. Thus, the officers relied on far more than simply the defendant's "looks."

Here, the officers relied on far more than simply the defendant's "looks." The officers knew that the defendant was associated with the 18th Street Gang. Defendant was wearing a t-shirt with the phrase "18th Street" printed on it, and his companion had a distinctive tattoo under his eye, one commonly associated with membership in the gang. In addition, both men had shaved heads and were wearing baggy clothes.

Moreover, the officers knew that members of the 18th Street Gang were dangerous, often carrying concealed weapons. One of the officers had earlier encountered a gang member in the same area who, after a pat-down search, was found to have a weapon concealed in his waistband.

Based on these facts, this case is distinguishable from *Bates* and *Valdez*. In *Valdez* and in *Bates*, the "look" that the officers relied on — a blue leisure suit and shiny black shoes in *Valdez* and long hair, a beard, and a leather jacket in *Bates* — could not be particularly associated with a weapon-related activity or with a particular group of people who regularly carry weapons. By contrast, here, the "look" at issue established a reasonable suspicion of gang activity and membership in the 18th Street Gang. Both the association with gang activity generally and the association with a particular gang known to carry weapons are specific, articulable facts that raise a reasonable suspicion that the defendant might pose an immediate threat.

Additional strategies that you should consider to ensure that you have effectively addressed weaknesses are set out in Table 7-K.

Table 7-K · Strategies to emphasize strengths and minimize weaknesses

---

❑ Do you place your strongest arguments first?

❑ If you are responding to an argument, do you focus on your client's perspective (that is, why your client's argument is correct) rather than giving additional "airtime" to the opposing party's assertions (for instance, by first explaining the opposing argument before refuting it)?

❑ If you have information that is less favorable to your client, is it located in the middle of a paragraph where it gets less attention?

❑ In sentences, do you minimize weaknesses by, for example, placing the weakness in a dependent clause or pairing a problematic fact with a stronger fact?

❑ If applicable, are your sentences constructed such that the beginning and ending include information that you want to emphasize?

❑ Do you explain why a weakness does not prevent the outcome you seek?

B. Editing for Style[3]

When editing for style, you will want to consider how to make your writing *flow*, as well as how to make it *clear, cohesive,* and *credible*.

1. Flow

"Flow" refers to the smooth transition from one idea to the next. You can enhance the flow of your arguments by effectively deploying (1) roadmaps, and (2) transitions.

Roadmap sections or sentences (you will decide which technique to use depending on the length and complexity of the argument) help with flow by alerting your reader how you have organized your argument that follows. If you need additional help with roadmap sections or sentences, review § 3.1, *Organizing Claims and Arguments*, which provides more detail about when to use and how to construct roadmap sections and sentences.

Transitions also alert the reader to a relationship between two ideas. Chapter 6, *Refining Persuasive Arguments*, Table 6-R provides a list of common transitions.

You should check all the places in your legal argument where roadmaps or transitions typically show up. Table 7-L lists typical locations when a roadmap section or sentence or transitions may be helpful to guide the reader. Check that you have provided roadmaps or transitions

---

3. Portions of this section are derived from Christine Coughlin, Joan Rocklin & Sandy Patrick, *A Lawyer Writes* 259–91 (3d ed. 2018).

in these locations. Check also that you have used transitions accurately and precisely.

Table 7-L · Guidelines for when to use roadmaps and transitions in your argument section

A roadmap section or sentence may be needed	A transition may be needed
• At the beginning of a legal argument or claim.	• Between two legal arguments.
• Before any argument that breaks down into one or more elements or factors.	• To explain the relationship among a series of rules.
• Before any argument that contains parts or intersecting components.	• As a "signpost" to remind the reader where she is within the structure of the analysis.
• Before any argument that contains complex explanations of law, case illustration, or analyses.	• Between the parts of a case illustration.
	• When moving from the case explanation to the application.

2. Cohesion and coherence in each paragraph; clarity for every sentence

Legal arguments are complex, but legal writing should not be. Your job as an advocate is to clearly articulate the most persuasive argument possible so that the judge can understand and retain your argument. Editing at this level entails checking each paragraph, sentence, and word. Tables 7-M and 7-N, below, each contain a checklist of techniques to ensure cohesion and coherence in your writing first at the paragraph level and then at the sentence level, respectively.

Table 7-M · Guidelines for paragraph-level cohesion and coherence

❏ Does each paragraph begin with a strong thesis sentence?

❏ Does the paragraph include only one main idea? If not, divide the paragraph, giving each idea its own paragraph and corresponding thesis sentences.

❏ With respect to rules, do you start with broad concepts and explain them in more detail using bridging language?

❏ Do sentences flow together? If not, consider creating sentence chains or adding transitions.

❏ Does the final sentence in the paragraph "close the loop" by establishing the thesis has been proved?

Table 7-N • Guidelines for sentence-level clarity

❑ Are sentences the optimal length? As a rule of thumb, a sentence that spans more than two lines is likely too long and should be revised.

❑ Does each sentence reflect one main point? Do your sentences contain too many ideas? For example, do your sentences contain a series of prepositions (of, after, in, between, about, to, etc.), which can signify that the sentence contains too many ideas?

❑ Do your sentences contain too many empty words? Compare "working" words to "glue" words and try to minimize the number of glue words in a sentence.

❑ When you read each sentence, is it clear who is doing what in each sentence? For example, are your subject and verbs close together at the beginning of the sentence?

❑ Are your sentences written using the active voice (unless you make a strategic decision to use the passive voice)?

❑ Do you select verbs that show action?

❑ Do your sentences avoid using the "it is" or "there is" structure?

❑ Have you minimized or eliminated nominalizations (nouns that could be expressed as verbs)?

❑ Do you use the simplest and most precise words possible for the issue you are analyzing and arguing?

❑ Do your pronouns agree with the noun they are replacing and the verb to which they relate?

---

3. Credibility

Polishing also allows you to enhance your credibility or *ethos*. Editing for credibility includes proofreading, checking quotations and citations for accuracy, and checking (or rechecking) the format of your document for its visual appearance (which includes checking those procedural and local rules again!). Reviewing your work product against the guidelines below will not only have a positive effect on the persuasive content of your message but will also go a long way toward establishing yourself as a careful, detail-oriented professional.

a. Proofread

Proofreading, which is one of the most important ways you can establish credibility, requires you to carefully reread what you have written. You know what you intended to say, but many times it is quite difficult to see what the document does say. While spell check, grammar apps, and other similar programs will catch some mistakes, your own eyes are also essential tools. Table 7-O provides some recommended proofreading techniques you can use.

Table 7-O • Proofreading techniques

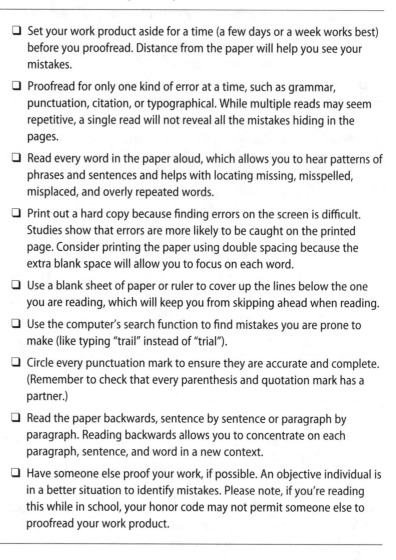

❑ Set your work product aside for a time (a few days or a week works best) before you proofread. Distance from the paper will help you see your mistakes.

❑ Proofread for only one kind of error at a time, such as grammar, punctuation, citation, or typographical. While multiple reads may seem repetitive, a single read will not reveal all the mistakes hiding in the pages.

❑ Read every word in the paper aloud, which allows you to hear patterns of phrases and sentences and helps with locating missing, misspelled, misplaced, and overly repeated words.

❑ Print out a hard copy because finding errors on the screen is difficult. Studies show that errors are more likely to be caught on the printed page. Consider printing the paper using double spacing because the extra blank space will allow you to focus on each word.

❑ Use a blank sheet of paper or ruler to cover up the lines below the one you are reading, which will keep you from skipping ahead when reading.

❑ Use the computer's search function to find mistakes you are prone to make (like typing "trail" instead of "trial").

❑ Circle every punctuation mark to ensure they are accurate and complete. (Remember to check that every parenthesis and quotation mark has a partner.)

❑ Read the paper backwards, sentence by sentence or paragraph by paragraph. Reading backwards allows you to concentrate on each paragraph, sentence, and word in a new context.

❑ Have someone else proof your work, if possible. An objective individual is in a better situation to identify mistakes. Please note, if you're reading this while in school, your honor code may not permit someone else to proofread your work product.

b. Check quotations

Quotations, when used thoughtfully, are quite persuasive. However, when used inappropriately quotations can clutter your writing and cause readers to skip over critical arguments. Moreover, if used inappropriately or out of context, you can lose credibility with your legal reader or even find yourself in a violation of ethical rules. Table 7-P provides techniques for reviewing your quotations for accuracy (in substance and form) and effectiveness.

Table 7-P · Techniques for effectively using quotations[4]

- ❑ Check all quotations for accuracy.
- ❑ While you should paraphrase most of your analysis, you may want to quote exactly key portions of a source when the specific wording matters. For example, you may want to quote the exact language of a statute, a witness's statement, or terms of a contract.
- ❑ Remember, you can combine quotes with paraphrased text. Generally, try to incorporate a quotation into a paraphrased sentence of your own, rather than quoting an entire sentence from a case.
- ❑ When a court's reasoning is relevant to your client's case, quote the relevant portion of the reasoning in the case illustration and then reintegrate the quote or a key part of the quote in your application of the law.
- ❑ Use block quotes sparingly.
- ❑ If a block quote is the best choice strategically, explain the point of the quotation before the block quote so that your reader is encouraged to read and confirm that the block quotation supports the point.
- ❑ When altering a word or the quote itself by using ellipses or brackets, make sure to consult a legal citation manual such as the Bluebook or ALWD guide to citation and use the format appropriate for your jurisdiction.
- ❑ Never misrepresent a source by using ellipses or brackets to make the quote "work" better for your client's position.

c. Check citations

Citations help the judge and the judge's staff find the authorities on which you have relied. Accurate citations also showcase your attention to detail. Have your citation manual close by, but you may also want to create a quick reference sheet for citations that you use frequently. Table 7-Q describes a process for checking your citations for accuracy.

Table 7-Q · Techniques for checking citations

- ❑ Verify that all the authorities that you have relied on are still good law.
- ❑ Review any local citation rules or conventions and adhere to them. Confirm that all legal propositions are cited. A citation should follow most sentences explaining the law.

---

4. See Angela Kershner, *Effective Use of Quotations*, University of Baltimore School of Law, Legal Writing Center, http://law.ubalt.edu/academics/academic-support /legal_writing_center/duediligenceguides/Due%20Diligence%20Guide%20Effective%20 Use%20of%20Quotations%20Spring%202018.pdf (last visited June 16, 2022).

❏ Go back to the original source. Check that each citation supports the cited proposition.

❏ Make sure that the first time you cite an authority, you use a full citation form.

❏ Confirm that any short forms use the correct citation and each "*id.*" relates to the preceding citation. Check punctuation used within a citation. Take special care to ensure that marks that come in sets, like quotation marks or parentheses, have a proper partner.

❏ Check that signals accurately describe the relationship between the original source and your cited explanation.

d. Check formatting

We can't emphasized this enough: Check the applicable procedural and local rules again. You may have checked the applicable rules of procedure earlier, but you will often want to check them one more time as you review the format of your document. As noted at the beginning of this chapter, procedural and local rules also focus on format. The rules may, for example, dictate typeface, word count, line spacing, where page numbers may be placed, and the size of the margins.

If you fail to follow the applicable rules, you will lose credibility. At the very least you will raise concerns in the judge's mind that you are sloppy and lack attention to detail. Failure to follow formatting rules may subject your client's motion to denial or even subject your case to dismissal. Table 7-R describes a process for checking your format.

Table 7-R · Techniques for checking your document's format

❏ Reread procedural and local rules and check your document against those rules.

❏ Use traditional formatting for point headings (as well as other components such as tables of content, and tables of authorities). If you are unsure what traditional formatting looks like, return to Chapter 6, *Refining Persuasive Arguments*, which addresses how to format point headings or look ahead to Chapters 8, *Trial Court: The Motion and Supporting Memorandum of Law* and 9, *Courts of Appeals: The Appellate Brief*, which address typical formatting for court documents.

❏ Do not divorce a heading from its text. Always have at least one line of text on the same page as a heading. If you do not have at least one line of text after a heading, insert a page break before the heading so that the heading appears on the next page with the text.

❏ Keep an eye out for inconsistencies. Check for inconsistent spacing before and after section titles and point headings; check that all section headings use the same font; check that all paragraphs are indented by the same amount; and check whether you consistently use either one or two spaces after a sentence's final punctuation.

C. Create and Customize Your Editing Checklist

Editing checklists are an excellent way to ensure that you systematically and thoroughly edit and polish your work. The best checklist is one that you have created and customized.

You can begin with the checklists provided above; however, ultimately, your checklist should reflect the issues that crop up in your writing and the struggles you face. Creating a customized editing checklist that addresses the struggles you face is one of the best ways to turn a struggle into a strength.

Constructing Persuasive Court Documents

The previous part, Part II, *Developing Persuasive Arguments*, addresses how to develop the heart of a document to be submitted to a court: the legal argument. This part, *Constructing Persuasive Court Documents*, addresses the form in which those legal arguments are submitted.

Chapter 8 describes motions and their supporting memoranda of law, and Chapter 9 describes appellate briefs. For each kind of document, the chapters explain the typical parts of the court document; how to find the procedural rules that govern the content and format of your document; and necessary background information about the court receiving the document, that is, your audience. Chapter 9 also explains some particular rules that govern appeals. These fundamental appellate concepts will influence the shape of an appellate argument.

Finally, both trial memoranda and appellate briefs include statements of fact. Chapter 10, *Statements of Fact and of the Case*, addresses how to build persuasive statements of facts — whether the statement is to be included in a document filed in a trial court or in an appellate brief.

Chapter 8

Trial Motions & Motion Practice

One kind of document lawyers submit to a court is a motion. A "motion" is simply a request that a court act.

Before discussing how to construct a motion, we must clarify what lawyers mean when they use the word "motion." Lawyers use the word "motion" in two very different ways. Technically, the word "motion" refers to a short document (often, only one to two pages long) in which the lawyer requests the court to take some action and it provides a brief explanation for why the court should act.

Lawyers also use the word "motion" in a more colloquial way. In this more colloquial usage, the word "motion" refers to not just the request, but all the documents that are submitted along with the request. Those additional documents include, most typically, a supporting memorandum of law and supporting evidence.

Because lawyers use the word "motion" in two different ways—to refer to the motion itself and to refer to the motion and all the accompanying documents—be attentive to the word "motion." If you are ever uncertain about the way in which a lawyer is using the word, just ask.

This chapter begins by explaining the motion itself. Then, it explains the parts that most commonly support the motion: (1) a legal argument, which is usually presented in an attached memorandum of law, and (2) the evidence supporting the motion, which is usually presented in attached exhibits. The chapter provides examples of each and describes how to construct each part.

Each part is shaped by the audience who will read the trial brief and by the court rules that apply to each part. Thus, the chapter next describes the audience that will decide the motion—the trial judge and the judge's staff—and it explains how to find the rules that govern the motion and its accompanying documents. Finally, this chapter explains what happens after you submit your motion and supporting documents to the court.

By the end of this chapter, you will be well-versed in how to draft and submit a request to a court.

I. A Trial Motion and Its Parts

Whether by custom or by formal rules of court, the form of a motion and its related documents varies from jurisdiction to jurisdiction. This section addresses the most typical parts of a trial motion—the motion itself, a supporting memorandum of law, and any evidence that supports the motion.[1]

---

1. When a lawyer files a motion with a court, the motion may also include a notice of motion, a draft order, and proof of service. To keep things simple, we have focused on the primary parts of an ordinary motion: the motion, the supporting memorandum of law, and supporting evidence.

A. The Motion

As explained above, a motion is a request that a court act. The request can be anything that the court has in its power to order. For example, a motion can request the mundane, such as an order to reschedule a hearing or an order to permit additional pages. Other motions go to the heart of a dispute. For example, a motion can request that a complaint be dismissed, that certain evidence be suppressed, or that a jury's verdict be overturned.

Most motions are written. Sometimes, however, events during a trial may prompt a lawyer to make a motion orally. This chapter addresses written motions only.

"Motion" is not a verb

A party *never* "motions" for summary judgment. A party "moves" for summary judgment. Similarly, a party does not "motion" the court to dismiss plaintiff's complaint; a party "moves" the court to dismiss the complaint.

Written motions typically include the following parts: (1) a caption, (2) a statement of the relief the party seeks, (3) a brief statement of the grounds for that request, and (4) the attorney's signature. Examples 8-A and 8-B show two different motions and their constituent parts. The text that follows describes each of these parts in turn.

Example 8-A · A motion to suppress

IN THE CIRCUIT COURT OF THE STATE OF OREGON
FOR LANE COUNTY

Caption

THE STATE OF OREGON,   )
)   Case No. 23-15-18156
                 Plaintiff,   )
)   DEFENDANT'S MOTION TO
vs.   )   SUPPRESS EVIDENCE
)
TRAVIS Z. TREATSKY,   )
)
                 Defendant.   )
_____)

This paragraph is a typical lead-in to a motion's actual request.

The defendant, through his attorney, Jordan R. Silk, moves this Court for the following orders:

The statement of the relief defendant seeks.

1. An order suppressing any and all evidence of the field sobriety tests performed by the defendant on May 21, 2023, and

2. An order suppressing all evidence of the breath test performed by the defendant on May 22, 2023.

The motion cross-references the memorandum of law, which explains the grounds for relief. That memorandum is provided at Example 4-C.

This motion is based on the attached memorandum of law and is, in the opinion of counsel, well-founded in law and not made or filed for the purpose of delay.

DATED this _____ day of November, 2023.

The lawyer's signature

_____
Jordan R. Silk
Bar # 105031
Lane County Public Defender's Office
555 Willamette Street
Eugene, OR 97401
Appearing for Defendant

Example 8-B · A motion to dismiss

United States District Court
For the District of Utah

KATELYN MASON and	:	Civil Action No. 23 CV 921
JENNIFER WELCH, individually	:	
and on behalf of those	:	
similarly situated,	:	
	:	DEFENDANT'S MOTION TO
	:	DISMISS PLAINTIFF
	:	WELCH'S COMPLAINT
Plaintiffs,	:	
	:	
v.	:	
	:	
CENTRAL STATE UNIVERSITY	:	
OF UTAH,	:	
	:	
Defendant.	:	MAY 5, 2023

Pursuant to Federal Rule of Civil Procedure 12(b)(6), defendant Central State University of Utah hereby moves to dismiss that portion of the Complaint that relates to plaintiff Jennifer Welch because plaintiff Welch lacks standing.

> The first paragraph of the motion states both the relief it seeks (dismissal of portions of the complaint) and the grounds for that relief (Rule 12(b)(6)).

Specifically, all claims asserted by plaintiff Welch must be dismissed because plaintiff Welch, by her own allegations, did not suffer any present or past injury, and she cannot establish future injury because she is graduating this year. For these reasons, and as explained more fully in the attached memorandum of law, she lacks standing to bring her Title IX claim.

> The next paragraph briefly elaborates on the grounds, but cross-references a memorandum of law for further explanation.

Therefore, defendant Central State University of Utah respectfully requests that this Court grant its Motion to Dismiss Plaintiff Welch's Complaint.

Hepworth & Peterson LLP

By: _____

> The lawyer's signature

Justin Hepworth, Esq.
jhepworth@wiggin.com
Federal Bar No. ut01386
350 Lake Street
Provo, UT 84601
Phone: (203) 363-7512
Fax: (203) 262-7676
Attorney for Defendant

1. Caption

The caption to a motion appears at the top of the motion and provides procedural details of the motion. It identifies the name and division of the court in which the case is proceeding, the parties, and the file number.

The caption also includes the title of the motion. The attorney who drafts the motion creates its title. No list of acceptable titles exists. Rather, you create a title that clearly identifies the purpose and scope of the motion. In a case involving a single plaintiff and a single defendant, the title might be as simple as "Defendant's Motion for Summary Judgment" or, as in Example 8-A, "Defendant's Motion to Suppress Evidence." If a case involves multiple parties and the motion has a more limited scope, however, the title will need to be more specific. For example, a title might read, "Defendant Vasco's Motion to Dismiss Count Two of Plaintiff Siegel's Complaint" or, as in Example 8-B, "Defendant's Motion to Dismiss Plaintiff Welch's Complaint."

Your firm or organization will likely have a template for the caption that complies with the local court rules. Even so, take time to ensure that the information in the caption is accurate, that names are spelled correctly, and that the caption is neat in appearance.

2. Statement of the relief requested

You submit a motion to ask a court to act on your client's behalf. Thus, the body of the motion states the action you seek. That action may be, for example, for the court to dismiss the case, to extend a filing date, or to suppress certain evidence.

3. Legal grounds for the relief requested

The statement of the grounds supporting the motion is short and simple. Usually, a motion will simply state the statutory basis, such as "Federal Rule of Civil Procedure 12(b)(6)" for a motion to dismiss, or it might refer to a statute or legal principle that a party has violated. If the statement of the grounds supporting the motion requires a more detailed legal analysis, that more detailed analysis usually is attached in a separate supporting memorandum.

4. Signature

You must sign (either physically or electronically) and date any motion that you submit. Local rules will also usually require that you provide contact information directly under your signature. Take note when you sign a motion: You are confirming that the motion is not frivolous, not intended to harass, and not intended to delay the proceedings.[2]

---

2. *See, e.g.,* Fed. R. Civ. P. 11(b).

B. The Supporting Memorandum of Law

Motions are often, but not always, accompanied by a supporting memorandum of law. The supporting memorandum of law explains why the motion should be granted. It explains the relevant law and applies that law to the facts of the case.[3]

Different jurisdictions have different names for the supporting memorandum of law. It may be called a "memorandum of law" in support of the motion, or it may be called a "brief," a "trial brief," a "memorandum of points and authorities," or something else entirely. Whatever the name, the supporting memorandum of law is where the court will find all your persuasive legal arguments.

Although many motions are accompanied by a supporting memorandum, other motions are not. Some requests to a court are so straightforward that no accompanying memorandum is necessary. For example, a motion asking the court to reschedule a hearing would likely not need to be supported by a memorandum because the motion itself would simply explain the conflict and request the change. A court would not need a legal analysis to determine whether the scheduling change is justified.

Other requests are less straightforward and require further explanation. When a request is less straightforward and requires further explanation, the memorandum explaining the request usually has these parts: (1) a caption, (2) a preliminary statement, (3) a statement of facts, (4) an argument, (5) a conclusion, and (6) the lawyer's signature. Example 8-C provides an example of a full memorandum of law and identifies each of those parts. The text that follows explains each part in turn.

---

3. In some jurisdictions, the legal argument explaining why the motion should be granted is presented in the same document as the motion. For simplicity, this book assumes that the request asking the court to act is one document called a "motion" and the legal argument supporting that request is in a separate document called a "memorandum of law."

Example 8-C • A memorandum of law in support of a motion to suppress

IN THE CIRCUIT COURT OF THE STATE OF OREGON
FOR LANE COUNTY

The caption identifies the court to which the motion is submitted, the parties to the litigation, the docket number, and the title of the document.

THE STATE OF OREGON,)	Case No. 23-16-18156
Plaintiff,)	
)	
vs.)	MEMORANDUM OF LAW IN
)	SUPPORT OF DEFENDANT'S
TRAVIS Z. TREATSKY,)	MOTION TO SUPPRESS
)	EVIDENCE
)	
Defendant.)	
_____)	

PRELIMINARY STATEMENT

The introduction to a supporting memorandum provides context for the arguments that follow by explaining the nature of the case and its procedural history. It may also provide a short summary of the arguments that follow.

On May 21–22, 2023, the state violated Article I, Section 9 of the Oregon Constitution when Trooper Evan Sether administered field sobriety tests and then a breath test to defendant Travis Treatsky. Trooper Evan Sether did not obtain warrants to administer those tests. With respect to the field sobriety test, Trooper Sether lacked probable cause to administer the test, and Mr. Treatsky did not voluntarily consent to field sobriety tests. Because the State obtained evidence from the tests in violation of Article I, Section 9 of the Oregon Constitution, all evidence resulting from the field sobriety tests — including results from the breath test — should be suppressed.

FACTUAL BACKGROUND

The statement of facts explains all the facts relevant to the motion and the arguments supporting the motion.

On the evening of May 21, 2023, Mr. Travis Treatsky was driving westbound on Highway 126 after a long day of travel and visiting with family. Earlier that day, Mr. Treatsky had driven from northern California where he attends the College of the Siskiyous to his home in Springfield, Oregon. After the long drive home, Mr. Treatsky visited with his mother and sister, and then drove to visit his stepfather. (Aff. Jordan Silk ¶ 3, Nov. 11, 2023.) Returning home from his stepfather's house, Trooper Sether stopped Mr. Treatsky because the lens on one of Mr. Treatsky's taillights was broken. Trooper Sether observed Mr. Treatsky's fatigued demeanor and concluded that Mr. Treatsky was under the influence of an intoxicant. (Police Rep. of Trooper Sether 1–2, May 22, 2023.)

Trooper Sether asked Mr. Treatsky to perform two separate field sobriety tests. Trooper Sether read to Mr. Treatsky his rights with respect to taking a field sobriety test, and Trooper Sether explained the consequences if Mr. Treatsky failed to take the field sobriety test. Those consequences included immediate seizure and then a likely suspension of his driver's license. Mr. Treatsky then took the field sobriety tests. According to Trooper Sether, Mr. Treatsky failed both field sobriety tests. (Police Rep. Sether 2.)

Trooper Sether then placed Mr. Treatsky under arrest, took him to the police station, and administered a breath test yielding a result of 0.08% BAC. (Police Rep. Sether 2).

ARGUMENT

The evidence in this case was illegally seized and must, therefore, be suppressed. Article I, Section 9 protects individuals from unreasonable searches and seizures by the state. Under that section, when the state searches an individual without a warrant, such "searches and seizures are *per se* unreasonable unless the state proves an exception to the warrant requirement." *State v. Bridewell*, 759 P.2d 1054, 1057 (Or. 1988). To show an exception to the warrant requirement, the state generally must show either that probable cause and exigent circumstances justified the search or that the individual voluntarily consented to the search. *See id.*; *State v. Nagel*, 880 P.2d 451, 456 (Or. 1994). In this case, Trooper Sether did not obtain a warrant to administer any of the tests. Thus, for each test, the state must show either that probable cause and exigent circumstances justified the search or that the defendant consented to the search. The State cannot meet that test. Thus, the field sobriety tests and the evidence from them were unlawfully seized, and that evidence must be suppressed.

> The argument section is the heart of the supporting memorandum. It explains all the reasons the court should order the relief you seek.

A. Trooper Sether administered field sobriety tests in violation of Article I, Section 9 of the Oregon Constitution.

Because the field sobriety tests were administered in violation of Article 1, Section 9 of the Oregon Constitution, evidence from those tests should be suppressed.

1. Trooper Sether lacked probable cause to administer field sobriety tests.

First, Trooper Sether lacked probable cause to administer the two field sobriety tests. A field sobriety test is a search and seizure within the scope of Article I, Section 9. *Nagel*, 880 P.2d at 456. To lawfully administer such a test without a warrant, the officer must have probable cause to believe that the person is under the influence of an intoxicant. *Id.*; *State v. Stroup*, 935 P.2d 438, 440 (Or. App. 1997). An officer has probable cause when the "officer subjectively believes that a crime has been committed and evidence of the crime can be procured by the seizure of the person or the thing"; however, "the officer's belief must be objectively reasonable under the circumstances." *Stroup*, 935 P.2d at 456 (citing *State v. Owens*, 729 P.2d 524, 529 (Or. 1986)). In *Stroup*, the court held the officer did not have probable cause to administer field sobriety tests because the only evidence was "a slight odor of alcohol, bloodshot eyes, and an admission of drinking alcoholic beverages." *Id.* at 441–42. In ruling that the officer lacked probable cause to administer the field sobriety test, the court emphasized that the defendant was initially stopped for an equipment violation, not for unsafe driving. *Id.* at 440.

> The defendant's attorney uses an analogical argument to support his argument that the officer lacked probable cause to support the administration of a field sobriety test.

Here, Trooper Sether had even less evidence supporting probable cause than did the officer in *Stroup*. In *Stroup*, the officer pointed to an alcoholic odor and bloodshot eyes to establish probable cause. Trooper Sether's only evidence was the defendant's general weariness. (Sether's Report, p 1). And, in both cases, the defendants were stopped for an equipment violation, not for unsafe driving. Thus, Trooper Sether believed he had probable cause based on far less evidence than was present in *Stroup*, where the Court of Appeals found no probable cause to administer field sobriety tests. Accordingly, Trooper Sether's belief was not objectively reasonable, and absent consent from Mr. Treatsky, the State obtained Mr. Treatsky's field sobriety tests in violation of Article I, Section 9 of the Oregon Constitution.

2. Mr. Treatsky did not voluntarily consent to perform field sobriety tests.

In addition to not having probable cause to administer the field sobriety tests, Trooper Sether also never obtained Mr. Treatsky's voluntary consent. In determining the voluntariness of consent to a warrantless search "the test is whether, under the totality of the circumstances, the defendant's consent was an act of free will *or, instead, resulted from police coercion, either express or implied*." *State v. Hall*, 115 P.3d 908, 918 (Or. 2005) (emphasis added).

Police coercion includes informing a person of economic harm and loss of privileges that will result if the person refuses a request to take a test. In *State v. Machuca*, a police officer suspected the defendant of drunk driving and requested the defendant take a blood test. 218 P.3d 145, 147 (Or. App. 2009), *overruled on other grounds*, 227 P.3d 729 (Or. 2010). Before the defendant gave his consent, the police officer read to the defendant the "rights and consequences" of refusing consent. *Id.* The consequences included seizing defendant's driver's license and likely suspension of the defendant's right to drive. *Id.* The defendant then consented to the blood test. *Id.*; Or. Rev. Stat. §813.130(2). Before trial, the defendant moved to suppress the evidence from his blood test. *Machuca*, 218 P.3d at 148. Upon review, the Oregon Court of Appeals held that consent to the blood test was not effective because the consent was obtained "through a threat of economic harm and loss of privileges." *Id.* at 150. Such consent, the court held, "is coerced by the fear of adverse consequences and is ineffective to excuse the requirement to obtain a search warrant." *Id.*

Here, too, Mr. Treatsky's consent was not voluntary. Just like the officer in *Machuca*, the officer in this case read to the defendant the "rights and consequences" of refusing consent. In this case, as in the *Machuca* case, those rights and consequences included the seizure of his driver's license and the likely suspension of his right to drive. Thus, Mr. Treatsky's consent, like the defendant's consent in *Machuca*, was "coerced by the fear of adverse consequences and is ineffective to excuse the requirement to obtain a search warrant."

Because Trooper Sether lacked probable cause to administer field sobriety tests and Mr. Treatsky did not voluntarily consent to the tests, evidence of the tests should be suppressed.

The defendant's attorney uses another analogical argument, this time to support his argument that the defendant did not consent to field sobriety tests.

B. Because Trooper Sether lacked probable cause, all evidence obtained as a result of the illegal search must be suppressed.

The results of the breath test must also be suppressed. Oregon employs an exclusionary rule that prevents the state from offering evidence obtained as a result of illegal police conduct. *Hall*, 115 P.3d at 920. "[T]he critical inquiry is whether the state obtained the evidence sought to be suppressed as a result of a violation of the defendant's rights under Article I, section 9." *Id.* If so, evidence from the illegal search and seizure must be suppressed. *See id.*

Here, the illegal search produced evidence that resulted in unconstitutionally obtained evidence. Had Trooper Sether not administered illegal field sobriety tests, he would not have arrested Mr. Treatsky and taken him to the police station, and the breath test would not have taken place. Because Trooper Sether lacked probable cause and voluntary consent to perform field sobriety tests, the breath test and its results were obtained in violation of Article I, Section 9. The Court should therefore suppress all evidence that was obtained as a result of any search conducted in violation of Article I, Section 9.

CONCLUSION

Because evidence of Mr. Treatsky's performance of field sobriety tests and from the breath test were obtained in violation of Article I, Section 9 of the Oregon Constitution, this Court should suppress all such evidence.

The conclusion is a short statement of the relief sought.

DATED this _____ day of November, 2023.

_____
Jordan R. Silk
Bar # 105031
Appearing for Defendant

The lawyer's signature

1. Caption

The caption for a memorandum supporting a motion is identical to the caption for the motion itself—except for the title. With respect to the title, take care to coordinate the memorandum title to the title of the motion. The supporting memorandum should begin with a phrase like "Memorandum in Support of" or "Brief in Support of" and then repeat *exactly* the title of the motion. Compare the title of the motion in Example 8-A and the title for the supporting brief reproduced in Example 8-D. You can see that the title for the memorandum in Example 8-D is generated by simply adding "Memorandum in Support of" to the title of the motion, "Defendant's Motion to Suppress Evidence." The names of documents can get long, especially in complex cases, but you will make the court's job easier by repeating the name of the motion in all documents supporting that motion.

Example 8-D · A caption for a memorandum of law in support of a motion to suppress

IN THE CIRCUIT COURT OF THE STATE OF OREGON
FOR LANE COUNTY

THE STATE OF OREGON,	)	
	)	Case No. 23-15-18156
Plaintiff,	)	
	)	
vs.	)	MEMORANDUM OF LAW IN
	)	SUPPORT OF DEFENDANT'S
	)	MOTION TO SUPPRESS
TRAVIS J. TREATSKY,	)	EVIDENCE
	)	
Defendant.	)	
	)	

2. Preliminary statement

Most memoranda begin with a preliminary statement that provides an overview of and context for the arguments that follow. The name of the preliminary statement varies from jurisdiction to jurisdiction. It might be called a "Preliminary Statement," or it might be called an "Introduction," a "Summary of the Argument," the "Statement of the Nature of the Matter Before the Court," or something else entirely. Check your jurisdiction's local rules or consult colleagues to determine the local custom.

Just as the name of the preliminary statement varies by jurisdiction, so does its content. In some jurisdictions, the preliminary statement focuses on the procedural posture of the case. In other jurisdictions, the preliminary statement focuses instead on the arguments to come and provides a preview of those arguments. And, of course, in some jurisdictions, the preliminary statement does both — explaining the procedural posture of the case and providing highlights of the arguments to come.

In those jurisdictions in which the preliminary statement focuses on the procedural posture, the preliminary statement will simply identify the motion before the court and the substantive issue underlying that motion. Usually, such a preliminary statement has a more objective tone, as in Example 8-E.

Example 8-E • A preliminary statement that focuses on the procedural posture of the case

PRELIMINARY STATEMENT

On November 29, 2023, Plaintiff Julie Stark was dismissed from her employment with defendant Michigan Power & Electric Company (MPE). Immediately after her dismissal, Ms. Stark filed a complaint alleging that Michigan's Whistle-blowers' Protection Act protected her from discharge. This motion for summary judgment seeks to dismiss her Whistle-blowers' claim because no material issues of fact exist, and as a matter of law, Ms. Stark cannot prove that she was engaged in an activity protected by Michigan's Whistle-blowers' Protection Act.

The "nature of the case" is identified by stating that Ms. Stark filed a complaint alleging that Michigan's Whistle-blowers' Protection Act protects her from being fired.

Both the "procedural posture" and the "type of motion" before the court are identified by explaining that this motion is a motion for summary judgment.

If you are in a jurisdiction that describes the procedural posture and provides a short preview of the arguments, your introduction might look like Example 8-F.

Example 8-F • A preliminary statement that describes the procedural posture and previews the argument

PRELIMINARY STATEMENT

Defendant Paul Adams's statement to an undercover police officer should be admitted into evidence at his trial for bank robbery. The State of Oregon filed charges against Adams for an alleged bank robbery on August 15, 2023. Adams was arraigned on August 20, 2023. He has pleaded not guilty, and the trial is set for September 16, 2023.

Shortly after the robbery, Adams spoke to an undercover police officer. That statement implicated him in the robbery. Defendant Adams now moves to suppress that statement. Oregon law, however, allows a defendant's statement to be admitted into evidence where, as here, the statement was made during "mere conversation" with a police officer. Because Adams's statement was made during a conversation and not during a police stop, his statement should be admitted into evidence, and defendant's motion to suppress should be denied.

The "nature of the case" is a criminal prosecution for bank robbery.

The "procedural posture" and the "type of motion at issue" is a motion to suppress in advance of trial.

This motion also explains why the motion should be denied.

In some jurisdictions, however, attorneys use the preliminary statement to present a more complete summary of the arguments and a summary that is more aggressively persuasive, as in Example 8-G.

**Example 8-G • A preliminary statement that previews the arguments
more fully and more aggressively**

PRELIMINARY STATEMENT

The first sentence states the ultimate conclusion the writer wants the court to reach.

The remainder of the first paragraph briefly explains background the court will need to understand argument.

Plaintiffs' action under Title IX of the Education Amendment of 1972 fails because the University complies with Title IX. Central State University of Utah made the difficult decision to eliminate its women's golf team after the State of Utah cut funding to the University by thirty percent. Thus, the University was forced to sell its golf course. However, after eliminating the women's golf team, the University established a women's competitive cheer team of twenty-four players, expanding its women's athletic program by twelve positions.

The second paragraph explains the most important reason why the court should reach the ultimate conclusion. It asserts that the defendant meets a legal standard (that the university has a "history and continuing practice of program expansion") and it provides a short explanation for why that legal standard is met.

Central State University complies with Title IX because it has a history and continuing practice of program expansion. The addition of the women's cheer team is yet one more step in that history of expanding opportunity. Since Central State University began its women's athletic program in the 1970s, the University has more than doubled the number of athletic opportunities available to its female students. The competitive cheer team is yet one more addition to this history and continuing practice of program expansion because it, too, increases the number of equal athletic opportunities available to women.

The preliminary statement ends by returning to the ultimate conclusion.

Because Central State University can show a history and continuing practice of program expansion, the University is in compliance with Title IX and is entitled to judgment as a matter of law.

Especially in those jurisdictions in which attorneys preview the arguments to come, the preliminary statement plays an important persuasive role. It sets forth your vision of the precise legal question and the most important facts and concepts the judge should consider while reading your brief. And, of course, the preliminary statement is the first part of the memorandum that the judge will read.

To construct a more persuasive preliminary statement, you will need to consider (1) what are the most important points in your argument, (2) what background the court needs to understand those points, and (3) how to explain those important points and essential background as concisely and persuasively as possible. You should think of a persuasive preliminary statement as your "elevator speech." Imagine yourself in a three-minute elevator ride. That's the time you have to convince the judge — who has never met you or heard about your case — to adopt the conclusion you seek.

To determine the most important points in your argument, you might ask yourself, "What ideas must the court accept for my client to win?" Then, explain those critical points in your preliminary statement. Another way to identify the most important points in your argument is to review a draft of your argument, paying particular attention to your point headings and thesis statements. Those sentences should assert the main points of each section and each paragraph. Together, they should outline why your client should win. You can use those point headings and thesis sentences as a starting point for drafting your preliminary statement.

Then, you will need to consider what background information the judge will need to understand those points. For example, you might need to explain the crux of the conflict between the parties, that is, what event occurred that drove the parties to court? Was there a breach of contract? Did one party fire another party? Does one party seek to admit evidence that the other party believes should not be admitted? Is there a claim in the complaint that cannot be supported by facts or law?

The challenge to writing a preliminary statement is that the statement must still perform its role, which is to provide a persuasive *summary* of your argument. Thus, you will need to ensure that your preliminary statement remains concise.

To keep your preliminary statement concise, you may need to make decisions about which aspect of your argument to highlight and which to exclude. For example, in the argument section, you may explain both why your argument is correct and why opposing arguments are weak. In your preliminary statement, you might focus on why your argument is correct and wait for the body of the argument to explain why opposing arguments are weak. Doing so will make your preliminary statement more concise and highlight the strengths of your client's position.

Another way to streamline your preliminary statement is to consider the level of generality at which you explain an argument. For example, in the body of your argument, you might support an argument with a detailed comparison to a prior case. In your preliminary statement, you might simply assert that reaching your desired conclusion is consistent with prior case law.

You can also consider the number of sub-arguments you provide to support a particular conclusion. For example, in a statutory construction argument, you might explain several reasons why the plain language of the statute leads to the interpretation you favor. Of those three reasons, one or two reasons might be significantly more compelling than the others. If so, your preliminary statement might focus on the most compelling reasons why the plain language leads to your preferred interpretation and save the remaining reasons for the body of your argument.

In addition to selecting the most compelling aspects of the argument to include in your preliminary statement, you will want to review your statement for its persuasive effect. To be persuasive, your preliminary statement should drive home the points that will be explained more fully in your brief.

To drive home the essential points of your argument, first, include a conclusion at the top and bottom of your preliminary statement. The conclusion at the top and bottom of your preliminary statement should state the ultimate conclusion you would like the court to adopt.

Next, review your thesis sentences. Each paragraph should begin with a thesis sentence that asserts a legal conclusion the writer wants the court to adopt. Sentences that follow support the assertion in the thesis sentence. Together, the thesis sentences outline the argument that is to come. By clearly outlining the argument to come, the thesis sentences drive the persuasive impact of the introduction.

Although the preliminary statement can (and should) play a persuasive role, the tone should still be reasonable. A preliminary statement that is framed too passionately can trigger heightened skepticism in a judge. By presenting yourself as a reasonable advocate, you will enhance your credibility — or *ethos* — and the judge will be more likely to trust the path you are encouraging the court to take.

Finally, if your preliminary statement previews the argument that follows, be sure to check your preliminary statement against your ultimate argument. Often, attorneys will draft their preliminary statement and then continue to work on their argument. If you continue to modify your argument, be sure that the description of your argument in your preliminary statement is consistent with the argument that follows.

Examples 8-H and 8-I are two preliminary statements from opposing sides of an argument. Review those examples to see how each party explains the essential points in that party's argument and provides essential background necessary to understand the argument, while keeping the preliminary statements concise and persuasive. You can review the full arguments that accompany the preliminary statements in Appendix B.

Example 8-H • **Defendant's preliminary statement explaining why the court should grant defendant's motion for summary judgment**

Preliminary Statement

The first paragraph states the ultimate conclusion the writer hopes the court will adopt. It also provides essential background information.

Discovery has now confirmed that Starr Publishing Corporation should be granted judgment in its favor. Plaintiffs allege that they were defamed when Starr published a pocket part to update "Starr's Pennsylvania Criminal Practice & Procedure" and listed the plaintiffs as authors; however, plaintiffs' claim fails as a matter of law and undisputed fact.

The middle two paragraphs explain the reason why the court should reach the desired conclusion.

First, plaintiffs cannot establish the essential elements of a defamation claim. Plaintiffs cannot, for example, establish that attributing the authorship to the plaintiffs is a defamatory statement. In addition, plaintiffs cannot establish that they suffered damages. The record includes no evidence that plaintiffs suffered economic damage or that their reputations were harmed.

Plaintiffs' defamation claim also fails because they consented to the use of their names in connection with the 2022–2023 pocket part even if they did not participate in its production. Finally, plaintiffs' defamation claim must fail because the statement that the 2022–2023 pocket part was "by Amit Prakash and Helen Vinocur" and "The Publisher's Staff" is true or substantially true.

For all of these reasons, plaintiffs' claim for defamation fails as a matter of law, and summary judgment in Starr Publishing's favor should be granted.

The final paragraph returns to the ultimate conclusion the court should reach.

Example 8-1 • Plaintiffs' preliminary statement explaining why the court should deny defendant's motion for summary judgment

---

Preliminary Statement

Summary judgment is inappropriate. Despite defendant's assertion to the contrary, discovery has confirmed both the strength of plaintiffs' claims and the egregiousness of defendant's misconduct. That misconduct provides sufficient evidence for a jury to conclude that Starr Publishing Corporation has defamed the plaintiffs.

The first paragraph asserts the ultimate conclusion that the writer wants the court to reach.

In 2023, defendant sold a 2022–2023 pocket part that allegedly updated "Starr's Criminal Practice & Procedure." The pocket part's cover stated that it was "by AMIT PRAKASH and HELEN VINOCUR" even though Mr. Prakash and Ms. Vinocur made absolutely no contributions to the pocket part. Defendant now argues that plaintiffs' defamation claims must be dismissed. None of defendant's arguments has any merit.

The second paragraph describes the background necessary for the court to understand this preliminary statement.

First, the record includes sufficient evidence that ascribing the names of plaintiffs to an incomplete and misleading pocket part is defamatory.

Second, the record also has sufficient evidence for a jury to conclude that plaintiffs were damaged. Both plaintiffs have testified that they were angry and outraged by the defamatory statements, and that evidence is more than sufficient to support an award of general damages.

Third, the 2014 agreement does not control this dispute. Nothing in the 2014 agreement between defendant and plaintiffs gave defendant the right to defame plaintiffs. Moreover, the 2014 agreement was superseded by a 2021 agreement between plaintiffs and defendant and, thus, does not apply to the 2022–2023 pocket part at issue in this case. If the conflict between the 2014 and 2021 agreements creates any ambiguity, such ambiguity is a question for the jury, and cannot be resolved on a motion for summary judgment.

The next three paragraphs explain the reasons why the court should reach the desired conclusion.

Finally, the defendant's only other argument on defamation — that the statements at issue were "true or substantially true" — is frivolous because, as everyone agrees, plaintiffs had nothing to do with the 2022–2023 pocket part.

For all these reasons, the evidence is sufficient for a jury to conclude that the defendant defamed the plaintiffs, and summary judgment should be denied.

The last paragraph repeats the conclusion the writer wants the court to reach in this case.

---

3. Statement of facts

The statement of facts typically follows the introduction. Chapter 10, *Statements of Fact and of the Case*, provides detailed advice about constructing a persuasive statement of facts, and we recommend that you review that chapter when writing your statement of facts.

4. Argument

The argument section is, of course, the heart of the memorandum, and it will likely require the greatest portion of your time and effort as you are constructing your memorandum. Accordingly, this book devotes five chapters to developing and refining your persuasive arguments. Those chapters are Chapter 3, *Organizing Persuasive Arguments*; Chapter 4, *Themes for Persuasive Arguments*; Chapter 5, *Drafting Persuasive Arguments*; Chapter 6, *Refining Persuasive Arguments*; and Chapter 7, *Editing Persuasive Arguments*. We recommend that you return to those chapters as you develop your argument in support of your motion.

5. Conclusion

In most instances, the conclusion to a supporting memorandum of law consists of a simple request for the relief the plaintiff seeks. (For that reason, the conclusion is also sometimes called the "prayer for relief.") This section is very short, often consisting of only one sentence in which you respectfully request that the court take the requested action or rule in your favor on the issues presented, as in Example 8-J.

Example 8-J · Traditional conclusion

CONCLUSION

For the reasons stated in this memorandum of law, Defendant respectfully requests that this Court grant Defendant's motion for summary judgment.

Sometimes attorneys use the conclusion to quickly summarize the argument made in the brief, as in Example 8-K.

Example 8-K · Short, summary conclusion

CONCLUSION

Because evidence of Mr. Treatsky's performance of field sobriety tests and from the breath test were obtained in violation of Article I, Section 9 of the Oregon Constitution, this Court should suppress all such evidence.

---

6. Signature

Like the motion, the supporting memorandum must be signed and dated by the lawyer submitting the motion and supporting memorandum of law. Again, sign with care. Your signature—whether on paper or provided electronically—confirms that your arguments are non-frivolous and are supported by the law and facts.[4]

---

4. *E.g.*, Fed. R. Civ. P. 11(b).

C. Factual Support

Sometimes an argument in the memorandum of law needs to be supported by evidence. For example, if the court must interpret a contract, you will need to attach a copy of the contract to the supporting memorandum. If the court is considering a motion for summary judgment, you may need to attach excerpts from depositions to prove that no material issues of fact exist. Sometimes a party or the lawyer submitting the motion will submit an affidavit or a declaration as evidence of the facts. Both an affidavit and a declaration are sworn statements and are treated as testimony presented to the court. (The two differ in that an affidavit is sworn before a notary or other official, whereas a declaration is simply signed.) Example 8-L shows a declaration in support of plaintiffs' motion opposing summary judgment in *Prakash v. Starr Publishing Corp.*, which appears in Appendix B.

Documents providing factual support are sometimes attached directly to the supporting memorandum of law, which are then submitted as a single document. Other times, the motion, the supporting memorandum of law, and the factual support for the argument are submitted as separate documents. The court's procedural or local rules will provide detailed instruction about how to file supporting documents.

Example 8-L · Affidavit in support of a motion[5]

IN THE UNITED STATES DISTRICT COURT
FOR THE EASTERN DISTRICT OF PENNSYLVANIA

Amit Prakash and	)	CIVIL ACTION
Helen Vinocur,	)	NO. 23-CV-727
Plaintiffs,	)	
	)	DECLARATION OF
v.	)	AMIT PRAKASH
	)	
Starr Publishing Corporation,	)	
Defendants	)	
	)	

Amit Prakash, being duly sworn, deposes and says:

1.   I am a lawyer admitted to practice in Pennsylvania and in the federal courts of the Third Circuit and the United States Supreme Court.

2.   I have practiced law for over 40 years and have specialized in criminal defense, civil rights, and civil liberties litigation. I also teach courses in Criminal Law, Constitutional Criminal Procedure, and Evidence at the University of Pennsylvania. I incorporate by reference my professional resume. See Exhibit 1.

---

5. This example is based on Amended Declaration of David Rudovsky, *Rudovsky v. West Publishing Corp.*, 2010 WL 2804844 (E.D. Pa. 2010) (No. 09-cv-00727-JF).

3.   In 2002, I, along with Helen Vinocur, ("Authors") contracted with Starr Publishing Company to publish a Pennsylvania criminal procedure book. Between 2003 and 2020, the Authors prepared annual pocket parts to update the text.

4.   In 2014 and 2021, Authors entered into written agreements with Starr Publishing Company. Copies of those Agreements are attached as Exhibits 2 and 3, respectively.

5.   Criminal procedure is a dynamic area in Pennsylvania law with major developments every year. Accordingly, to prepare the annual pocket parts, the Authors read every reported appellate court case decided in Pennsylvania that concerned Pennsylvania criminal procedure. In addition, we read all U.S. Supreme Court cases on constitutional criminal procedure, and selected cases from the lower federal courts. Further, we tracked all changes to the Pennsylvania Rules of Criminal Procedure and Pennsylvania Rules of Appellate Procedure, as well as pertinent statutory developments.

6.   For each pocket part, the Authors added approximately 100 to 150 new case citations and all new relevant rule changes, amendments, or statutory developments. The Authors also provided commentary on the relevance of new cases to the specific subject matter areas.

7.   The Pennsylvania criminal procedure book and its annual pocket parts has been purchased by lawyers, public defender offices, prosecutors, and courts, as well as by prisons and jails in Pennsylvania for use in prison law libraries. Over the years, the Authors have received many comments, from subscribers about the Treatise. These comments made it clear to the Authors that subscribers use the Treatise because the Treatise would explain any significant reported cases, rule application, or statutory law. Because the Authors included all new cases and rule changes of any significance, subscribers and users rely on the pocket part for the latest developments in the law.

8.   In 2022, West and the Authors could not agree on business terms for the 2022–2023 pocket part.

9.   In December 2022, West published a 2022–2023 pocket part, with a title page that prominently stated that the publication was "by" Amit Prakash and Helen Vinocur, and in smaller print, by the "The Publisher's Staff."

10.   This pocket part was virtually unchanged from the 2020–2021 pocket part as it contained almost no new cases or rule changes of any significance. Moreover, the pocket part failed to note or discuss several decisions from the Pennsylvania Supreme Court that reversed, remanded, or granted review of decisions by the Pennsylvania Superior Court. *See, e.g., Commonwealth v. Mallory*, 941 A.2d 686 (Pa. 2021); *Commonwealth v. Brown*, 925 A.2d 147 (Pa. 2021); *Commonwealth v. West*, 938 A.2d 1034 (Pa. 2007); *Commonwealth v. Bennett*, 930 A.2d 1264 (Pa. 2021); *Commonwealth v. Lee*, 935 A.2d 865 (2021); *Commonwealth v. Gravely*, 918 A.2d 761 (Pa. Super. 2021).

11.   The Authors retained counsel to seek relief from the harm caused. West did not provide the relief requested, and this lawsuit followed.

12.   Publications that I authored or co-authored, including "Policing Wrongs: Legal Proceedings in Police Misconduct Cases" (West, 2022, 3d ed.), and "Search and Seizure in Pennsylvania: The Laws that Govern" (PBI Press,

2022, 5th ed.), are important to my academic standing, my legal practice, and my ability to earn income. My reputation for integrity in my scholarship is important to the sales of these publications and, therefore, to the royalty income I receive.

I declare under penalty of perjury pursuant to 28 U.S.C. § 1746 that the above is true and correct to the best of my knowledge, information, and belief.

Dated: May 23, 2023

/s

_____

Amit Prakash

II. Your Audience: The Trial Judge

The primary audience for your motion and its supporting memorandum of law is, of course, a trial judge. Trial judges often work with a law clerk who assists the judge by researching the law and producing draft opinions. Some law clerks have worked with a judge for years and have vast experience in analyzing legal problems. Other law clerks are hired directly out of law school and may have only a few months of experience before reviewing your arguments.

The trial judge and that judge's law clerk have one trait in common: They are busy. For example, one New York court estimated that a judge assigned to hear civil motions for one week will hear "upwards of 650 motions."[6] Thus, trim your memorandum of law to its essentials, and present your argument simply, clearly, and directly. Your goal should be to help the judge *quickly* decide your motion in your favor.

Sometimes you may be able to learn more about the judge who will be hearing your case or your motion. In some jurisdictions, a single judge is assigned to hear pretrial motions and another judge will preside over the trial. In other jurisdictions, a judge will be assigned to the entire case and will, therefore, also hear your pre-trial motions. When you know the judge who will be hearing your motion, take the time to determine whether that judge has standing orders that govern motions submitted to that judge. (Standing orders are discussed more fully below.) You should also consult more experienced colleagues. Colleagues will often have invaluable information about the preferences of a particular judge.

---

6. Judge Assignments, NY Courts, http://www.courts.state.ny.us/COURTS/nyc/civil/assignmentsdef.shtml (last visited June 16, 2022).

III. The Rules that Govern Trial Motions

One issue your audience will care about is whether your documents comply with all relevant procedural rules. A document that complies with procedural rules increases the author's credibility (or *ethos*) and suggests that the author is reliable. Thus, before drafting a motion familiarize yourself with all the rules and customs that govern the motion you are planning to submit.

You will usually look for three different kinds of rules: the jurisdiction's procedural rules, "local" court rules, and "standing orders" of the judge before whom you will be appearing. Then, ask around about any unwritten rules.

A. Procedural Rules

The first set of rules to become familiar with are the jurisdiction's procedural rules that govern trial practice. The federal courts and all state courts have their own rules of procedure. Those rules — the rules of civil procedure and the rules of criminal procedure — govern practices in those jurisdictions.

The procedural rules at the federal and state level provide only the most general guidance with respect to most motions. For example, the Federal Rules of Civil and Criminal Procedure require that motions be in writing, unless made during trial; state the grounds for seeking an order; and state the specific relief or order sought.[7]

For a limited number of motions, however, the jurisdiction's procedural rules will provide more detailed guidance. For example, the Federal Rules of Civil Procedure require that, when filing a motion for summary judgment, the motion must prove that no fact is in dispute "by citing to particular parts of the record," such as depositions, answers to interrogatories, affidavits, or other materials in the record. If a party seeks an order protecting it from discovery, a motion filed in federal court must also include a statement that the parties attempted, in good faith, to resolve the dispute.[8]

Thus, although the jurisdiction's rules may not ultimately provide significant guidance for the particular motion you are writing, you should always start your research there, just in case they do.

---

7. Fed. R. Civ. P. 7(b); Fed. R. Crim. P. 47(b).

8. Fed. R. Civ. P. 26(c)(1).

B. Local Rules

Next, you will want to become familiar with the court's local rules. For management purposes, federal and state trial court systems are further divided. For example, the federal trial court system is divided into ninety-four districts. Each state has between one and four federal districts within it. State trial courts are often divided by county or judicial district. Each subdivision usually has its own set of rules. These rules are often called "local rules."

Local rules are rules adopted by courts and apply regardless of the particular judge hearing the case.[9] These local rules tend to provide more specific guidance than the jurisdiction-wide procedural rules. Local rules will often dictate details about the content and format of a motion and its accompanying memorandum of law, including the sections that must be included in a memorandum of law, page limits, margin sizes, and fonts.

Local rules also often provide a wealth of practical information, including the hours that a court is open, where documents are received, how cases are assigned, when motions will be heard, what methods of delivery constitute service, appropriate attire for court, and whether cell phones and other electronic devices will be permitted.

C. Standing Orders

In addition to local rules, courts and individual judges within a court-system may also issue standing orders. Standing orders are simply ongoing orders about procedure. Standing orders can include the same kinds of information that local rules include. They apply court-wide if issued by the court or to a single judge if issued by just one judge.

The difference between a "standing order" and a local "rule" is the process by which it came to be. A "local rule" is adopted following a public comment period. A "standing order" is issued by a court or an individual judge without comment from the public.

Not all courts and not all judges have standing orders, but you should always determine whether any relevant standing orders exist. Example 8-M provides an example of an individual judge's standing order.

---

9. The Federal Rules of Civil Procedure explain that, in federal courts, "a district court, acting by a majority of its district judges, may adopt and amend rules governing its practice. A local rule must be consistent with — but not duplicate — federal statutes and rules...." Fed. R. Civ. P. 83.

Example 8-M · A standing order[10]

Example 8-M shows the first of eleven pages of "individual practices" for Judge Edgardo Ramos's chambers. The document also addresses

- requesting an adjournment or an extension of time
- pre-trial procedures
- formatting requirements for motions, such as page limits and font size

Notably, Judge Ramos's standing orders include this recommendation: "[W]here junior lawyers are familiar with the matter under consideration, but are not experienced in arguing before a court, they should be encouraged to actively participate."

May 27, 2020

INDIVIDUAL PRACTICES OF JUDGE EDGARDO RAMOS

Contact Information
Thurgood Marshall U.S. Courthouse
40 Foley Square
New York, NY 10007
Tel (212) 805-0294
Courtroom 619
ChambersNYSDRamos@nysd.uscourts.gov

Courtroom Deputy Clerk
Ms. Jazmin Rivera
(212) 805-4590
jazmin_rivera@nysd.uscourts.gov

Unless otherwise ordered, matters before Judge Ramos shall be conducted in accordance with the following procedures:

1. **Communications with Chambers**

   A. **Letters.** Except as otherwise provided below, communications with chambers shall be by letter, filed electronically via ECF. Letters seeking relief should be filed as letter-motions in accordance with Section 1.E below. Letters between or among counsel shall not be filed on ECF or otherwise sent to the Court (except as exhibits to an otherwise properly filed document).

   Letters to be filed under seal shall follow the procedure for Electronic Filing Under Seal in Civil and Miscellaneous Cases in accordance with Section 3 of this document.

   Parties shall not submit courtesy copies of letters that are filed as described above.

   B. **Telephone Calls.** Except as provided below, telephone calls to chambers are permitted only in situations requiring immediate attention. In such situations, call chambers at (212) 805-0294.

   C. **Faxes and E-mails.** Faxes to chambers are **not** permitted. Except as otherwise provided in Section 1.A. above, if a party wishes to e-mail a .pdf document to the Court, it must obtain prior permission. E-mails should indicate who in chambers provided such permission, and must be copied to all counsel. *If a document is e-mailed to chambers, do **NOT** also send a hard copy.*

   D. **Docketing, Scheduling, and Calendar Matters.** Please call Jazmin Rivera,

1

D. Finding the Rules

All the rules mentioned above are usually available on the website of the court to which you will be submitting your motion. So, go to the court's website first to determine the relevant rules. If you cannot find the rules on the court's website, you can check with the Clerk of Court

---

10. *Individual Practices of Judge Edgardo Ramos,* United States District Court Southern District of New York (May 27, 2020), https://www.nysd.uscourts.gov/sites/default/files/practice_documents/ER%20Ramos%20Individual%20Pracetices%20updated%205-27-2020.pdf. (last visited Dec. 20, 2021).

to determine how to get a copy of the local rules. Local federal district court rules are also available on Westlaw. If your case has been assigned to a particular judge, you can also ask the Clerk of Court whether the judge has any standing orders. Alternatively, you can call the judge's chambers to determine whether the judge has issued any standing orders.

All these rules — and especially the local rules and standing orders — are subject to change. Whenever submitting a motion, always check to make sure you are relying on the most up-to-date set of rules.

You might want to take a minute right now to find your local court's website to see what they look like. For example, if you searched the Internet for "local rules Southern District of New York," your search will lead you to the home page for the United States District Court for the Southern and Eastern Districts of New York, shown in Figure 8-N. That website also lists standing orders issued by individual judges.

Figure 8-N · A page from a court's website[11]

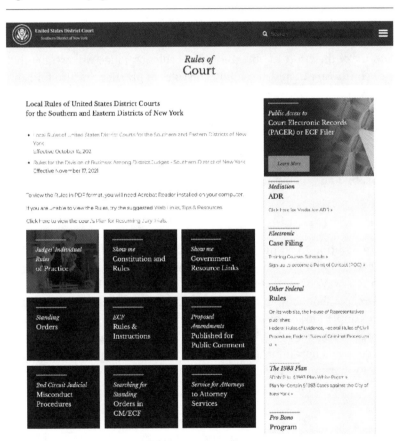

Example 8-N shows the website for the district courts for the Southern and Eastern Districts of New York.

The box in the upper-left corner leads to the standing orders for individual judges. Here, they are called "Judge's individual Rules of Practice."

The box below (middle left) leads to court-wide standing orders.

---

11. *Rules of Court*, United States District Court Southern District of New York (Oct. 29, 2018), https://www.nysd.uscourts.gov/rules.

E. Following the Rules

Following all the relevant rules is important. In some instances, failing to follow the rules could result in your motion being rejected or denied. If you are filing on a deadline, you may not have time to resubmit. On that basis alone, you could have your motion denied and possibly even lose the case.

While other consequences are less dire, you still must scrupulously follow the rules—a theme that you will find emphasized repeatedly in this book. First, following the rules will make your arguments easier to absorb. Judges are very busy, and they read many motions and their accompanying legal arguments. They expect the motion and the accompanying argument to look a certain way, to have the sections in a certain order, and to contain all the information required by the rules. To the extent that a motion or memorandum of law does not do those things, the judge has to work harder to follow it and will have less mental energy to devote to the legal argument.

Carefully following the rules also enhances your credibility—that is, your *ethos*. Following the rules shows the court that you know how to, and make the effort to, find and follow rules. A judge will assume that someone who can find and follow the rules of practice can also find and follow the substantive law. By contrast, if a judge sees that you cannot find and follow the rules of practice, the judge may begin to wonder whether you can find and follow the substantive law. You want the judge to read your motion and memorandum of law with complete confidence that what follows was written by a smart, careful, trustworthy lawyer. Thus, find and follow all relevant rules of practice.

F. Unwritten Rules

In addition to all the formal rules that you must follow, it is worth your while to find out about local customs. Often local jurisdictions have common ways of presenting a motion. Sometimes particular judges have preferences about how information is presented. So, ask a trusted colleague for a sample motion or memorandum of law. If you know which judge has been assigned to hear your motion, ask whether that judge has preferences about how information is presented. Although you are not bound by these customs or preferences, you and your client will be well served if you know of them in advance.

IV. After the Motion Is Drafted

After you have drafted the motion and gathered any supporting documents, you will serve a copy of those documents on opposing counsel and provide a copy to the court.

A. Service and Its Proof

Each jurisdiction's rules of civil and criminal procedure provide detailed instructions about how to properly serve opposing counsel.[12] "Proof of service" is a document that shows you have served opposing counsel the same documents that you have filed with the court. Failure to provide such proof can be grounds for dismissing the motion. That proof is usually provided in a sworn statement by the person who served the opposing party, as in Example 8-O. That statement is then appended to the documents provided to the court.

Example 8-O · Proof of service when opposing party served by mail

---

CIVIL COURT OF THE CITY OF NEW YORK   Index No. 23-SC-52975
COUNTY OF NEW YORK: PART 28

Randall Runco,
            Plaintiff,   AFFIDAVIT OF SERVICE
                                             BY MAIL

-against-

HammerTime Construction, Inc.,
            Defendant.

Glenna Gilbert, being duly sworn, states as follows:

I am over 18 years of age and not a party to this action.

On September 16, 2023, I served Plaintiff's Motion to Compel Evidence on HammerTime Construction, Inc., the defendant in this proceeding. I enclosed a true copy of the attached papers in a properly sealed postpaid envelope. I deposited that sealed envelope in an official depository of the United States Postal Services within the State of New York. The envelope was addressed to HammerTime Construction, Inc., the defendant, at 5555 Broadway, New York, NY, 10036.

                              Signature:_____

Sworn to me this ___ day of _____ 20__

_____
Notary Public or Court Employee

---

12. The purpose of this book is to give you a picture of that process and of any documents you might have to draft. Thus, we skip over the exact ways in which you will serve opposing counsel and address the document you will have to draft to prove you have served opposing counsel.

Alternatively, and as discussed further below, most courts now accept (or even require) electronic filing. If papers are filed electronically, proof of service might be provided as in Example 8-P.

Example 8-P · Proof of service when filing electronically

CERTIFICATE OF SERVICE

I certify that on May 5, 2023, the above defendant's Motion to Dismiss Plaintiff Overdevest's Complaint was filed electronically, and notice of this filing will be sent by e-mail to all parties by operation of the Court's electronic filing system or by mail to anyone unable to accept electronic filing as indicated on the Notice of Electronic Filing.

_____

Jonathan Bardavid, Esq.

B. Filing with the Court

You will then file your notice of motion, motion, memorandum of law in support of the motion, supporting documents (if any), draft order (if any), and proof of service with the court. Again, you should first consult the local rules to determine how to file with the court.

Traditionally, to file your documents with the court, you or someone you work with goes to the courthouse. Once at the courthouse, you go to the clerk of court and submit two or three copies of your motion and all accompanying documents. The clerk of court examines the motion and the accompanying documents to ensure compliance with the court rules. Once approved, you pay a filing fee. Then, the clerk of court stamps the documents as filed. The stamp shows the date on which the documents were filed. One stamped copy is returned to you so that you have proof that your motion was properly filed.

Most courts have adopted electronic filing systems. In some courts, however, parties are permitted, but not required, to file electronically. In other court systems, parties must file electronically. In such electronic filing systems, counsel can submit documents to the court electronically. Often, counsel can also serve opposing counsel electronically. Courts with electronic filing systems have detailed explanations about how to use the electronic filing systems on their websites, as in Figure 8-Q.

Figure 8-Q • An electronic filing system[13]

ECF Information

Setting Up My Account:

▸ New Registration Instructions for Attorneys
▸ New Registration Instructions for Pro Se (Self-Represented) Litigants
▸ NextGen ECF Instructions
  (Action required by all current ECF users)
▸ Special Mailing Group (SMG) Registration Instructions for Press and Public

Managing My Account:

▸ Signing up for case-specific emails/NEFs
▸ Setting up Mobile Query on a smartphone or tablet

Preparing My Filing:

▸ Best practices for creating PDFs
▸ Redacting sensitive information
▸ Exhibits and attachments
▸ Limitations on e-filing
▸ Filing paper documents and other items
▸ Signing documents
▸ Courtesy/chambers copies

E-Filing My Documents:

▸ Which event do I choose in ECF?
▸ Index of all ECF Events
▸ Opening A New Civil Case
▸ Filing Documents Under Seal in Civil Cases
▸ Filing Documents Under Seal in Criminal Cases
  effective May 2021
▸ Online Fee Payments/Pay.gov
▸ ECF E-Filing Tutorial

Troubleshooting:

▸ I made an e-filing mistake
▸ Troubleshooting FAQs
▸ Avoiding common errors
▸ Contacting the ECF Help Desk

Downloads

📄 ECF Registration Information Handout (.pdf)

C. The Opposing Party's Response

In some instances, you may be the one who drafts, serves, and files a motion and its accompanying documents. In other cases, you will represent the party who is being served. If you represent the party being served, you will have to respond to the motion. You can do so in one of several ways.[14]

---

13. *ECF Information*, United States District Court Northern District of California, https://www.cand.uscourts.gov/cases-e-filing/cm-ecf/ (last visited Aug. 1, 2021).

14. The discussion of an opposing party's possible responses was drawn from Thomas A. Mauet, Pretrial 340 (8th ed. 2012).

1. Statement of non-opposition

If you do not oppose the motion, you can notify opposing counsel of your lack of opposition. At the hearing, opposing counsel can inform the judge of the lack of opposition, and you will not need to attend the hearing. A good practice, however, is to submit a statement of non-opposition. Doing so creates a record of your position and ensures that your position is not misrepresented.

You are most likely to take this route when the matter is a ministerial one, as in Example 8-R.

Example 8-R · A statement of non-opposition[15]

SUPERIOR COURT OF THE STATE OF CALIFORNIA
FOR THE COUNTY OF INYO

CITY OF LOS ANGELES DEPARTMENT OF WATER AND POWER, Plaintiff, vs. GREAT BASIN UNIFIED AIR POLLUTION CONTROL DISTRICT, Defendant.	Case No. SJCVPT-23-41092 Assigned for all purposes to the Honorable Dean T. Stout **PLAINTIFF CITY OF LOS ANGELES DEPARTMENT OF WATER AND POWER'S NOTICE OF NON-OPPOSITION TO DEFENDANT GREAT BASIN UNIFIED AIR POLLUTION CONTROL DISTRICT'S MOTION FOR MANDATORY TRANSFER OF VENUE** Date: July 10, 2023 Time: 1:00 P.M.

TO ALL PARTIES AND THEIR ATTORNEYS OF RECORD HEREIN:

PLEASE TAKE NOTICE THAT Plaintiff City of Los Angeles Department of Water and Power has received and reviewed Defendant Great Basin Unified Air Pollution Control District's Notice of Motion and Motion for Mandatory Transfer of Venue and does not oppose the motion. In fact, the Department of Water and Power supports the motion and joins in the request to transfer this action to the Kern County Superior Court pursuant to Code of Civil Procedure § 394(a).

Dated: June 23, 2023   MANATT, PHELPS & PHILLIPS, LLP
                                      Mark D. Johnson

                                      By:_____
                                      Mark D. Johnson
                                      Attorney for the City of Los Angeles
                                      Department of Water and Power

---

15. Example drawn from a motion of non-opposition filed in *City of Los Angeles Department of Water & Power v. Great Basin Unified Air Pollution District*, No. SICVPT-06-41092 (Cal. Sup. Ct. June 26, 2006).

2. Consent order

Another possibility is to consult with counsel to determine whether the parties might be able to craft a consent order. This approach, common in state courts but not in federal courts, allows the parties to negotiate a proposed order and then submit it to the court for its approval. Although a judge is not required to grant an order simply because the parties agree on it, a judge usually will.

3. Memorandum of law in opposition

Finally, you might oppose the motion. When you oppose a motion, you ordinarily do not submit a motion in opposition. Instead, you submit a memorandum of law in opposition to the motion. That memorandum of law explains why the moving party's motion should not be granted. A memorandum of law in opposition to a motion has all the same parts as the moving party's memorandum of law in support of the motion.

D. The Moving Party's Reply Memorandum

If the rules permit, the moving party may file a final reply. A reply memorandum, when it is allowed, may have all the same parts as an opening memorandum of law; often, however, it does not. A reply memorandum responds to new issues raised in the opposing memorandum of law; it should not repeat arguments already presented in the opening memorandum of law. Because the reply memorandum addresses only those issues not already addressed in the opening memorandum, the reply is often limited to a short argument section and a conclusion.

Practice Points

- A motion has these typical parts:
  - A caption
  - A statement of the relief requested
  - A brief statement of the legal grounds upon which the relief is requested
  - An attorney's signature

- When the legal grounds for granting a motion need to be explained in any detail, the motion is accompanied by a "memorandum of law" or "brief." A memorandum of law has these parts:
  - A caption
  - A preliminary statement
  - A statement of facts
  - An argument explaining the legal grounds that support the motion.
  - A conclusion
  - An attorney's signature

- Before drafting your own motion
  - Review the governing procedural rules.
  - Review the local rules.
  - Determine whether any standing orders govern your motion.
  - Ask colleagues about any local customs or preferences of the judge assigned to your case.

- After drafting your motion, make sure it is properly filed with the court and served on opposing counsel.

- If you are served with a motion, carefully consider whether you, in fact, oppose the motion.
  - If you do oppose the motion, you must submit a reply.
  - If, however, you do not oppose the motion, you can submit a statement of non-opposition.
  - If you can work out a settlement with opposing counsel, you can submit a motion asking the judge to approve a consent order.

Chapter 9

Appellate Briefs & Appellate Practice

This chapter introduces you to the world of appeals. An appeal, as you likely know, is the way in which a lawyer asks an appellate court to review the decisions of a lower court.

The chapter begins by introducing you to the appellate brief. Before you begin any writing project, you should have a clear idea of how the end product should look. To help you envision that end product, § 9.1 provides an example of an appellate brief. (You can see additional examples of appellate briefs in Appendix C.)

In addition, to write an effective appellate brief, you will need to know more about the context in which the appellate brief will function. To that end, § 9.2 describes the appellate process — from the initial decision to appeal to requesting review from the highest appellate court. That discussion is followed by a brief tour of some uniquely appellate concepts that play into appellate brief writing.

The final section of this chapter, § 9.3, will provide detailed guidance about constructing an appellate brief for your client.

Appellate Briefs:
An Example

After a trial, a party dissatisfied with the results can ask an appellate court to review the trial court's legal decisions. That party would file an appeal. In that party's appellate brief, the party would explain any error the lower court made and why one or more errors should result in the lower court's decision being reversed. Although the components and their order vary by jurisdiction, the typical appellate brief includes the following components:

- Cover
- Table of contents
- Table of authorities
- Statement of jurisdiction
- Statement of the issues (or questions) presented
- Statement of the case
- Summary of the argument
- Argument
- Conclusion and relief sought
- Lawyer's signature

Each of those parts is identified in Example 9.1-A.[1]

---

1. Although the brief illustrated in Example 9.1-A was filed with the Oregon courts, the format has been adapted to illustrate what a typical appellate brief looks like. Therefore, this example does not follow the format required by Oregon's local rules governing appellate briefs.

Example 9.1-A · An appellate brief

IN THE COURT OF APPEALS OF THE STATE OF OREGON

STATE OF OREGON,   Malheur County Circuit Court
                                          No. 04065087C

    Plaintiff-Respondent,

        v.

RUBEN E. RODRIGUEZ,   CA A126339

    Defendant-Appellant.

The cover identifies the parties, their lawyers, the court from which the case is being appealed, the court in which the appeal is being heard, and the docket numbers for the trial and the appellate cases.

RESPONDENT'S BRIEF

———————

Appeal from the Judgment of the Circuit Court
For Malheur County
Honorable PATRICIA A. SULLIVAN, Judge

LELAND R. BERGER #83020   HARDY MYERS #64077
Attorney at Law   Attorney General
3527 NE 15th Ave. #103   MARY H. WILLIAMS #91124
Portland, OR 97212   Solicitor General
Telephone: (503) 287-4688

                                          LAURA S. ANDERSON #88150
ANTHONY L. JOHNSON #05070   Assistant Attorney General
Attorney at Law   1162 Court St. NE
8425 SE 19th Avenue   Salem, Oregon 97301-4096
Portland, Oregon 97202   Telephone: (503) 378-4402
Telephone: (503) 238-2781

                                          Attorneys for Plaintiff-Respondent

Attorneys for Defendant-Appellant

TABLE OF CONTENTS

The table of contents provides an overview of the argument to come. It also tells the judge where to find the different parts of the argument within the brief.

i

TABLE OF AUTHORITIES

Cases Cited

Anderson v. Jensen Racing, Inc.,
          931 P.2d 763 (Or. 1997). 4

Chaffee v. Shaffer Trucking, Inc.,
          948 P.2d 760 (Or. Ct. App. 1997). 2

In re Marriage of Denton,
          951 P.2d 693 (Or. 1998). 3

Galfano v. KTVL-TV,
          102 P.3d 766 (Or. Ct. App. 2004). 4

Krieger v. Just,
          876 P.2d 754 (Or. 1994). 3

Owens v. Motor Vehicle Div.,
          875 P.2d 463 (Or. 1994). 3

Portland Gen. Elec. Co. v. Bureau of Labor & Indus.,
          859 P.2d 1143 (Or. 1993). 2, 3

State v. Ausmus,
          85 P.3d 864 (Or. 2003). 3

State v. McBroom,
          39 P.3d 226 (Or. Ct. App. 2002). 4

State v. Robison,
          120 P.3d 1285 (Or. Ct. App. 2005). 4

State v. Stamper,
          106 P.3d 172 (Or. Ct. App. 2005). 3

State v. Thompson,
          971 P.2d 879 (Or. 1999). 2

State v. Vasquez-Rubio,
          917 P.2d 494 (Or. 1996). 3

Stephens v. Bohlman,
          838 P.2d 600 (Or. 1992). 3

Vsetecka v. Safeway Stores, Inc.,
          98 P.3d 1116 (Or. 2004). 3

Statutory Provisions

Other Authorities

RESPONDENT'S BRIEF

JURISDICTION

This statement of jurisdiction
establishes that the court has
jurisdiction to hear this case.

This court has jurisdiction pursuant to Oregon Revised Statutes § 138.035.

QUESTION PRESENTED

The question presented states
the legal question that needs to
be resolved on appeal.

Should the language of *former* Oregon Revised Statutes § 809.235(1)(b), providing that a person's driver's license shall be permanently revoked if the person is convicted of a misdemeanor DUI "for a third time," be construed to preclude revoking a person's driver's license after a fourth, fifth, or other succeeding misdemeanor DUI?

STATEMENT OF THE CASE

The statement of the case states
the facts relevant to the appeal.
In some jurisdictions, this
section is called the statement
of facts. Other jurisdictions
require both a statement of facts
and a statement of the case.

Defendant has been convicted of driving under the influence (DUI) on four separate occasions. In Oregon, he was convicted of a DUI in 1976 and 1980. While in California in 1989, he was also convicted of a DUI. Finally, last year, defendant pleaded guilty and was then convicted of a DUI when he drove with a blood alcohol content of .27 percent. At sentencing, the trial court permanently revoked defendant's driving privileges. Defendant now appeals that sentence.

SUMMARY OF ARGUMENT

The summary of the argument,
not surprisingly, gives a
summary of the argument to
come. Judges will return to this
section if they need a quick
overview of the argument.

After defendant pleaded guilty to a misdemeanor DUI, the trial court permanently revoked his driver's license pursuant to *former* Oregon Revised Statutes § 809.235(1)(b) (amended 2005) because defendant had been previously convicted of a DUI at least two times. *Former* Oregon Revised Statutes § 809.235(1)(b) requires a court to permanently revoke a person's driver's license if the person "is convicted of misdemeanor [DUI]…*for a third time.*"

On appeal, defendant argues that the trial court was not permitted to permanently revoke his license because he had three previous DUI convictions, and the statute allowed permanent revocation only upon a third conviction, not upon a fourth. This court should affirm the permanent revocation.

First, revocation was mandatory under *former* Oregon Revised Statutes § 809.235(1)(b). That statute is ambiguous because it can plausibly be read to mean that permanent revocation is mandatory in cases where either (1) a person had *only* two prior convictions for DUI, or, as the state argues, (2) a person had *at least* two prior convictions for DUI.

Because the statute is ambiguous, this court should look to the legislative history of *former* Oregon Revised Statutes § 809.235(1)(b) to discern the legislature's intent. That history shows that the legislature recognized that repeat drunk drivers pose a significant danger to the public, and revocation of driving privileges is one means for protecting the public from habitual drunk drivers. Given the legislature's intention to protect the public and sanction repeat DUI offenders, construing the statute as defendant proposes, to revoke third-time offenders, but not revoke fourth-, fifth-, or more-time offenders, would be contrary to the legislature's intent as evidenced by the legislative history.

ARGUMENT

I. The trial court's permanent revocation of the defendant's driver's license was proper.

At sentencing, the trial court correctly revoked defendant's driving privileges pursuant to *former* Oregon Revised Statutes § 809.235(1)(b).[1] That statute provided as follows:

> The court shall order that a person's driving privileges be permanently revoked if the person is convicted of felony driving while under the influence of intoxicants under Oregon Revised Statutes § 813.010 or *if the person is convicted of misdemeanor driving while under the influence of intoxicants under Oregon Revised Statutes § 813.010 for a third time.*

Or. Rev. Stat. § 809.235(1)(b) (amended 2005) (emphasis added).

This argument provides an example of a statutory construction analysis.

A. Oregon's method of statutory construction

A trial court's construction of a statute is reviewed for errors of law. *State v. Thompson*, 971 P.2d 879, 885 (Or. 1999); *Chaffee v. Shaffer Trucking, Inc.*, 948 P.2d 760, 761 (Or. Ct. App. 1997). That construction is governed by Oregon statutes pertaining to statutory construction, Oregon Revised Statutess §§ 174.010-.090, and the methodology set out in *Portland General Electric Co. v. Bureau of Labor & Industries*, 859 P.2d 1143, 1145-47 (Or. 1993).

The aim of statutory construction — both under Oregon statute and case law — is to discern what the legislature intended when it enacted the particular statute: "In the construction of a statute, a court shall pursue the intention of the legislature if possible." Or. Rev. Stat. § 174.020(1)(a); *Portland Gen. Elec. Co.*, 859 P.2d at 1146-47.

To ascertain the legislature's intent, the text and context of the relevant statutes must be analyzed first because the text and context together represent the best evidence of the legislature's intent. *Portland Gen. Elec. Co.*, 859 P.2d at 1145-46. In examining the text of a statute, the construing court generally assumes that the legislature intended the words of the statute to carry their

---

1. Oregon Revised Statutes § 809.235(1)(b) (amended 2005) was amended by Oregon Laws 2005, chapter 436, section 1, and now reads as follows:

> (b) The court shall order that a person's driving privileges be permanently revoked if the person is convicted of felony driving while under the influence of intoxicants in violation of Oregon Revised Statutes § 813.010 or if the person is convicted of misdemeanor driving while under the influence of intoxicants in violation of Oregon Revised Statutes § 813.010 or its statutory counterpart in any other jurisdiction for a third or subsequent time.

ordinary meanings unless the phrasing of the statute suggests that the legislature intended different meanings to apply. *Id.* at 1146; *see also State v. Ausmus,* 85 P.3d 864, 869 (Or. 2003) (stating that a court usually "gives words of common usage their plain, natural and ordinary meaning"); *State v. Stamper,* 106 P.3d 172, 174 (Or. Ct. App. 2005) (phrasing of statute may indicate legislature intended different meaning to apply).

The text, however, should not be considered in isolation, but in its context. *Vsetecka v. Safeway Stores, Inc.,* 98 P.3d 1116, 1119 (Or. 2004). The context of a statute includes other parts of the same statute, along with other related statutes, prior versions of the statute, prior judicial interpretations of the relevant statutory language, and pre-existing common law. *See In re Marriage of Denton,* 951 P.2d 693, 697 (Or. 1998); *Krieger v. Just,* 876 P.2d 754, 758 (Or. 1994); *Portland Gen. Elec. Co.,* 859 P.2d at 1146; *Stephens v. Bohlman,* 838 P.2d 600, 603 n.6 (Or. 1992). At this first step in the analysis, rules of construction, both statutory and judicial, may be applied to assist in discerning the meaning of the language at issue. *Portland Gen. Elec. Co.,* 859 P.2d at 1146.

If, after examining the text in context, the court concludes that the statute is ambiguous, that is, capable of multiple constructions that are not "wholly implausible," the court may resort to legislative history and, if necessary, other aids to assist in its construction. *Owens v. Motor Vehicle Div.,* 875 P.2d 463, 468 (Or. 1994) (explaining that resort to legislative history is necessary unless alternative interpretations are "wholly implausible").

If the intent of the legislature still remains unclear even after considering the text, context, and legislative history, then this court may resort to general maxims of statutory construction to resolve the remaining uncertainty. *Portland Gen. Elec. Co.,* 859 P.2d at 1146. Among these general maxims is the principle that the court will not adopt a statutory meaning that is inconsistent with the apparent policy of the legislation as a whole and that leads to an incongruous result. *See State v. Vasquez-Rubio,* 917 P.2d 494, 497 (Or. 1996) (explaining that absurd-result maxim best suited for helping court determine which of a number of plausible meanings legislature intended).

B.   Oregon Revised Statutes § 809.235(1)(b) is ambiguous because the phrase "for a third time" is capable of multiple constructions that are "not wholly implausible."

The subject phrase, "for a third time," is ambiguous because it has more than one plausible meaning. It could mean, as defendant argues, that (1) a person had *only* two prior convictions for DUI, or, as the state argues, that (2) a defendant had *at least* two prior convictions for DUI, and the present conviction for which revocation is mandatory constitutes the "third." The latter construction is plausible for several reasons.

First, the legislature created an indefinite reference. The indefinite article "a" is an indefinite determiner with an indefinite reference. *See* Sidney Greenbaum, *Oxford English Grammar* 165 (1996) ("The definite article is used when the speaker (or writer) assumes that the hearer (or reader) can identify the reference of a noun phrase[.]...The indefinite article is used when that assumption cannot be

3

made[.]"); *see also* Ronald Carter & Michael McCarthy, *Cambridge Grammar of English* 907 (2006) ("Indefinite article refers to the determiner *a/an* that is used to express an indefinite meaning."). It is "used as a function word before…mass nouns when the individual in question is undetermined, unidentified, or unspecified…." *Webster's Third New Int'l Dictionary* 1 (unabridged ed. 1993); *see also Galfano v. KTVL-TV,* 102 P.3d 766, 772 (Or. Ct. App. 2004) (relying on *Webster's* definition of the article "a" in ruling that the phrase *"a* judgment pursuant to Rule 67" in Oregon Rules of Civil Procedure 68 C(5)(b) authorizes a trial court to render a supplemental judgment after *any* Oregon Rules of Civil Procedure 67 judgment has been entered). *Compare Anderson v. Jensen Racing, Inc.,* 931 P.2d 763, 767 (Or. 1997) (explaining that the definite article "the" functions as an adjective that denotes a particular, specified thing).

The indefinite article "a" used with the ordinal determiner "third" suggests that the legislature intended an indefinite third. The word "third" is an ordinal number; ordinals refer to positions in a sequence. *See* Greenbaum, *supra,* at 199. Thus, the combination of the indefinite "a" with the ordinal "third," creates an indefinite third. Because the statute refers to an indefinite third position in a sequence, the ordinary meaning of the statutory text mandates license revocation upon any conviction, following two prior convictions.

Reading the text of *former* Oregon Revised Statutes § 809.235(1)(b) in its context also leads to the conclusion that the statute mandates revocation of a person's driver's license upon any conviction after two prior convictions. The stated policies of the legislature are context within which the text of each statute should be read. *State v. McBroom*, 39 P.3d 226, 228 n.2 (Or. Ct. App. 2002) (explaining that statutory statement of general policy in vehicle code is context for interpretation of specific provision pertaining to offense of failure to drive within a lane). With respect to Oregon's vehicle code, the legislature's stated polices are to protect the public, Or. Rev. Stat. § 801.020(11)(a), to "deny the privilege of operating motor vehicles on the public highways to persons who by their conduct and record have demonstrated their indifference for the safety and welfare of others," Or. Rev. Stat. § 801.020(11)(b), and to "discourage repetition of criminal acts," Or. Rev. Stat. § 801.020(11)(c). Thus, understanding *former* Oregon Revised Statutes § 809.235(1)(b) to require the revocation of a driver's license upon any conviction following two prior convictions is also consistent with the statute's context.

The alternate construction advanced by defendant is not consistent with the statutory context. If defendant's argument prevails, a person with a *greater* number of DUI convictions (i.e., more than three convictions) prior to the enactment of the statute would lose his or her license for a substantially *lesser* period of time than a person who has been convicted of only two DUIs before the effective date of the statute. *See* Or. Rev. Stat. §§ 809.400(1), .428(2). Not only is such a construction patently inequitable, such an eventuality would be contrary to the stated policies of the legislature to protect the public and to deny driving privileges in relation to driving offenses.

Moreover, the fact that the legislature has in other instances used the phrase "at least three times," does not mean the absence of that language here requires the court to adopt the defendant's interpretation. Previously, this court has explained that, when the legislature uses a particular phrase in one statute but not another, it permits an inference that the omission was intentional, but this court "c[ould] not say that the text speaks conclusively in that regard." *State v. Robison*, 120 P.3d 1285, 1287 (Or. App. 2005). Thus, the absence of the "at least three time language" merely creates an ambiguity, which allows this court to consider the statute's legislative history when interpreting the statute.

C. The legislative history demonstrates that the legislature intended to mandate license revocation any time after two prior convictions.

The legislative history for House Bill 2885, which eventually became Oregon Revised Statutes §809.235, reflects an intent that sanctions for DUI increase as the number of DUI convictions increases.

For example, Representative Barker, a chief sponsor of the bill, testified before the House Judiciary Committee in support of the bill. He expressed frustration with current law, which allowed courts to revoke driving privileges only upon a fourth conviction. He wanted revocation to occur sooner:

> I introduced this bill, brought this bill forward, that would revoke driving privileges after a third conviction of driving under the influence. At the present time, it's four convictions. And * * * to keep it really brief the only objections I've heard about this so far at town halls and so on in meetings with citizens in my district is they can't imagine why we're waiting for the third time, why it isn't done sooner.

House Judiciary Committee, April 3, 2003, Tape 123 Side A at 50, Internet RealOne Player at 1:51:52.

When Representative Barker carried the bill on the House floor, he explained waiting until a fourth DUI conviction to revoke a driver's license was "unacceptably tolerant towards reckless behavior":

> HB 2885 comes to you from your Judiciary Committee where it passed with a unanimous vote. Currently someone convicted of driving under the influence of intoxicants does not permanently lose their driving privileges until after their fourth conviction. This means that after the initial DUI arrest which often results in a diversion program someone has to be convicted four more times to lose their privileges. As an Oregonian and the father of two daughters I find this to be unacceptably tolerant towards such reckless behavior. As a retired police lieutenant I could tell you that someone who gets convicted of drunk driving four times has a substance abuse problem[,] and colleagues[,] they need to be off the road.

> This bill revokes rather than suspends the driver's license of a person convicted for the third DUI. This revocation can be appealed after ten years. I don't feel it's necessary to give you a long speech about the dangers of driving while intoxicated. Most of us know someone who's been victimized by an intoxicated driver.

House Floor Debate on HB 2885, April 10, 2003, Tape 49 Side A at 314 to 356, Internet RealOne Player at 3 6:27 to 3 9:56.

On the Senate floor, prior to passage of the bill, other senators expressed their frustration with drivers who, despite prior convictions and other sanctions, continued to drink and drive:

> Senator Stan: HB 2885 is a DUI bill that changes the penalty for conviction for DUI from suspension to revocation of a driver's license after three convictions. We understand on the first conviction an individual may go through a diversion program and have the conviction removed so it's very likely a person convicted of three DUI has also offended one other time. It's very clear that people who continue to offend in this way have a very serious addiction problem and we believe that it's important to revoke their privilege to drive and so members I urge your support of HB 2885.

> Senator Dukes: This is a good bill because it makes a very small incremental improvement. But I stand today in utter frustration, if you listen to the carrier when to get around to a Class A misdemeanor — which by the way folks we're not even prosecuting at the moment because we don't have enough court time to do all of that. We're going to do that after the fifth DUI. We're going to finally — it's just the penalty really small for turning someone lethal loose on the roads in Oregon. And I think that one of the failures that the legislature has made over the years is an inability to be able to deal with that. I mean after you've gone out and driven and then convicted, and driven and then convicted, and driven and then convicted — we're going to give you a Class A misdemeanor. And then if you go drive and get convicted again we'll finally get to a felony. And we'll get serious about it maybe, and I just think in that process we have given people far too many opportunities to kill and maim people. And that is a mistake. However, as I said this bill is an improvement, but at this rate we're going to have a lot more deaths from drunk drivers that we could have stopped if we would simply have the guts to strengthen these laws.

> Senator Minnis: Mr. President, I just wanted to stand and say that I agree one hundred percent with the senator from Astoria [Senator Dukes]. There were over 25,000 DUI arrests in Oregon in 2001. That is simply not acceptable. Thank you.

Senate Floor Debate on H.B. 2285, May 21, 2003, Tape 165 Side B at 16 to 74, Internet RealOne Player at 59:18 to 1:00:52.

Nowhere does the legislative history suggest that the legislature was enacting a bill that would allow revocation of driving privileges at the third conviction but not upon a fourth. Such an interpretation would lead to the incongruous result that a person with a greater number of DUI convictions would be subject to a lesser penalty.

Accordingly, this court should construe *former* Oregon Revised Statutes §809.235(1)(b) to mandate permanent driver's license revocation in cases in which a person is convicted of a misdemeanor DUI and has previously been convicted at *least twice* for DUI.

In this case, Mr. Rodriguez had three times been convicted for DUI when, on September 13, 2004, he pleaded guilty to a fourth misdemeanor charge of driving under the influence of intoxicants. Because he had been convicted for DUI at least twice before, pursuant to *former* Oregon Revised Statutes §809.235(1)(b), the court properly imposed a permanent revocation of Mr. Rodriguez's driving privileges.

CONCLUSION

Final conclusions to a brief are often short and formulaic, such as this one. The final conclusion will always ask for the relief sought.

The trial court's judgment wherein defendant's driver's license is permanently revoked should be affirmed.

Respectfully submitted,

The lawyer's signature

_____

LAURA S. ANDERSON
Senior Assistant Attorney General

Attorneys for Plaintiff-Respondent
State of Oregon

Appellate Practice

This section explains a key part of appellate practice — drafting the appellate brief.

The chapter begins with an overview of some uniquely appellate concepts. These concepts will affect both the decision whether to appeal and the likelihood of success. Next, this chapter describes the judges who will read your brief and the staff that will help them reach a decision in your case. Finally, this chapter explains the appellate process — from the notice of the appeal to an ultimate decision by the highest appellate court.

I. Fundamental Appellate Concepts

Several appellate concepts shape how appellate courts handle appeals. Understanding these concepts will allow you to make an initial assessment of whether an appeal is likely to succeed and will allow you to advise your client appropriately. If you decide to proceed with an appeal, understanding these appellate concepts will also allow you to speak a language that appellate judges understand and to shape your writing to fit comfortably into the appellate setting in which it will be considered.

A. The Decision to Appeal

A lower tribunal—a trial court, administrative agency, or other tribunal—has just disposed of a matter in a way that is contrary to your client's position. Do you appeal the decision? Lawyers should put a lot of thought into answering that question.

1. Whether to appeal

The first question in deciding whether to file an appeal is whether the tribunal's ruling is appealable. As a general matter, a losing party has no inherent right to appeal. You cannot, for example, appeal a trial court's decision simply because you do not like the trial court's decision. The trial court must have made some identifiable legal error.

In addition, even if a court did commit a legal error, your right to appeal may be limited by statute. Usually, statutes permit litigants to appeal decisions that end the litigation but not those decisions that occur during the litigation process. For example, you may appeal after a decision granting a motion to dismiss or for summary judgment if the decision ends the litigation by disposing of all the claims before the court. By contrast, you typically may not appeal a decision denying summary judgment because that decision does not end the litigation but rather permits the case to proceed to trial.[1]

Assuming you have an appealable decision in hand, you must still decide whether you should appeal. In reaching that decision, consider whether an appeal will be worthwhile to your client:

- What is the projected cost of the appeal?
- What is the likelihood of obtaining a better outcome on appeal?
- How will the delay inherent in pursuing the appeal affect your client?

---

1. Some exceptions do exist. Statutes permit some "interlocutory" appeals—that is, appeals before the litigation is concluded—if continuing the litigation would be particularly prejudicial to a party.

- Is another route — such as seeking a settlement or asking the trial court or other tribunal to modify its ruling — a better approach?

In short, before filing an appeal, you must carefully consider whether an appeal is the best way to serve your client's needs. Producing a persuasive brief in an otherwise ill-advised appeal may not be to your client's advantage.

2. Which issues to raise on appeal

Once you have decided that it makes sense to appeal, another decision that you will have to make before filing an appellate brief is which issues you will raise on appeal. Some appellate briefs raise only one issue, such as whether the evidence was sufficient to support a criminal conviction, while other briefs may raise dozens of issues.

In choosing which issue or issues to raise on appeal, remember that you are not required to challenge every ruling made by the trial court or agency. Experienced appellate practitioners will choose their strongest arguments and forgo those arguments that have only a small chance of succeeding for three reasons: First, a good argument buried in a host of weak arguments may be overlooked. Second, appellate judges have a lot of reading to do; if you force them to read several arguments that have little merit, they are less likely to react favorably — consciously or subconsciously — to the one strong argument that you present. Finally, appellate courts impose length limits on briefs. If you waste words on six weak arguments, you may not have space to make that incredible winning argument on the one meritorious issue.

Notwithstanding the general advice to limit the number of issues raised on appeal, you must sometimes raise issues that you think have little chance of success so that it is preserved for later courts to consider. In doing so, however, the savvy practitioner will acknowledge in the intermediate court that the argument has previously been rejected by that court and that it is being raised only for the purpose of preservation.

B. Standards of Review

Appellate judges live and breathe standards of review, so it is important to be familiar with the concept. Appellate standards of review can be described in various ways:

- The degree of deference that an appellate court gives to a lower tribunal's resolution of an issue
- The level of scrutiny an appellate court gives to a lower tribunal's determination
- The lens through which the appellate court will view the lower tribunal's determination

Review of Agency Decisions

As you read this chapter understand that appellate courts review decisions not just from trial courts. Appellate courts also review agency decisions, and sometimes the review of agency decisions constitutes a significant part of an appellate court's docket. Although there are some differences when an appellate court reviews an agency decision, many of the same principles discussed below apply to review of agency decisions.

So that you will have a feel for how an appeal arises from an agency decision, here is a brief description of the process:

After the legislature passes a statute, often the legislature will delegate to an agency the authority to implement that statute. For example, Congress has delegated to the Environmental Protection Agency the responsibility for implementing environmental laws. States often have analogous agencies, which implement state laws. Agencies implement statutes by promulgating rules or regulations.

To enforce those regulations, agencies have authority to issue orders. Disputes often arise from those orders. For example, the Environmental Protection Agency has authority to issue permits that allow parties to discharge some material into wetlands. If the permit is denied, the party seeking the permit can challenge the EPA's decision.

The process for challenging an agency decision varies greatly from agency to agency. Some agencies have an internal process for reviewing an initial agency decision. In some agencies, that review may be before an administrative law judge and be nearly as formal as a trial. In other agencies, that review is much less formal. Still other agencies provide no review after the initial decision is made. In those cases, the initial decision is also the agency's final order.

Whatever the process may be in any given agency, once the agency issues its final order, a dissatisfied party can seek review in a state or federal appellate court, depending on whether a state or federal agency issued the order. Review of an agency's final order normally skips over the trial court and proceeds directly to an appellate court.

You are, no doubt, familiar with standards of review in non-legal settings. You may have asked a friend or colleague to review something you wrote to see if it is "in the ballpark." In that case, you are not asking the reviewer to tell you whether you have crossed every "t" and dotted every "i," but rather you seek a general level of scrutiny. Contrast that standard of review with the case in which you ask someone to look something over "with a fine-toothed comb." In that case, you are asking the reviewer to perform a very different type of review — a level of review with much greater scrutiny.

The sports world also has standards of review. For example, in the National Football League, a referee's initial call on the field may not be overruled absent "incontrovertible visual evidence" that the call on the field was incorrect. Such a standard gives high deference to the call on the field because it permits the call on the field to be overruled only when it is "incontrovertibly" clear that the call on the field was wrong.

As with standards outside the legal world, some appellate standards of review are more deferential to the trial court, while others are less deferential. Before turning to specific standards of review, a few important points about standards of review are in order.

First, standards of review permeate the appellate process. The standard of review can affect everything from the decision whether to appeal, to your likelihood of prevailing on appeal, to how you couch your argument, to how the appellate court will think about your case. If you do not consciously consider (and set out) the proper standard of review for every issue you raise on appeal — and tie your substantive argument and relief sought to it — your brief will be far less persuasive.

Second, standards of review are tied to specific issues, not to entire cases. For example, on appeal, a party might question whether summary judgment was appropriately granted and whether the trial court's award of attorney's fees was appropriate. The summary judgment question would be reviewed "de novo," giving no deference to the trial court's decision, while the second issue may be reviewed for an "abuse of discretion." In other words, the different issues you raise on appeal are often governed by different standards of review.

Third, because standards of review vary by issue you will need to research the standard of review for each issue you raise on appeal. Although it happens rarely, you may find an issue for which the standard of review is unsettled. If the standard of review is disputed, you will begin your argument to the court by arguing for the standard of review that you believe is appropriate — and beneficial for your client. After presenting your argument about the appropriate standard of review, then, you will proceed to your substantive argument.

Various standards of review exist; the following discussion focuses on the most common standards of review that apply in appeals from trial court decisions.

1. Rulings on issues of law

The most familiar standard of review is for errors of law. Whether the lower tribunal correctly interpreted the law is reviewed de novo by the appellate court. That is, the appellate court determines "anew" what the correct interpretation is, and the appellate court owes no deference to the lower court's interpretation.[2] This same standard is also described by saying that the appellate court reviews the lower court's ruling "as a matter of law" or by saying that the appellate court's review is "plenary." If you lost in the court below—and assuming that you have a persuasive legal argument — this standard of review is the one under which you are most likely to prevail because, under this standard, the appellate court owes no deference to the lower court.

2. Discretionary rulings

The second common standard of review is for abuse of discretion. For some rulings, no rule of law provides a single correct disposition. Rather, a trial court may choose from among several legally justifiable actions. In those cases, unless the trial court made a choice that is outside those that are legally available, an appellate court will not disturb the trial court's choice.

The abuse of discretion standard is often applied to a trial court's decision about court processes because trial courts are permitted significant leeway when managing courtroom proceedings. Assume, for example, that a rule of civil procedure states that, upon proper request, the trial court must give a party oral argument on any motion. Assume that the rule also states that the court may determine the amount of time the party may have for oral argument. Whether a trial court chose to give a party 15 minutes or 90 minutes, the appellate court would be unlikely to consider either ruling to be in error; that choice is within the "sound discretion" of the trial court. If, on the other hand, the trial court gave a party only 30 seconds for oral argument on a complex issue, that choice might constitute an abuse of discretion. In the first instance, the trial

---

2. Although the phrase "de novo" is commonly used, as described above, *de novo* review may have a different meaning in different jurisdictions, so be careful to check how the phrase is used in your jurisdiction. For example, in Oregon the phrase *de novo* review applies to reviewing errors of fact and not errors of law:

> In Oregon, "*de novo* review" remains tied to its origins in equity cases, which appellate courts tried anew upon the record; it thus refers to the review of factual findings. The phrase is inapplicable to actions at law, such as this case, in which there is the right to a jury trial on the facts. The [United States Supreme] Court, however, uses the phrase to refer to appellate review of the trial court's legal decisions; it contrasts that standard of review with review for abuse of discretion.

Waddill v. Anchor Hocking, Inc., 78 P.3d 570, 573 (Or. Ct. App. 2003) (internal citations omitted).

court choose from among legally permissible options, while in the second case, an appellate court might conclude that the trial court's choice was outside the range that the rule permitted.

Other decisions regarding court processes to which the abuse of discretion standard of review might apply include a court's decision to grant (or deny) motions to amend a complaint; to amend a judgment; to seal court records; or to grant a continuance.

Trial courts also often have leeway with more substantive decisions. For example, federal law allows a trial court to "exclude relevant evidence if its probative value is substantially outweighed by a danger of," among other things, "unfair prejudice" or "wasting time." Thus, the standard invites the judge to make a judgment, and different judges might reasonably reach different outcomes. Because more than one permissible outcome is available, such rulings are reviewed for an abuse of discretion.

As a rule of thumb, if a lower court takes an action pursuant to a statute or rule stating that the court "may" do something, the action probably will be reviewed for an abuse of discretion.

The abuse of discretion standard of review is significantly more deferential to the lower tribunal than the de novo standard of review but probably slightly less deferential than the clearly erroneous standard, discussed below. Therefore, an appellant may be slightly more likely to persuade an appellate court that a trial court abused its discretion than that a trial court's factual finding is clearly erroneous.

3. Factual findings by a trial court

The third common standard of review relates to how the appellate court will consider the trial court's factual findings. A court is engaged in fact-finding — and not legal analysis — if its conclusion is based solely on the record, with no reference to a legal standard. For example, was the traffic light red when the pickup truck barreled through it? What exactly were the dimensions of the room in which the police officer interrogated the defendant, and how many hours did the interrogation last? Did the driver have three India Pale Ales before he jumped in his car and drove, or was it seven? The responses to all of those questions are findings of fact.

When an appellate court reviews a trial court's factual findings, the standard of review is very deferential to the trial court. Because the trial court saw or heard from the various witnesses and exhibits and was able to assess the credibility of the witnesses and evidence first-hand, an appellate court will reverse a trial court's factual finding only if the trial court's findings of fact were "clearly erroneous." Under this standard, an appellate court will not reweigh the evidence in the record. Rather, the trial court's judgment about how to resolve any conflicts in the record will stand, and the appellate court will reverse only if the trial court's factual determination is implausible, and the appellate court is left with a "firm and determined" conviction that the trial court's factual findings was a mistake.

The strong deference that appellate courts give to factual findings may affect the likelihood that your argument will prevail on appeal. If your argument on appeal depends on the appellate court finding the facts contrary to the way they were found by the trial court, you will have a steep uphill battle.

4. Factual findings by a jury

Juries are also fact finders. Some trials are decided entirely by a judge. In other cases, defendants choose for a judge to find facts and reach a verdict. When a jury finds facts and reaches a verdict, the jury's fact finding can also be reviewed.

If an appellate court reviews a jury decision, the appellate court will review whether there was evidence from which reasonable minds could reach the conclusion that the jury did. If such evidence exists, the jury's decision will stand. To overturn a jury verdict, a party must show "no substantial evidence" supports the jury's decision. Again, the battle will be uphill if you wish to overturn a jury's factual findings and ultimate verdict.

5. Mixed questions of fact and law

Things in standard-of-review land get murky when considering mixed questions of fact and law. The United States Supreme Court has "noted the vexing nature of the distinction between questions of fact and questions of law,"[3] and commentators have written volumes about the proper standard of review when the two are combined. This section addresses the issue briefly, simply to provide a feel for it.

In many cases, a trial court must perform a three-step process to resolve an issue before it. First, it must determine the facts. As you know, facts as found by the trial court will not be disturbed on appeal absent "clear error." Second, having determined the facts, the trial court must determine the appropriate rule of law. As you also know, a trial court's interpretation of a legal rule is reviewed de novo. Finally, the trial court must apply the rule it has determined to the facts it has found.

This last step—when the court applies the relevant rule to the facts—is the so-called mixed question of fact and law. That is the tricky part: What is the proper standard of review for that part of the process? It depends. If the application of the law to the facts in a given case is more

---

3. *Pullman-Standard v. Swint*, 456 U.S. 273, 288 (1982).

like fact-finding, then the clearly erroneous standard applies. If, in contrast, the application is more like interpreting the law, the de novo standard applies. Unfortunately, courts and commentators may disagree about when the application of law to facts is more "fact-finding-like" and when it is more "law-interpreting-like."

Thus, if you are faced with an issue that turns on a mixed question of fact and law, do your research. Determine whether the courts in your jurisdiction have reached a conclusion. With luck, the courts will have already decided the appropriate standard of review for your issue. If not, as suggested previously, you should argue for the standard that benefits your client.

The discussion above provides a brief overview of the standards of review that you will most often see in practice. Table 9.2-A summarizes those standards and provides examples of when each standard would be used. If you write appellate briefs, determine the appropriate standard of review for each issue on appeal before you begin drafting—indeed, before you decide whether to appeal. Remember, standards of review are critical to appellate judges.

C. Preservation of Error and Plain Error

Another important concept that occupies appellate courts is the principle known as "preservation of error." The general rule is that an appellate court will not consider a claim of error that was not raised at trial. For example, if you want to argue that the trial court erred in admitting a piece of evidence, you must have objected to admission of the evidence in the trial court.

Why require that a claim of error be preserved? First, the requirement promotes judicial efficiency by making the trial court aware of the claimed error when it still has a chance to take action to correct it. Second, the requirement ensures that the appellate court will have a complete record to review. For example, if the claim is that the trial court erred when it excluded a witness's testimony, challenging the exclusion at trial may allow the lawyer to describe the excluded evidence on the record (but outside the presence of the jury). With that description, the appellate court will know what it was that the trial court excluded. Finally—for judicial efficiency and just plain fairness—the rule prevents a litigant who notices a claimed error from "lying in the weeds," that is, waiting until after a loss to jump out and claim an error.

Table 9.2-A • Standards of Review: Federal Courts*

STANDARD OF REVIEW	DE NOVO	ABUSE OF DISCRETION
Type of decision under review	Question of law and some mixed questions of fact and law	Discretionary action
Trial-court decision-maker	Trial judge	Trial judge
Degree of deference given to trial-court decision-maker	No deference	Substantial deference
Party typically benefitted by this standard	Appellant	Respondent
Definition	"[W]e review the matter anew, the same as if it had not been heard before, and as if no decision previously had been rendered." *Freeman v. DirecTV, Inc.*, 457 F.3d 1001, 1004 (9th Cir. 2006). "When de novo review is compelled, no form of appellate deference is acceptable." *Salve Regina Coll. v. Russell*, 499 U.S. 225, 238 (1991).	"Under this standard, a reviewing court cannot reverse absent a definite and firm conviction that the district court committed a clear error of judgment in the conclusion it reached upon a weighing of relevant factors." *Valdivia v. Schwarzenegger*, 599 F.3d 984, 988 (9th Cir. 2010). "An abuse of discretion occurs where the district court clearly erred or ventured beyond the limits of permissible choice under the circumstances." *Wright ex rel. Trust Co. of Kan. v. Abbott Labs., Inc.*, 259 F.3d 1226, 1233 (10th Cir. 2001). "Under an abuse of discretion standard, a trial court's decision will not be disturbed unless the appellate court has a definite and firm conviction that the lower court made a clear error of judgment or exceeded the bounds of permissible choice in the circumstances. That is to say, we will not alter a trial court's decision unless…the court's decision was an arbitrary, capricious, whimsical, or manifestly unreasonable judgment." *Id.* at 1235-36 (citations and internal quotation marks omitted).
Examples	Motions for summary judgment; constitutional questions; statutory interpretation; mootness, ripeness, and standing; contract interpretation.	Amount of Rule 11 sanctions; attorney's fees; courtroom management and discovery issues (such as whether to grant a motion for continuance or whether to grant a motion to compel the production of documents); injunctions; temporary restraining orders.

* Over the years, numerous professors have contributed to and updated this chart. Among them, professors at Hamline University and Professor Terri Pollman have been credited with significant work on this chart.

CLEARLY ERRONEOUS	SUBSTANTIAL EVIDENCE	ARBITRARY AND CAPRICIOUS
Question of fact	Question of fact	Agency resolution of a question of fact
Trial judge	Jury	Administrative law judge
Significant deference	Extreme deference	Extreme deference
Respondent	Respondent	Respondent
A reviewing court "will not reverse a lower court's finding of fact simply because [it] would have decided the case differently. Rather, a reviewing court must ask whether, on the entire evidence, it is left with the definite and firm conviction that a mistake has been committed." *Easley v. Cromartie*, 532 U.S. 234, 242 (2001) (citations and internal quotation marks omitted). "If the district court's account of the evidence is plausible in light of the record viewed in its entirety, the court of appeals may not reverse it even though convinced that had it been sitting as the trier of fact, it would have weighed the evidence differently. Where there are two permissible views of the evidence, the factfinder's choice between them cannot be clearly erroneous." *Anderson v. Bessemer City*, 470 U.S. 564, 573-74 (1985). *See generally* Fed. R. Civ. P. 52(a)	Appellate courts will review the record to determine whether there was evidence from which reasonable minds could have reached the same conclusion as the jury. The verdict must stand unless the appellant can show that there is no substantial evidence to support it, considering the evidence in the light most favorable to the verdict and with all reasonable inferences deducible from the evidence drawn in support of the verdict. *See Glasser v. United States*, 315 U.S. 60, 80 (1942). When evidence is supported by substantial evidence, it means that there is "more than a mere scintilla. It means such relevant evidence as a reasonable mind might accept as adequate to support a conclusion." *Richardson v. Perales*, 402 U.S. 389, 401 (1971) (quoting *Consolidated Edison Co. v. NLRB*, 305 U.S. 197, 229 (1938)). The "unsupported by substantial evidence" is more deferential than the "clearly erroneous" standard. *Stern v. Marshall*, 131 S. Ct. 2594, 2627 (2011), *reh'g denied,* 132 S. Ct. 56.	The absence of a rational connection between the facts found and the choice made. There should be a clear error of judgment; an action not based upon consideration of relevant factors and so is arbitrary, capricious, an abuse of discretion or otherwise not in accordance with law or if it was taken without observance of procedure required by law. *Natural Resources Defense Council, Inc. v. United States EPA*, 966 F.2d 1292, 1297 (9th Cir. 1992)
Findings of fact made by a trial court.	A finding of fact from a jury, or a finding of fact made by an administrative agency under an Administrative Procedure Act adjudication or formal rulemaking.	A government agency's resolution of a question of fact decided by informal rulemaking under the Administrative Procedure Act.

Whether the action a lawyer took in the trial court was adequate to preserve the claim of error is something that appellate lawyers are happy to argue about and appellate courts are happy to write about. What it takes to preserve a claim of error varies from jurisdiction to jurisdiction and from legal issue to legal issue. Nonetheless, a good guideline is that an objection or other action that may preserve a claim of error must be both timely and specific; how timely and how specific, however, varies with the context.

For our purposes, you should be aware of the following: (1) claims of error generally must be preserved for an appellate court to address them;[4] and (2) appellate courts take the requirement seriously and many claims do not get addressed for lack of preservation. Thus, before proceeding with an appeal or raising a certain issue on appeal, you must consider whether the issue was preserved for appeal.

D. Harmless Error

Another concept affecting how appellate courts will dispose of claims of error is known as "harmless error." Consider this example: The trial court commits an error; you object, preserving the claim of error; on appeal, you raise the claim of error, make a brilliant argument, and seek reversal of the trial court's judgment. You win, right? Not necessarily. If the trial court's error—although indisputably an error—did not ultimately affect the outcome of the case, the appellate court will not reverse the decision based on the error. Thus, if one witness's testimony was admitted erroneously, but the jury heard the same information from three other witnesses, the error in admitting the first witness's testimony may be harmless. Under what circumstances an error will be considered "harmless" varies, but all appellate courts recognize the doctrine. You should consider whether an error is harmless when deciding whether to appeal and when choosing which issues to raise on appeal. In other words, consider whether there was no harm, and thus, no foul.

E. Right for the Wrong Reason

One final important appellate concept is known as "right for the wrong (or a different) reason." Under this principle, an appellate court may affirm a trial court's ruling, even if the trial court's reasoning was incorrect, if the trial court ultimately reached the legally correct result. Thus, when deciding whether to appeal and when considering which issues to raise on appeal,

---

4. That said, some exceptions to the preservation requirement may allow an appellate court to address unpreserved claims. The most common exception is known as "plain error." If the trial court made a mistake that is obvious, an appellate court may consider an argument based on that error.

you should also consider whether the trial court was right for the wrong reason. Similarly, a respondent who is seeking to uphold a trial court's ruling should carefully consider whether there is a colorable argument that the trial court was right for the wrong reason—sometimes, that argument may be the only one available for affirmance.

II. The Court and Its Players: Judges, Law Clerks, and Staff Attorneys

As mentioned above, before crafting any document, you should have a sense of your audience. Understanding your audience will help you craft a more useful and persuasive document. In an appellate setting, the audience will typically be judges, their law clerks, and staff attorneys.

Of course, appellate courts have judges or justices. Normally, courts have an odd number of judges; however, if a court has vacancies or recusals, your appeal may be heard by an even number of judges. Courts may sit in panels (usually of three judges), or the entire court may sit together (en banc).

In addition to the judges or justices, most appellate courts have two other categories of lawyers who may be involved in your appeal: law clerks and staff attorneys. Law clerks may be attorneys hired for the position indefinitely or term clerks who are often recent law school graduates employed by an individual judge for one to two years.[5] Staff attorneys are permanent lawyer-employees who may work for the court as a whole or for individual judges. Some staff attorneys have many years of experience and may have expertise in an area of law. Although titles and functions vary from court to court, in most appellate courts, law clerks and staff attorneys assist the judges by conducting legal research,

---

Be Precise! Know Your Judges from Your Justices

In most jurisdictions, a judge who is appointed or elected to the highest appellate court is called a "justice." A judge who sits on an intermediate appellate court is called a "judge." Exceptions do exist. In California, for example, the Court of Appeal jurists are called justices. Be sure to know the correct title for the person who will be deciding your case. It can only help.

---

5. Increasingly, judges are hiring permanent law clerks. When a law clerk is hired on a permanent basis, the most significant difference between a "law clerk" and a "staff attorney" is the title. Otherwise, both are experienced lawyers assisting a judge or group of judges with research, drafting opinions, and preparing for oral arguments.

preparing bench memoranda (a memorandum that summarizes the legal issues a case presents, usually prepared before oral argument), preparing initial drafts of opinions, and editing and finalizing opinions.

When drafting an appellate brief, keep those various audiences in mind. Specifically, keep in mind that, in most cases, the judges and most of the legal staff working with the judges are generalists. That is, they are educated attorneys, but they may not be experts in the subject matter central to your client's case; in any event, they will not know the facts of your case as well as you do. You should always assume that you know your case better than the appellate judges who will hear your appeal. Thus, in most instances, to persuade the court of your client's desired outcome, you must first educate the court about the facts of your case and the underlying law that applies to the case.

III. The Appellate Process

When drafting an argument, it's helpful to have a picture of the path ahead. This section provides that procedural picture.

A. The Notice of Appeal

The appellate process typically begins with a notice of appeal. The notice of appeal is filed with either the trial court or the appellate court, depending on the rules in that jurisdiction. In addition, the notice of appeal is served on the other parties to the case. With these steps, both the court and the other parties to the case are notified that the dispute has not been finally resolved and that jurisdiction now lies with the appellate court.

The exact format of a notice of appeal will vary from jurisdiction to jurisdiction. Example 9.2-B shows you a typical notice of appeal.

In federal court, the notice of appeal must be filed within 30 days after the decision being appealed is entered in the trial court's docket.[6] After that document is filed, certain timelines begin to run and certain actions must be taken before the briefs are filed. For example, in federal court the appellant must order a transcript of the court proceedings within fourteen days after the notice of appeal is filed.[7]

---

6. Fed. R. App. P. 4(a)(1)(A).

7. Fed. R. App. P. 10(b)(1).

Example 9.2-B · A typical notice of appeal

United States District Court for the
Southern District of Texas

Jonathan B. Wilson, Plaintiff,	No. 23-10664
v.	Notice of Appeal
Zal Medical Group, Inc., Defendant.	

Notice is hereby given that Zal Medical Group, Inc., defendant, in the above named case, hereby appeals to the United States Court of Appeals for the Fifth Circuit from the final judgment entered in this action on the 7th day of March, 2016.

Gail Izaguirre
Gail Izaguirre
Attorney for Zal Medical Group
1100 Louisiana Street
Suite 410
Houston, TX 77002

> ### The Petition for Judicial Review of a Final Agency Order
>
> When seeking judicial review of a final agency order, you would file a "petition for judicial review," which is the administrative law counterpart to a notice of appeal from a trial court decision. As with the notice of appeal, the petition for judicial review of the agency order triggers certain timelines and triggers the agency's duty to transmit relevant parts of the administrative record to the appellate court.

B. The Parties

Once a party files a notice of appeal, the parties are designated with new names. The party who lost at trial and appeals is designated as the appellant. The party responding to the appeal is designated as the respondent or appellee.[8]

Although the parties have new designations, often when writing about them, lawyers will continue to use names such as "plaintiff" and "defendant," "employee" and "employer," or other names that make it easier for the court to keep track of who is who. In fact, the federal rules of appellate procedure state that "counsel should use the parties' actual names, or the designations used in the lower court or agency proceeding, or such descriptive terms as 'the employee,' 'the injured person,' 'the taxpayer,' 'the ship,' 'the stevedore.'"[9]

> ### Appellee vs. Respondent
>
> "Appellee" and "respondent" refer to the same party: the party who is responding to the appeal.
>
> The Federal Rules of Appellate Procedure use the word "appellee." "Respondent," however, is the more intuitively meaningful word. When using the word "respondent," the reader does not have to sort out the difference between "appellant" and "appellee," two very similar sounding words. For these reasons, this chapter uses the word "respondent" throughout.

C. The Record

When an appellate court considers whether a trial court erred, the trial court bases that decision on the evidence in the trial record. The trial record consists of documents, exhibits, and a transcript of any oral

---

8. The order of the names in the caption may also change. In trial court captions, the plaintiff—the party bringing the case—is listed first. On appeal, the appellant—the party bringing the appeal—is usually listed first.

9. Fed. R. App. P. 28(d).

testimony or argument. On appeal, lawyers compile excerpts of the trial record (sometimes called an appendix) and submit it to the appellate court so that the appellate court can review the proceedings below.

The record on appeal is critically important because, with few exceptions, appellate courts may not consider evidence that was not before the trial court. Thus, when trying to persuade appellate courts, remember that if something is not in the record, it essentially does not exist. References to matters that are not in the record may draw the ire of appellate judges and will detract from the persuasiveness of your argument.

Court rules differ regarding who is responsible for preparing the appendix or excerpt of the record. The rules also vary regarding the contents of the appendix or excerpt. Typically, the appendix or excerpt contains only those parts of the trial record that are necessary to support the arguments made on appeal; however, some appellate courts require the full record to be transmitted.

Do Appellate Courts Really Care About the Record?

Yes. Here's what one California court had to say about the record:

When practicing appellate law, there are at least three immutable rules: first, take great care to prepare a complete record; second, if it is not in the record, it did not happen; and third, when in doubt, refer back to rules one and two. In this case, the parties totally missed the appellate mark by failing to provide an adequate record for review.

Protect Our Water v. Cty. of Merced,
1 Cal. Rptr. 3d 726, 726 (Cal. Ct. App. 2003).

D. The Briefs

After the relevant parts of the record have been transmitted, the parties submit their briefs. The appellant begins the exchange by filing an opening brief (also called the "appellant's brief"). Then comes the respondent's brief. Finally, the appellant will sometimes—but not always—submit a reply brief. This exchange usually occurs over the course of two or three months.[10]

---

10. In federal court, the appellant's opening brief must be filed 40 days after the record is filed. The respondent then has 30 days to file, and the appellant has another 21 days to file a reply. Fed. R. App. P. 31(a)(1).

E. Oral Argument

After briefs are filed — often many months after briefs are filed — the parties may have an opportunity to present oral arguments to the court.

Judging from movies and television, one would think that appeals are really all about oral argument. It turns out — no surprise here — that television and movies do not always depict the court system accurately. As an initial matter, many appeals are decided without oral argument; the briefs are the only opportunity the parties have to persuade the court. In addition, even for those cases in which the court hears oral argument, the briefs are almost always considered to be more important in persuading the court. Oral argument is discussed in detail in Part IV, *Oral Argument*.

F. The Opinion

Finally, after briefs are submitted and after oral argument (if oral argument is permitted and if the parties elect to present oral argument), the court will issue its opinion. The opinion is the court's explanation of its decision in an appeal.

The form of opinions varies enormously from court to court and even from case to case. The United States Supreme Court often issues opinions that run dozens or hundreds of pages in length. At the other extreme, some appellate courts issue short opinions or one-page orders that do little more than affirm or reverse a lower court's decision. Many courts also issue unpublished opinions that have little or no precedential value.

G. Petitions for Reconsideration or Rehearing

If you lose an appeal in an intermediate appellate court, you might appeal to a higher court, a route that is discussed below. But, before doing so, you can consider whether to ask the intermediate appellate court to reconsider its decision (or rehear the case — the two phrases are often used interchangeably). If you ask the intermediate appellate court to reconsider its decision, you have two options.

First, you can ask the panel that decided the appeal to reconsider its decision. However, a panel will usually do so only if a party can show that the panel failed to consider a salient fact or misunderstood the law.

Second, you can ask all the judges of the intermediate appellate court to review the panel's decision. When all the judges on a court review a panel's decision, the review is called an "en banc review." Under the federal rules, petitions for rehearing en banc are "not favored and ordinarily will not be ordered" unless you persuade the court that "en banc consideration is necessary to secure or maintain uniformity of the court's decisions" or that "the proceeding involves a question of exceptional importance."[11]

In summary, petitions for reconsideration or rehearing are appropriate in only a limited number of circumstances. However, if your client's case meets the necessary criteria, you may be able to obtain a better result for your client without the time or expense of seeking review in a higher court.

Be Precise! Appellant vs. Petitioner

A party who appeals a trial court's decision and has an appeal as of right, is called an "appellant." The party responding is the "appellee" or "respondent."

By contrast, when a party seeks review in a discretionary court, the party instigating the review is called the "petitioner" not the "appellant." The instigator is called the "petitioner" because that party must petition for the right to be heard. The party responding is called the "respondent," never the appellee.

H. Review in a Discretionary Court

Above, we have discussed the typical appellate process as a case moves from the trial court through an appellate court. Most states, though, and the federal judiciary have two levels of appellate review: an intermediate appellate court and a supreme court.[12] Thus, after an intermediate appellate court issues its final decision in a case, a party may still request that the court of last resort—typically the supreme court—review the intermediate appellate court's decision.

We must emphasize the word "request." One of the big differences between intermediate appellate courts and supreme courts is that intermediate courts tend to be non-discretionary and supreme courts tend to be discretionary. That is, intermediate appellate courts generally have to consider every appeal that is filed, and their primary goal is to correct trial court or agency error rather than to announce rules of law. In contrast, the court of last resort (usually supreme courts) typically have control over which cases they review. Supreme courts usually limit their docket to those cases that represent an important issue or a conflict in the law that needs to be resolved.

---

11. Fed. R. App. P. 35(a).

12. Delaware, Maine, Montana, New Hampshire, Rhode Island, North Dakota, South Dakota, Vermont, and Wyoming are states without typical intermediate courts.

> **Supreme Courts**
>
> Nearly every jurisdiction designates its highest court as the "supreme" court of that jurisdiction. Exceptions, however, exist. New York and Maryland, for example, both call their highest court the "Court of Appeals." And, in New York, the trial courts are called "Supreme Courts."
>
> For convenience, we use the term "supreme court" to refer to the highest court in a jurisdiction.

Some exceptions do exist to a supreme court's ability to determine its docket. In many states, statutes will require that state's highest court to review a limited range of cases. For example, death penalty cases are often reviewed automatically and directly by the supreme court, rather than the intermediate appellate court. However, the kinds of cases that a supreme court must hear are limited. Therefore, remember that your one shot at winning may be in the intermediate appellate court; use it wisely.

Practice Points

- Before you begin drafting an appellate brief, ask yourself
  - ◦ Whether it makes sense to appeal.
  - ◦ Which issues should be raised on appeal.
  - ◦ Whether those issues have been preserved.
- In addition, and also before you begin drafting, determine the standard (or standards) of review that apply to each issue on appeal.
- When you write to an appellate court, you are writing not just to the judge or justice but also to law clerks and staff attorneys—all of whom are generalists.
- A typical appeal follows this path:
  - ◦ Notice of appeal
  - ◦ Gathering the record
  - ◦ Drafting briefs
  - ◦ Presenting oral arguments (sometimes)
  - ◦ Receiving an opinion from the appellate court
- If you lose an appeal, you might petition for reconsideration, a rehearing, or for review in the highest court

Section 9.3

Constructing an Appellate Brief

I.   The Rules that Govern Appellate Briefs
II. Building a Brief
     A. Cover
     B. Table of Contents
     C. Table of Authorities
     D. Statement of Jurisdiction
     E. Issue (or Question) Presented
         1. The "short form" or single-sentence question presented
         2. The "long-form" question presented
         3. The question presented as syllogism
         4. Incorporating the standard of review
         5. Organizing multiple questions presented
         6. A good question presented leads to a better brief
     F. Statement of the Case
     G. Summary of the Argument
     H. Argument
     I. Conclusion and Relief Sought
III. Briefs for Different Parties
     A. Appellant's Brief
     B. Respondent's Brief
     C. Appellant's Reply Brief

This chapter now turns to the nuts and bolts of drafting an appellate brief. The first section of this chapter, §9.1, included an image of what an appellate brief looks like. Section 9.2 then introduced you to the particular concepts that govern appeals, your appellate court audience, and the process by which an appeal moves through the court system. This section now returns to the appellate brief to look more closely at each part and how each part can be used to advance your argument.

Appellate briefs, however, vary among jurisdictions. To determine what your brief should include, you will have to consult the rules that govern appeals in your jurisdiction. Thus, this chapter begins with a short introduction to the procedural rules that govern appeals and how to find those rules and then turns to the different appellate briefs that attorneys construct.

I. The Rules that Govern Appellate Briefs

To construct a persuasive appellate brief, you must begin by examining the appellate court rules. Rules of appellate procedure will tell you everything from the proper font, the size of the margins, and the length of the brief.[1]

Complying with the rules will make your brief more persuasive. Why? First, it shows the reader that you know how to, and make the effort to, find and follow rules. Following the rules enhances your credibility with the court, and the more credible you appear, the more likely the judges will be open to the argument that you have drafted.

Second, following the rules reduces distractions. Judges are very busy, and they read many briefs. They expect the brief to look a certain way, to have the sections in a certain order, and to contain all the information required by the rules. To the extent that a brief does not do those things, the judges have to work harder to follow it and will have less mental energy to devote to the legal argument. The easier you make your brief to digest, the less heartburn it will cause the judges.

Keep in mind that some jurisdictions have more than one set of rules governing their appeals. For example, appeals in the federal courts of appeal are governed first by the Federal Rules of Appellate Procedure. Then, the various federal circuit courts have their own local rules that supplement the Federal Rules of Appellate Procedure. Similarly, in state courts, the state's highest court usually adopts a set of rules that govern its proceedings, while the intermediate appellate court adopts different rules for its proceedings.

Two resources can help you find and understand the governing appellate rules. First, most courts have valuable information on their websites. In addition to appellate rules of procedure, you will often find sample documents and how-to advice on courts' websites. Second, a number of good treatises on appellate practice are available, some of which address practice in certain courts (such as the United States Supreme Court or the Ninth Circuit Court of Appeals) and others that are more general. A law librarian will be able to direct you to the most suitable treatise. The bottom line for your practice: Long before you even think about writing a brief, make sure you have consulted the rules that govern the appeal.

---

1. *See, e.g.*, Fed. R. App. P. 32(a)(5)(A) (requiring 14-point font size for appellate briefs); Fed. R. App. P. 32(a)(4) (requiring one-inch margins on all sides); Fed. R. App. P. 32(a)(1)(7) (page length and word count).

II. Building a Brief

As discussed above, the rules in your jurisdiction will largely dictate the parts that you must include in your brief. In addition, briefs may vary depending on whether you are writing appellant's opening brief, respondent's brief, or appellant's reply brief. This section discusses the typical parts of an appellate brief. Later sections discuss how your client's position in the litigation — as appellant or respondent — might affect whether your brief will include all the parts described here.

Usually, an appellate brief includes these components:

- Cover
- Table of contents
- Table of authorities
- Statement of jurisdiction
- Statement of the issues (or questions) presented
- Statement of the case
- Summary of the argument
- Argument
- Conclusion

To be honest, some components of an appellate brief are pretty dry and do not provide much opportunity for creativity. Other components — primarily the issue presented, the statement of facts, and of course, the argument — let you really strut your analytic and writing skills.

But all aspects of the brief are important. To the extent that the dry, constrained parts of the brief are not properly prepared, the reader will be less positively inclined to accept a brilliant argument. To be persuasive, an argument must be served up right. Put another way, the obligatory, formulaic parts of the brief are to the argument as a picture frame is to a work of art. A good frame enhances, but does not distract from, the work; an ugly frame can ruin the whole effect. Below, you will see how each section of the appellate brief offers an opportunity, no matter how small, to persuade the court.[2]

---

2. This chapter discusses the typical components of an appellate brief. This discussion does not address one section required in the federal circuit courts, but not usually required in state appeals: a corporate disclosure statement. See Fed. R. App. P. 26.1(a) (requiring that "[a]ny nongovernmental corporate party to a proceeding in a court of appeals must file a statement that identifies any parent corporation and any publicly held corporation that owns 10% or more of its stock and states that there is no such corporation").

A. Cover

Briefs begin with a cover page. That cover page typically states the name of the court hearing the appeal, the parties to the case, the docket number, the court from which the appeal is being taken, and the names of the attorneys and their contact information.[3]

The cover is the first place to begin persuading. If you scrupulously follow the rules and provide exactly the information the rules prescribe, the judge's first impression will be that you are professional and competent and that you know what you are doing.

Blue brief, red brief, grey brief

Traditionally—that is, when attorneys went to courthouses and filed physical copies of their briefs—appellate brief covers came in various colors. The appellant's or petitioner's brief had a blue cover, and the respondent's brief had a red cover. The appellant's reply brief had a gray cover; amicus curiae briefs sported a green cover.

In fact, appellate practitioners and judges often refer to briefs by their color. So, in the hallways of an appellate court you may hear someone say, "I have the blue brief and the red brief; do you know if they filed a gray brief?"

Today, most appellate briefs are filed electronically, and briefs filed electronically are no longer required to have colored covers. However, because you may see a brief with a colored cover or hear a reference to a blue, red, or grey brief, you should know the history.

B. Table of Contents

Like any other table of contents, the table of contents in an appellate brief lists all the sections of the brief and the page on which each section begins. In an appellate brief, the table of contents is created by listing—verbatim—all the point headings and subheadings found within your brief and the page on which those point headings and subheadings can be found. As discussed in Chapter 6, *Refining Persuasive Arguments,* point headings should read as an outline of your argument. Thus, if you have constructed effective headings in your brief, the table of contents will serve as a summary of your argument.

The table of contents is particularly important because it is the very first place the judges will be exposed to your legal argument. If, for example, the first heading under the argument section in the table of contents is, "Plaintiff never objected to admission of the toxicologist's report, so his

---

3. *See, e.g.,* Fed. R. App. P. 32(a)(2).

claim of error is unpreserved," the judges are already thinking that this appeal may have a simple answer: "lack of preservation."

The table also serves utilitarian functions, which will bring the judges back to your table of contents over and again. For example, as the judges are considering your case, they are likely to address one issue at a time. As the judges consider each issue, they will use the table of contents to find that section of your brief. In addition, if the judges lose track of your argument, they are likely to come back to the table of contents to get an overview of your argument. Thus, the table of contents is not just the first place where the judges will see your argument; instead, it is likely to be the place where they return repeatedly and are exposed to your argument again and again.

For those reasons, your table of contents should always present a persuasive summary of your argument. For example, it is hardly ever appropriate to produce a table of contents that has no subheadings between "Argument" and "Conclusion." As you can imagine, judges will not find that of table of contents useful, and you have lost a prime opportunity to persuade.

Compare the table of contents in Examples 9.3-A, 9.3-B, and 9.3-C. Which is more likely to persuade the judges that your analysis is correct? Which table of contents will be easier for the judges to use? Importantly, which table of contents is more likely to convince the judges that you think carefully about the details?

Example 9.3-A • A table of contents without an effective overview of the argument fails to persuade

---

TABLE OF CONTENTS

These subheadings do not actually explain the party's legal argument. Rather they assert specific sub-points within the argument. By failing to connect these sub-points to the larger legal conclusions, the table of contents misses an opportunity to persuade.

9.3 · CONSTRUCTING AN APPELLATE BRIEF

Example 9.3-B · A persuasive table of contents

TABLE OF CONTENTS

I.   STATEMENT OF JURISDICTION 1

II. STATEMENT OF THE ISSUES 2

III. STATEMENT OF THE CASE 3

IV. STATEMENT OF THE FACTS 3

V.   SUMMARY OF ARGUMENT 5

VI. ARGUMENT 8

A.   Under the Sixth Amendment, the officers were permitted to question defendant about a charged offense outside the presence of counsel because defendant initiated the conversation. 8

1.   A defendant initiates conversation about a charged offense when a reasonable officer could conclude that she has evinced a willingness to discuss the charged offense. 9

2.   The totality of the circumstances entitled the trial court to conclude that defendant initiated a conversation with the officers about the charged offense. 11

B.   Under the Sixth Amendment, the officers were permitted to question defendant about a charged offense because defendant waived her right to counsel's presence during questioning. 15

1.   A defendant's waiver of her right to counsel must be knowing and intelligent. 15

2.   The totality of the circumstances entitled the trial court to conclude that defendant was aware of her right to counsel but nonetheless chose to discuss the charged offenses without counsel present. 17

VII. CONCLUSION 20

Read the point headings under "ARGUMENT" to see how the point headings provide a clear summary of the argument.

Notice also how the table of contents has a crisp look to it. That crisp look is achieved by using consistent tabs (each level is indented an additional 1/2 inch); by using hanging indents, which are explained in Chapter 6, *Refining Persuasive Arguments*, at Example 6-G; and by leaving a column of blank space (interrupted only by leader dots) between the text of each point heading and the page numbers.

Example 9.3-C • A carelessly formatted table of contents fails to persuade

TABLE OF CONTENTS

<u>Page</u>

Inconsistent formatting makes the table look sloppy. Judges are apt to think that a sloppy brief is a prelude to sloppy thinking.

Page numbers do not line up.

The initial indentation at each level of the outline — after the Roman numeral, the capital letter, and the Arabic numeral — is inconsistent.

When the text of a point heading comes out as far as the page number, the page number is more difficult to see. Why make the judge's job more difficult?

When a point heading is a complete sentence, use final punctuation.

Bold and all caps are used inconsistently. Compare "VI. ARGUMENT" with "**VII. Conclusion.**"

C. Table of Authorities

The table of authorities is one of those dry sections of the brief. The table of authorities simply lists every authority that you rely on in your brief. Often, as the court is considering your case, the court will want to see how you addressed a particular case, statute, or other authority. The table of authorities allows the court to easily find where you have addressed each authority.

As with a table of contents, a professional-looking table of authorities will persuade the judges that you know the rules and pay attention to detail. Like other parts of the brief, the form the table takes typically is specified in the appellate rules.[4] While the table is often produced by support staff or computer programs, you must still make sure that it is accurate and looks good. Your name will be on the brief, meaning that you are ultimately responsible for everything in the brief from cover to cover. The same consistency in formatting that makes a table of contents look professional and credible will also make your table of authorities (and you) look professional and credible. To see the difference between a professionally and unprofessionally presented table of authorities, compare Example 9.3-D with Example 9.3-E.

Additionally, because your goal in providing a table of authorities is to be helpful to the court, whenever possible avoid using the term *"passim." Passim* is a Latin word meaning "throughout," "frequently," or "here and there."[5] A table of authorities may use the word *passim* rather than provide specific page numbers when an authority appears so frequently in a brief that listing every page on which that authority appears would be more overwhelming than helpful. No uniform rule exists about when to use *passim* as opposed to listing specific pages, but many courts discourage the use of *passim*.[6] Simply keep in mind what will be most helpful to the court, and then make your decision. As a rule, judges will likely find it more helpful to see the exact pages in which you have cited an authority, even if you have cited the authority frequently.

---

4. *See, e.g.*, Fed. R. App. P. 28(a)(3) (explaining that a table of authorities should have "cases (alphabetically arranged), statutes, and other authorities — with references to the pages of the brief").

5. *Passim, The American Heritage Dictionary* (5th ed. 2020), https://www.ahdictionary.com/word/search.html?q=passim (last visited Dec. 21, 2021).

6. *See, e.g.*, Or. R. App. P. 5.35(3) ("Reference to 'passim' or 'et seq.' in the index of authorities is discouraged.").

Example 9.3-D · A professionally presented table of authorities

TABLE OF AUTHORITIES

Cases

<u>Page</u>

Reid v. Georgia,
    448 U.S. 438 (1980) 23

State v. Bates,
    304 Or. 519 . . . .   2, 9, 14, 17, 20, 21, 24, 25, 26, 28

State v. Ehly,
    317 Or. 66 (1993) 16, 17, 18, 19, 20, 21, 22, 25

State v. Goodman,
    328 Or. 318 (1999) 19

State v. Gulley,
    324 Or. 57 (1996) 16

State v. Miglavs,
    186 Or. App. 420,
    rev. allowed, 335 Or. 479 (2003) 10, 14, 15, 27, 28

State v. Valdez,
    277 Or. 621 (1977) 17, 18, 20, 21, 24

Terry v. Ohio,
    392 U.S. 1 (1968) 17

United States v. Bignoni-Ponce,
    422 U.S. 873 (1975) 17

Constitutional and Statutory Provisions

Or. Const., Art. I, §9 . . . .   2, 14, 15, 16

Or. Rev. Stat. §131.005(11) 16

Or. Rev. Stat. §166.250(11) 9

Other Authorities

4 Wayne R. La Fave, *Search and Seizure: A Treatise on the Fourth
    Amendment* (3d ed. 1996) 15, 23, 24

Webster's Third New Int'l Dictionary (unabridged ed. 1993) 24

In a professionally presented table of authorities, authorities are grouped by kind of authority, e.g., cases are listed separately from constitutions and statutes. Within each kind of authority, the individual authorities are listed alphabetically.

Consistent formatting and effective use of blank space make a table easy to read.

Compare with Example 9.3-E. Note that the blank line between each authority and space between the citations and the page numbers (where only the leader dots appear) make the information easy to pick out.

Of course, all citations must be accurate.

Notice that no pinpoint page numbers are given. These citations are to an authority generally and not to a particular page within the authority.

Example 9.3-E • A table of authorities that is not professionally presented

One good way to frustrate a judge and the judge's staff is to make your brief more difficult to use. Here, the lawyer has done just that in the following ways:

- Providing inaccurate citations (compare the *Terry and Bignoni-Ponce* cites)

- Providing inconsistent citations

- Failing to correctly alphabetize the list (where is *Reid v. Georgia*?)

- Failing to list the pages where the judge can find arguments citing *Bates* and *Ehly*

- Making the table difficult to read because citations and page numbers overlap and the absence of blank space between each authority makes each authority difficult to pick out

TABLE OF AUTHORITIES
Cases

Page

State v. Bates, 747 P.2d 991 (1987)....................................*passim*

State v. Ehly, 317 Or. 66, 854 P.2d 421 (1993) ....*passim*

State v. Goodman, 328 Or. 318 (1999) 19

State v. Gulley, 324 Or. 57 (1996) 16

State v. Miglavs, 186 Or. App. 420, 63 P.3d 1202, *rev. allowed*, 335 Or. 479 (2003) 10, 14, 15, 27, 28

State v. Valdez, 277 Or. 621, 561 P.2d 1006 (1977) 17, 18, 20, 21, 24

Terry v. Ohio, 392 U.S. 1, 422 U.S. 873, 95 S. Ct. 2574, 45 L. Ed. 2d 607 (1975) 17

United States v. Bignoni-Ponce, 422 U.S. 873, 95 S. Ct. 2574, 45 L. Ed. 2d 607 (1975) 17

Reid v. Georgia, 448 U.S. 438, 100 S. Ct. 2752, 65 L. Ed. 2d 890 (1980).......23

Constitutional and Statutory Provisions

Or. Const., Art. I, § 9..2, 14, 15, 16

Or. Rev. Stat. § 131.005(11) 16

Or. Rev. Stat. § 166.250(11) 9

OTHER AUTHORITIES

4 Wayne R. La Fave, *Search and Seizure: A Treatise on the Fourth Amendment* (3d ed. 1996)..15, 23, 24

Webster's Third New Int'l Dictionary (unabridged ed. 1993)..................24

D. Statement of Jurisdiction

The federal rules require a statement of jurisdiction. In this section, you must state the basis for the district court's jurisdiction, the basis for the appellate court's jurisdiction, the relevant dates demonstrating that the appeal is timely, and the basis for claiming that the judgment or order appealed from is appealable,[7] as seen in Example 9.3-F. Often, the easiest way to provide this information is in chronological order. For example, of the events that need to happen to establish appellate jurisdiction, the district court must first have jurisdiction, so describe that first. Then, the district court must enter a judgment or appealable order, so describe that next. And so on. As with the other sections discussed above, to make this section persuasive, make it complete, concise, and error-free.

---

7. Fed. R. App. P. 28(a)(4).

Example 9.3-F · Statement of jurisdiction

The district court had jurisdiction of this action under 28 U.S.C. §§ 1331 and 1346(a)(2). The district court granted plaintiff's motion for summary judgment and entered a permanent injunction on June 10, 2015. Defendants filed their notice of appeal on July 5, 2015, within the 30-day time limit allowed by Federal Rule of Appellate Procedure 4(a)(1)(A). This court has jurisdiction under 28 U.S.C. § 1291, which provides for review of all final decisions of district courts.

The trial court's jurisdiction is established in the first sentence.

The court's appellate jurisdiction is established in the second and last sentences. Under 28 U.S.C. § 1291, federal courts of appeals have jurisdiction from all final decisions of district courts. Summary judgment and a permanent injunction are final decisions.

The timeliness of the appeal is established by stating the rule establishing a 30-day timeline for filing the notice of appeal (Fed. R. App. P. 4(a)(1)(B)), the date of the final decisions, and the date the notice of appeal was filed.

E. Issue (or Question) Presented

In the issue (or question) presented[8] you finally have an opportunity to write some beautiful prose, foreshadowing your argument or arguments. Here, you must begin to put some careful thought into how you want to pitch your case. "In law," Supreme Court Justice Frankfurter explained, "the right answer usually depends on putting the right question."[9]

The issue presented serves several functions. First, of course, it tells the court what legal issue is presented by the appeal. For example, it may tell the court that the question in the case is not whether violent video games generally are bad for children, but specifically whether, under the First Amendment, a state is required to demonstrate a direct causal link between violent video games and physical and psychological harm to minors before the state can prohibit the sale of the games to minors.[10]

Second, the issue presented allows you to frame the issue in a way that advantages your client. A good issue presented will concisely present a legal issue with just enough facts to give it context and to persuade. To persuade, the question presented should suggest an answer that is favorable to your client. Some appellate lawyers will specifically aim for a question presented that leads to a "yes" answer, believing that creating a question that leads to a "yes" answer has the most persuasive value.

Because you can choose how to define the legal issue the court is to consider, the issue presented is a prime opportunity for persuasion. Be careful, however, not to mislead the court in your question presented; it must always accurately reflect the facts in the record and the relevant law.

---

8. The terms "issue presented" and "question presented" are used interchangeably. Choose the phrase that is used in your jurisdiction. Also, if more than one issue is raised in the appellate brief, make your chosen term plural, as in "issues presented" or "questions presented."

9. Rogers' Estate v. Helvering, 320 U.S. 410, 413 (1943).

10. *See Brown v. Entm't Merchants Ass'n*, 564 U.S. 786 (2011).

Questions Presented in Objective vs. Persuasive Writing

You have probably already figured this out, but the questions presented in objective writing, such as a memo, are very similar to the questions presented in persuasive writing, such as a brief. In both cases, the question presented must be concise and accurate and describe the key facts on which the issue will turn.

The difference between the two lies in the dual function of the question presented in an appellate brief. In an appellate brief, the question presented not only narrows the issue and informs the reader, but also is an opportunity to begin persuading.

Finally, after reading the issue presented, a judge should be intrigued and motivated to read the rest of the brief to discover your argument about what the answer should be.[11]

An effective issue presented will usually have three parts:

- The controlling law
- The determinative facts
- The legal conclusion that is at issue

As discussed below, those parts may be presented either in a single sentence or in several sentences.

1. The "short form" or single-sentence question presented

One easy way to present all three parts of an effective issue presented is in the "Under-Does-When" format.[12]

Under the controlling law

Does/Is/Can the legal conclusion result

When the determinative facts occur

You can see each of these parts in Example 9.3-G.

---

11. For a more detailed discussion about effectively constructing a question presented, *see* Christine Coughlin, Joan Malmud Rocklin & Sandy Patrick, *A Lawyer Write: A Practical Guide to Legal Analysis* 229–40 (3d ed. 2018).

12. We believe the originators of this format are Laurel Currie Oates, Anne Enquist, & Kelly Kunsch, *The Legal Writing Handbook: Analysis, Research, and Writing* (1st ed. 1993).

Example 9.3-G · An effective question presented in three parts

---

Under Wisconsin state common law, which requires specificity in contracts, does an apple grower breach his contract when an apple grower contracts to supply 10,000 bushels of Scarlet Gala apples to a distributer, but delivers only Royal Gala apples?

Of the three parts necessary for an effective question presented, the most critical—and often most difficult—is the selection of determinative facts. Those facts can suggest the "yes" or "no" answer that is favorable to your client. And those facts provide you with the opportunity to leave the court intrigued about the arguments that will follow. Selecting those facts can, however, be difficult because you cannot include every determinative fact. Doing so would create an overly long and unreadable question presented. Rather, you must select those facts that are *most* determinative and favorable to your client, and you must describe those facts accurately and precisely.

You can see how Example 9.3-G above has effectively framed the issue. After reading Example 9.3-G, you may suspect that the answer is "yes." You likely know that the law requires "specificity in contracts." You also know from the facts given that the contract specified Scarlet Gala apples, yet no Scarlet Gala apples were delivered—only Royal Gala were. Thus, this question presented persuades while it explains the legal issue the court must address.

One key to leading a judge to the answer you seek is to include facts supported by the record, rather than your characterization of the facts. If your question presented is supported by facts in the record, rather than your interpretation of them, the judge must accept them. For example, in Example 9.3-H, the facts lead the judge to conclude that the citizen has been "stopped" for Fourth Amendment purposes. By contrast, in Example 9.3-I, the judge first has to determine whether your characterization of the facts is accurate before she knows whether the answer is "yes" or "no." That diversion—during which the court must ascertain whether you have presented facts or characterized the facts—will undermine your credibility and, ultimately, make your question presented less persuasive.

Example 9.3-H · An issue presented that relies on facts

Under the Fourth Amendment to the United States Constitution, does a police officer perform a "stop" when, dressed in uniform, with a clearly visible badge and gun, she approaches a citizen and states, "Sir, I strongly suggest that you tell me whether you have any controlled substances on your person"?

Example 9.3-I · An issue presented that characterizes the facts

Under the Fourth Amendment to the United States Constitution, does a police officer perform a "stop" when, flaunting her gun and badge, she advances on a citizen and demands to know whether he is hiding drugs?

After ensuring that you have the content that you want, then you must ensure that the content reads well. That inquiry often focuses on how many facts you have chosen to include in your question presented. If the custom or requirement in your jurisdiction is to write a question presented in a single sentence, then you will have to work especially hard to make your question presented readable. Your question presented should include only the determinative facts; other details should be omitted. If the court's conclusion depends on its analysis of a lot of facts, then you may not be able to include all the determinative facts. Rather, you should choose the facts that are most likely to sway the court toward the outcome you seek and rely on just that subset of facts.

When the law is complex or the record includes numerous determinative facts, it may not be possible to write a coherent question presented in one sentence. In those situations, you should consider using the long-form question presented.

2. The "long-form" question presented[13]

Traditionally, the issue presented was written as a single sentence; however, lawyers now frequently use more than one sentence to explain the issue (or issues) before the court. Sometimes, a single sentence is sufficient, but if your local rules and customs allow, using more than one sentence to present the issue may allow you to present the question more fully and more persuasively.

To see how a long-form question presented can make the judge's job easier, compare the two versions of the same question presented provided in Examples 9.3-J and 9.3-K.[14]

---

13. The most well-known proponent of the long-form question presented—which he calls the "deep issue"—is Bryan Garner. For an extended discussion of the deep issue, *see* Bryan A. Garner, *The Winning Brief* 77–131 (3d ed. 2014); Bryan A. Garner, *The Deep Issue: A New Approach to Framing Legal Questions*, 5 Scribes J. Legal Writing 1 (1994).

14. The questions presented in Examples 9.3-J and 9.3-K are derived from *State ex rel. Juvenile Dep't v. Nicholls*, 87 P.3d 680 (Or. Ct. App. 2004).

Example 9.3-J • A weak question presented: too much information forced into one sentence

Whether, when the legislature amends the law so that a sentence may ← Under this rule, extend to a youth defendant's 25th birthday, when previously it could extend only to the youth defendant's 21st birthday, and the youth defendant here was found guilty of violating a provision of the juvenile code before the law ← when these facts occur, was amended, but who was committed to juvenile detention until his 25th birthday after the amendment, that sentence violates the *ex post facto* clauses ← does this conclusion result? of the Oregon Constitution.

Example 9.3-K • An effective question presented: information is divided into sentences of reasonable length

The Oregon Constitution prohibits a retroactive increase in "punishment" ← Under this rule, for a "crime." In 1994, the youth was committed to juvenile detention until his 21st birthday—the maximum time then allowed under Oregon's juvenile code. In 1995, the legislature allowed juvenile commitments to extend to a juvenile's ← when these facts occur, 25th birthday. In 1997, the juvenile court committed the youth to juvenile detention until his 25th birthday. Was the four-year increase to the youth's ← does this conclusion result? commitment an increase in "punishment" for a "crime" such that it violates Oregon's constitution?

The second version, Example 9.3-K, is preferable because it is written in understandable sentences of reasonable length, yet it still contains all the same information that is included in the single-sentence "under-does-when" format. Perhaps most importantly, drafting with more than one sentence provides greater flexibility in both sentence length and content and, thus, provides greater opportunity for persuasion.

Here are two more examples of the long-form question presented. As you read Examples 9.3-L and 9.3-M, consider how each would read as a single sentence.

Example 9.3-L • A long-form question presented[15]

Oregon Revised Statutes § 161.405(1) provides that "[a] person is guilty ← Under this rule, of an attempt to commit a crime when the person intentionally engages in conduct which constitutes a substantial step toward commission of the crime." Here, defendant attempted to hire a "hit man" to kill several people. ← when these facts occur, Is hiring someone else to commit a crime a "substantial step" toward commission of the crime? ← does this conclusion result?

---

15. This example is based on the issue presented in *State v. Kimbrough*, 431 P.2d 76 (Or. 2018).

Example 9.3-M · Another long-form question presented[16]

Under this rule, ──────▶   Under state law, a court may revoke a defendant's probation if the defendant violates a condition of probation. In this case, Defendant was convicted of manufacture of a controlled substance and placed on optional probation for 36 months. As conditions of that probation, Defendant was to obey all laws, was not to use or possess controlled substances (except pursuant to a medical prescription), and was to submit to urine tests. Defendant admitted to possessing and using methamphetamine during that 36-month period, and she tested positive for methamphetamine metabolites in her urine. Did the trial court abuse its discretion in revoking probation?

when these facts occur,

does this conclusion result? ──────▶

3. The question presented as a syllogism

The issue presented may also be constructed persuasively by using a syllogism. As discussed in §3.3, *Structuring Rule-Based Arguments*, a syllogism consists of a major premise, a minor premise, and a conclusion that logically follows if the major and minor premises are true. Bryan Garner describes the long-form or deep issue presented as a type of syllogism:

> It's a multi-sentence issue statement that begins with a legal premise, then states a factual premise or miniature story demonstrating the applicability or inapplicability of that legal premise, and ends in a short question devoid of new information. Essentially, it's a syllogism ending in a question mark.[17]

Syllogisms work well when drafting an issue presented because the structure essentially puts forth two premises and a conclusion. If the two premises are true, then the conclusion must also be true. Consider Example 9.3-N:

Example 9.3-N · An issue presented as a syllogism[18]

The major premise (bolded) is a statement of law.

The minor premise (underlined) is a factual statement—a description of a particular New York law.

The proposed conclusion—that the law is unconstitutional—flows from the major and minor premises.

    This Court has held that the second amendment to the United States Constitution protects "the individual right to possess and carry weapons in case of confrontation." <u>New York prohibits its ordinary law-abiding citizens from carrying a handgun outside the home without a license, and it denies licenses to every citizen who fails to convince the state that he or she has "proper cause" to carry a firearm.</u> Does New York's law violate the Second Amendment?

---

16. This example is based on the respondent's brief in the Oregon Court of Appeals, *State v. Galati*, 66 P.3d 1029 (Or. App. 2003).

17. Bryan A. Garner, *Going Deep: The key to effective pleadings is a clear and succinct statement of the issues—and here's how to do it*, 103 ABA L. J. 26 (2017).

18. This example is based on the petition for certiorari to the United States Supreme Court in *New York State Rifle & Pistol Ass'n, Inc. v. Corlett*. Petition for Certiorari at 1–3, *N.Y. State Rifle & Pistol Ass'n, Inc. v. Corlett*, 804 F.3d 242 (2d Cir. 2015).

In Example 9.3-N, the major premise cannot be challenged — it includes a statement of law announced by the very court that the brief is filed in. The minor premise also seems incontrovertible, assuming it is an accurate description of the law at issue. Finally, the conclusion follows if the major and minor premises are true.

Framing a question presented in the form of a syllogism is an effective means of both informing the court of the legal issue in the case and in beginning to persuade the court that the issue should be resolved in your client's favor.

4. Incorporating the standard of review

In framing the issue presented, consider the relevant standard of review. Framing the issue presented in terms of the relevant standard of review shows the court that you recognize the importance of standards of review and reminds the court what the relevant standard is, as illustrated above in Example 9.3-M.

Moreover, the standard of review may persuade an appellate court that it has limited room to act, such as in Example 9.3-O. In Example 9.3-O, the issue presented frames the issue in terms of an abuse of discretion, a high hurdle for a challenging party to overcome. By incorporating the "abuse of discretion" phrase, the writer immediately establishes that the appellate court may have limited capacity to act. After reading the question presented in Example 9.3-O, the judge likely will be thinking two things: "This lawyer speaks my language!" and "It will take a lot to convince me that the lower tribunal abused its discretion."

Example 9.3-O · Incorporating the standard of review

Oregon Uniform Trial Court Rule 5.050 provides, "There must be oral argument if requested by the moving party in the caption of the motion or by a responding party in the caption of a response," but gives the court discretion in determining the time allowed for the argument. The court granted 15 minutes for oral arguments on the question of whether the defendant would be permitted to substitute counsel two days before trial was to begin. Did the trial court abuse its discretion in allowing 15 minutes for oral argument?

You are most likely to incorporate the standard of review into your question presented when you won below (thus, you are the respondent) and the applicable standard requires deference to the trial court. For example, if you won below, and the appellate court will review for an abuse of discretion or for clear error, reminding the appellate court of the deferential standard of review will tilt the question presented in your favor.

Because appellate judges are so familiar with the de novo standard for questions of law, appellate practitioners are less likely to incorporate the standard of review into the question presented when the standard of review is de novo. Nonetheless, if you lost below, and you want to emphasize that the question before the appellate court must be resolved with no deference to the lower tribunal, you should consider referring to the de novo standard in your question by, for example, using the phrase "as a matter of law."

If the applicable standard of review is debatable and you intend to argue that a certain standard should apply, you should draft a question presented devoted solely to that issue.

5. Organizing multiple questions presented

As explained above in Chapter 3, *Organizing Persuasive Arguments*, you should have one argument to support each legal claim in your brief. Similarly, you should have one question presented to address each legal issue that you raise on appeal. When a case involves more than one question presented, the problem arises in what order to present them. First, the order of your issues presented should match the order of the arguments in the body of your brief. To do otherwise only confuses the audience. Second, as with the arguments in your brief, order your issues presented with the following three principles in mind: (1) threshold issues first, (2) stronger arguments before weaker ones, and (3) broader relief before narrower relief.

For example, if doubt exists about the trial court's jurisdiction over the case, you would raise that issue before presenting a question about the merits of the trial court's ruling. Similarly, if you have a strong argument that the trial court erred (or did not err) in its ruling, that issue should be presented before a weaker one. Finally, if, for example, in a criminal case, you are arguing that the trial court erred both in finding the defendant guilty and also in the sentence it imposed, you should present the issue about guilt or innocence (the broader relief) before the sentencing issue (the narrower relief).

6. A good question presented leads to a better brief

In addition to informing the court of the question that you want it to answer, the question presented serves one other very important function: It forces you, the advocate, to think very carefully about the issue you are bringing to the court. In drafting a brief, advocates often only vaguely consider the issue before the court, rather than precisely pinpointing the issue that the court must address.

For example, suppose you frame the question presented as, "Did the court err in ordering a new trial on the issue of damages?" If you argue generally about the amount of damages, you will not be addressing the proper question. Rather, the question you should present to the court is this question, which is significantly more focused: "The undisputed evidence was that plaintiff's special damages were $163,000. The jury however, awarded only $100,000. Did the trial court abuse its discretion in ordering a new trial on the issue of damages?"[19] By precisely stating the legal issue on appeal, both you and the court will properly focus on that issue.[20]

F. Statement of the Case

Appellate rules also require a statement of the facts, a statement of the case, or both.[21] Those sections explain the facts — both historical and procedural — relevant to the issues on appeal. Chapter 10, *Statements of Fact and of the Case,* discusses how to draft those sections.

G. Summary of the Argument

Most appellate court rules require a summary of the argument or arguments in the brief. The following provision is typical: "[An appellant's brief must contain] a summary of the argument, which must contain a succinct, clear, and accurate statement of the arguments made in the body of the brief, and which must not merely repeat the argument headings[.]"[22]

The summary should not be so long that it simply repeats the argument. Nor should it be so short that it does not give the judge a flavor of the argument ahead. The summary should be a readable, succinct summary of your argument. If the brief raises a number of issues, it may be appropriate to have separate summaries of argument for each issue.

Example 9.3-P is a summary of one argument.

Example 9.3-P • Summary of argument

This Court should affirm the judgment of the trial court on any one of the following three independently adequate grounds.

First, defendant never preserved the claimed error of law, and thus this Court should not address it. Defendant claims that the trial court erred in excluding testimony of defendant's brother that defendant was not at the scene of the crime. Although defense counsel made a vague allusion to the proffered testimony, she never made an offer of proof regarding exactly what the witness would have said. This court has stated on numerous occasions that a specific offer of proof is necessary to preserve a claim that evidence was improperly excluded. Defendant's claim of error is thus not preserved for appellate review.

The summary of argument, which generally does not include citations to the record or to authority, describes the legal argument the judge will be considering. The summary primes the reader, making the full argument easier for the reader to digest.

---

19. *See McClain v. Owens-Corning Fiberglas Corp.,* 139 F.3d 1124 (7th Cir. 1998).

20. We thank Oregon Court of Appeals Judge Steven Powers for reminding us that a more focused question presented can be as helpful to the advocate as it is to the court.

21. *See, e.g.,* Fed. R. App. P. 28(a)(6).

22. Fed. R. App. P. 28(a)(7).

Second, even assuming that this Court addresses defendant's claim of error, the trial court did not abuse its discretion in excluding the testimony. The trial court excluded the evidence on the ground that its probative value was substantially outweighed by the danger of unfair prejudice. This Court consistently has held that a trial court has "great latitude" in excluding or admitting evidence under that rule and, here, the trial court's choice was well within the bounds of discretion.

Finally, even if the trial court had erred in excluding the testimony, the error would have been harmless. Four other witnesses — a nurse, a pastor, a physician, and an accountant — all testified they saw defendant at the scene of the crime; the video from three different surveillance cameras corroborate that testimony.

Thus, the evidence that defendant wished to introduce was appropriately excluded, and the judgment of the trial court should be affirmed.

Notice the effective use of thesis sentences in Example 9.3-P. Each thesis sentence urges the court to adopt a particular conclusion that is beneficial to the state's cause. If you read down the thesis sentences in Example 9.3-P, the thesis sentences alone outline the argument. Strong thesis sentences that assert a conclusion you want the court to adopt will make your summary of the argument more persuasive.

Practitioners differ as to whether they prefer to write the summary before or after they have written the argument. You may choose to use the summary to outline your argument, writing it before drafting the complete argument. Doing so allows you to see your argument in its purist form, without supporting authority or detail. Alternatively, you may write your argument first, and then simply summarize it. Whichever approach you choose, you must be sure that, in finalizing the brief, the summary and the argument are consistent. If the summary of argument has not been updated to reflect changes that you have made to the argument, you will have a confused judge on your hands.

H. Argument

By the time the judge reaches the argument section of your appellate brief, the judge has seen the cover of your brief; the table of contents and the summary of the argument, both of which give an overview of the case; a statement of the issues presented; and the statement of the case, which presents the facts as you see them. If you have correctly prepared those parts of the brief, the judge will arrive at your legal argument knowing what the case is about, knowing what arguments are before the court, and knowing that you are an intelligent, trustworthy lawyer. In short, the judge should be predisposed to be convinced.

Two earlier chapters, Chapter 5, *Drafting Persuasive Arguments*, and Chapter 6, *Refining Persuasive Arguments*, explain in detail how to build a persuasive legal argument, whether for a trial motion or an appellate brief. No matter the format, your argument should be organized, concise, well-written, and supported by citations to the record (for factual assertions) or to authorities (for legal assertions). The argument section should include headings and, because those same headings will make up the table of contents, they should be descriptive and persuasive. You should use transitions, correct grammar, engaging sentence and paragraph structure, and accurate punctuation. In short, the argument section should be a professional, persuasive, easy-to-read chunk of persuasive prose.

One special aspect of appellate brief arguments deserves discussion. As you may remember, standards of review are important to appellate courts. Accordingly, incorporating the standard of review into your arguments is helpful. Indeed, the federal rules require that, in your argument, you identify the standard of review. Specifically, the rule states that, "for each issue, a concise statement of the applicable standard of review (which may appear in the discussion of the issue or under a separate heading placed before the discussion of the issues)" must be included.[23]

But making the standard of review work *for* you is better than just setting it out in a separate section. The next several examples illustrate how to incorporate the standard of review into your argument. Consider Examples 9.3-Q and 9.3-R, two versions of the same assertion, with a subtle difference.

Example 9.3-Q • A less effective assertion because it does not incorporate the standard of review

---

The trial court erred in granting summary judgment in favor of the defendants on the ground that the statute does not violate the First Amendment.

Example 9.3-R • A more effective assertion because it incorporates the standard of review

---

The trial court erred as a matter of law in granting summary judgment in favor of the defendants on the ground that the statute does not violate the First Amendment.

Both statements assert that the trial court erred. The second one, however, inserts the phrase "as a matter of law." That phrase subtly reminds the appellate court that the trial court's ruling is reviewed de novo, with no deference to the trial court's view. That is, the phrasing reminds the court that the standard of review is relatively favorable to the appellant, and it shows the court that you know the standard of

---

23. Fed. R. App. P. 28(a)(8)(B); *see also, e.g.,* Or. R. App. P. 5.45(5) (requiring that the appellant's brief "identify the applicable standard or standards of review, supported by citation to the statute, case law, or other legal authority for each standard of review").

review. The phrasing demonstrates that you are speaking the same language as the appellate judges.

Here is another example. Suppose that you represent a defendant who won the jury trial below. During that trial, the trial court decided to exclude the plaintiff's evidence under Federal Rule of Evidence 403 on the ground that its probative value was substantially outweighed by the danger of unfair prejudice. The plaintiff is now appealing. Now compare Examples 9.3-S, 9.3-T, and 9.3-U. Those examples show three versions of a statement you might make in response to the plaintiff's brief claiming that the trial court erred in excluding the evidence:

Example 9.3-S · Assertion, but no reference to the standard of review

The trial court did not err in excluding the evidence under Federal Rule of Evidence 403.

Example 9.3-T · Assertion with direct reference to the standard of review

The trial court did not abuse its discretion in excluding the evidence under Federal Rule of Evidence 403.

Example 9.3-U · Assertion with a reminder about what the standard of review means

Although this court or another court might have ruled differently, the trial court did not abuse its discretion in excluding the evidence under Federal Rule of Evidence 403.

The first version, Example 9.3-S, is adequate. It states your position.

The second version, Example 9.3-T, is better. It includes the standard of review when it says that "[t]he trial court did not abuse its discretion." By incorporating the "abuse of discretion" language, Example 9.3-T reminds the appellate judge that a great deal of deference is owed to the trial court's decision.

The third version, Example 9.3-U, is a more forceful way of including the standard of review. As you will recall, an issue is reviewed for an abuse of discretion when the issue could be resolved in a number of permissible ways, and the only question is whether the trial court chose one of several permissible resolutions. Thus, by reminding the appellate judge that "this court or another court might have ruled differently," Example 9.3-U also reminds the court that the standard of review is abuse of discretion and that a great deal of deference is owed to the trial court's decision.

What makes the third version, Example 9.3-U, the most effective is that it talks to the appellate judge like a real person. That version addresses what the appellate judge might be thinking—"I sure wouldn't have ruled that way"—but reminds the judge that the trial court's decision cannot be reversed simply because the judge would not have ruled that way. Thus, Example 9.3-U translates the legal standard, "abuse of discretion," into what it means for the appellate judge as the judge wrestles with the issue presented.

Once you have decided to incorporate the standard of review, the question is where to do so. Because the standard of review is usually coupled with the conclusion you are seeking under that standard, the best place to remind the court of the standard of review is anywhere that you would assert the conclusion to that legal issue. As discussed in Chapter 6, *Refining Persuasive Arguments*, the three places where you will most often assert a conclusion is in a point heading at the outset of an argument, the topic sentence that begins an argument, and the final sentence that sums up an argument.

Consider incorporating the standard of review into those three places. Doing so (1) enhances your credibility by showing the court that you understand the importance of standards of review; (2) strengthens your argument if the standard of review is favorable to your position; and (3) forces both you and the court to focus on the legal issue in light of the standard of review.

I. Conclusion and Relief Sought

The final section of the brief is the conclusion and relief sought. As with some of the other parts of the brief, this section often receives too little attention. Spending a few extra minutes to carefully think about this section and to draft it accordingly will enhance your brief and avoid confusion regarding what you really want the court to do.

The look of this section varies among appellate courts. In some courts, this part of the brief consists of something like the summary of argument, followed by a request for relief, as in Example 9.3-V.

Example 9.3-V · Conclusion that summarizes and states relief sought

---

In conclusion, this court should reverse Defendant's conviction. As explained above, the trial court erred in denying Defendant's motion to exclude the evidence of Defendant's mental illness on the ground that it was irrelevant. But even if the court upholds Defendant's conviction, it should reverse and remand for resentencing. That is so because, for the reasons set out above, Defendant's sentence is cruel and unusual in violation of the Eighth Amendment.

In other courts, the conclusion is simply another formulaic section, often consisting of a single sentence, as in Example 9.3-W or 9.3-X.

Example 9.3-W · Formulaic conclusion and request for relief

For the foregoing reasons, the trial court's judgment should be reversed.

Example 9.3-X · Another formulaic conclusion and request for relief

Therefore, the judgment should be reversed.

Check the rules, ask for sample briefs from your colleagues, or search for briefs written by well-respected attorneys in your jurisdiction to determine how this section should look.

Think carefully about what relief you seek from the court and make sure (1) that the court can grant the requested relief in light of its authority and the procedural posture of the case and (2) that the relief sought is consistent with the arguments made in the brief. For example, asking the appellate court to simply "reverse the judgment" is not always appropriate. Your request may be to vacate the judgment, to modify the judgment, to remand for reconsideration, or to remand for entry of an order directing a party to take a certain action.

Whether you write a short summary followed by a request for relief, or you simply make a request for relief, put some thought into what relief you are requesting. If the only argument in your brief is that the trial court erred in the sentence it imposed in a criminal case, the only relief you can request is a remand for a modified sentence. Your conclusion should not assert, "Defendant's convictions should be reversed." In short, make sure that your request for relief follows from the arguments in the brief.

III. Briefs for Different Parties

Most briefs will include the parts described above. Those parts may, however, vary based upon the governing procedural rules and whether the party is drafting the opening brief, the respondent's brief, or a reply brief. The sections that follow discuss the circumstances under which you might decide to omit one or more parts in the appellate brief you are drafting.

A. Appellant's Brief

If you are drafting an appellant's brief—the opening brief—you must include all the parts that are required by the appellate rules in your jurisdiction. Those parts are typically the parts listed above in section II, *Building a Brief.*

B. Respondent's Brief

A respondent's brief usually includes all the same parts as the appellant's opening brief, but the respondent has the option of accepting one or more of the appellant's statements and omitting that section from the respondent's brief. The federal rules, for example, state that, unless the respondent is dissatisfied with the appellant's statement, a respondent's answering brief need not include the jurisdictional statement, the statement of the issues, the statement of the case, or the statement of the standard of review.[24]

Some lawyers are loath to "accept" anything that their opponents have proposed. As a result, respondents often repeat parts of the appellant's brief, with no substantive changes. You should not do that. If you accept certain parts of the appellant's brief and omit those parts from your own brief, you serve a number of goals. First, you save space in your brief that can be devoted to persuasive writing, rather than repetition. Second, you help yourself and the court pinpoint where the disagreement is. For example, if you accept the appellant's statement of the case, everyone is on the same page about which facts will be relevant to the appeal. Third, accepting parts of the appellant's brief saves the judge time and energy. If the judge does not have to spend time determining whether your slightly different statement of jurisdiction means that you really disagree or whether you are just being overzealous, the judge has more energy to consider your argument.

C. Appellant's Reply Brief

Finally, an appellant will often file a brief in response to the respondent's brief. Reply briefs are not always allowed.[25] Before assuming that you can file a reply brief, check the rules.

If a reply brief is permitted and the appellant decides to file one, then the reply brief will look very much like the opening or responding brief. However, you will include only those parts of the brief that are necessary to respond to the opposing arguments. Usually, after a cover, table of contents, and table of authorities, the reply brief jumps straight into the argument.

When constructing a reply brief keep in mind two additional points. First, never "save" an argument for the reply brief. The appellant should make all the arguments the appellant intends to make in the appellant's opening brief. The reply brief should be used only to address points made

---

24. Fed. R. App. P. 28(b).

25. For example, under the Oregon Rules of Appellate Procedure, the appellant in a habeas corpus case is not allowed to file a reply brief without leave of court. Or. R. App. P. 5.70(3)(a). Other jurisdictions may have similar rules.

in the respondent's brief that were not addressed in appellant's opening brief.

Reply briefs may be useful to respond to the following types of arguments that a respondent makes: that the case has become moot after your opening brief was filed; that a claim of error raised in your opening brief is not preserved or that the claimed error is harmless; that a new authority, which came out after you filed your opening brief, supports the respondent's position; or that the record supports a different view of the facts from that set out in your opening brief.

Second, do not file a reply brief unless you have something to say. If your reply brief will merely repeat the points you made in your appellant's brief, do not file one; the court will be grateful.[26]

Practice Points

- Before you begin drafting, take these steps:
  - Know the rules that govern appellate procedure.
  - Know the standard (or standards) of review that apply to each issue in your case.
- An appellate brief usually has these parts:
  - A cover
  - A table of contents
  - A table of authorities
  - A statement of jurisdiction
  - A statement of the issues (or questions) presented
  - A statement of the case
  - A summary of the argument
  - The argument
  - A conclusion
- When writing a respondent's brief or an appellant's reply brief consider carefully which sections of a traditional appellate brief are necessary to assist the court and convey your argument. Draft only those sections.

---

26. Some advocates suggest that not filing a reply brief is a sign of strength because it suggests the other party has not come up with any arguments that weaken your position. Other appellate advocates, however, disagree, pointing out that it is helpful to get the last word in. They also suggest that if an appellant does not file a reply brief, judges will assume that the appellant agrees with the respondent. However, we suggest that to avoid burdening the court with unnecessary reading, avoid filing a reply if you have nothing further to add.

Chapter 10

Statements of Fact and of the Case

At the heart of every legal issue lies a story. The word "story" does not refer to fiction. Rather, you are explaining the factual story that gave rise to the controversy before the court. Whether you are drafting a motion or an appellate brief, you will be responsible for telling that story. This chapter explains how to tell that story so that the court can see the facts from your client's vantage point, whether you are telling that story in a trial or appellate brief.

In explaining your client's story, you have two goals. First, you are laying the factual foundation for the legal argument that will follow. You will need to explain all the facts that will be relevant to the court's analysis of the legal issue, and you will need to explain those facts with scrupulous accuracy. That means you must include all legally relevant facts, whether those facts hurt or help your client.

In explaining those facts, you have a second goal. Your second goal is to allow the judge see the story from your client's perspective. You will want to make the busy judge care about your client. If you remember from Chapter 1, *The Nature of Persuasion,* the statement of facts lets you take advantage of a powerful mode of persuasion—*pathos,* that is, persuading by appealing to the audience's emotions. Although the emotional appeal will be subtle, you can influence how the judge connects with your client. You can highlight those facts that make your client seem reasonable and sympathetic and place difficult facts in context. In fact, if your client's story is explained effectively, a judge should be inclined to rule in favor of your client before the judge has even read the legal arguments.

To meet those goals, you will need to make deliberate choices about how you frame the conflict, portray the parties, and organize the story. This chapter addresses those choices.

I. Statements of Fact vs. Statements of the Case

The section of your brief in which you present your client's story will usually be designated as either the "statement of facts" or the "statement of the case." Whether you present a statement of facts, a statement of the case, or both will depend on the rules in your jurisdiction.

Some jurisdictions ask for both a statement of facts and a statement of the case. If the rules call for both, then the statement of facts will describe the historical facts—the conflict between the parties up until the time the case entered the court system—and the statement of the case will describe the procedural facts—those facts that relate to the case once it entered the court system.[1]

---

1. The section that describes procedural facts sometimes has names other than statement of the case. For example, some jurisdictions require that procedural facts be explained in a "statement of the nature of the matter before the court" or through a "preliminary statement."

Sometimes, though, the court rules will ask for only a statement of facts or only a statement of the case. If so, then you will explain both the historical facts and the procedural facts in that one section.

Accordingly, you should read the rules in your jurisdiction before you begin writing to determine whether the court will expect both a statement of facts and a statement of the case or whether one section will contain both the historical and procedural facts.

For convenience, we will refer to the "statement of facts" throughout. The same advice applies no matter the name of the section.

II. Present the Conflict and Your Client

Before you draft, take a step back and consider the role of "conflict" and "character" in your client's story. If you took a literature class in high school or college, you may remember that the three main elements of any good story are character, conflict, and resolution.[2] Those elements also come into play in drafting a persuasive and engaging statement of facts.

A. Frame the Conflict

The conflict that gave rise to your client's case may very well fall into one of several traditional kinds of conflicts. Thinking about the kind of conflict that exists in your case may give you new ways of thinking about your client, the problem before you, and how to present your client and your client's problem to the court. Chart 10-A lists some traditional kinds of conflicts found in stories.

Chart 10-A · Traditional kinds of conflicts[3]

- Person versus Nature
- Person versus Society (or Society versus Person)
- Person versus Self
- Person versus Machine
- Person versus Person
- Person versus God

---

2. Much has been written in recent years about the power of story in legal analysis. This chapter touches on those ideas only briefly. For more information on the topic, consider these resources: Brian J. Foley & Ruth Anne Robbins, *Fiction 101: A Primer for Lawyers on How to Use Fiction Writing Techniques to Write Persuasive Facts Sections*, 32 Rutgers L.J. 459 (2001); Ruth Anne Robbins, Steve Johansen, & Ken Chestek, *Your Client's Story* 121–31 (2d ed. 2019); Legal Writing Inst. Monograph Series, *Vol. 10: Legal Storytelling* (Anne E. Ralph, ed., 2021).

3. Foley & Robbins, *supra* note 2, at 472.

Your story will likely present one of these conflicts. For example, say you represent a student with autism in a claim against the public school system. The heart of your client's claim is that the school is not providing sufficient opportunities for the student in the mainstream classroom, in violation of a federal statute. In that case, you might frame the conflict as "person versus machine." Here, your client, the child with autism, is the person, and the machine is the behemoth school system that grinds forward without considering the individual needs of each student.

On the other hand, if you represented the school system, you would frame the conflict very differently. Then, you might frame the conflict as "person versus society," but your client, the school system, would be the person. You would humanize the school system by presenting it as a collection of people who do care, but who lack the financial and human resources to meet the needs of one student at the expense of hundreds or thousands of others. You would present the battle as one against a society that does not adequately fund education or give educators the resources they need to help individuals.

Too often, attorneys default to the most common conflict, "person versus person." Although that conflict nearly always exists in litigation, that framework may not lead a judge to intuitively side with your client. In a "person versus person" conflict one person must be portrayed as the hero and the other as the villain.[4] A judge, however, usually knows that neither party is entirely hero or villain. If the judge does not immediately agree with your portrayal, your narrative will have lost its power.

Although you probably will not explicitly name the kind of conflict that exists in your client's case, assessing the type of conflict may provide a valuable perspective that will help you use facts in the case in the most advantageous way. To assess the type of conflict, answer the following questions before you draft a statement of facts.

- What kind of conflict would best fit this story?
- What facts illustrate this conflict?
- If you must use "person versus person," what facts can you use to present the story in the most reasonable and objective way without overly glorifying one side or vilifying the other?

Once you have assessed how the conflict can best be framed, you are ready to think about how to portray your client and the other characters in the story.

---

4. *Id.*

B. Cast the Characters

In addition to a conflict, every legal story also has a cast of characters—major players and minor players.[5] The major player is the "protagonist," or the good guy, and the "antagonist," or the bad guy with whom the good guy is in conflict. Attorneys usually want to cast clients as the protagonists, or the good guys; at a minimum, they do not want their clients to be perceived as the bad guys.

When casting the story's characters, take the same thoughtful approach as you did when framing the conflict. Although no character is completely a hero or villain, you may be able to cast your client in a more favorable light.

Think about what heroic (or otherwise positive) qualities you want to highlight. Then think about what facts support those characterizations. Do the same for the other major characters in the story, avoiding the blatant labels of villain or bad guy.

Although we encourage you to think about your conflict and your client in heroic terms, that process is to get you thinking. Remember that the next step is to find the facts that will lead the judge to see your client and the conflict in a way that most benefits your client. You will never write, "My client is 'every man' in a conflict against machine." Rather, you will state facts that will allow a judge to reach that conclusion on his own. The rest of this chapter explains how to find and shape those facts.

III. Decide Which Facts to Include

As mentioned above, as you are thinking about the conflict and the role your client plays in the conflict, you will need to cull the record to find the facts that will make your perspective evident to the court.

As you read through the entire record, make a list of the facts that appear to be relevant. Include both positive ones that help your client's position and negative ones that undermine your client's position. You can then use this list to help you categorize and label your facts as well as to assess their value in the story.

---

5. *See id.* at 466–67; Robbins, Johansen, & Chestek, *supra* note 2, at 121–31. *See generally* Ruth Anne Robbins, *Harry Potter, Ruby Slippers and Merlin: Telling the Client's Story Using the Characters and Paradigm of the Archetypal Hero's Journey*, 29 Seattle U. L. Rev. 767 (2006).

Usually, your facts will fall into three categories: legally significant facts, background facts, and emotional facts.

A. Include All Legally Significant Facts

When drafting a statement of facts, begin by focusing on the "legally significant facts." Legally significant facts are the facts necessary for the court to resolve the legal issues in the case. These facts may sometimes be called "key facts," "determinative facts," or "critical facts." No matter what name is used, these facts are the ones on which the court's decision will turn.

Your statement of the facts must include *all* legally significant facts, whether those facts help or hurt your client. If you omit a negative fact, you lose the opportunity to present that fact in context and minimize its impact. Moreover, the judge will see the negative facts anyway when reading the opposing party's brief and examining the record or supporting documents. Your work will be more credible and trustworthy if the judge sees that you have forthrightly presented *all* the facts. Instead of running from negative facts, take advantage of the opportunity to present the negative facts in a way that supports your theory of the case.

To ensure that you have included every legally significant fact, begin, as mentioned above, by reviewing the record. In addition, re-read your own argument. Highlight every fact that you relied on and make sure that that fact is in your statement of facts. Remember, judges do not like to be surprised, so be sure to include all the facts where the judge expects to see them—in the statement of facts.

Finally, consider whether your statement of facts should point out the absence of a legally significant fact. Sometimes pointing out the absence of a fact can be helpful to your client. For example, in an intentional infliction of emotional distress case, the plaintiff must establish that he suffered "severe" emotional distress. As the defendant, you might point out that the plaintiff never contacted a doctor or therapist for treatment regarding any emotional distress. Later, you would argue that the absence of a visit to a doctor or therapist demonstrates that the plaintiff did not suffer severe emotional distress and that, therefore, the claim should fail. In such a case, the absence of a fact is important to note.

B. Include Enough Background Facts to Provide Context

Background facts are facts that explain the context in which the controversy takes place. Background facts allow the court to understand your client's situation and how the conflict arose; they provide a frame for the details necessary to resolve the case. Provide enough background facts for the legally significant facts to make sense. That said, be selective about the background facts that you include. Judges assume that the statement of facts focuses on legally significant facts. Including too many background facts will distract and confuse the judge about which facts are actually relevant to the legal issues.

In all forms of communication, readers absorb a message when they are provided with context before detail; so too with statements of facts. Present the facts with enough contextual information so that the court can understand the detail.

C. Include Emotional Facts Selectively

Emotional facts are a kind of background fact that cause a reader to feel positively toward one party or negatively toward another; that is, they invoke *pathos*. Emotional facts are not necessary to resolve the legal issues, but they may help the judge understand what motivated a party to act or react in a particular way. Often, the judge will connect with your client through the emotional facts you choose.

Although emotional facts may help a judge sympathize with or understand your client better, you must choose your emotional facts with care. Too many emotional facts, especially when those facts seem irrelevant to the legal issues, may make a judge skeptical of the brief's objectivity. Accordingly, when constructing a persuasive statement of facts, choose emotional facts selectively.

Consider Examples 10-B and 10-C. Both offer openings to a statement of facts in which the primary issue is whether a university violated Title IX when it eliminated its women's golf team. The opening in Example 10-B provides facts that help put the plaintiff, a member of the golf team, in a positive light and the university in a negative light.

Example 10-C attempts to do the same thing, but by spending too much time on facts that are not relevant to the legal issues, the emotional facts ultimately detract from the narrative.

Example 10-B · Choosing emotional facts to support the story

Plaintiff Katelyn Mason is a scholarship student who came to Defendant Central State University of Utah to play on its varsity golf team. Mason Depo. 8:4–6. Less than a year after Ms. Mason arrived, Central State eliminated the women's golf team. Blasher Depo. 15:12–16:18. The University plans to replace golf with a sport not yet recognized by the National College Athletic Association (NCAA): cheerleading. *Id.* 22:8–19. Ms. Mason is now seeking to enjoin Central State from eliminating its golf team on the ground that eliminating golf and replacing it with cheerleading would violate Title IX. Am. Compl. ¶ 8.

In the 1970s, Title IX prompted Central State to establish its women's athletic program....

Because the central issue in the case is whether the University violated Title IX by not providing enough athletic opportunities to its female students, the particular details about Ms. Mason's success as a golfer are not legally relevant. Those facts are "emotional facts." Those emotional facts are included to generate sympathy for the plaintiff who—if the suit is not successful—may have difficulty continuing with her golfing career.

Example 10-C • Too many emotional facts detract from the story

The emotional facts are those that put Ms. Mason in a positive light and the university in a negative light; however, the extent of those details is likely to annoy a judge because the judge will struggle to understand their relevance and wonder why her time is being wasted.

For example, the plaintiff's status as an "A" student, her role as president of her class, the colleges that recruited her, and her golfing record both before and during college add details that are unnecessary and, together, will bog the judge down.

Plaintiff Katelyn Mason came to Defendant Central State University of Utah to play on its varsity golf team. Mason Depo. 8:4–6. Before arriving at Central State, Ms. Mason was an "A" student, president of her class, and a noted golf player. *Id.* 9:10–12. She had won first place in the 2020 and the 2021 U.S. Juniors Invitational, and she had won second place at the Junior Ryder Cup in Perthshire, Scotland. *Id.* For all of these reasons, Ms. Mason was heavily recruited by other colleges and universities, including Williams College, The University of Hawaii, and Stanford University. *Id.* 10:15–11:4. Nevertheless, she chose to attend and play golf for Central State. *Id.* 11:21–24. Once at Central State, she had a successful year, contributing to the varsity golf team's 10–1 record and leading the team to its second-place finish at the NCAA Golf Championship. *Id.* 12:02–13:15.

Despite the success of the golf team, Central State decided to eliminate the women's golf team after Ms. Mason had played for just one season. Blasher Depo. 15:12–16:18. The University decided to replace golf with a sport not yet recognized by the National College Athletic Association (NCAA): cheerleading. *Id.* 22:8–19. A wide range of students and alumni protested the decision; the University nevertheless moved ahead, eliminated the golf team, and replaced it with a cheerleading team. *Id.* 26:2–25. Ms. Mason is now seeking to enjoin Central State from eliminating its golf team on the ground that eliminating golf and replacing it with cheerleading would violate Title IX. Am. Compl. ¶ 8.

In the 1970s, Title IX prompted Central State to establish its women's athletic program....

In addition to being selective about the emotional facts that you include, be sure to stick to the facts. Because emotional facts attempt to place one's client in a sympathetic light, some lawyers make the mistake of providing their opinion about their client (and the opposing party) rather than stating the facts. A lawyer's opinion or characterization of the facts is far less persuasive than the facts themselves; indeed, your opinion about the facts has no place in a statement of facts. Example 10-D attempts to provide the same facts as Example 10-B, but instead Example 10-D (in the shaded text) states the writer's opinion about the facts.

Example 10-D • State the facts, not your opinion about the facts

Plaintiff Katelyn Mason is a gifted student and junior golf player. She came to Defendant Central State University of Utah to play on its varsity golf team. Mason Depo. 8:4–6. Less than a year after Ms. Mason arrived, Central State suddenly and inexplicably eliminated the women's golf team. Blasher Depo. 15:12–16:18. The University plans to replace golf with an activity that is not even a recognized sport: cheerleading. *Id.* 22:8–19. Ms. Mason is now seeking to enjoin Central State from eliminating its golf team on the ground that eliminating golf and replacing it with cheerleading would violate Title IX. Am. Compl. ¶ 8.

In the 1970s, Title IX prompted Central State to establish its women's
athletic program....

For a good example of a brief that uses emotional facts selectively,
look again at the brief of John Roberts in the *"Red Dog Mine"* case mentioned in Chapter 1, *The Nature of Persuasion*. Without choosing overtly-
emotional facts or inserting his opinions and characterizations, Roberts
firmly establishes the economic importance of the mine to the remote
community in a subtle way.

> Operating 365 days a year, 24 hours a day, the Red Dog Mine is
> the largest private employer in the Northwest Arctic Borough,
> an area roughly the size of the State of Indiana with a population
> of about 7,000. The vast majority of the area's residents are Inupiat
> Eskimos whose ancestors have inhabited the region for thousands
> of years. The region offers only limited year-round employment
> opportunities, particularly in the private sector.... Prior to the
> mine's opening, the average wage in the borough was well below
> the state average; a year after its opening, the borough's average
> exceeded that of the State.[6]

Roberts selected these facts with care. After reading this passage, a judge
will undoubtedly realize than any decision adverse to the mine will
negatively impact the people who live there. Thus, with a subtle use of
pathos, his phrasing creates a commanding narrative that helps the legal
reader connect to that litigant's side of the story.

In sum, be selective about the emotional facts you include, particularly
when your purpose for using those facts is to paint your client in a positive
light or to cast the opposing party's actions in an undesirable light.
Moreover, when you do include such facts, be sure to stick to the facts
rather than characterizing or inserting your opinion about those facts.

D. Include Procedural Facts

Together, the legally significant facts, the background facts, and the
emotional facts tell your client's story from your client's perspective. In
addition to that story, you will also need to tell the story of the case once
it entered the court system. As with any story, the procedural story will
be better told if you are selective. Once litigation begins, attorneys file

---

6. From Brief for Petitioner, *Alaska, Dept. of Environmental Conservation v. U.S.
E.P.A.*, 540 U.S. 461 (2004), available at 2003 WL 2010655 (citations omitted); *see
also* Ross Guberman, *Five Ways to Write Like John Roberts*, http://www.legalwriting
pro.com/pdf/john-roberts.pdf.

a variety of different pleadings, they engage in discovery, and they file motions that address issues large and small. You do not want to detail all of it.

Rather, highlight the particular points that brought you to the current brief you are filing. Thus, if you are drafting a motion for summary judgment, the only procedural history you might include is that the plaintiff filed a complaint and, after discovery, the defendant is now filing a motion for summary judgment. By contrast, if the case went to trial and the current dispute is whether the jury verdict should stand, you would likely note that a complaint was filed (in a civil case), that the case went to the jury, and that the verdict was returned. You would not note a motion for summary judgment, unless the motion for summary judgment raised the same issue that the current motion involves. Finally, if you are drafting an appellate brief, your statement of the procedural facts would identify each trial court decision that you believe was in error.

Notice that in drafting the procedural facts you again have the opportunity to persuade. Compare Examples 10-E and 10-F. Both examples point out the key procedural events: plaintiff filed a complaint, defendants moved to dismiss that part of the complaint that sought punitive damages, and the current appeal followed. Notice, though, the plaintiff's emphasis on the jury's decision to award her damages. She emphasizes the defendants' bad act (discriminating against her) and that she won below. A jury found in her favor, and jury decisions are difficult to overturn. By contrast, the defendants, who lost in the lower court, focus on what they believe was the trial court's error: allowing the plaintiff to seek punitive damages.

Example 10-E • Procedural facts from the plaintiff-respondent's perspective

---

Statement of the Case

On February 15, 2023, plaintiff-respondent Amy Russo filed a complaint against defendants-appellants, Williams University and Adam Lam. R. 3. The complaint alleges that Williams University and athletic director Adam Lam willfully and intentionally discriminated against the respondent on the basis of her gender by paying her unequal wages. R. 2. The complaint also alleged that, in response to Ms. Russo's stated intent to file a discrimination claim, Williams University and Adam Lam retaliated by firing her. R. 2.

On December 3, 2023, the district court judge denied the defendants' motion to dismiss Ms. Russo's claim seeking punitive damages under 29 U.S.C. §215(a)(3). The case proceeded to jury trial. R. 85. The jury awarded Ms. Russo compensatory, liquidated, and punitive damages. R. 86. After the jury returned its verdict in favor of Ms. Russo, the defendants appealed. R. 92.

Respondent's recitation of procedural facts identifies all the important procedural steps that led to the appeal, but it also emphasizes that she won below.

Example 10-F · Procedural facts from defendants-appellants' perspective

Statement of the Case

In February 2023, plaintiff-respondent Amy Russo filed a complaint against defendants-appellants, Williams University and Adam Lam. R. 3. Before trial, the defendants moved to dismiss that part of Ms. Russo's complaint that sought punitive damages, arguing that the plain language of the Fair Labor Standards Act does not permit punitive damages. R. 80. The district court denied the motion, and after a jury verdict in favor of Ms. Russo, which included punitive damages, R. 86, the defendants filed this appeal. R. 92.

Appellants' recitation of procedural facts similarly describes all the important procedural steps leading to the appeal, but appellants focus on the decision that they believe to be in error and minimize their loss below.

E. Weed Out Irrelevant Facts

As you decide which facts to include, think carefully about which facts to exclude. Irrelevant details make it harder for the court to see which facts are important. They distract. Thus, aim to exclude any details that are not relevant to the legal story or that do not explain the story from your client's perspective. The most common types of irrelevant material are dates, places, and names.

Specific dates can—and should—be excluded if that date is not legally significant. The date on which something occurred is not relevant if all that matters to your story is the order in which events occurred and not the precise date on which they occurred. Look at Example 10-G, an excerpt of the statement of facts for a case in which the legal issue stems from the quality of a good delivered under a contract. Since the issue in the case is not one of *when* the contract was negotiated and signed, all the dates are irrelevant and should be eliminated.

Example 10-G · Irrelevant facts distract

On December 25, Defendant and Plaintiff began negotiating a contract for the sale of hops. Clark Dep. 2:16–22. They reached a tentative agreement on December 31, but on January 1, they determined that they were unsatisfied with that tentative agreement. Clark Dep. 22:1–23:2; Bruce Dep. 42:1–8. It was not until February 29 that they reinitiated negotiations. Clark Dep. 36:6–10; Bruce Dep. 55:16–56:10. The contract was finalized on April 1. Clark Dep. 41:6–10; Bruce Dep. 60:18–22.

Irrelevant dates are distracting. The judge will wonder whether these characters work only on holidays (and, by the way, was that a leap year?). Most likely, the judge is wondering, "Do I need to remember these dates?" Unless specific dates are needed, consider instead focusing on the sequence of events, as in Example 10-H.

Example 10-H · Re-write to omit irrelevant facts

The parties began negotiating the sale of hops in late 2022. Clark Dep. 2:16–22. Following on-again, off-again negotiations, they signed a contract in early April 2023. Clark Dep. 22:1–36:10, 41:6–10; Bruce Dep. 42:1–56:10, 60:18–22.

Keeping track of too many minor players' names also becomes tiresome and distracting for the judge. Thus, when introducing a minor character, it is usually best to introduce the minor character by that character's role in the story and to omit the person's proper name. For example, a minor player like "Investigating Detective Leonard Briscoe" or "Director of Operations, Erin Nalle," can be introduced as "the investigating officer" or "Director of Operations" in the facts and argument sections.

The primary parties and other significant players should be introduced by their names and their role in the story. Avoid using their status in the litigation. For example, in a civil proceeding you might introduce the parties by name and by their role in the story. Then, throughout the rest of the statement of facts, you could call that major player by name or by their role (for instance, "landlord" or "employer"). You would not, though, tend to call the parties by their litigation status of plaintiff or defendant, unless doing so would be helpful. A person's status in the litigation will not usually create as strong an image in the judge's mind and is, therefore, less useful.

Despite that general advice, one time when you might designate a major player by that person's litigation status (as opposed to that person's status in the story) is if you are a prosecuting attorney in a criminal case. If you are a prosecutor, "the defendant" may be the best designation because it reminds the court that the person has been charged with, or perhaps has even been convicted of, a crime. On the other hand, a defense attorney would want to personalize the defendant and refer to the person by name.

Compare the two excerpts from a statement of facts in Examples 10-I and 10-J. The argument in that case is about whether evidence obtained from a search must be excluded because the police obtained the search warrant by relying on evidence from an involuntary confession. Accordingly, details about who executed the search warrant and where and when it was executed are irrelevant.

Example 10-I · Irrelevant facts distract

Officers Zal and Izaguirre executed the warrant at 10:34 a.m. at the defendant's residence, located at 234 Fifth Street, Canton, Ohio, 44701. Zal Aff. ¶ 2.

Example 10-J · Omitting irrelevant facts is better

Police officers executed the warrant at the defendant's trailer. Zal Aff. ¶ 2.

To be sure, some dates, some names, and some places will be important enough to the story to warrant specificity. For example, if the issue before the court is whether an action was filed within the applicable statute of limitations, the exact dates when events occurred become extremely important. The point is to think about which details your reader will need (and which your reader won't need), so you can leave out those distracting details.

IV. Organize Your Statement of Facts

Once you have determined which facts to include in your statement of facts, you must decide how to organize the facts. A facts section is usually organized chronologically, topically, or perceptually, depending on the type of issues you are presenting and the complexity of the story. No matter how you choose to organize the facts section, always start the facts in a way that will grab the reader's attention and provide necessary context for your client's story.

A. Create an Opening Paragraph that Provides Context and Draws the Reader In

The first paragraph, and even the first sentence, of your facts section is a great place to attract the judge's attention and entice the judge to read more. A famous litigator once said that the opening paragraph of a statement of facts should be like a two-minute morality play for the court that establishes the characters and frames the conflict.[7] Remember, the statement of facts is your first opportunity to bring the parties and the legal issues to life.

In addition, the first paragraph or two of your statement of facts should provide context for your reader by introducing the parties, their status in the story, and the crux of the conflict between the parties. Giving even minimal context is more effective than jumping into the chronological details of the story without any context.

> **Once Upon a Time...**
>
> Sometimes when it comes time to write the statement of facts, you are so deep in the weeds that it is difficult to know where to begin. In that case, imagine that you are describing the case to a friend and beginning with, "Once upon a time...." Imagining that you are begining your statement of facts with "Once upon a time..." will likely help you back up and provide the context your reader needs.

---

7. Conversation with attorney Rudolph Aragorn, international litigator at White & Case law firm (April 2014).

For example, in Example 10-K, look at how the lawyer uses the first two paragraphs to introduce the parties and the crux of the dispute. In explaining the crux of the dispute, the attorney stayed focused on the facts and answered the judge's basic questions: Who are the parties involved? Why is one party suing the other party? In this example, the first paragraph grabs the reader's attention, tells who the parties are, and directly presents the crux of the issue at hand.

Example 10-K • Opening paragraphs of a statement of facts[8]

Defendant's two pit bulls, running loose and without permission, spotted Plaintiff's pet cat and mauled her to death. R. 10. Plaintiff ran from her house and attempted to stop the attack, but could not. R. 10. After the dogs dropped the mauled cat and ran away, Plaintiff saw that her cat was gravely injured but still alive. R. 13. She immediately rushed her cat to the veterinarian, but the cat died en route. R. 14–15.

The trial court concluded that Defendant was negligent and awarded Plaintiff $1,000 in compensatory damages but denied Plaintiff's claims for negligent infliction of emotional distress and loss of companionship. R. 40, 52–53. Plaintiff now appeals the trial court's denial of her claim for negligent infliction of emotional distress. R. 72.

Similarly, the opening paragraph in Example 10-L provides context and begins to generate sympathy for an employer who has fired an employee. In that case, the employer's perspective is that the employee is suing the company because she is a disgruntled employee who has been fired. Thus, the employer's statement of facts opens with the fact that the employee was dismissed after receiving a negative job review.

A statement of facts in that same case, but written from the employee's perspective, would open with different facts, as in Example 10-M. That opening introduces the employee as a successful, long-term employee, who was fired only after she became concerned that her employer was violating environmental regulations.

Example 10-L • The opening paragraph in a persuasive statement of facts (defendant's perspective)

On November 29, 2023, plaintiff Julie Stark was dismissed from her employment with defendant Michigan Power & Electric, Company (MPE). (Dep. Julie Stark, 10:21–22.) Her termination followed a negative performance review. (Dep. Julie Stark 10:1–2.) Ms. Stark now claims she is entitled to protection from being dismissed because she is a whistle-blower. (Pl.'s Compl. ¶¶ 15–22.)

---

8. Based on *Lockett v. Hill*, 51 P.3d 5, 6 (Or. Ct. App. 2002).

Example 10-M · The opening paragraph in a persuasive statement of facts (plaintiff's perspective)

Plaintiff Julie Stark, a long-time employee of defendant Michigan Power & Electric, has also been a long-time advocate for a healthy planet. (Dep. Julie Stark, 8:2-16; 22:4-23:10.) Thus, in October 2023, when Julie Stark discovered that MPE might be ignoring environmental regulations, she spoke out. (*Id.* at 11:6–12.) MPE then fired her. (*Id.* at 12:16–22.)

The opening paragraphs of both Example 10-L and Example 10-M provide context, name the parties, and begin to provide sympathy for each client. Although they sound very different, each is an accurate presentation of the facts.

Sometimes, however, the opening paragraph will not be so exciting, particularly when the underlying issue is a procedural one. Still, you can create an opening paragraph that will introduce the parties and conflict and focus the judge's attention on the critical facts, as in Example 10-N.

Example10-N · Opening paragraph of statement of facts in which only issue on appeal is a procedural issue

---

This case involves a dispute under the Clean Water Act, 33 U.S.C. § 1251 *et seq.*, in which plaintiff Yalohosee Riverkeepers alleged that defendant Zimels Performance Fabrics illegally discharged effluent into navigable river waters. R. 2–3. Although trial took three weeks and the record is voluminous and technical, the sole issue on appeal is whether the trial court correctly denied defendant Zimels's motion for a three-week continuance under the circumstances described below. R.55. Because the sole issue on appeal is procedural, this statement of facts details only the events surrounding the trial court's ruling on the motion for a continuance.

No matter whether the underlying issues in the case are exciting factual ones or drier procedural ones, fashion your first paragraph in a way that introduces the parties and the conflict, grabs (or at the very least focuses) the judge's attention, and begins to shape the version of the story your client wants to tell.

B. Choose a Logical Organization

After providing an opening that introduces the parties and the problem from your client's perspective, you must decide on an organizational structure for the facts that follow. You can organize chronologically (telling facts in the order in which the events occurred), topically (presenting facts by topics like issues or categories), or perceptually (presenting facts from the various participants' vantage points).

Facts are usually set forth in chronological order because readers (including judges) tend to better comprehend stories told in sequence. Accordingly, you will most often present facts in chronological order.

Although chronological order may be your default method of organization, be open to using other organizational options. A topical organization might make sense if, for example, you need to discuss both the company's corporate structure and the facts about the allegedly defective pressure cooker that the company produced. Likewise, a perceptual organization might make sense if your case involves a business transaction that occurred in three locations. You might, then, discuss how the transaction developed from the perspective of the people in those three locations.

You may even use a combination of these organizational schemes. Imagine, for example, that you have a contractual dispute that involves three very different issues under the contract with different sets of facts relevant to each issue. You could have a topical organization for each contract provision that is in dispute, but then you could tell the facts regarding the execution of that part of the contract chronologically.

One organizational approach that is rarely a good idea is to simply summarize the testimony of each witness in the order it is given, whether that be by deposition in advance of trial or on the witness stand during trial. For one thing, the testimony of every witness may not be relevant to the issues. Second, summaries can be choppy, thus interrupting the flow of a good story. Finally, summaries can be unclear, not showing how the events or characters of the story are connected. Because witnesses may be deposed or called to the stand "out of order"—usually for scheduling reasons—merely summarizing the record sequentially may simply frustrate and confuse the judge. Frustrated and confused judges are harder to persuade than happy and interested judges.[9] Your job is to figure out how the evidence connects and show those connections to the judges.

---

9. Look at how one court responded to a statement of facts presented, not as a cohesive story, but as individual witness summaries:

> We base this summary of the facts on our review of the record, assisted by plaintiff's helpful statement in her brief. In its brief, the City [the defendant] fails either to describe the facts most favorably to the jury's verdict or to do so in narrative form. Rather, it summarizes each witness' [sic] testimony seriatim, requiring the court to attempt to determine the relationship between the events that the various witnesses described. [Thus]...the City fails to comply with...basic principles of effective appellate practice.

Storm v. McClung, 4 P.3d 66, 68 n.1 (Or. Ct. App. 2000), *aff'd*, 47 P.3d 476 (Or. 2002).

When in doubt, you should organize your facts chronologically. You should not, however, be wedded to that approach. When deciding on an organization, think about how you could most easily explain the story to a friend over a dinner conversation. Using that organizational order allows you to tell the story clearly and succinctly.

C. Use Point Headings to Guide Your Reader

Point headings in your statement of facts operate much as they do in your argument. Point headings help the reader understand your organization, and they alert the reader to the main points the section will address.

The most significant difference between point headings in your argument and point headings in a statement of facts is that, in your statement of facts, the point headings do not assert a legal conclusion. Rather, they describe the kinds of facts that will be addressed in that section of your statement of facts. In other words, your point headings will be descriptive, rather than assertive.

Another difference is that, in your statement of facts, the point headings may not be complete sentences. When arguing, you want to assert a complete idea; thus, a full sentence that clearly asserts your point is both appropriate and necessary. By contrast, when your goal is to describe, rather than assert, a descriptive label may be sufficient, as in Example 10-O.

Example 10-O · A descriptive point heading

C. The night of June 21.

Of course, you are not prohibited from using a full sentence; however, if you do, be certain that you are asserting an indisputable fact and not making an argument. Compare Examples 10-P and 10-Q. Example 10-P states a fact. Example 10-Q, in contrast, likely asserts an argument.

Example 10-P · A full sentence as a descriptive point heading

C. Julie McGee died on the night of June 21.

Example 10-Q · A full sentence that may assert an argument

C. Defendant killed Julie McGee on the night of June 21.

One last point with respect to point headings: If you choose to include point headings, be consistent. If you use a full sentence for one point heading, use full sentences throughout. If you choose not to use full sentences, do that throughout.

D. Close Your Statement of Facts

Once you have crafted a strong opening paragraph and organized your facts logically, spend some time on your last paragraph or at least the last sentence of the statement of facts. The final paragraph or sentence should provide closure to the statement of facts, leaving the judge ready to read your arguments. Importantly, though, your statement of facts should end with a fact, and not a legal argument. For example, your final sentence in a statement of facts might be written as in Examples 10-R or 10-S. You would not want a final sentence as in Example 10-T.

Example 10-R · A final sentence that states a fact

Defendant now appeals. R. 72.

Example 10-S · A final sentence that states a fact

Plaintiff then filed a complaint alleging that she was fired in retaliation for exercising her protected First Amendment rights. Pl's. Compl. ¶¶ 4–5.

Example 10-T · A final sentence that (inappropriately) argues

As explained next, Plaintiff was fired in retaliation for exercising her protected First Amendment rights.

V. Create a Persuasive Statement of Facts

Because the statement of facts is the court's first introduction to your client and the controversy before the court, you will want to take advantage of every opportunity to persuade. The tone of the section, the placement of information, and even word choice can have an impact on the judge reading your motion or brief. Remember, your goal is to make the judge want to rule for your client. The way in which you write your statement of facts can influence how much the judge wants to rule for your client. The following strategies will help you draft a more persuasive statement of facts.

A. State Facts Accurately

Of all the techniques for creating a persuasive statement of facts, the most important technique is to state facts accurately and precisely. An accurate description of the facts means that any fact you describe in your statement of facts is consistent with the record in the case. An accurate statement of facts is one that includes *all* facts that will be relevant to the court's decision, whether those facts are helpful to your client or not.

Zealous advocacy should never trump your duty to be accurate. Although you want to present the facts from your client's perspective, never overstate or misrepresent a fact. Overstating or misrepresenting facts not only triggers ethical questions about your practice, but doing so can alienate your reader. The facts will not always be good for your client. Some facts may be quite detrimental. Nevertheless, never avoid the detrimental facts. As discussed above, the statement of facts is your place to put them in perspective. It can, of course, be tempting to stretch the facts to serve your client, particularly when you know your client has been wronged. However, you will best serve your client by becoming an advocate who the court trusts. You will build that reputation for trustworthiness and, thereby, serve your clients best by always telling the truth, and never exaggerating, misstating, or lying. Writing a scrupulously accurate statement of facts builds credibility from the beginning.

> **Reminder!**
>
> To preserve your credibility (*ethos*) with the court, never overstate, misrepresent, or omit a relevant fact, even if that fact is detrimental to your case. Instead, put that fact in context and explain it from your client's perspective.

B. Maintain a Reasonable Tone

Strive for a tone that suggests objectivity even while presenting the facts from your client's perspective. You may feel passionate about your client's claims, particularly after spending months (or years) on the case. Even so, judges are usually put off by highly emotional briefs; judges become wary or skeptical if the passion in the brief suggests that you are too close to the case to present your side objectively. Although your facts can be written to subtly evoke empathy for your client, keep an eye (or ear) on the tone of the section. Keep the tone objective and credible.

C. Use Strong, Factual Thesis Sentences

As explained in Chapter 6, *Refining Persuasive Arguments,* a "thesis" is a proposition put forward for consideration. In a legal argument, the proposition put forward for consideration is a legal conclusion. Thesis sentences can, however, also be used to great effect in a statement of facts. In a statement of facts, a thesis sentence proposes a factual conclusion. Beginning a paragraph with a thesis sentence can focus the judge on the fact you want the judge to learn after reading the paragraph.

Compare Examples 10-U and 10-V.[10] In Example 10-U, the prosecuting lawyer does not use a thesis sentence when presenting facts about a defendant who was convicted of a mass shooting at a school. By contrast, in Example 10-V the prosecutor uses a thesis sentence to help the judge see the point that the facts support. In Example 10-V, the facts show that a pattern of violence had begun years before. By asserting that idea up front, the judge is primed to see the point the prosecutor wants to make.

Example 10-U · A paragraph without a thesis sentence leaves the judge to reach an independent conclusion about the facts

Although the paragraph does a good job of presenting the facts chronologically, without a thesis sentence, the judge will not know exactly what the paragraph is about. The paragraph is about much more than what happened when the defendant was four.

Defendant's interest in guns and knives began as early as age four. (Ex. 301, p. 860.) Defendant got "in trouble" in the second grade for bringing a knife to school. (Ex. 301, p. 972.) According to Defendant's fourth-grade teacher, Defendant had an "anger management problem." (Tr. 513.) Defendant would be aggressive if things did not go his way on the playground. (Tr. 513.) His fourth-grade teacher remembered Defendant throwing punches, placing other children in headlocks, and wrestling students to the ground. (Tr. 512.) He testified: "I think we were working on a behavioral management plan with our school counselor." (Tr. 510.) During that year, Defendant's disruptive behavior in the classroom sometimes would require his removal. In about the sixth grade, his interest expanded to bombs and explosives. (Ex. 301, p. 982.)

Example 10-V · A strong thesis sentence can state the factual conclusion you want the the judge to reach

With a strong thesis sentence, the judge will know what point the paragraph is making. By immediately understanding the context of the paragraph, the judge can focus on the detailed information that follows.

Defendant's behavior problems and violent tendencies manifested themselves at an early age. Defendant's interest in guns and knives began as early as age four; in about the sixth grade, his interest expanded to bombs and explosives. (Ex. 301, p. 860.) Defendant got "in trouble" in the second grade for bringing a knife to school. (Ct.'s Ex. 301, p. 972.) According to Defendant's fourth-grade teacher, Defendant had an "anger management problem." (Tr. 513.) Defendant would be aggressive if things did not go his way on the playground. (Tr. 513.) His fourth-grade teacher remembered Defendant throwing punches, placing other children in headlocks, and wrestling students to the ground. (Tr. 512.) He testified: "I think we were working on a behavioral management plan with our school counselor." (Tr. 510.) During that year, Defendant's disruptive behavior in the classroom sometimes would require his removal. (Tr. 512.)

Although using thesis sentences within your statement of facts can be very effective, it can also be a little tricky. In a statement of facts, a

---

10. Examples 10-U, 10-V, and 10-W are based on Respondent's Brief at 3, *State v. Kinkel*, 56 P.3d 463 (Or. Ct. App. 2002) (CA A108593).

thesis sentence must assert a factual conclusion that you want the judge to reach, and not a legal conclusion or an argument. Moreover, the facts that follow must, of course, support the assertion in the thesis sentence. Example 10-W shows an inappropriate thesis sentence when it appears in a statement of facts. The sentence is inappropriate because it asserts a legal conclusion rather than a fact.

Example 10-W • An inappropriate thesis sentence asserts a legal conclusion

---

Defendant began cultivating a mindset to commit murder during childhood. Defendant's interest in guns and knives began as early as age four. (Ex. 301, p. 860.) Defendant got "in trouble" in the second grade for bringing a knife to school. (Ex. 301, p. 972.) According to Defendant's fourth-grade teacher, Defendant had an "anger management problem." (Tr. 513.) Defendant would be aggressive if things did not go his way on the playground. (Tr. 513.) His fourth-grade teacher remembered Defendant throwing punches, placing other children in headlocks, and wrestling students to the ground. (Tr. 512.) He testified: "I think we were working on a behavioral management plan with our school counselor." (Tr. 510.) During that year, Defendant's disruptive behavior in the classroom sometimes would require his removal. In about the sixth grade, his interest expanded to bombs and explosives. (Ex. 301, p. 982.)

This thesis sentence is inappropriate because it assumes intent, an element in the underlying murder case. Because the writer asserts a legal conclusion rather than letting the facts speak for themselves, a judge is likely to become wary of whether the statement of facts is accurately presenting the facts or inappropriately slanting them in the party's favor.

Using thesis sentences in a statement of facts can be a very effective way of focusing the judge's attention on the point that you want to make. You should, however, craft your thesis sentences with care. Avoid stating a legal conclusion, and be certain that the facts that follow clearly establish the proposition stated in the thesis sentence. Overstating what the facts will show will undermine your credibility.

D. Highlight Good Facts and Minimize Unfavorable Facts

Rarely, if ever, will you have a perfect set of facts. As discussed above, you are ethically required to include negative facts that are legally relevant to the court's analysis. Your job now is to highlight how the good facts support your legal arguments and minimize the impact of the inconvenient or undesirable facts, while ensuring that your statement of facts is accurate.

1. Use location to your advantage

One way to highlight favorable facts is to put them in "positions of emphasis."[11] We have previously discussed positions of emphasis in

---

11. Mary Beth Beazley, *A Practical Guide to Appellate Advocacy* 279–80 (5th ed. 2019).

Chapter 6, *Refining Persuasive Arguments*. As explained there, one of the best ways to emphasize your main points is to put them where a judge is most likely to see and process them. The eyes of most readers tend to rest on point headings, the first sentence of each paragraph, and the last sentence of each paragraph.[12] Thus, put the facts you want to emphasize in those positions. By contrast, disclose adverse information in the middle of a paragraph and in the middle of sentences, where that information is likely to receive less emphasis.

Consider Table 10-X. That table shows two different versions of the same statement of facts. The statement of facts comes from a case in which an employee alleged that her employer fired her because she was "about to report" a violation of the law to the authorities. The lawyer who wrote the statement of facts represents the employer. That lawyer will later be arguing that the employee was not "about to report," as required by statute.

Now, compare the two versions of the statement of facts provided in Table 10-X. First, read each statement of facts from start to finish. Which is better? Then, for each statement of facts, read the first and last sentence of each paragraph. Which statement of fact uses positions of emphasis more effectively? In particular, notice how the factual thesis sentences in version one sets the stage for the employer's argument: the plaintiff is merely a disgruntled employee; she filed a report against the company because she was upset about being dismissed; she was not "about to report" a violation of law at the time of her dismissal; nor was she fired for that reason.

2. Give more airtime to favorable facts

Another way to highlight favorable facts is to describe favorable facts in more detail and to give those facts more "airtime." By contrast, address unfavorable facts more quickly and in less detail. By giving favorable facts more airtime and unfavorable facts less, you keep the judge's attention on the facts that strengthen your client's case and away from the facts that do not.

Consider version one from Table 10-X. Notice the "airtime" given to the idea that Ms. Stark was not taking any action with respect to her complaint. Lack of action helps prove that Ms. Stark was not "about to report" at the time she was fired, an important point for the employer. Thus, the employer's statement of facts repeats the idea that the employee had taken no action: She "had let her concerns languish for months"; "[s]he never submitted the complaint—not that month, nor the following month"; and "[t]wo months followed . . . [but s]till, she did not submit any complaint." By repeating that important fact, the employer emphasizes the employee's lack of action.

---

12. *Id.* at 122–23.

Table 10-X • Using positions of emphasis in a statement of facts

Version 1	Version 2
STATEMENT OF FACTS	**STATEMENT OF FACTS**
Plaintiff Julie Stark was an MPE employee who, on October 6, 2023, received a negative employment review. (Dep. Julie Stark 10:1–2.) Soon thereafter, on November 29, she was dismissed from MPE. (*Id.* 10:21–22.) Four days after she was dismissed, Ms. Stark filed a complaint with the state attorney general alleging that defendant MPE had violated the federal Clean Air Act. (*Id.* 11:1–4.) Ms. Stark contends that she should be protected from dismissal because she was about to report her allegations when she was dismissed. (Pl.'s Compl. ¶ 15.)	On November 29, 2023, Plaintiff Julie Stark was dismissed from her employment with defendant MPE. (Dep. Julie Stark, 10:21–22.) A month and a half before she was fired, Ms. Stark received a negative employment review. (*Id.* 10:1–2.) After she was dismissed, Ms. Stark filed a complaint with the state attorney general alleging that MPE had violated the federal Clean Air Act. (*Id.* 11:1–4.) Ms. Stark contends that she should be protected from dismissal because she is a whistleblower. (Pl.'s Compl. ¶15.)
In fact, Ms. Stark had let her concerns languish for months. (Stark 11:22–12:1.) Sometime during the first few days of October, Ms. Stark downloaded a complaint form from the state attorney general's office, filled it out with allegations against MPE, and saved it to her computer. (Stark 11:6–11:18; Ex. 1.) She never submitted the complaint—not that month, nor the following month. (*Id.* 11:22–12:1.)	Sometime during the first few days of October, Ms. Stark downloaded a complaint form from the state attorney general's office, filled it out with allegations against MPE, and saved it to her computer. (Stark 11:6–11:18; Ex. 1.) Ms. Stark did not, however, submit the complaint until after she had been dismissed. (Stark 11:22–12:1.)
During that time, what she did do was express her anger at receiving a negative job review. (Dep. Eric Block 22:3–23:12.) On October 6, Ms. Stark and her supervisor, Eric Block, reviewed her job performance. (*Id.* 18:6–8.) Her evaluation stated, among other things, that she "fails to follow directions" and that she "lacks the degree of teamwork and cooperation that MPE seeks in its employees." (*Id.* Ex. 1.) Ms. Stark responded by yelling at her supervisor that MPE was a bunch of "mega-polluters" and "criminals," that they would "live to regret it," and that she would "tell everyone." (*Id.* 24:2–25:15.) It was not clear to her supervisor, Eric Block, what Ms. Stark was referring to (*Id.* 26:4–8).	On October 6, Ms. Stark and her supervisor, Eric Block, reviewed her job performance. (*Id.* 18:6–8.) Her evaluation stated, among other things, that she "fails to follow directions" and that she "lacks the degree of teamwork and cooperation that MPE seeks in its employees." (Ex. 1.) Ms. Stark responded by yelling at her supervisor that MPE was a bunch of "mega-polluters" and "criminals," that they would "live to regret it," and that she would "tell everyone." (*Id.* 24:2–25:15.) It was not clear to her supervisor, Eric Block, what Ms. Stark was referring to. (*Id.* 26:4–8.)
Two months followed after Ms. Stark's exchange with her supervisor. (Stark 11:22–12:15.) Still, she did not submit any complaint to the state Attorney General's office or to any other public official. (*Id.*) In fact, it was not until Monday, December 3, 2015, four days after she was dismissed from MPE, that Ms. Stark submitted her complaint. (*Id.* 10:21–11:4, 11:19–12:2.) Thus, until she was discharged, Ms. Stark allowed her complaint to languish for months.	Two months followed after Ms. Stark's exchange with her supervisor. On Monday, December 3, 2015, four days after she was dismissed from MPE, Ms. Stark submitted her complaint. (*Id.* 10:21–11:4, 11:19–12:2.) This litigation followed.

3. Pair unfavorable facts with favorable facts

You can also minimize the impact of an unfavorable fact by pairing that unfavorable fact with a more positive fact, either in the same sentence or the same paragraph. A good fact will provide a bad fact with context and, thereby, allows the reader to absorb the bad fact in context. Take Example 10-Y. In Example 10-Y, the employer has to acknowledge that its former employee, Ms. Stark, downloaded a complaint form and threatened to tell people about the employer's alleged environmental misdeeds. Those facts are bad for the employer because they help the employee establish that she was "about to report" the employer's environmental violations. Because those facts are bad facts, the employer places those facts in context. The employer's statement of facts notes that, although the employee downloaded the form, she did not submit it for months. Although she did say that she would report her employer, the employee made her threat when she was angry about a negative job review. The paragraphs suggest that the employee's threat was made in the heat of the moment, and the employee never actually intended to act on it. By pairing the bad facts with good facts, the lawyer minimizes the impact of the bad facts while still providing the judge with an accurate and complete view of the story.

Example 10-Y · Pair a bad fact with a good fact

In fact, Ms. Stark had let her concerns languish for months. Sometime during the first few days of October, Ms. Stark downloaded a complaint form from the state attorney general's office, filled it out with allegations against MPE and saved it to her computer. (Dep. Julie Stark 11:6–11:18; *id.* at Ex. 1.) Although Ms. Stark downloaded the form, she never submitted the complaint—not that month, nor the following month. (*Id.* at 11:22–12:1.)

During that time, what she did do was express her anger at receiving a negative job review. (Dep. Eric Stark 22:3–23:12.) On October 6, Ms. Stark and her supervisor, Eric Block, reviewed her job performance. (*Id.* at 18:6–8.) Her evaluation stated, among other things, that she "fails to follow directions" and that she "lacks the degree of teamwork and cooperation that MPE seeks in its employees." (*Id.* at Ex. 1.) Ms. Stark responded by yelling at her supervisor that MPE was a bunch of "mega-polluters" and "criminals," that they would "live to regret it," and that she would "tell everyone." (*Id.* at 24:2–25:15.) It was not clear to her supervisor, Eric Block, what Ms. Stark was referring to. (*Id.* at 26:4–8.)

The shaded facts are "bad facts" for the employer. They are paired with "good facts," which are underlined. The good facts help mitigate or put the bad facts in context.

One way to pair an unfavorable fact with a favorable fact is to place the unfavorable fact in a dependent clause. A dependent clause provides additional information in a sentence, but it cannot stand alone as its own sentence. Because information in a dependent clause is implicitly understood by readers to be "additional" rather than "the main" information of a sentence, information in a dependent clause receives less attention. In Example 10-Z, negative information is put in a dependent clause (where it gets less attention), and the positive information is placed in the main clause.

Example 10-Z • A dependent clause minimizes a negative fact

Although neighbors harvested and kept some of the vegetables, the Neros told them they could do so. (Nero. Dep. 42:2–10; Walker Dep. 55:6–18.)

In an argument about whether a client had "exclusive possession" of land, the fact that others were allowed to harvest vegetables is a negative fact. Thus, that negative fact is paired with a more positive fact that shows "exclusive possession."

You can see the effect of the dependent clause by comparing version one and version two in Example 10-aa. Each time, the information in the dependent clause is minimized and placed in context by information in the main clause.

Example 10-aa • Information in the dependent clause receives less emphasis

Version 1: Although Moore's blood alcohol level was .13, she did not demonstrate any outward signs of intoxication. Officer Hanley Rpt. 1.

Version 2: Although she did not demonstrate any outward signs of intoxication, Moore's blood alcohol level was .13. Officer Hanley Rpt. 1.

Although dependent clauses are a great way to minimize undesirable facts, do not overuse this technique. Having too many dependent clauses in a row can be distracting to the reader. For maximum impact, use dependent clauses sparingly.

E. Choose Your Words Carefully

Subtle choices in language can make your statement of facts more compelling. Judges, like all of us, would rather read a dynamic, well-written story than a boring, uninspiring description of the record. To create a commanding narrative, choose your words carefully.

1. Choose vivid detail

One way to tell a more compelling story is to draw out graphic details that allow the judge to actually *visualize* what happened. In Example 10-bb, compare the two versions of the same event.

Example 10-bb • Neutral vs. vivid facts

Version 1: The defendant went through the red light before colliding with the plaintiff's automobile. Tr. 31–33.

Version 2: The defendant, driving his 3/4-ton pickup truck at a speed that
police later determined to be twice the speed limit, sped through
the red light and slammed into the plaintiff's compact car. Tr. 30–
33.

Which facts more dynamically convey the story? Version one truthfully
describes what happened, and it satisfies the cardinal rule that factual
statements must be accurate. But does that sentence tell the story in a
dynamic way? By contrast, version two includes vivid details that make
one believe that the defendant is guilty of driving recklessly.

Concrete, vivid detail can help a judge see your client's story as you
do; however, you must add such detail carefully. First, make sure the
details are relevant to your client's story and to the legal issues being presented. Vivid, but irrelevant, detail will annoy the judge. Second, make
sure the record supports your description. Vivid, but unsupported, detail
will also annoy the judge. Finally, make sure the vivid detail will support
your client's position. You do not want an unfavorable fact to be
highlighted in vivid detail.

2. Choose strong verbs

Another way to use word choice to emphasize a fact is to choose
your verbs carefully. Compare the two different verbs in Example 10-
cc. Version one uses the verbs "applied" and "placed." By contrast,
version two uses "choke" and "wrap." If you represent the store where
the security guard works, you might want to use the wording in version
one to downplay the physicality of the act and to implicitly suggest that
the security guard was following proper restraint procedure. If you represent the person who had been accused of shoplifting, however, you
would want to emphasize, not downplay, the physicality of the restraint
procedure.

Example 10-cc · The effect of verb choice

Version 1: The security guard applied a chokehold to the suspect by placing an
arm against the suspect's neck. Tr. 62.

Version 2: The security guard choked the suspect by wrapping his forearm
around the suspect's throat. Tr. 62.

Likewise, look again at what was Example 10-bb above, and what is
now Example 10-dd. Compare the effect of the verbs "went" and "colliding"
with "sped" and "slammed."

Example 10-dd · The effect of verb choice

Version 1: The defendant went through the red light before colliding with the plaintiff's automobile. Tr. 31–33.

Version 2: The defendant, driving his 3/4-ton pickup truck at a speed that police later determined to be twice the speed limit, sped through the red light and slammed into the plaintiff's compact car. Tr. 30–33.

Again, you want to choose your verbs with care. Your verb choice must be appropriate, supported by the record, and favorable to your client's position.

F. Provide Clear, Accurate Citations to the Record

An effective statement of facts will always provide accurate citations to show the court where those facts can be found in the record. Citing the record shows that your description of the events is grounded in reality. If the court wants to check the facts or needs more detail than you have provided, citations to the source of your facts will help the judges get that information.

Because citations make it easier for the judges to find the facts you are describing, you should cite nearly every sentence in your statement of facts. The only kinds of sentences that you might not cite are those that summarize other facts. The underlying facts, the ones that support the summary statement, should be cited.

Courts provide different rules about how to cite the record, so make sure to consult the court rules, local rules, and your jurisdiction's citation manual to ensure that your citations are appropriate. Anything in your brief that is different from the court's usual practice distracts the judge, slows down the judge's reading, and lessens the persuasiveness of your brief.[13]

If the form of the citation is not governed by rules or custom, balance the usefulness of the citation against how much it distracts from your narrative. Judges and their staff should be able to easily find the cited item in the record, but putting too much citation detail in the text of the statement of facts will make it harder to read and will water down your story. So, for example, if you were to file a brief in the United States Supreme Court and you wanted to reference a statement on page 12 of the appendix to the petition for certiorari, choose Example 10-ee rather than 10-ff.

---

13. Follow the citation rules for your jurisdiction. In the absence of local rules governing the form of your citation, both the *ALWD Guide to Legal Citation* and *The Bluebook* describe how to cite to court documents, transcripts, and the record. *See* ALWD & Carolyn V. Williams, *ALWD Guide to Legal Citation* 286–95 (7th ed. 2021) (R. 25); *The Bluebook: A Uniform System of Citation* 24–26 (Columbia L. Rev. Ass'n et al. eds., 21st ed. 2020) (R. B17).

Example 10-ee · Effective citation to the record

See Pet. App. 12.

Example 10-ff · Overly long, distracting citation to the record

---

See Appendix to the petition for certiorari of the Petitioner Xylorg Corporation, LLC, at page 12, line 22 (quoting finding of fact by the Honorable Judge Ralph Simone, entered in the record on October 26, 2023, afternoon session, United States Courthouse, White Plains, New York).

G. Let the Facts Determine the Length

Statements of fact vary enormously in their length. For example, if the issue involves whether a police officer "seized" a citizen for purposes of the Fourth Amendment, the statement of facts may include a detailed discussion of exactly where the contact took place; the time of day; who else was present; what the defendant was wearing; and the exact words the officer used when addressing the defendant. By contrast, if the underlying legal issue is one of statutory construction, your statement of facts may be very short because the legal question will focus on the statute and its history.

Think carefully about which facts the court needs to know to resolve the issues and which facts are interesting, but extraneous. Judges want shorter briefs. They do not enjoy slogging through irrelevant detail or expending their intellectual energy figuring out which detail is important.

Accordingly, choose your facts deliberately. Every fact should serve a purpose in telling your client's story. Every fact should support your legal analysis or inform the judge about an important background or emotional fact. If a fact does not serve one of those purposes, take it out.

H. Draft and Re-Draft

Attorneys draft their statement of facts at different times—some draft before they draft their argument, some draft after their argument is finished, and some alternate between the two. One good piece of advice is this: No matter when you initially draft your statement of facts, revisit the statement of facts after you complete your argument.

Your review should ensure that your statement of the facts is accurate, complete, and succinct. You should also confirm that the statement presents a favorable introduction to your client. Remember that the court meets your client for the first time in the statement of the facts.

To guarantee that your statement of facts includes all the relevant facts, review your argument and highlight every fact that you rely on. Then, make sure that those facts are included in your statement of facts. Think carefully about negative facts and whether you have addressed those facts in your argument and in your statement of facts.

Next, consider your opening. Do the opening sentences provide context for the facts ahead? As we explained earlier in this chapter, a reader is better able to absorb details if you first provide context for those details. In a statement of facts, you can provide that context by introducing the parties, their role in the litigation (are they plaintiff? defendant? appellant? respondent?), and the crux of the conflict at the outset of your statement of facts. Do not rely on a preceding preliminary statement or question presented to provide that context. The statement of facts should be a self-contained unit. Thus, when editing your statement of facts, make sure that, instead of jumping into the facts, you first provide context.

Then consider whether any descriptions of the facts need to be adjusted so that the statement of facts is consistent with your argument. Often, as you are drafting your argument, certain facts will take on more significance than you initially thought they would. Your statement of facts is the place to highlight those facts that will be most important to your argument.

Next, consider paragraph cohesion and paragraph length. As always, paragraphs should chunk similar information together. A new paragraph should signal new information. Review your paragraphs to see whether the content of each paragraph is a cohesive unit of like information. Although paragraphs can be of any length, readers need momentary breaks in their reading to pause and absorb information. The end of a paragraph signals that moment to readers. Ideally, to give readers the breaks they need, paragraphs should not exceed half a page. As you are looking for places to break up text, consider that guideline. Of course, life is not always ideal, and at times, you may need to exceed the half-page guideline. The half-page mark is simply a guideline that, when exceeded, tells you to look carefully to see if other points of division exist.

After you have paragraphs of related content and manageable length, consider the first sentence of each paragraph. Ask yourself whether the first sentence of each paragraph (a) accurately indicates the content of the paragraph to follow, (b) is favorable to your client, and (c) asserts a fact, not a legal conclusion. If the first sentence fails on any of these points, revise the first sentence of the paragraph.

Finally, and most importantly, ensure the accuracy of all the facts and citations to facts. Doing so is essential to your credibility or *ethos*. The judge and the judge's staff should be able to find every fact that you rely on and conclude that the fact, as stated, is true.

Practice Points

- Before writing your statement of facts, step back and consider how you wish to frame your client and the conflict.

- Include all legally relevant facts, enough background facts to provide context, and only select emotional facts.

- When organizing your statement of facts, begin by providing context: Who are the parties and what is the crux of their problem? After providing context, chronological organization is usually best. Sometimes, though, you will use another organizational system—topical, perceptual, or a hybrid of more than one approach.

- Always state facts accurately and completely. Acknowledge bad facts, but put them in context to minimize their impact.

Oral Argument

Oral argument before a trial judge or an appellate court is the most visible part of the persuasive process. Television shows and motion pictures focus on the drama of the courtroom rather than on the long hours spent alone with a computer drafting a memorandum in support of a motion or polishing a brief. But how does oral argument fit into the bigger picture of the persuasive process? What are the keys to a good oral argument, and how do you prepare for it? What are the pitfalls you should be aware of? This chapter addresses those issues and more.

As is true with written work, your oral argument will be most effective if you keep in mind the purpose of oral argument and the needs of your audience. Accordingly, the chapter begins with § 11.1, which addresses the purpose of oral argument and how both the advocate's and the court's needs can be met. Next, § 11.2 addresses how to prepare for oral arguments. Then § 11.3 examines how to present your argument. The advice in those first three sections holds true no matter the tribunal in which you will argue. Lawyers, however, present oral arguments to trial judges and to appellate judges (as well as to administrative law judges and administrative boards). So, § 11.4 focuses on the differences between trial courts and appellate courts. Finally, § 11.5 addresses adjustments you will need to make if you are arguing remotely.

The Purpose of Oral Argument

I. The Court's Goals
   A. Clarify Factual and Legal Points
   B. Determine the Practical Impact of a Ruling
II. The Advocate's Goals
   A. Ensure that the Court Understands Your Argument
   B. Correct Misapprehensions and Address Concerns
   C. Respond to Claims That You Could Not Address in the Briefs

Before oral argument, both you and your adversary will have submitted briefs to the court, but brief writing is a one-way information exchange.[1] The court has not had a chance to ask questions or otherwise interact with the advocates who wrote the briefs. In contrast, oral argument is an interaction among advocates and judges. It is the opportunity for the judges to interact and have a conversation with advocates that distinguishes oral argument from the rest of the persuasive process.

At oral argument, the judges' overriding goal is to enlist the advocates' help in understanding the arguments that have been made in the briefs and the implications of those arguments. As an advocate, you, of course, want to make sure that the court understands your argument and that the court is comfortable with the implications of ruling in your favor. Thus, properly done, oral argument satisfies both the court's goals and the advocate's goals.

As explained in more detail below, oral argument is more a question-and-answer conversation than a speech. Although the broad goal of oral argument is for the court to better understand the case by asking questions—and for the advocates to explain the case and further their positions by responding to those questions—both the court and the advocates have other goals that they will attempt to achieve. Understanding the

---

1. As noted elsewhere, a persuasive document filed in a trial court is often referred to as a memorandum. In this chapter, all persuasive documents are referred to as briefs.

court's goals in asking questions and thinking about the goals you would like to accomplish in answering the questions will add value to your brief instead of simply repeating it.

I. The Court's Goals

In asking questions, courts have a variety of goals. As you move up the judicial hierarchy from trial courts to appellate courts, the goals (and thus the nature of the questions each court asks) tend to shift. This section addresses the different kinds of questions that each court is most likely to ask in furthering its goals. However, you can expect some kinds of questions no matter which court you are appearing in.

A. Clarify Factual and Legal Points

First, courts will seek to clarify factual and legal points that have been presented in the briefs. For example, the state in a criminal case may represent in its brief that the officer "invited" the defendant to accompany him to the police station, while defense counsel may state that the police officer "ordered" the defendant to accompany the officer to the police station. Legally, whether the officer's words were an invitation or an order may make a difference. Oral argument presents an opportunity for judges to seek the advocates' help in clarifying exactly what the officer said and how it was said. In addition to clarifying factual points, the court may seek to clarify a legal point, for example, whether the holding in a binding case is broad or narrow, or whether more recent cases have overruled an older case without expressly stating so.

B. Determine the Practical Impact of a Ruling

At oral argument judges are likely to ask the advocates to help them examine the practical impact of a ruling. A court is concerned not only with the practical impact of its ruling on the parties in the case before it, but also its effect on future cases.

Consider this example. In *Oregon v. Ashcroft*, the State of Oregon was defending its recently enacted Death With Dignity Act. The Act allows doctors to prescribe lethal doses of federally controlled narcotics to certain terminally ill patients, but the United States Attorney General sought to bar doctors from prescribing those drugs for purposes of assisted suicide. At oral argument, the Justices expressed concern about how a ruling outlawing prescription of those drugs would affect patients. Example 11.1-A illustrates how the United States Supreme Court justices considered the practical effect of their ruling.

Example 11.1-A • Examining the legal effect of an argument

[SOLICITOR] GENERAL CLEMENT: [T]he interpretation of the Attorney General…does not purport to foreclose the issue of assisted suicide—

JUSTICE SOUTER: Well, they say…that, in practical terms, that is exactly what it does, because the only way they can administer their law sensibly is by using these kinds of drugs, scheduled drugs.

GENERAL CLEMENT:…[P]hysician-assisted suicide and the use of federally controlled substances for physician-assisted suicide are not coextensive.

JUSTICE GINSBURG: But we're told that the—those methods are less gentle to the patient, the methods that the State of Oregon has authorized its physicians to prescribe. We are told, at least in some of the briefs, that, from the patient's point of view, it's much less upsetting.

Oral argument in *Gonzales v. Oregon*, 543 U.S. 1145 (2005),
aff'g Oregon v. Ashcroft, 368 F.3d 1118 (9th Cir. 2004).

Similarly, courts—especially appellate courts—are concerned with the impact a decision in one case will have on other, future cases. For example, imagine a case in which a child and her parents argue that, under the common law "public trust doctrine," the state must enact legislation to regulate greenhouse gases. In the case, the child and her parents would argue that, although the "public trust doctrine" was originally focused on waterways, the doctrine equally protects the atmosphere and obligates the state to regulate emissions. At oral argument, the court would likely be concerned about the impact of its ruling. If the court were to accept the argument that the public trust doctrine requires the government to regulate emissions, what else might the public trust doctrine require the state to do? Might the state need to regulate tree cutting and bee breeding? The court may similarly be concerned about its ability to determine under that doctrine when the state had sufficiently performed its duty to regulate the environment.

When they are concentrating on their client's legal arguments, advocates can easily lose sight of the real-world effect of a court's ruling. But courts need to know the practical effect of their rulings, and judges often use oral argument as a tool for getting at those practical effects.

II. The Advocate's Goals

Just as the court has its goals in hearing oral argument, the advocate also has goals in presenting oral argument. Generally, those two sets of goals are compatible. A good oral argument satisfies both the court's goals and the advocate's goals.

A. Ensure that the Court Understands Your Argument

As an advocate, your first goal is to make sure that the court understands your argument. For example, in rereading your brief, you may realize that you did not present a portion of your argument as coherently as you might have hoped. Oral argument is the chance to "fix" that defect. Or it may be that your opponent's briefing has pointed out some ambiguity in your argument as you briefed it. Oral argument provides an opportunity to clarify your argument in an interactive manner. Assuming that the argument you made in your brief is a good one, ensuring that the court understands it will make it more persuasive.

B. Correct Misapprehensions and Address Concerns

Oral argument is also an opportunity to demonstrate the soundness of your position in light of any concerns the court may have. As explained above, judges are concerned about the practical impact of their rulings. A judge's concerns will come to light from the questions the judge asks. Judges may be concerned that, if they adopt the position espoused in the brief, it will have negative side effects or that it will cut too broadly, or not broadly enough. At oral argument, you can address any concerns and provide the judge with a degree of comfort that ruling in your favor will not lead to untoward consequences, as in Example 11.1-B.

Example 11.1-B · Reassuring the court that ruling in your favor will not cause unanticipated results

COUNSEL: Thus, your honor, section 12.73 of the Penal Code is unconstitutional and should be struck down.

THE COURT: Counsel, if I rule in your favor, won't that effectively mean that roughly thirty percent of the inmates in our state prisons will have to be released immediately?

COUNSEL: No, Your Honor, such a ruling would affect only a small fraction of state inmates, for several reasons. First,…

C. Respond to Claims that You Could Not Address in the Briefs

Finally, you may need to respond to a claim that you did not have an opportunity to address in your brief. For example, suppose that you, as a respondent, argue that appellant's claim on appeal was not preserved in the trial court. The appellant, in the reply brief, has argued that the claim is, in fact, preserved. As the respondent, you do not have the opportunity to submit a written response to the new argument presented in appellant's reply brief. Thus, oral argument will be the first—and only—opportunity you will have to respond to the argument that the claim really was not preserved, so one of your goals at oral argument should be to respond to that argument. Similarly, suppose that the United States Supreme Court issues a decision in a case similar to yours the day before your oral argument. Oral argument may be the only opportunity you have to address the effect of that case on your case.

By keeping in mind what the court and advocates seek to achieve in oral argument—and how those goals fit into the context of the persuasive process—you are more likely to persuade the court that your position is correct and thus to have the court rule in your favor.

Practice Points

- At oral argument, the judges' overriding goal is to understand the advocates' arguments and the implications of those arguments.

- As an advocate, your goals are to ensure that the court understands your argument, address any concerns about the implications of your argument, and respond to any claims not addressed in your brief.

- Prepare for oral argument with those goals in mind.

Preparing for Oral Argument

I. Create a Strong Foundation
   A. Review the Briefs
   B. Know the Record
   C. Know the Law
   D. Review the Court's Rules

II. Prepare Your Argument
   A. Determine "Where the Game Will Be Played"
   B. Determine the Strengths and Weaknesses of Your Position and Your Opponent's Position
   C. Know the Boundaries of Your Position
   D. Anticipate Every Question the Court Will Ask and Prepare Responses
   E. Involve Others

III. Prepare Written Materials
   A. Script Your Opening
      1. Movant's or appellant's opening
      2. Respondent's opening
   B. Create Lectern Materials

IV. "Where Do I Park?" and Other Practical Matters
   A. Visit the Courtroom
   B. Investigate Court Protocol
   C. Choose Your Attire

When should you start preparing for oral argument? The answer is simple: Start preparing for oral argument as soon as you begin drafting your brief.

The first question you must ask is whether you will be allowed to present oral argument. Many courts do not allow oral argument in support of a motion or on appeal as a matter of course.[1] Thus, first make sure that you are entitled to present oral argument.

---

1. For example, parties do not have an automatic right to a hearing on a summary judgment motion. *E.g., Villanueva v. CNA Ins. Companies*, 868 F.2d 684, 688 (5th Cir.

Assuming you are permitted to argue, then you should be thinking about oral arguments as you draft your brief. As you draft each section of your brief and each argument, ask yourself, "When the judge reads this, what questions might she have?" If you can anticipate questions that a judge might ask at oral argument and address those questions in the brief, your brief will be more persuasive. It is never too early to begin preparing for oral argument, at least by having it in mind as you draft your brief.

Once all the briefs have been filed and a date for oral argument is set, your preparation begins in earnest. As you prepare, your overarching goal will be to plan for the questions that a judge is most likely to ask. But you also must be familiar with both sides' arguments, the facts in the case, and all relevant legal authority. This section explains how you can prepare for the court's questions and achieve the necessary familiarity with the facts and the law.

As you read, keep in mind that your level of preparation will vary depending on the importance and complexity of the issues and the court that you are appearing before. For example, an argument about a dispositive trial court motion may entail more preparation if it involves complex or novel legal issues, if the decision is likely to create an important precedent, or if the record is unusually lengthy. In contrast, your preparation may be minimal and your argument may be brief and straightforward for a simple, one-issue argument on a motion or on appeal. In addition, preparation tends to increase as you move up the judicial hierarchy. As you move from trial to appellate courts, oral arguments become more formal and frequently are longer. An argument before the United States Supreme Court, for example, may entail months of practice and multiple moot court sessions, preferably with lawyers who have previously argued before the Supreme Court.

Consider Saving Hypotheticals and Examples for Oral Argument

Some material is more effectively presented at oral argument. Certainly, all essential components of your argument must be presented in writing, and failure to do so may waive your right to present those issues. Some supporting material, however, may be best presented at oral argument. For example, as you prepare your brief you may think of a hypothetical that brilliantly illustrates your point. That hypothetical may not fit into the argument as you are drafting it. Make a note of that hypothetical and plan to use it at oral argument. The same approach applies to examples you think of that flesh out your argument. Make a note of those examples so that you will have them at hand for oral argument.

1989). Similarly, the federal circuit court panel to whom an appellate case is assigned may choose to have it submitted without oral argument. Fed. R. App. P. 34(a).

This section is directed at preparing for arguments on significant trial court motions and appellate arguments. Whittle down or expand the suggestions set out below as appropriate to the particulars of your case.

Finally, keep in mind that different advocates prepare for oral argument differently; if you know that a certain method of study helps you remember and synthesize material, use it. Despite those individual differences, experienced oral advocates have learned a number of common approaches to preparing for oral argument, which are discussed below.

I. Create a Strong Foundation

At oral argument, the court will expect you to be the expert on your case. Among other things, the court will look to you to explain or clarify the relevant law and facts. Because the court will expect you to be the expert about your client's case, your first step is to ensure that you can fulfill that role by knowing the facts of the case and the applicable law. In addition, the court will expect you to be familiar with courtroom procedure. So along with knowing the law and facts of your case, you will need to review the court's rules governing the presentation of oral arguments.

A. Review the Briefs

Because some time—and in appellate courts, often a long time— has passed since you filed your brief, your first step should be to review all briefs that have been filed in the case. As you review, "put your judge hat on." Read the briefs in the order that the judge will, and to the extent possible, try to view the briefs from a neutral judge's perspective.

As you read each brief, ask yourself these questions:

- Which arguments are "must win" arguments?
- Which points can be conceded if necessary?
- What are the strengths and weaknesses in each argument?
- Which arguments would benefit from additional explanation or clarification at oral argument?

Highlight important passages in the briefs, take notes, or outline the arguments, if those methods help you remember and understand the briefs. As you review, begin to develop a list of questions the judges may ask— because the facts are not clear, because an argument is not clear, or because the impact of an argument is not clear.

As you review the briefs, remember that courts tend not to look kindly on arguments raised for the first time at oral argument. Rather, at oral argument, courts expect you to clarify arguments already presented. If, as you prepare your argument, you think of new arguments that you wish you had made in your brief, try to present them as extensions of or variations on arguments that you have already made in writing.

Don't Raise an Argument for the First Time at Oral Argument

JUSTICE:...Well, what I'm saying is, I'm confused. I've read the briefs.... And so we're hearing new theories here for the first time....

[COUNSEL]: I am — I, I, I appreciate that....

JUSTICE: I mean, we're here to discuss the issues that were briefed on appeal. You, you don't get multiple briefings....It's not okay to come and make your arguments that have been ne — never made to any court....I don't — the arguments you're making here, and I've read those briefs pretty carefully, and I wouldn't claim to remember everything I read, but some of these seem to me — to be new to me. Am I, am I incorrect on that?

Oral argument in *Henry v. J.P. Morgan Chase Bank*,
No. B249535, 2014 WL 1481139
(Cal. Ct. App. Apr. 16, 2014).

B. Know the Record

In light of the number of cases they hear, judges cannot be expected to know your case as well as you do. You are the expert on your case, and a judge must be able to rely on your expertise. Accordingly, you must be familiar with the record, either the relevant evidence in a trial court argument or the record on appeal in an appellate argument.

Make sure you know where in the record the court will find important documents or testimony. For example, if the case turns on a provision in a complex contract, and the contract was introduced as an exhibit at trial or attached to a motion, you should be able to tell the judge where to look in the file or appellate record for that provision. In a similar vein, if certain testimony is a crucial part of the argument, make sure that you know what the testimony says and where it can be found. Again, highlighting and taking notes on the record are useful ways of processing it in a way that will keep it in your memory.

C. Know the Law

You should reread the cases and other legal authorities that were cited in the briefs and make sure you are familiar with them. Although you need not memorize every authority, you should be familiar with every legal authority that you or your opponent has cited in the briefs. The more central an authority is to an argument, the more familiar you should be with that authority. Again, processing the authorities in a way that will ingrain them in your memory (for example, highlighting, outlining, or summarizing them) will benefit you at oral argument.

You must also update all authorities to ensure that they are still good law, using Shepard's, KeyCite, Bcite, or another citator. It would be embarrassing if, at oral argument on a summary judgment motion, a judge asked, "Counsel, didn't the governor sign a bill last week that takes effect immediately and that repeals the statute at issue in this case?" and you were unaware of the bill. Similarly, no advocate should be caught having to answer "I don't know" to the following question from an appellate court bench: "Counsel, didn't we issue an opinion in a different case yesterday that rejected your position?" Be prepared and up-to-date.

D. Review the Court's Rules

The last step in creating a strong foundation is to review the court's rules that govern oral argument. As stated throughout this book, knowing and following the court's procedural rules is a fundamental prerequisite to persuading a judge of anything. You should check the court's website for the rules of trial or appellate procedure for that jurisdiction, as well as the court's local rules.

In reviewing the court's rules, be sure to determine how much time you will have in which to present your argument. Preparing for a thirty-minute argument (the time allotted each side in the U.S. Supreme Court) is different from preparing for a ten-minute argument (as each side is allotted in some cases in the federal courts of appeals and other courts). Knowing how long you have for your argument will prevent you from trying to shoehorn seven major points into a ten-minute argument on a simple motion. Similarly, knowing that you have a half-hour will allow you to prepare to spend your time convincing the court of the four points you need to prevail, rather than having to choose only one.

II. Prepare Your Argument

As explained above, as you review the briefs, the record, and the law, you should begin to ask yourself certain questions:

- Which arguments are "must win" arguments?
- Which points can be conceded if necessary?
- What are the strengths and weaknesses in each argument?
- Which arguments would benefit from additional explanation or clarification at oral argument?

Those questions will allow you to determine "where the game will be played" at oral argument, that is, what points the court will focus on. As you prepare, you will need to dig deeper into your arguments by examining the limits of your argument and imagining questions that the court will have. The text below guides you through those thought processes.

A. Determine "Where the Game Will Be Played"

Begin your preparation by considering "where the game will be played." Often, one point in your argument is a "pivot point" (as one judge calls it).[2] If you lose that point, you lose the argument. For example, in an appeal in which the parties dispute whether a claim of error was preserved for review, that argument about preservation is a "pivot point": If the appellant does not convince the court that the error was preserved for appellate review, the court will not consider the merits, and the appellant will lose. It might be, in such a case, that the merits of the claim are not in serious dispute. In such a case, each side's preparation should focus on convincing the judges that the claim of error was (the appellant) or was not (the respondent) preserved. That is, the "game" at oral argument will be "played" around the pivot point of preservation.

Similarly, the primary legal issue in your motion for summary judgment may be well-briefed and fairly straightforward, but whether the trial court has jurisdiction may be a much thornier proposition. Although the merits of the case may be much "sexier," you should prepare to use your time at oral argument addressing the threshold technical issue of jurisdiction. That is where the game will be played.

Always consider where the game will be played as you prepare, and make sure that you plan to spend the bulk of your time at oral argument addressing those issues.

B. Determine the Strengths and Weaknesses of Your Position and Your Opponent's Position

Next, consider which parts of your argument are strongest and which are weakest. If you have presented a strong argument in your brief on a certain point and your opponent has not refuted it, you will waste precious oral argument time if you choose to discuss that point. Instead, in preparing, think about weaker or more difficult aspects of your argument and how you can build on what is in the brief to persuade the court that your position is correct.

Of course, even if you believe that your brief adequately addresses an issue that is central to the case, you should consider devoting some time to it in oral argument. In short, when preparing, take into account both those points that you believe need bolstering and those points that are central to your case.

---

2. Former Chief Judge Rick Haselton of the Oregon Court of Appeals.

C. Know the Boundaries of Your Position

Having taken the steps set out above, you must now begin to rigorously question your position. In particular, you must determine the limits of your position. To determine the limits of your position, you must clarify what rule you are asking the court to adopt and then consider how that rule will apply under different scenarios that the court might, one day, be confronted with.

Imagine, for example, that you are defending a criminal defendant who has been charged with burglary, a crime that requires that the perpetrator enter a "building or occupied structure" with the intent to commit a crime therein. Your client entered a recreational vehicle (RV) and took

---

Know Your Position: An Example

The *Oregon v. Ashcroft* case, introduced in § 11.1, provides an example of the importance of knowing your position. That case focused on the legality of a state law permitting physicians to prescribe lethal doses of controlled substances to terminally ill patients. The state took the hard position that the U.S. Attorney General had no authority to determine whether a medical practice allowed by state law was or was not "legitimate." Thus, the state argued, the Attorney General could not revoke a physician's license to prescribe controlled substances if the doctor had prescribed a controlled substance in accordance with the state's Death with Dignity law.

Clearly, the judges hearing the case would be concerned about the limits of the state's argument. Was the state arguing that, no matter what a state allows a physician to do, the U.S. Attorney General has no authority revoke the physician's license under the federal Controlled Substances Act? That was, in fact, the state's position. Although it might make the advocate nervous to take such an extreme position, that logically had to be the state's position.

At oral argument, this exchange occurred:

Q: Counsel, under your analysis, if Oregon passed a law allowing physicians to prescribe morphine (a controlled substance) for the sole purpose of increasing a patient's psychological well-being, could the U.S. Attorney General determine that such a use was not "legitimate" and revoke a physician's license to prescribe controlled substances?"

A: No, Your Honor, that would be outside of the U.S. Attorney General's authority....

Without thinking in advance about the logical end of the state's position, the advocate might be worried that answering the question "no" would seem unpalatable to the judges. But, given the state's theory, the answer had to be "no" and recognizing that point before oral argument made the advocate's response more confident and persuasive.

fifty dollars in cash. You move to have the indictment dismissed, arguing that an RV is not a building or occupied structure.

At oral argument, the judge may ask, "If the RV has not been moved for one year and has a family living in it, would it qualify as a building or occupied structure?" If you have not thought carefully about the limits of your position, you might struggle with your response. But if you have thought carefully about the rule you are proposing, the answer will be straightforward. If you are advocating for a rule that says that any vehicle *capable* of being moved cannot be a building or occupied structure, you will confidently respond, "No, Your Honor, and let me explain why...." If, however, your preferred rule is more narrow, you might respond, "Yes, Your Honor, that might be a building or occupied structure, but that was not the case here."

In short, think carefully about what rule you want the court to apply to your case. Test the rule under different factual scenarios to see how it works. If you know the boundaries of that rule, you will be able to confidently respond to the hypothetical fact scenarios that the court throws out at oral argument.

D. Anticipate Every Question the Court Will Ask and Prepare Responses

As you think about where the game will be played, the strengths and weaknesses of your argument, and the limits of your position, begin to develop a list of questions that the court is likely to ask. As stated above, what makes oral argument unique in the persuasive process is its interactive nature: Judges ask questions and advocates respond. It follows that perhaps the most important part of preparing for oral argument is to anticipate the questions that the judge or judges will ask and to have prepared responses to those questions. Although you may sometimes be forced to answer an unanticipated question on the fly, you will be more articulate, and your answers will be more persuasive, if you have predicted which questions the judge or judges will ask and have prepared for them. As suggested above, you should begin anticipating the judges' questions from the moment you start drafting the brief. You can also anticipate questions later in your preparation by reviewing the briefs and asking yourself about the weaknesses in your case or anything that might, on rereading your brief, be less clear than you had hoped.

In addition, you should consider the court and its role. If you are arguing before a trial court, the judge is likely to be concerned about the controlling law and which facts are in dispute. By contrast, if you are arguing before an appellate court, that court is likely to be more concerned about how a decision in this case will affect future, similar cases. Therefore, you should try to imagine what rule your case will stand for in the future and whether that rule is one that a court will feel comfortable adopting.

The way in which you prepare for the court's questions will vary depending on the complexity and importance of the case. In a relatively simple case, you might simply keep a list of likely questions as you brief the case and prepare for argument, thinking about what your response will be. In more complex or important cases, you might write out answers to each potential question as a way of bringing your thoughts together and ensuring that you have a good answer. In the biggest cases, you might actually host one or more moot courts in which experienced attorneys act as judges, posing questions while you practice responding.[3] In sum, the bulk of your preparation energy should be devoted to planning carefully for the court's questions.

E. Involve Others

Finally, you should consider seeking help from others. Because you are so close to your case and because you are wedded to one position, having others listen to your argument can be invaluable. Explaining your argument to another person—even, or perhaps especially, a person who is not law-trained—will help you recognize rough patches in your presentation, will allow you to identify difficult aspects of your argument, and will generate additional questions for which you can prepare responses should those questions arise at oral argument. As suggested above, when a case is particularly important or complex, you may want to arrange for a formal moot court with attorneys who have read the briefs and will act as judges. In fact, conducting such moot courts—sometimes a number of them before different attorneys—is the standard practice in United States Supreme Court cases.

III. Prepare Written Materials

Although, as explained above, oral argument is more of a conversation than a presentation, some materials should be prepared in advance. In particular, you should script and memorize your opening. In addition, you should create materials that you will bring with you to the lectern.

A. Script Your Opening

To ensure a smooth start to their arguments, most advocates write out their opening statement and memorize it. In trial courts, you are

---

3. The "moot courts" that are used by experienced attorneys to prepare for oral arguments should be distinguished from the moot court competitions in law school, which are discussed in Appendix D.

likely to introduce yourself as in Example 11.2-A, and in appellate courts, you are likely to introduce yourself as in Example 11.2-B.

Example 11.2-A · The standard trial court salutation

Your Honor. My name is _____. I represent defendant [or plaintiff] XYZ Corporation.

Example 11.2-B · The standard appellate court salutation

May it please the court. My name is _____. I represent appellant [or respondent] XYZ Corporation.

After uttering those stock phrases, your opening will vary depending on whether you represent the party that is arguing first (the moving party or the appellant) or the responding party.

1. Movant's or appellant's opening

Let's assume that you are first to the lectern as the moving party (at trial) or the party who lost below, the appellant (on appeal). In that case, you should memorize the first twenty to thirty seconds of your argument. That opening will set the tone for the argument, and especially in an appellate court, it may be the last time during the argument that you have control over what is being discussed. Take advantage of that opportunity. Preparing and memorizing—not reading—the opening also will give you a chance to launch into your argument on "autopilot" so that you can hit your stride without worrying about what you're going to say.

After introducing yourself with one of the stock phrases mentioned above, your opening should introduce your theme and then give an overview of what you plan to address. Example 11.2-C provides a typical opening that the moving party might make on a motion for summary judgment. Example 11.2-D provides a typical opening that an appellant might make.

Example 11.2-C · A moving party's opening

Notice how the lawyer begins with a conclusion.

The lawyer then provides a roadmap of the argument.

Your Honor. My name is Sol Cohen, and I represent J&B Corporation. In this case, there is no genuine issue of material fact, and my client is entitled to judgment as a matter of law. I will begin by explaining why the exhibits that plaintiff introduced—although they suggest a possible issue of fact—do not demonstrate that there is an issue of *material* fact. I will then explain why the material facts are undisputed, and why, given those facts, the law clearly dictates that we are entitled to judgment. This court should grant J&B's motion for summary judgment.

Example 11.2-D · An appellant's opening

May it please the Court. My name is Andreas Rojas, and I represent the State. Although this case takes place in the context of important issues surrounding the end of life, the issue before this court — and the issue I will address today — is much more mundane: What is the authority of the Attorney General to override state law governing medical practice? Unless the Court has questions, I do not intend to address the jurisdictional issue, which is adequately addressed by the briefs. Rather, I will explain why the Attorney General exceeded his authority in this case.

> Here, the lawyer introduces the theme of his argument.
>
> The lawyer then provides a roadmap of his argument.

Local customs may vary with respect to whether you should ask the court for a recitation of the facts. However, when arguing before a trial court, lawyers commonly begin with an overview of the facts. In appellate courts, normally you do not ask the court if it would like a recitation of the facts; you should assume that an appellate court is familiar with the facts of your case unless you have reason to suspect otherwise. You should, in any event, be prepared to provide a summary of the facts in the event a judge asks for it.

Example of a Short U.S. Supreme Court Opening

MR. GARTLAN: Mr. Chief Justice, and may it please the Court: This case presents three questions. The first is, "Does article 36 of the Vienna Convention on Consular Relations confer rights to individuals such as Mr. Sanchez-Llamas?" The second is, "Can Mr. Sanchez-Llamas enforce the right in a State criminal prosecution?" And the third is, "Can the right be enforced by suppression?"

Oral argument in *Sanchez-Llamas v. Oregon*, 548 U.S. 331 (2006).

Example of a More Complex U.S. Supreme Court Opening

MS. KAPLAN: Mr. Chief Justice, and may it please the Court:
I'd like to focus on why [the Defense of Marriage Act (DOMA)] fails even under rationality review. Because of DOMA, many thousands of people who are legally married under the laws of nine sovereign States and the District of Columbia are being treated as unmarried by the federal government solely because they are gay.

These couples are being treated as unmarried with respect to programs that affect family stability, such as the Family Leave Act, referred to by

Continued on next page

Justice Ginsburg. These couples are being treated as unmarried for purposes of federal conflict of interest rules, election laws, and anti-nepotism and judicial recusal statutes.

And my client was treated as unmarried when her spouse passed away, so that she had to pay $363,000 in estate taxes on the property that they had accumulated during their 44 years together.

Oral argument in *United States v. Windsor*, 570 U.S. 744 (2013).

2. Respondent's opening

If you are representing the responding party (either the non-moving party in a trial court or the respondent in an appellate court), a prepared opening is less important. A responding party must be more flexible in her argument, adapting it in light of the opposing party's argument, the court's questions during that argument, and the responses to the questions. Thus, a previously prepared opening for a responding party may be completely inappropriate in light of the direction that the argument already has taken. Nonetheless, it can be comforting and useful to prepare an opening in the event that nothing unanticipated takes place during the opposing party's argument.

One very effective way to begin if you are responding is to introduce yourself and then build on some part of the argument that has preceded you. For example, you can begin by focusing on a point that appeared to be important to the court during opposing counsel's argument, as in Examples 11.2-E and 11.2-F.

Example 11.2-E • Respondent's opening on appeal

May it please the court: My name is Matan Bar-Lev, and I represent BustaMove, LLC. I would like to turn first to the question that Judge Ruiz asked about appellant's third argument. Judge Ruiz is right to be skeptical of appellant's position for two reasons.

Example 11.2-F • Respondent's opening in a trial court

Your Honor, my name is Dan Olson, and I represent the County. Before turning to the main focus of my argument, I'd like to note that the testimony that Your Honor asked about can be found in the Arnold Deposition, pages 12 to 14. And Your Honor can see that there simply is no mention of waiver in that passage.

> **Example of U.S. Supreme Court Respondent's Opening That Builds on the Previous Argument**
>
> MR. FEIGIN: Thank you, Mr. Chief Justice, and may it please the Court: I'd like to begin, if I could, by addressing Justice Kagan's question, which Justice Sotomayor then followed up on. We think that the probable cause finding and the fact that they want to repeat essentially the speech that was made earlier are the two critical factors in this case and without that, none of their claims would be justiciable. As it is, we think that their purely legal First Amendment challenges are ripe for those particular case-specific reasons.
>
> Oral argument in Susan B. Anthony List v. Driehaus, 573 U.S. 149 (2014).

> **Example of U.S. Supreme Court Respondent's Opening That Builds on the Previous Argument Without Any Introduction**
>
> [SOLICITOR] GENERAL VERRILLI: Mr. Chief Justice, and may it please the Court:
>
> The line drawn in *Abood* is sound. It has the force of stare decisis behind it, it is completely consistent with this Court's First Amendment jurisprudence, and it requires affirmance. If I could, I'd like to turn to the questions that Justice Kennedy has raised because I do think it gets to the key issue in the case.
>
> Oral argument in Harris v. Quinn, 573 U.S. 616 (2014).

Although as counsel for the responding party you have the opportunity to begin by picking up on a point the court had previously been discussing, it may be that nothing unanticipated or that requires a response happened before you stand up. In that case, your prepared opening may be both comforting and an appropriate place to begin.

B. Create Lectern Materials

Although some advocates may present oral argument with no notes at all, that is a good idea only in the simplest of cases. Even experienced advocates have notes with them to which they can refer. Having those materials accessible during oral argument is important, but it is the preparation of the notes that is the key to a successful and low-stress argument. Many experienced oral advocates carefully prepare an outline of their argument, but find that they never consult it during the argument. But that is a good sign: In preparing the outline, the advocate has internalized the argument.

Experienced advocates also work hard to condense their lectern materials. Minimizing the number of items you bring with you to the lectern will prevent you from fumbling through the pages as you search for information. In addition, and perhaps more importantly, condensing your case into a small enough bundle to take to a lectern forces you to understand your case and be prepared to present and discuss the pivotal aspects of the case.

Accordingly, most advocates use either a manila folder or a thin (perhaps one inch thick) three-ring binder to organize their lectern materials. Everything should be prepared in a way that makes it easy to find and easy to read when you are nervous. Many experienced advocates recommend using at least fourteen-point type and double-spacing your materials.

What goes onto an advocate's manila folder or into a binder varies, but at a minimum you should include an easily accessible list of "must-make" points. As explained below, sometimes the court's questions can take you away from your planned argument. Thus, create a short (no more than three to five items) list of the major points you must make during argument. This list can be placed on the inside front cover of a binder or stapled to the front of a manila folder. In either case, the list should be in big, bold print. With that list easily accessible, you will find it easier to return to your argument and to ensure that you have made all critical points before the argument is over.

The next document to include is an outline of your argument. The outline can be as short as one page and should never be more than a few pages long (in fourteen-point type). Although some advocates write out the entire argument *as part of their preparation*, your binder should not include a full-text version of your argument. The temptation to read your

---

Lectern vs. Podium

Strictly speaking, a podium is a raised platform on which a speaker stands to deliver a speech. A lectern is a raised stand, often with a slanted top, that the speaker can use to hold her notes. Courtrooms have lecterns, not podiums. Nonetheless, many discussions of oral argument refer to the "podium" rather than the "lectern." We use the term "lectern."

argument will be too great, and if you succumb to that temptation, your argument will suffer. Outline your argument using phrases in your notes instead of full sentences to avoid that temptation to read. Practice your argument from the outline.

After your outline, include materials that you might need to access during argument. For example, if the case involves the interpretation of a statute, you should include the text of the statute in your binder. If there are two pages of key testimony that will be important in the argument, include those pages of transcript in the binder. If your argument will depend heavily on a discussion of the concurring and plurality opinions in a U.S. Supreme Court case, include those opinions in the binder. Likewise, if the case turns on the interpretation of paragraph 34.1.2.55(j) of a contract, you should include the exact wording of that paragraph in your materials.

When preparing those supplemental materials, some advocates simply photocopy or print them from their original sources. Another approach—and probably the better one—is to import or type them into a word processor and format them for easy reading at the lectern. If a judge has a question about a statutory provision, or if you want to quote it, your argument will be smoother if you have the provision in your lectern materials, tabbed for easy access, and printed in fourteen-point type. Rather than squinting at a Westlaw or Lexis printout, you will be able to pay attention to what you are saying and maintain eye contact with the court. Moreover, the additional "processing" of the material will help you understand and remember it better.

Finally, at the very top of your materials include any personal reminders that might be helpful. For example, if you have a tendency to talk too fast, make a note to yourself: "Slow down!" If you are nervous about how you are going to begin your argument and you think you will stumble, write, "May it please the court...." Put that personal reminder on the first page of your binder or, better, on the inside left cover in big, bold print. Many advocates find those highly personal reminders comforting during what can be a tense experience.

Preparing lectern materials is a vital part of preparing for oral argument. Yet you may find, as do many advocates, that after spending hours preparing a gorgeous lectern binder, you hardly ever look at it during oral argument. Rather than viewing all that preparation as a waste of time, recognize that in preparing the binder you mentally processed the material and winnowed it down sufficiently to produce a focused oral argument. The more time you spend preparing those materials, the less likely you are to need them at the lectern.

An example of what your lectern materials might look like is presented in Figure 11.2-G.

Figure 11.2-G · Lectern materials

speak slowly!!!

Points I Must Make: *Don't click*

(1) Claim of error is not preserved.

(2) Trial court did not abuse its discretion.

(3) Any error is harmless.

Argument:

Preservation

- This Court has said that counsel must cite specific constitutional provision to preserve claim. (*Gonzales*)

- Only vague mention of constitution.

  ○ "Your honor, admission of defendant's statement would violate the constitution." (Trans. p. 217)

- Court need not reach merits, as the claim is not preserved.

Merits

- Trial court's decision admitting the statement is reviewed for an abuse of discretion.

- Although this court might have ruled otherwise, the trial court's decision was a legally permissible one.

- To make later statement to police inadmissible, defendant must unequivocally invoke right to counsel. (*Davis*)

- Defendant's statement: "I have nothing to say." (Trans. p. 112)

- "I have nothing to say" is not unequivocal invocation.

  ○ See *Davis* ("if a suspect makes a reference to an attorney that is ambiguous or equivocal in that a reasonable officer in light of the circumstances would have understood only that the suspect might be invoking the right to counsel, our precedents do not require the cessation of questioning").

Harmless Error

- If the disputed testimony is merely cumulative of other evidence that already established the same fact, then the error is harmless. (*Holcomb*)

- Defendant's statement that the trial court admitted was identical to the statements of three other witnesses. (*Izaguirre*, *Bigelow*, and *Sparks*)

- Even if the trial court should have excluded the statement, any error was harmless.

Unless the court has further questions, I have nothing to add. Thank you. (sit down!)

IV. "Where Do I Park?" and Other Practical Matters

On the day of your argument, you will want to be focused on your argument and not on such questions as "Where do I park?" To that end, take care of practical details—such as determining where you park, where the courtroom is located, and what to wear—before the day you are to argue.

A. Visit the Courtroom

Before oral argument, you should visit the courtroom and, if possible, observe an argument. By actually going to the courtroom, you will ensure that you know how to get there, where to park, how much travel time you will need to arrive on time, where the restrooms are, whether water will be provided at counsel table, where the clerk or bailiff sits, and other aspects of the setting. Learning the lay of the land beforehand will make you more comfortable and allow you to focus on your argument when you give it.

As you watch others' oral arguments, note the timing, pace, and style of attorneys' arguments, and what seems effective. Note the concerns of the judge or panel of judges, how they present their questions, and how counsel most effectively answers their questions. If you can, try to observe the judge or judges who will be hearing your case. You will learn about the particular preferences of the judges, the degree of formality expected, and the dynamics of that particular courtroom.

B. Investigate Court Protocol

In addition to visiting the courtroom, you may also want to search the Internet to find useful guides to oral argument specific to the court in which you are to argue. For example, the North Carolina Bar Association produces a useful guide entitled, "Guide for Counsel for Oral Arguments Before the North Carolina Court of Appeals" that covers everything from where to park, to the table at which appellant's counsel sits, to how to address the court. Similarly, the U.S. Supreme Court provides a "Guide for Counsel in Cases to Be Argued Before This Court," which "is designed to assist attorneys preparing cases for argument before [the] Court, especially those who have not previously argued" there. Look for such guides and follow them.

Finally, ask around. The particular courtroom customs in one county, district, or level of court often are not written down. Attorneys who have gone before you are great resources for those unwritten rules.

C. Choose Your Attire

The overriding goal in choosing your attire is to wear clothing that will not distract the court from your message. Just as failing to follow court rules will distract a judge from your written message, anything unusual or unexpected about your dress will distract the court from your oral message. In courtrooms, business attire is always appropriate. You want the judges focused on what you are saying, not squinting at you trying to figure out what the symbol on your tie is or what that strange-shaped pin on your blouse is supposed to be. Your attire for oral argument cannot be too boring or conservative. As the U.S. Supreme Court guide says, "Appropriate attire for counsel is conservative business dress in traditional dark colors (e.g., navy blue or charcoal gray)."

Preparing for your first oral argument can be nerve-wracking. Table 11.2-H can help ensure that you are prepared. In sum, remember what the court's goals are and what your goals are. Process the material until you are comfortable with it, remembering that the judges expect you to be the expert on your case. Know your position and try to anticipate and prepare a response to every possible question. Prepare for a conversation, not a speech. Prepare user-friendly lectern materials. When you have done all that, you will sleep soundly the night before the argument.

Table 11.2-H · Oral Argument Preparation Checklist

A. General preparation

❑ Determine whether oral argument will be held in your case. (You should make this determination before submitting your brief, if possible.)

❑ Review court rules regarding oral argument; conduct any other research, such as consulting a guide on the court's website or talking to other lawyers who have argued in that court.

B. Big-picture preparation

❑ Review all briefs.

❑ Review the lower court opinion(s), if any.

❑ Review key documents or the appellate record.

❑ Review the authorities cited in the briefs.

❑ Draft a list of questions that might be asked.

❑ Prepare (orally or in writing) responses to questions.

❑ Think about and know the weaknesses and strengths in your position and in your opponent's position.

❑ Make sure that you can articulate your position precisely.

C. Short-term preparation

❑ Shepardize, KeyCite, BCite, or otherwise update all authorities.

❑ Conduct moot courts or discuss the case with others.

❑ Prepare an opening and memorize it.

❑ Prepare your oral argument notes, including your outline, important documents, "must-make" points, and personal reminders.

D. Final preparation

❑ Select your attire, make sure you know how to get to the courthouse, where to park, etc.

❑ Review your oral argument notes materials.

❑ Get a good night's sleep.

Presenting Oral Argument

I. Your Frame of Mind

II. Inhabit Your Space Confidently

III. Leave Your Baggage Behind

IV. Make Eye Contact

V. Speak Slowly and Simply

VI. Have a Conversation

VII. Use Humor with Care

VIII. Assert Conclusions, Not Your Beliefs

IX. Deliver Your Opening

X. Respond to Questions from the Bench
   A. Stop Talking and Listen
   B. Pause
   C. Ask for Clarification, If Necessary
   D. Respond With "Yes" or "No"; Then Explain Your Answer
   E. Never Praise a Judge's Question
   F. Always Answer a Question When It Is Asked
   G. Embrace Hypotheticals
   H. Recognize Friendly Questions
   I. Admit When You Do Not Know the Answer
   J. Recognize the Logical End of an Answer
   K. After Answering the Court's Question, Return to Your Planned Argument or Adjust as Necessary

XI. Conclude

XII. Listen When the Court Questions Opposing Counsel

XIII. Rebuttal

When the day of argument finally arrives, get to court early, and get settled in the courtroom as you wait for your case to be called. Remember that, even though you may not be at counsel table or the lectern yet, you are still in the formal setting of the courtroom. It will not advance your case if, by the time you approach to argue your case, the judges have already seen you texting, whispering, or rolling your eyes at others' arguments.[1] Act professionally at all times.

This section addresses how to present your argument from the moment you stand to speak to when you return to your chair. As explained above, the core of oral argument is answering questions. Moreover, that is the part of oral argument that many new advocates find the most daunting, so this section spends the most time on that subject.

I. Your Frame of Mind

Your frame of mind throughout the argument should be that you are an intelligent person with special knowledge of your case trying to help a judge or judges reach the right result. You should think of yourself as a helpful expert, there to guide the court to your preferred outcome. If you maintain that frame of mind—the perspective that you are there to be helpful to the court—your argument and responses to questions will be more persuasive. By contrast, if your tone is combative or suggests that your agenda is more important than the court's questions, you will be less persuasive and you will not endear yourself to the people who ultimately will decide the fate of your case.

Remember, too, that there is no "best" argument style. Some advocates are like pit bulls, forcefully (though respectfully) presenting their arguments. Others are effective by calmly showing the court how reasonable their approach to the problem is. Think about what style comes naturally to you and use it, remembering to be respectful and professional within that style. Advocates tend to run into trouble when they attempt to adopt a style that does not feel natural to them. Unless you are particularly obnoxious or overbearing, the best advice is this: Be yourself.

II. Inhabit Your Space Confidently

When your turn arrives, stand, and if the custom in the court is to speak at a lectern, approach the lectern confidently and with your materials in hand.

Once you are standing, either at counsel table or at the lectern, get comfortable and stand up straight. Your hands should not be in your pockets or clasped behind you. If you are at a lectern, a good default position is to *rest* your hands on the sides of the lectern; do not grip the sides, holding on for dear life. Do not sway or rock back and forth. Plant your feet, take a deep breath, and begin. Speak clearly and confidently, making eye contact with the judge or each member of the panel of judges.

---

1. *See, e.g.,* Ga. R. App. P. 28(g)(2) ("Talking, reading newspapers or other material, and audibly studying briefs and arranging papers are prohibited in the courtroom.").

III. Leave Your Baggage Behind

As discussed in §11.2, *Preparing for Oral Argument*, you should prepare a thin notebook or folder of essential materials. Do not have additional materials in front of you, other than the relevant briefs, especially if you are addressing the court from a lectern. We have seen attorneys with loose notes, extra books, piles of briefs and files, and several notebooks arrayed before them. If you have prepared properly, you do not need all of those materials at the lectern or directly in front of you at counsel table. They can only cause problems. You do not want to be leafing through reams of materials as you search for the answer to a judge's question or have books fall to the floor because you have put too much material on the limited space provided to you. Your binder and perhaps the briefs are all you should need.

Should you have a pen or pencil in hand? Most attorneys do, but leaving the pen behind may be a wiser decision. Attorneys seem uncomfortable without a writing implement. But what will you do with that pen? What do you need to write? More likely, you will play with the pen in your nervousness. The pen is just one more item that can cause you — or worse, the judges — to be distracted from your message.[2] Place your pen on counsel table before you stand. If you really feel that a pen or pencil is necessary, take care not to continually click it or flip it around during your argument.[3]

IV. Make Eye Contact

Take care to make eye contact with the judge or judges who are hearing your argument. Making eye contact is important for two reasons. First, it engages the judge or judges in your message; listeners are more captivated by a speaker who looks them in the eye. Making eye contact helps you engage with each judge and allows you to have a conversation. Second, if you are making eye contact with a judge, you will be able to see when the judge has a question, so that you can pause or prepare for the question. And, as previously explained, the advocate should welcome questions from the bench.

---

2. One of the authors of this book described to the other authors her own experience with bringing a pen to the lectern: "I would click the cap incessantly, and once, in a passionate hand gesture, I flung my pen across the lectern toward the panel of judges. After that day, if I took a pen, I let it rest on the table."

3. Be especially vigilant if you have brought water to the lectern. One author watched an advocate squeeze a water bottle so tightly, the water shot out of the water bottle like a fountain. Another author watched as a colleague poured a glass of water over his notes.

V. Speak Slowly and Simply

Next, remember that you are attempting to persuade *orally*. Speakers communicate differently to listeners than writers do to readers. When communicating orally, you should speak in short sentences, using simpler language with fewer syllables than you might if you were writing a brief. In short, speak the spoken word.

In addition, speak slowly. Unlike the written word, spoken language takes longer for the listener to process. It is exceedingly rare to hear an advocate speak too slowly. Rather, given the excitement of the argument and the often too-short time allotted, most oral advocates tend to speak too fast. If in doubt, slow down.

A slow delivery has another advantage. Some attorneys speak so fast that they never pause, making it more difficult for a judge to pose a question. As emphasized throughout this chapter, however, you should welcome questions and make sure that judges are able to pose them easily. Thus, your delivery should be slow enough that the judges can interject with questions.

VI. Have a Conversation

In presenting your argument, be conversational but not too familiar. Having a conversation means that you do not read from notes and (except for your opening) you do not recite from memory. As the Federal Rules of Appellate Procedure caution, "Counsel must not read at length from briefs, records, or authorities."[4] Explain. Listen. Respond. Make eye contact. In other words, have a conversation.

VII. Use Humor with Care

Although oral argument is a kind of conversation, use humor with care. When using humor, you always run the risk of offending someone—for example, a judge or a crime victim in the courtroom—or distracting from your argument. Generally, if the subject matter of your argument is not too delicate and you are familiar with the judges, humor may be a helpful way to make a point. But when in doubt, avoid it. Only if you are confident that your humor will not offend, and if you have appeared a number of times before that court, should you consider using humor during oral argument.

---

4. Fed. R. App. P. 34(c).

Oral Argument Humor

At the oral argument before the U.S. Supreme Court in the *Ashcroft* case, the following exchange took place between the Court and the attorney arguing for the State of Oregon:

JUSTICE O'CONNOR: Would you speak up just a little, please?

MR. ATKINSON: I'm sorry, Your Honor, I will.

JUSTICE SCALIA: Maybe elevate your — the microphone.

JUSTICE O'CONNOR: Maybe you could raise the podium.

JUSTICE SCALIA: You're too tall.

[Laughter.]

MR. ATKINSON: I'll work on that, Your Honor.

Oral argument in *Gonzales v. Oregon*, 546 U.S. 243 (2006),
aff'g Oregon v. Ashcroft, 368 F.3d 1118 (9th Cir. 2004).

VIII. Assert Conclusions, Not Your Beliefs

Many lawyers will begin a statement to the court with "I believe" or "it is our contention that." Lawyers do that either because they are not confident in their assertions or because they are stalling for time. Whatever the reasons, those empty words will dilute your argument. Present your argument as truth, not your opinion. Thus, rather than stating, "It is our position that the contract is unenforceable," simply say, "The contract is unenforceable." Don't say, "A review of the record shows that the officer did not turn on his overhead lights until after he had stopped defendant." Rather, omit the empty words: "The officer did not turn on his overhead lights until after he had stopped defendant."

IX. Deliver Your Opening

As mentioned in § 11.2, *Preparing for Oral Argument*, you should have a prepared opening, and it should be memorized. That opening will set the tone for the argument, and depending on the court, it may be the last time during the argument that you have control over what is being discussed. Take advantage of that opportunity. Preparing and memorizing — not reading — the opening may also give you a chance to slide gently into your argument so that you can hit your stride after having warmed up.

Of course, in some courts, especially in appellate courts, you may be interrupted by questions after you utter your first word, and you will never get to your prepared opening. Nevertheless, have your opening down pat in case you are not.

X. Respond to Questions from the Bench

As we have suggested throughout this chapter, oral argument is primarily about the judges' questions. Sometimes, the advocate can manage to get out only a sentence or two before the court interrupts with questions, as in Example 11.3-A.

Example 11.3-A • The Court interrupts almost immediately with questions

---

MR. BOIES: Mr. Chief Justice, may it please the Court:

The district court below found, and it is not disputed here, that the plaintiff fulfilled all of the requirements of Rule 23(a) for class certification. The district court also found, and the court of appeals affirmed, that the plaintiffs demonstrated all of the requirements for class certification under 23(b)(3) except for the Fifth Circuit's loss causation requirement. The court below recognized that whether or not there was an efficient market was not disputed. It was conceded that we have an efficient market here. There were no challenges—

CHIEF JUSTICE ROBERTS: Mr. Boies, if could I just stop you there.

MR. BOIES: Certainly.

Oral Argument in *Erica P. John Fund, Inc. v. Halliburton*, 563 U.S. 804 (2011).

Although the inexperienced advocate might be put off by immediately being interrupted and redirected, the veteran advocate appreciates the interruption so that she can address the topic in which the court is interested. That information is invaluable because it gives the advocate the opportunity to address the court's concerns, rather than wasting time on matters that may be less important to the court.

As you know, the court's questions and the advocates' responses really form the core of oral argument. Some advice about how to handle those questions follows, but recognize that putting the advice into practice requires, well, some practice.

Lawyers Get a Break at the Supreme Court

Historically, U.S. Supreme Court justices have felt free to jump in with questions almost as soon as an advocate started speaking. The most recent edition of the Court's *Guide for Counsel in Cases to be Argued*, however, states, "The Court generally will not question lead counsel for petitioners (or appellants) and respondents (or appellees) during the first two minutes of argument."

A. Stop Talking and Listen

When a judge asks a question at oral argument, counsel must imme-diately do two things: stop talking and listen carefully. As soon as you see a judge's mouth open, stop talking, even if you are mid-word. It is a serious breach of oral argument etiquette to "talk over" a judge.

Moreover, you must stop talking so that you can listen carefully. Hearing the question correctly and responding to the question asked is harder than one might imagine. Advocates are sometimes so nervous that they simply have difficulty listening carefully. As a result, they will answer the question that they hoped was asked, or the question that they had prepared to answer, rather than the question that actually was asked. Thus, as soon as a judge starts talking, focus on the judge's question and make sure that you respond to the question actually asked.

B. Pause

After you have listened, you can take another moment or two to think through your answer. Although you may feel panicked inside, pausing for a moment will actually suggest to the judge who asked the question that it is an important question and that you are carefully con-sidering your response. You project the image of a thoughtful, careful advocate.

Rather than pausing, many attorneys confronted with an unanticipated question start talking, often wandering around orally, as they search for an answer. Judges find that approach frustrating, and it wastes some of the precious time you have at the lectern.

Of course, if you have prepared properly, you will have anticipated the question, and you may not need to pause long to think. But if the question takes you by surprise, pause for a moment (it may seem like an hour to you, but it really is just a moment), think about what the answer should be, and then, as explained below, respond "yes" or "no."

C. Ask for Clarification, If Necessary

If you are not sure what the judge is asking, ask for clarification. For example, you might ask the judge to repeat the question. At the very least, the repetition will give you more time to process the question. Or, rather than simply asking the judge to repeat the question, you might state your understanding of the question: "If I understand correctly, Your Honor, you are asking whether we agree that dismissal is an appropriate remedy in this case?" Such a question will allow the judge to tell you whether you have understood her question. (But, as discussed below, asking a clarifying question is the only instance in which you should ask a question of a judge.)

D. Respond with "Yes" or "No"; Then Explain Your Answer

If possible—and it almost always is—respond to questions with a "yes" or "no" and then explain your answer. Judges want to know your bottom line up front. So, concisely state your bottom line, then explain your answer. For example, "No, Your Honor, that is not the case here. Our case differs in two important ways. First,...." Answering "yes" or "no" and then explaining your response projects confidence in your response and lets the judge know that you are not being evasive.

Answer "Yes" or "No," and then Explain

JUSTICE ALITO: Let me be clear about exactly what your argument is. Your argument is that there is nothing that a State can do to limit minors' access to the most violent, sadistic, graphic video game that can be developed. That's your argument?

MR. SMITH: My position is—

JUSTICE ALITO: Is it or isn't it?

MR. SMITH: My position is that strict scrutiny applies, and that given the facts in the record, given the fact that the—the problem is already well controlled, the parents are already empowered, and there are greatly less alternatives out there—

JUSTICE SOTOMAYOR: So, when you—

MR. SMITH: —there isn't any basis to say scrutiny is satisfied.

JUSTICE SOTOMAYOR: So, when you say that—

CHIEF JUSTICE ROBERTS: So, just to be clear, your answer to Justice Alito is, at this point, there is nothing the State can do?

MR. SMITH: Because there's no problem it needs to solve that would justify—

CHIEF JUSTICE ROBERTS: Could I—could I just have a simple answer?

MR. SMITH: The answer is yes, Your Honor.

Oral argument in *Brown v. Entm't Merch. Ass'n*,
564 U.S. 804 (2011).

E. Never Praise a Judge's Question

Judges like to assume that all their questions are good, and they do not take kindly to attorneys telling them so. Although oral argument is a conversation, the parties are not on equal footing. Thus, even though sometimes you might be tempted, do not say, "That's a good question, Your Honor," even if it really *is* a good question. Doing so may sound obsequious. Simply answer the question. Do not comment on the quality of the question.

F. Always Answer a Question When It Is Asked

Never put off a question. You may, for example, think that the dispositive issue in the case has to do with the proper interpretation of a constitutional provision, and you have prepared your argument accordingly. But when the judge asks instead about a technical procedural issue, you should not put the question off or, by your demeanor or response, suggest that the question is not important. Or you may think that the question relates to your fourth point and you want to discuss your first three points before that. Nonetheless, recognize that the judge asking the question may see things differently, and your task is to address the judge's concern. Thus, never postpone responding to a judge's question.

Answer the Question When It Is Asked:
Go Where the Court Wants to Go

MR. COOPER: Thank you, Mr. Chief Justice, and may it please the Court: New York's highest court, in a case similar to this one, remarked that until quite recently, it was an accepted truth for almost everyone who ever lived in any society in which marriage existed . . .

CHIEF JUSTICE ROBERTS: Mr. Cooper, we have jurisdictional and merits issues here. Maybe it'd be best if you could begin with the standing issue.

MR. COOPER: I'd be happy to, Mr. Chief Justice.

Oral argument in *Hollingsworth v. Perry*, 570 U.S. 693 (2013).

G. Embrace Hypotheticals

Embrace hypotheticals that judges propose. Remember the tough job that judges have: They have to issue a decision that resolves the case before them and (in the case of most appellate courts and some trial courts) write an opinion that persuades the reader why their decision is correct. They also have to make sure that their decision fits within existing, binding case law and, to the extent that their decision will act as precedent in future cases, that it will yield correct results in other cases.

Appellate courts are particularly concerned about the rule of law that one case will establish for future cases. Thus, appellate judges in particular tend to use hypotheticals at oral argument to test the limits of your position, determine if there would be any untoward consequences if they adopt your position, and ensure that the rule they announce "works." By carefully listening to any hypothetical and explaining to the court how your position would play out under those facts, you help the court achieve its goals.

As you prepare for oral argument, you should be thinking about hypothetical situations that test the limits of your position, and you should consider what the result would be under your proposed rule. If, as explained in §11.2, *Preparing for Oral Argument*, you have carefully determined the precise limits of your position, you will be prepared for hypotheticals. If you are confronted with a hypothetical that you had not considered, your response will be obvious if you know your position precisely. Take a deep breath, think for a moment, and explain to the judge the result of his hypothetical under your position. And if, under that hypothetical, your client would lose, say so. But end on a strong point, such as, "But, Your Honor, this case differs from your hypothetical in three ways. First,.... Second,.... Third,.... Thus, in this case, my client should prevail."

Don't Fight the Hypothetical

In *Carpenter v. United States*, 138 S. Ct. 2206 (2018), the Supreme Court addressed whether the government violated the Fourth Amendment by accessing cell tower records containing the physical locations of cellphones without a search warrant. The following exchange took place between Justice Gorsuch and the government's lawyer.

JUSTICE GORSUCH: Let's say I have a property right…, so that if someone were to steal my location information from T-Mobile I'd have a conversion claim, for example, against them for the economic value that was stolen.

Wouldn't that, therefore, be a search of my paper or effect under the property-based approach approved and reminded us in Jones?

.....

MR. DREEBEN: I don't think you can make that assumption.

JUSTICE GORSUCH: — [L]et's stick with my hypothetical, counsel, okay? I know you don't like it. I got that.

(Laughter.)

JUSTICE GORSUCH: But let's say that, in fact, I've got positive law that indicates it is a property right. Would you there, therefore, agree that that's a search of my paper and effect?

MR. DREEBEN: I wouldn't, and I —

JUSTICE GORSUCH: But why not?

MR. DREEBEN: Because it's not your paper or your effect.

JUSTICE GORSUCH: If property law says it is.

MR. DREEBEN: Well, I don't think property law does say that it is. And I think that —

JUSTICE GORSUCH: Well, that's fighting the hypothetical, counsel. And I know I — I didn't like hypotheticals, too, when I was a lawyer sometimes, but I'm asking you to stick with my hypothetical.

> MR. DREEBEN: Justice Gorsuch, I think that the problem with the hypothetical is that it creates a property interest out of transfers of information.
>
> JUSTICE GORSUCH: Please—please, could you stick with my hypothetical and then you can tell me why it's wrong.
>
> MR. DREEBEN: All right.
>
> Oral argument in *Carpenter v. United States*, 138 S. Ct. 2206 (2018).

H. Recognize Friendly Questions

Recognize and respond appropriately to so-called "friendly questions." Sometimes advocates are so bent on being adversarial that they do not recognize a friendly question. Judges, however, sometimes ask questions that are helpful to your position. When you hear such a question, you should accept it at face value, answer "yes" or "no," and use it as a launch pad for your argument: "Yes, that's correct, Your Honor, for two reasons. First,…." It is frustrating indeed to watch an oral argument in which the advocate is unwilling to take "yes" for an answer.

I. Admit When You Do Not Know the Answer

Do not be afraid to say these three words: "I don't know." Judges understand that advocates do not always know the answers to their questions. Although attorneys hate to say that we do not know something, doing so is better than the alternatives of bluffing or being flat-out wrong, both of which damage your credibility with the court. In some courts, advocates may offer to file a post-oral argument memorandum in response to a judge's question. If that is the practice in the court in which you are appearing, and if it seems appropriate to do so, offer to file such a memorandum—and then remember to do it.

> **Do Not Be Afraid to Say, "I Don't Know."**
>
> JUSTICE GINSBURG: Mr. Dreeben, something that you said about the encryption. What—what is the experience of the police? Isn't it so that most cell phones when they're found on a person are not open, that—that they are locked?
>
> MR. DREEBEN: Justice Ginsburg, I would not be able to answer a question about what condition most cell phones are found in. The fact that this issue has arisen repeatedly in cases across the country indicates that at least in a significant number of cases, the phones are not locked and the officers are able to obtain access to the information.
>
> Oral argument in *Riley v. California*, 573 U.S. 373 (2014).

Some questions are factual. When responding to a factual question, you must note whether your answer is based on facts in the record or if it has a different source. Sometimes you can respond to a question by first making it clear that the answer to the judge's factual inquiry is not in the record, but then offering information that the judge might find useful.

J. Recognize the Logical End of an Answer

If, at the outset, you took a moment to think through your answer, you will also recognize the end of your answer when you get there. As you think about a question, consider whether the question requires a single sentence to answer or several paragraphs. For example, if the court asks you, "Was anyone else present during the interrogation?" you can assess whether a simple "No, Your Honor," is sufficient or whether that question needs to be addressed in detail. When you unnecessarily tack on several paragraphs to what could have been a simple "No, Your Honor," you waste your time and the court's time.

K. After Answering the Court's Question, Return to Your Planned Argument or Adjust as Necessary

After answering a question, you should try to return to the points that you want to make. Returning smoothly to your plan after minutes of wide-ranging argument on other points is one of the hardest skills to master; it takes practice. Remember, however, that it will be easier to return to your argument and keep track of your "must-make" points if you have listed them at the beginning of your lectern materials.

When you return to your argument, you will need to make a choice: "Do I return to where I was in my argument before the questions? Or, do I pick up at the place in my argument where the questioning left off?"

That depends. Sometimes you can give a quick answer to a judge's question and return to exactly where you left off before the question. Other times the questions will persist, and then you will need to make a decision. If, after the questioning on an issue is over, you have more or less provided all the information you planned to provide on the issue about which you were questioned, you can now leave that issue and return to an unfinished issue or move on to another issue. If, however, the questions did not bring out all you wanted to say on that issue, address it completely before moving on. If judges spend time asking questions about a particular issue, they consider that issue important.

As you proceed through your argument, be aware of the remaining time and manage your time appropriately. You can, of course, pause for a moment, take stock of where you are and what points remain, and then decide how to continue. Remember this: The court does not expect a polished speech, but a helpful, enlightening conversation.

XI. Conclude

You should conclude your argument when you have said everything that you have to say, and you are satisfied that the court has no further questions. Ideally, your conclusion will provide a very brief summary of your argument or a simple conclusion stating the relief you seek.

The specific language that you use may depend on whether you are arguing before a trial court or an appellate court and whether you have exhausted any time limits. Section 11.4, *Trial Courts vs. Appellate Courts*, provides more detailed suggestions about how to conclude an oral argument depending on whether you are arguing before a trial court or an appellate court.

No matter the tribunal, be aware of one common mistake that novice advocates make. That mistake is to continue talking simply because they have the time to do so. Judges will appreciate your not wasting their time by going back over matters that have been thoroughly addressed or by addressing matters that are not in contention. Spending unnecessary time arguing may not only annoy the judges, but it might also open you up to questions that take away from the points you wanted to leave the court with. When you have nothing useful left to say, conclude confidently and sit down.

XII. Listen When the Court Questions Opposing Counsel

Counsel for a responding party has a distinct advantage at oral argument: the opportunity to listen to the questions posed during opposing counsel's argument and thereby gain insight into the court's concerns.[5] That is, by the time counsel for the responding party begins her argument, she may have a much better idea about "where the game is being played." Thus, if you are representing the responding party, listen carefully to opposing counsel's argument and the questions the court asks; that information is invaluable.

Then, shape your argument in light of what you have heard. In other words, counsel for the responding party has to be flexible enough to construct aspects of an argument while opposing counsel is arguing. To be sure, if you are counsel for a responding party, you may make a number of planned arguments regardless of what opposing counsel argued. But, if you represent the responding party, take advantage of having listened to the court and tweak your argument in light of what you have heard. For example, if during opposing counsel's argument, the court has

---

5. This advantage is somewhat offset by the appellant's opportunity to present rebuttal (the appellant's or moving party's opportunity to respond to the respondent's or nonmoving party's argument), thus getting the last word in.

indicated that it is not persuaded by one of the arguments, you may choose to spend less time on that argument than you had initially planned.

Responding counsel who fails to take into consideration what has taken place and simply presents a canned argument loses an opportunity to address the court's concerns and may annoy the judge or judges. Instead, use your position as responding party to get to the heart of what the court cares about.

XIII. Rebuttal

Similarly, if you have an opportunity to rebut, listen carefully while responding counsel is arguing to determine how you can best use your rebuttal time.

In a trial court, counsel who opens the argument will usually be given time to respond to opposing counsel's argument. At the end of the responding party's argument, the judge will ordinarily turn to counsel who opened the argument and ask, "Counselor, do you have anything further?"

Rebuttal time in appellate courts is more formal. Appellate court rules often govern how much time an appellant may reserve for rebuttal, and rebuttal time typically comes out of the appellant's total allotment. Thus, if the appellant has thirty minutes total, reserving five minutes for rebuttal leaves twenty-five minutes for the principal argument. Most courts allow the appellant to use part of her rebuttal time as principal argument if she desires, reserving the remaining time for rebuttal. Thus, an exchange like that in Example 11.3-B might take place for an appellant who has reserved five minutes of rebuttal.

Example 11.3-B · Using some of your rebuttal time

THE COURT: Counsel, your red light is on. You are welcome to continue, but you are into your rebuttal time.

COUNSEL: Thank you, Your Honor. I'd like to just finish the point I was making. [Counsel continues for one minute and concludes.]

THE COURT: Thank you, counsel. You will have four minutes remaining for rebuttal.

In general, in an appellate court, reserve no more than five minutes for rebuttal and, in many cases, one to three minutes is appropriate, especially for shorter arguments. Because they normally can go into rebuttal time during the principal argument if circumstances call for it, appellants should always reserve rebuttal time.

How should you use rebuttal time? During the responding party's argument, listen carefully to the questions and counsel's responses and take notes, perhaps on a single sheet of paper in your binder. You will have the opportunity to get the last word in, and keeping track of the court's concerns during your opponent's argument will allow you to use that time to your benefit.

When it is your turn for rebuttal, you should quickly choose the one to three most important points that came up during the respondent's argument to address. If you have less time for rebuttal, you may choose to address only one point; even with more time, it is rarely appropriate to address more than three points in rebuttal.

Rebuttal is not a time to repeat what you said during your principal argument or a time to make additional arguments, but a time to rebut statements made by the respondent or to address questions that came up during the respondent's argument. Just as judges do not appreciate a reply brief that does nothing but repeat the opening brief, they are unlikely to be persuaded by a rebuttal that tells them what they have already heard. Novice advocates often try to do too much with rebuttal, attempting to address every little quibble they have with what the respondent said. But that approach is rarely useful. Instead, choose up to three major points, address them quickly and clearly, chose a strong ending, and then sit down.

The discussion above provides general advice about preparing for and presenting oral arguments. As noted at the beginning of this chapter, oral arguments differ—both in their preparation and presentation— depending on whether you are arguing before a trial court or an appellate court. In the next section, you will learn how to adjust your argument to suit the court in which you are arguing.

Practice Points

- An oral argument is a conversation with the court.
  - Listen to the questions carefully.
  - Pause before you speak.
  - Answer with a "yes" or "no," and then explain as necessary.
  - Speak slowly.
  - Return to your argument.
- Show your respect for the court.
  - Never speak when a judge is speaking.
  - Always answer a question when it is asked.
  - Do not ask any questions except to clarify the court's question or to ask permission to finish a response.
- Listen carefully as the court questions opposing counsel.

Trial Courts vs. Appellate Courts

The preceding sections provide guidance about preparing for and delivering argument in trial and appellate courts. The guidance in those sections applies generally to both types of courts—as well as to other tribunals, such as administrative agencies. This section delves deeper into the differences between oral arguments in trial courts and in appellate courts. As you read, remember that the differences addressed below tend to be matters of degree.

I. Arguing Before Trial Courts

The following discussion about arguing before a trial court refers particularly to presenting an argument to a court after one party has filed a motion and both parties have had an opportunity to brief the court on the motion. An argument on a motion is usually called a "hearing."

Other arguments do occur during a trial—many of which you have seen on TV, in a movie, or perhaps in real life. For example, at trial, an attorney may present an opening statement or closing argument to a jury. In addition, while a witness is on the stand, one attorney may object to opposing counsel's question and may need to quickly explain the basis for that objection. All of those activities are "arguments" in the broadest sense.

The advice that follows is largely focused on the more formal arguments that are presented after a motion has been filed and briefs have been submitted. Those arguments, for the most part, occur before or after trial and much less frequently during a trial.

A. Jurisdictional Variation

The most important thing to know about arguing at the trial level is that practice varies greatly—from federal district to federal district, from state to state, from county to county, and even from judge to judge in the same courthouse. For that reason, research the procedure in the particular courtroom in which you will be arguing before you arrive. Many courts have information about practicing in that court on their websites. Some bar associations publish information, and especially in larger states and in the federal courts, practice guides and treatises may be available. However, some courts and judges adhere to unwritten rules, and the best resource is often your colleagues. Thus, the suggestion earlier in this chapter to talk to others is especially important in trial courts.

B. Your Audience: One Judge

One obvious characteristic of oral argument at the trial level is that you will be arguing to only one person.[1] Because argument on a motion in a trial court is before a single adjudicator, it is worth knowing the particular preferences of that judge. Does the judge you are appearing before typically like a recitation of the facts? Does the judge generally ask a lot of questions or few? Has the judge ordinarily read the briefs beforehand, or does the judge need a summary of the brief?

Usually, the best way to find out about the idiosyncrasies of a particular judge is to ask others who have appeared before the judge and visit that

---

1. Rare exceptions exist. For example, 28 U.S.C. § 2284(a) requires a district court to convene a three-judge panel for a limited number of issues:

> A district court of three judges shall be convened when otherwise required by Act of Congress, or when an action is filed challenging the constitutionality of the apportionment of congressional districts or the apportionment of any statewide legislative body.

judge's courtroom when the judge is hearing motions. As suggested earlier, the Internet is also an invaluable resource. For example, the website for the Federal District Court for the Central District of California lists each judge with a link to that particular judge's procedures.[2]

C. Busy Dockets

Trial judges—especially state court trial judges—have very busy dockets. Thus, trial judges may not have the luxury of preparing thoroughly for your argument. They may not have had time to read the brief you submitted the day before argument or may not have been able to review the 500 pages of deposition testimony that your motion for summary judgment depends on. Thus, when arguing before a trial judge, you are more likely to recite the facts or recap the argument you gave in your brief. Although you should be prepared to provide such overviews, each judge is different. You can determine the likelihood that you will need to provide such an overview by talking to colleagues who have practiced before that particular judge.

D. Shorter Timelines to Oral Arguments

Trial courts move quickly. Thus, after submitting your brief, oral arguments might be scheduled within a few weeks or, in some cases, the within the next few days. The accelerated timeline means that you will compress your preparation. Fortunately, the law, the record, and your arguments will be significantly fresher in your mind, making the compressed timeframe more manageable.

E. Addressing the Court

Depending on a number of factors, such as whether you are in state or federal court, which particular judge you have drawn, and local custom, a trial courtroom is likely to be less formal than an appellate courtroom. For example, some trial judges allow counsel to address the court while standing at counsel table or even while seated; appellate courts rarely, if ever, do. Accordingly, find out before argument what the custom is.

As stated in § 11.2, *Preparing for Oral Argument*, even though a trial courtroom may be less formal, when you first stand to address the court, you should say, "Your Honor, my name is _____, and I represent

---

2. *See Judges' Procedures and Schedules*, U.S. Dist. Court, Cent. Dist. of Cal., http://court.cacd.uscourts.gov/CACD/JudgeReq.nsf/FAQs+about+Judges%27+ Procedures+and+Schedules?OpenView (last visited July 25, 2021).

[name the party you represent].” Thereafter, address the judge as “Your Honor.” Although in some courts it is common to address the judge as “Judge _____” or just plain “Judge,” practice varies, and you cannot go wrong with “Your Honor” as a default.

F. Typical Questions from the Trial Court's Perspective

Trial courts decide cases; they are less concerned with setting precedent and setting out rules of law than are appellate courts. Thus, trial judges are more likely to be concerned about what law governs the outcome of the case and about the facts of your case than about the rule of law that the case will stand for. It follows that trial judges will more likely have questions about the facts of the case, especially about what facts are in dispute. Trial judges are also more likely to be concerned about—and thus ask questions about—what the law requires them to do, with less attention to the effect of their rulings on future parties.

G. Time Allotted for Oral Argument

In trial courts, oral argument—if it is permitted at all—may be much more of a free-ranging discussion among counsel and the judge than it might be in an appellate court. The judge may not have a strict limit on the time each lawyer may speak; rather, the judge may allow the lawyers to argue for as long as they wish. Or, the judge may allow only a very short time to argue a simple motion. Similarly, a trial court judge may permit more back-and-forth between the lawyers than would be permitted in an appellate court. Thus, for example, the nonmoving party may have another chance to argue after the moving party does rebuttal. In short, as with other aspects of trial court oral argument, expect more variation in the amount of time and conduct.

H. Your Closing

Closings for trial court arguments can vary depending on the circumstances in which the oral argument arose.

Some trial court oral arguments are more formal. Usually, more formal oral arguments are preceded by written briefs, and the court schedules a time for arguments related to those briefs. At the end of these more formal oral arguments, you would likely close by briefly summarizing the main points of your argument. Example 11.4-A imagines a closing that plaintiff's attorney would make at the end of oral arguments on the summary judgment motion described in Appendix B. Notice that it states the relief the party is seeking (dismissal of the motion for summary judgment) and states the major reasons why that relief should be granted.

Example 11.4-A · Closing an oral argument before a trial court

---

In sum, Your Honor, defendant's motion for summary judgment should be denied. Based on the evidence discovered, a jury could find that defendant Starr Publishing defamed our clients. Moreover, our clients never consented to being defamed, and the evidence does not support such a conclusion. For these reasons, summary judgment would be inappropriate. Thank you.

If, based on the questions the court has posed, you believe you have already made your main points clear, you can simply close by saying "Thank you, Your Honor."

Other times, an issue arises unexpectedly, and the parties have not briefed the issue in advance. Or, perhaps, the argument is on a minor or administrative matter, such as a motion for a continuance. In those circumstances, you may choose to summarize your point and the relief you seek, as in Example 11.4-A; however, the colloquy is more likely to end in a simple "Thank you, Your Honor."

When an issue arises unexpectedly you may also want to clarify next steps before leaving: Are you and opposing counsel supposed to craft proposed orders to submit to the judge? Does the judge want copies of any relevant cases or a legal memorandum or brief? Do you need to schedule another hearing? You should try to clarify those issues before leaving court.

Practice in trial courts varies more than it does in appellate courts; trial practice is often less formal, and the trial judge often has not had an abundance of time to prepare for an argument on a motion. Because of the greater variation among trial courts, it is essential to familiarize yourself with the practice in the particular court in which you will be arguing.

II. Arguing Before Appellate Courts

By the time oral argument rolls around, the appellate judges most likely will have read your brief, your opponent's brief, any reply brief or amicus briefs, and the opinion or other disposition below. They may have read a bench memorandum, prepared by a law clerk or staff attorney, summarizing the issues in the case and the record. They may have already engaged in a pre-argument conference and discussed their initial impressions of the case; in some courts, a draft opinion may have been prepared. In most appellate courts, the judges are quite prepared to address your case at oral argument.

In preparing for argument in appellate courts, in addition to other resources, you also may be able to read transcripts of arguments or listen to recordings of them. For example, both audio recordings and written transcripts of U.S. Supreme Court arguments are readily accessible from the Court's website. Westlaw and Lexis also provide access to some other oral argument transcripts. Be careful, however, not to assume that the nature of argument in your court (for example, in a state intermediate appellate court) is the same as that in the U.S. Supreme Court.

A. Jurisdictional Variation

As suggested previously, appellate courts are more like one another than trial courts are. Accordingly, the relevant portion of the Federal Rules of Appellate Procedure (as supplemented by any additional circuit rules) will give you a pretty good idea of what to do at oral argument in any appellate court in a given federal circuit. The same goes for state courts: An argument in the Fourth District of the California Court of Appeal is likely to resemble an argument in the First District, despite their distance from one another. Thus, although it still is important to research the court you will be arguing in, you generally can expect less variation in the oral argument practices in appellate courts than you will find in trial courts.

B. Your Audience: A Panel of Judges

When arguing an appeal, you will argue before a panel of judges. The panel of judges will range in size from the usual three-judge panel in an intermediate appellate court to a panel of five, seven, or nine judges in courts of last resort, including the United States Supreme Court. In fact, some advocates will argue before as many as fifteen judges for an en banc argument in the United States Court of Appeals.

Arguing before a panel of judges, rather than a single judge, has at least three implications. First, a single judge's idiosyncrasies are less important because at least two other judges are involved in the process. Second, you need to persuade at least two (and maybe as many as six or more) judges that your position is correct. Thus, in preparing for an appellate court argument, think about the different arguments that might appeal to different judges. For example, one judge might be persuaded that you should prevail because the trial court did not err; a second judge of the three-judge panel might be persuaded that the trial court erred, but that the error was harmless. In such a case, by presenting both an argument on the merits and a harmless error argument, you are more likely to prevail.

Third, maintaining eye contact, especially while answering questions, differs in the context of an appellate argument. Maintaining eye contact with three or more judges sitting in a semicircle in front of you is more difficult than maintaining eye contact with a single judge. Thus, when responding to questions—especially a series of questions from the same judge—focus primarily on the judge who asked the question, but be careful not to exclude the other judges. Sometimes, a judge and an advocate can engage in a back-and-forth that lasts several minutes. If you don't make eye contact with the other judges, they will feel excluded, and you will lose a chance to persuade them.

C. Appellate Courts Have More Time to Prepare

As compared to trial courts, appellate courts have significantly more time to prepare for oral argument. In most appellate courts today, the judges have read your brief (or a bench memorandum summarizing it), have thought about it, and may have already discussed it with the other judges. Thus, repeating the brief is a poor use of your time at an appellate oral argument. Rather, oral argument should complement the brief, emphasizing important points, expanding on arguments made in the brief, and explaining difficult points.

Most importantly, you should use your limited time to listen to the court's questions, assess the concerns that the court has, and respond to those concerns. Appellate judges have had more time to prepare for oral argument than their colleagues on the trial bench, and they expect that you will have, too.

D. Longer Timelines to Oral Arguments

At the appellate level, months may pass between when an appellate brief is filed and oral argument is heard. Thus, you will need to engage in significantly more review to remind yourself of the law and facts of the case. In addition, you must update the law to ensure that the cases you cited are still good law, that no other relevant cases have been decided, and that no relevant legislative changes have occurred.

E. Addressing the Court

In virtually all appellate courts, you will address the court only when standing at a lectern.

Once at the lectern, begin with, "May it please the court." (An exception is the U.S. Supreme Court, where advocates begin with, "Mr. Chief Justice, and may it please the Court.") Following that stock greeting, you should introduce yourself by saying, "My name is_____. I represent _____." If you are the appellant, and if it is the practice in that court, you should then reserve rebuttal time.

When responding to a judge's question, you may use the judge's name, or you may refer to the judge as "Your Honor." Given how embarrassing it is to address a judge by the wrong name, when in doubt, stick with "Your Honor."

Calling a Judge by the Wrong Name

During oral argument in *United States v. Comstock*, 560 U.S. 126 (2010), then-Solicitor General Elena Kagan mistakenly referred to Justice Scalia as the Chief Justice in responding to Justice Scalia's question:

[SOLICITOR] GENERAL KAGAN: Mr. Chief—excuse me, Justice Scalia—I didn't mean to promote you quite so quickly.

(Laughter.)

CHIEF JUSTICE ROBERTS: Thanks for thinking it was a promotion.

(Laughter.)

JUSTICE SCALIA (looking at CHIEF JUSTICE ROBERTS): And I'm sure you didn't.

(Laughter.)

GENERAL KAGAN: Justice Scalia, …

That gaffe did not, of course, prevent Elena Kagan from later being appointed to the Supreme Court.

F. Typical Questions from the Appellate Court's Perspective

Appellate courts have a somewhat different task than do trial courts. As stated above, trial courts resolve cases. Appellate courts—although they must dispose of the case before them—decide the law. It follows that the questions posed by appellate judges during argument tend to have a different flavor. Because the opinions issued by appellate courts create binding precedent, appellate judges are more concerned than trial judges about the effect of their ruling on other cases. They use oral argument to examine the implications of the rule that the case will stand for; to clarify which issues are properly before them and which are not; to assess the practical effect of their decision in the case, both for parties and nonparties; to determine the reach of their ruling; and to consider other, more jurisprudential, aspects of the case.

Thus, appellate judges are more likely to pose hypothetical situations and ask the advocates what the result would be in those situations under the advocate's proposed rule. They are more likely to poke and prod the advocate's positions, looking for unintended consequences or other problems. Finally, as explained in Chapter 9, *Appellate Briefs and Appellate Practice*, the appellate judge's universe is only that which is in the record on appeal. Accordingly, appellate judges are likely to have questions about the record.

What Rule Should the Court Adopt?

QUESTION: Exactly what is the constitutional rule you would have this Court adopt? It's not clear to me.

MR. D'ALEMBERTE: Your Honor, it is the rule that we believe the Court has adopted in Ford. It's also a rule that was adopted earlier in *Robinson v. California*, and it's the idea that our protections against cruel and unusual punishment protect against anything that's barbaric. We believe that execution of someone who is innocent, execution of someone who has —

QUESTION: Well, that goes back to my initial question. We don't have an innocent person here. We have a person who has been convicted of the murder. You have allegations coming up later of new evidence. So in that context what is the rule you are asking us to adopt?

MR. D'ALEMBERTE: Your Honor, I believe that the rule is analogous to the rule announced in *Ford*. We did not know in *Ford* whether the person —

QUESTION: Well, just, just can you tell me the rule you would have us adopt, then we can talk about authorities.

MR. D'ALEMBERTE: I'm sorry. Your Honor, the rule that we would suggest is the rule that says that an inmate with a colorable claim of innocence may not be executed without provision for a hearing, due process to determine the merits of that claim.

Oral argument in *Herrera v. Collins*,
506 U.S. 390 (1992).

G. Do Not Question the Court

Other than when you ask a judge to clarify a question posed or ask a procedural question, do not ask questions of the judges. In particular, do not ask, "Does that answer your question, Your Honor?" Most judges believe that their role is to ask questions, and your role is to respond to them. They may be offended or at least surprised if you ask them questions. The first exception is, as mentioned above, when you ask a judge to clarify her question. The second exception is when you are asking a procedural question, such as, "I see that my time is up. May I respond to Your Honor's question?" As long as you speak slowly and make eye contact, judges will be able to ask the questions they have.

One goal of the court at oral argument on appeal is to identify the scope of the parties' claims. For example, in the *Ashcroft* case, discussed earlier, a judge might wonder whether the state is taking the position that the U.S. Attorney General never has authority to issue a directive that purports to interpret a statutory provision, or whether only a directive that conflicts with a state law is impermissible. Oral argument allows the judges to determine the scope of the rule of law that each party is advocating, either through direct questions or through the use of hypotheticals. That is why, as discussed in §11.2, *Preparing for Oral Argument*, advocates must be confident that they know the scope of the rule they advance.

When the Red Light Goes On, Stop!

MS. JACKSON: Your Honor, I don't think that *Chadha* is identical, with respect. In—for two main reasons. In *Chadha*, the Court was, I think, quite careful to avoid deciding whether the United States had Article III standing. It intensively analyzed a statute, since repealed, 1252, which gave this Court mandatory jurisdiction in cases in which a federal statute was held unconstitutional and the U.S. was a party. And it framed its analysis of whether the statute permitted the appeal.

[Counsel's red light goes on.]

What I think was—oh, may I reserve my time for rebuttal?

CHIEF JUSTICE ROBERTS: You can finish your sentence.

MS. JACKSON: Thank you.

What was—what was going on there was the Court said, well, the statute wanted to reach very broadly, perhaps implicit, not stated, perhaps more broadly than Article III. Congress said whenever you have this configuration, you go up to the Supreme Court. Then the Supreme Court in *Chadha* says, of course, in addition to the statute, there must be Article III case or controversy, the presence of the congressional intervenors here provides it. And that—

CHIEF JUSTICE ROBERTS: Thank you, counsel. That was more than a sentence.

MS. JACKSON: Oh, I'm sorry. I'm sorry, Your Honor. Thank you.

Oral argument in *United States v. Windsor*,
570 U.S. 744 (2013).

H. Time Allotted for Oral Argument

Be aware of time limits. Appellate courts set strict time limits for the argument, and those limits usually are found in the relevant rules of appellate procedure. In some appellate courts, counsel is expected to keep track of the time. Most appellate courts, however, provide a system of lights or a countdown timer to inform counsel of the time remaining. In those courts with a system of lights, a white or yellow light usually illuminates when counsel has two minutes remaining, and a red light illuminates when counsel's time is up.

Appellate courts usually strictly enforce the time limits. When the red light illuminates, counsel is expected to utter no more than a couple of words before leaving the lectern. Some courts expect counsel to stop mid-syllable if the red light goes on. If you are answering a question when your red light goes on, you should ask the presiding judge or justice (the one at the center of the bench) if you may finish your response, even if another judge asked the question. But even if permission is granted to do so, you should not add more than a few more sentences at the most.

I. Your Closing

Appellate practitioners typically have different closings memorized. At the end of their oral argument, they choose the most appropriate closing depending on the time available.

If you have said everything you hoped to say and you have one or more remaining minutes, you might provide a conclusion that reiterates or emphasizes important points and then state the relief that you are seeking, as in Example 11.4-B. If the court's questions throughout your argument repeatedly returned to one point, you might choose to emphasize your position on that point in concluding, as in Example 11.4-C.

Example 11.4-B · A closing when you have the time for a closing

---

In conclusion, this court should deny the motion for two independent reasons. First, as we explained in our trial memo and as we've discussed here today, trial counsel's conduct did not fall below an objective standard of reasonableness. Failing to object to the victim impact evidence was a reasonable tactical choice. Second, even if that choice not to object was objectively unreasonable, it had no tendency to affect the outcome of the trial. That is, petitioner has not demonstrated prejudice. If the court agrees with us on either point, it should deny the motion. Unless the court has additional questions, I have nothing further to add. Thank you.

Example 11.4-C · A closing that emphasizes a point on which the court focused

---

In closing, I would like to draw the court's attention to the discussion it had with opposing counsel regarding preservation of error. As the court's questions suggested, the vague reference to the Constitution at trial below was not sufficient to preserve a claim of constitutional error. For that reason, as well as the reasons discussed in our brief, this court should affirm the trial court's judgment. Unless the court has other questions, I have nothing further to add. Thank you.

If you have only a few seconds left, your closing may have to be shorter. You might say a simple, "Thank you," and then sit down. Or, you might say, "Unless the court has further questions [pause to ensure that the judges have no further questions], I have nothing else to add. Thank you." Then, assuming the court does not have any further questions, gather your materials and return to your seat.

In an oft-quoted statement, U.S. Supreme Court Justice Robert H. Jackson, who argued numerous appellate cases before going on the bench, accurately summarized the experience of oral argument:

> I used to say that, as Solicitor General, I made three arguments of every case. First came the one that I had planned—as I thought, logical, coherent, complete. Second was the one I actually presented—interrupted, incoherent, disjointed, disappointing. The third was the utterly devastating argument that I thought of after going to bed that night.[3]

The goal of the oral advocate is to thoroughly plan the first argument, to recognize that the second argument will inevitably occur, and to try as much as possible to incorporate that golden third argument into the first and second arguments. Although speaking style, good posture, engagement with the court, and all the other techniques discussed above are necessary elements of a successful oral argument, the true key to ensuring that oral argument is persuasive to the court and satisfying to the advocate is thorough preparation. If you prepare properly, you will represent your client well, you will be helpful to the court, you will reduce the inherent stress of an oral presentation, and you may really enjoy the experience.

---

3. Robert H. Jackson, *Advocacy Before the Supreme Court: Suggestions for Effective Case Presentations*, 37 A.B.A. J. 801, 803 (1951).

Practice Points

- Oral arguments may differ if you are arguing in a trial court as opposed to an appellate court.

- If you are arguing in a trial court
  - Your audience is a single judge who, because of a busy docket, may have had less time to prepare.
  - The oral argument is less likely to adhere to strict to time limits.
  - The judge will likely be most concerned about ascertaining the existing governing law and understanding the specific facts to which that law applies.

- If you are arguing in an appellate court
  - Your audience is a panel of judges who have likely had more time to prepare for oral argument.
  - The oral argument is more likely to adhere to strict time limits.
  - In addition to ascertaining the current law that governs, the appellate court will be interested in the impact its decision will have on future cases.

Section 11.5

Remote Oral Arguments

Many court proceedings that had previously taken place exclusively in person and in a courtroom are now taking place through online services such as Zoom or WebEx. Online proceedings offer some benefits to the parties and to the court systems. Lawyers, their clients, and witnesses no longer have to travel to the courthouse or wait around the courthouse in the event of delays. Eliminating travel and wait time reduces costs to individuals who need to appear and increases efficiency within, and accessibility to, the legal system. Thus, many courts are conducting some proceedings—including oral arguments—online.

If you are asked to present oral arguments remotely, you should be prepared to adjust to that environment. Below, we provide a few tips so that your remote arguments appear as professional and polished as your in-person arguments.

- **Consider your video background.**

As you prepare for your remote oral argument, consider the background that will show in your video. Your video background implicitly speaks to your professionalism whether you are at work or at home. Your background should be neat, professional, and above all, not distracting.

Before your argument, turn on your screen and review what will show up in your camera's video feed. Consider the artwork, office tchotchkes, personal photos, coffee cups, or piles of papers in your space, and remove any item that would be distracting to a viewer.

Alternatively, some online services allow you to replace your actual background with a downloaded image. If you choose a virtual background image, choose an appropriate one that will reflect your professionalism. An image of a beach with palm trees swaying in the background is beautiful, but not appropriate for a court hearing. Choose colors or patterns that are neutral, even boring. You want judges paying attention to your argument and not wondering about where exactly that beach in the background might be located.

Consider whether a virtual background is, in fact, better. Sometimes virtual backgrounds create distracting gaps where the live individual and the virtual background meet.

- **Consider your wider surroundings.**

In addition to considering the background that the judges and opposing counsel will see, consider what they might hear. For example, attending a court hearing from your home may not be ideal if you have a dog that might bark or a nearby toilet that might be flushed in the middle of your oral argument.[1] If possible, choose a location where no unexpected sounds will distract from the arguments.

- **Consider your lighting.**

Watch for two common problems: having too little (or too much) light and having the lighting behind you. The best source of light is natural, diffused light that washes evenly across your face.

Avoid having too dark of a room and inadequate light on your face; judges and opposing counsel will want to see a clear image, not a grainy one. Conversely, avoid having too much light on your face. Super bright lighting or cool-toned bulbs can make your image stark. Aim for softer, warmer-toned lighting spread evenly on your face.

The major source of light in your room should be in front of you. If the major source of light is behind you, your face will likely appear in shadow—as if you are in a witness protection program. Detailed guides for products and methods to light your space are plentiful on the internet.

- **Adjust your camera so it frames your face.**

When two people are talking, the person listening absorbs a lot of information by observing facial expressions. The court will be better able to absorb your argument if your camera frames your face. Ideally, the camera will be at eye level, so that you are naturally looking into the camera. The top of the screen will be just above your head, and the bottom of the screen will show your shoulders. Avoid looking down at your laptop, and prop up the camera to achieve eye level.

Figure 11.5-A shows an image from a Georgia Supreme Court oral argument that took place remotely. Each person is appropriately framed in the video screen, and their chosen backgrounds are appropriate.

1. Fred Barbash, Oyez. *Oy Vey. Was That a Toilet Flush in the Middle of a Supreme Court Live-Streamed Hearing?*, Wash. Post (May 7, 2020), https://www.washingtonpost.com/nation/2020/05/07/toilet-flush-supreme-court/.

Figure 11.5-A · Georgia Supreme Court hears oral arguments remotely[2]

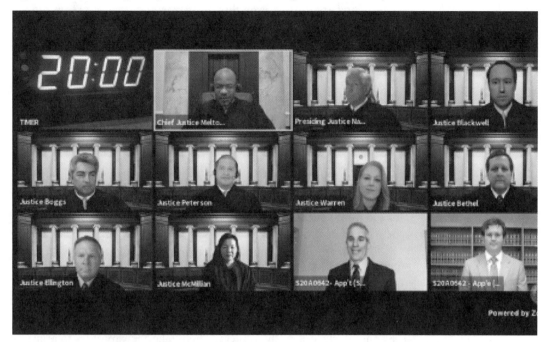

- **Decide whether you will sit or stand.**

When lawyers argue in court, they typically stand as they argue. Some local rules require that advocates stand while speaking to the court. In addition, standing when presenting an argument to the court is seen as a sign of respect for the court and allows for the speaker to be clearly seen and heard.

When arguing remotely, consider carefully whether you want to sit or stand. The first consideration is that, whatever position you choose, you will have to remain there throughout the argument. Most web cameras do not easily adjust their focus or framing, so if you were to change your position after you argue, you would no longer be on camera or you would be out of focus. Since attorneys generally keep their cameras on throughout an argument, you will need to remain in one place.

The second consideration is that you will likely want space for your computer, your argument outline, and a note pad to take notes while opposing counsel argues. You may also want space for a glass of water.

2. Photograph of the Georgia Supreme Court in Max Mitchell, National Appellate Advocacy Group Issues Best Practice for Remote Oral Arguments, Law.com (July 21, 2020, 1:56 PM), https://www.law.com/nationallawjournal/2020/07/21/national -appellate-advocacy-group-issues-best-practices-for-remote-oral-arguments/.

With these considerations in mind, many lawyers choose to sit during remote oral arguments, even though they would stand if presenting arguments in court.

- **Consider where you will look during arguments.**

To appear as though you are talking directly to the judges, you should look directly at the camera as you speak. Doing so will feel awkward at first. Our natural tendency is to look at the face of the person to whom we are speaking. When arguing on camera, if you look at the judge's faces, you will appear to the judges as though you are looking below or to the side of the judge.

You may also want to consider adjusting your settings so that others can see your image, but you cannot see your own image. By hiding your image from yourself, you are more likely to focus on the judges rather than on what you look like.

Consider recording yourself practicing your oral argument. Practice with a friend or colleague so that you will have someone on screen to look at. Consider making the friend's screen smaller and off to the side to simulate an argument in which the judge's image is not immediately below your camera. Take a few minutes at the outset of your argument to consciously look at the camera. Then, take a few minutes to argue as you look at the other person on your screen. Watch the recording to see whether you notice a difference. If you do, adjust accordingly.

- **Place your notes in front of you.**

Just as you would for an in-person argument, you should print your notes and have a physical copy of your notes in front of you. Ideally, you will have memorized your opening and closing, and your notes will largely be a list of points you want to be sure to make. Looking down at your notes for a moment is a natural part of oral arguments and will seem appropriate to the judge or judges before whom you are arguing.

Think carefully about whether to keep detailed notes visible on your computer screen—or worse, on a second monitor. If your notes are off to one side, the judges will likely notice that you are regularly looking off to one side. They will also notice if you are squinting, trying to find your place amid detailed notes on your screen. In either case, the judges may be distracted from your message.

So, when preparing an outline for a remote argument, prepare as you would for a traditional, in-person argument.

- **Remain quietly in one place when you are not arguing.**

When you are not arguing, remain quietly in one place. Your camera will still be on and focused on you. Appropriate conduct while opposing counsel is arguing includes looking at the screen, taking notes, and taking small sips of water from a plain glass. Actions that will be distracting include rocking back and forth, swiveling in your chair, leaving the video, reaching across your desk to look for anything, guzzling water from a water bottle, checking email or text messages, looking at your phone or tablet, or doing anything else that you would not do if you were in an actual courtroom.

Your goal is to make this online proceeding as similar to a courtroom proceeding as possible.

- **Create a back-up plan.**

Technology fails, and sometimes it fails at extraordinarily inconvenient times. In advance of your argument, think through what you will do if your video or audio link should fail. Some online services have a call-in option, which will allow you to continue via telephone if your video fails. If so, you should have that number available and easy to find. You might also ask for a phone number for the courtroom or a law clerk who you can call if your video fails in the middle of an argument.

- **Practice your set up in advance.**

Well in advance of oral arguments, you will want to put your set-up through a test run. Give yourself enough time so that, if you discover any problems, you can adjust. To test your set-up, arrange a video call with two or more colleagues, peers, or assistants. Use the same device, lighting, and background filter as you will during oral arguments. In addition, make sure you are located in the same space. If possible, practice with the same platform that the court uses. Test your video and volume and solicit feedback from the others who are helping you. Your goal is to make sure that the focus of your future argument is on you and your ideas—and not on the strange photo hanging behind you.

Appendices

Appendix A

A Litigation Overview

Before you draft documents for your client, you must understand the litigation that has generated the need for your document. Lawyers submit different documents depending on whether litigation is "civil" or "criminal" litigation. Lawyers also submit different documents depending on whether litigation has just begun or is nearing its conclusion. These variables— whether a case is a civil case or a criminal case and whether the motion or brief is submitted earlier or later in the litigation—affect which facts are available, what law applies, and the arguments you may make. Thus, you must be aware of the litigation process and where your case is located within that process before you draft.

To that end, this appendix briefly describes the difference between civil and criminal litigation and then explains the different documents that are produced along each of those litigation tracks. As you read, you should note the different purposes for the different documents. Some documents present persuasive arguments and ask the court to take action or to refrain from taking an action. Those documents are usually called a "motion" or "brief." A motion is often accompanied by a "memorandum of law," which explains the arguments in detail.

Other documents merely inform. For example, "pleadings," such as a complaint or an answer, inform the court and opposing party of alle-

> **Oral vs. Written Motions**
>
> Not all motions are in writing. During a hearing or trial, motions are usually made orally and ruled upon by the judge. Other motions, especially those before and after a trial, are usually in writing. This book focuses on written motions.

gations, denials, or defenses in a lawsuit, but make no arguments about those allegations, denials, or defenses. Similarly, lawyers will notify opposing counsel of depositions they intend to take, documents the other side must produce, and witnesses they plan to call at trial.

In providing an overview of the civil and criminal litigation processes, this appendix describes both kinds of documents—those that seek to persuade and those that inform. In that way, you can see the different roles that different documents play.

I. Civil vs. Criminal Litigation

Table A-1 sets out some of the more significant differences between a civil case and a criminal case.

Civil and criminal cases are governed by different rules of procedure, which permit different kinds of motions and appeals.[1] The rules of civil and criminal procedure differ from jurisdiction to jurisdiction. Moreover, local custom may affect how a particular procedural step is performed.

Table A-1 · Differences between a civil case and a criminal case

	Civil Litigation	Criminal Prosecution
Definition	Civil litigation addresses disputes between two or more parties, whether those parties are individuals, organizations, or a government.	Criminal litigation addresses crimes against society. Criminal litigation is often called criminal "prosecution" because the government prosecutes an individual or other entity for alleged crimes.
Case filed by	A private party or the government	The government
Burden of proof	The plaintiff has the burden of proof. The plaintiff must prove each claim by a preponderance of the evidence.	The burden of proof is on the government. The government must prove its case beyond a reasonable doubt.
Examples	Landlord/tenant disputes, divorce proceedings, personal injuries, and medical malpractice.	Theft, assault, robbery, trafficking in controlled substances, and murder.
Redress	The plaintiff seeks monetary damages or an injunction. An injunction requires a person to act or refrain from acting.	The prosecutor seeks jail time, probation, fines, or in exceptional cases and in some states, a death sentence.
Appeal	The losing party appeals.	Usually, only the defendant appeals.
Effect of judgment	Liability	Guilt

---

1. Specialized courts—such as tax courts, bankruptcy courts, or specialized business courts—have their own, somewhat different, procedural steps; however, because the majority of cases follow either the civil or criminal procedural tracks, this appendix focuses on those two paths.

For those reasons, cases within different jurisdictions will always look a little bit different. Nevertheless, regardless of whether a case is a civil or criminal case and no matter the jurisdiction, the litigation will have four distinct stages: pre-trial, trial, post-trial, and appeals.

The two sections that follow provide a tabular overview of a civil matter and, then, a criminal matter. The tables are by no means exhaustive. The tables do, however, describe the major stages of litigation and the motions or briefs that are produced along the way. To give you a sense of the pace of litigation, the tables provide the time frames within which documents must be filed. The time frames are from the federal rules of civil, criminal, and appellate procedure. State procedural rules will govern the time frames in state court, and those rules may result in slightly different time frames.

As you read, remember that, although you may be permitted to file a motion or brief at a particular stage, whether you actually file a particular motion or brief always depends on the facts and law available to you. Remember also that procedures vary from jurisdiction to jurisdiction. We've said it before and we'll say it again: Read the rules that govern in your jurisdiction.

Time Is of the Essence

In the descriptions of civil and criminal litigation, we generally cite to federal rules regarding required timelines. The corresponding timelines in state courts vary, so check the required timelines in your jurisdiction to ensure that no filing is ever dismissed as untimely.

II. Civil Litigation

Every civil case begins with a dispute between two or more parties. For example, one neighbor builds an addition to his house that blocks the view that another neighbor had previously enjoyed; a business owner receives a delivery of goods that do not look or perform as expected; a bicyclist runs into you while you're on your skateboard. Although the kinds of disputes are limitless, the general process of litigation is the same.

A. Pre-Trial

As an attorney, you begin by listening to the client's problem and investigating the relevant facts and law. After your preliminary investigation, you will likely contact the other party or that party's attorney. You may send a "demand letter" that asks the other party to stop certain conduct or pay damages. If a dispute cannot be settled informally, then one of the parties may decide to initiate a claim in court. The typical pre-trial path is set forth in Table A-2.

Table A-2 • Typical civil pre-trial stages

Pre-trial stage	Explanation
Complaint	The first formal step in civil litigation is to file a complaint. A complaint notifies the opposing party that some individual (or entity) has initiated a legal action in court. The complaint outlines the plaintiff's legal claims and the factual basis for those claims.
Motion to dismiss	After the complaint is filed, the defendant's attorney has an initial opportunity to ask the court to take action to dismiss all or part of the complaint. A defendant can ask the court to dismiss a complaint for a variety of reasons. Some common reasons for asking the court to dismiss the complaint are because the complaint fails to state a claim upon which relief can be granted, the court lacks jurisdiction, the complaint was not properly served on the defendant, or because the plaintiff waited too long to initiate the litigation (i.e., "the statute of limitations" has run). If the judge grants the motion to dismiss, the dismissal may be granted "with prejudice" or "without prejudice." If the motion is granted with prejudice the case is dismissed, the litigation in the trial court ends, and the plaintiff's only recourse is to appeal. If the motion is granted without prejudice, the plaintiff can still amend and re-file the complaint to continue the litigation.
Answer	If the defendant does not move to dismiss or a motion to dismiss is not granted, the defendant must file an answer to the plaintiff's complaint. In the answer, the defendant must admit or deny each of the allegations in the complaint. Failure to do so results in the defendant admitting to the complaint's allegations. In the answer, the defendant can set out affirmative defenses and counterclaims. An affirmative defense asserts claims that, if true, will defeat one or more plaintiff's claims. An example of an affirmative defense might be a claim that the statute of limitations has run. A counterclaim is a claim brought by the defendant that, if later proved true, would entitle defendant to some relief.
Reply	If the defendant's answer included counterclaims, the plaintiff may be able to file a "reply," similar to the defendant's answer. In a reply, the plaintiff admits or denies the allegations that support the counterclaim and may assert counterclaims or move to dismiss.
Discovery	After the lawsuit is filed, a great deal of activity occurs in the form of discovery. Discovery provides relevant information to both parties in terms of facts, expected testimony, and exhibits. Common types of discovery include: (1) interrogatories, which are a list of questions that one party is asking the other party to answer; (2) requests to produce documents; (3) requests that the opposing party admit to certain facts; and (4) depositions, during which an attorney questions a witness who is under oath. The majority of discovery is handled without judicial involvement. Sometimes, however, if the parties cannot agree, one party will file a motion asking the court to take action related to the discovery process. Typical discovery-related motions include a motion to compel discovery, a motion for a protective order to prevent discovery, or a motion to limit discovery. A court may also order parties to engage in a mediated settlement conference. Mediation is an informal settlement conference led by a trained mediator who seeks to find a resolution to the case that is acceptable to all parties.

Chart continues on the next page

Table A-2 · Typical civil pre-trial stages, *continued*

Pre-trial stage	Explanation
Motion for summary judgment	A motion for summary judgment asks the court to dismiss the case based on the known facts. In a motion for summary judgment, the moving party argues that, based on the undisputed facts, that party is entitled to judgment as a matter of law. The well-known standard is that a party is entitled to summary judgment if "there is no genuine dispute as to any material fact and the movant is entitled to judgment as a matter of law." Fed. R. Civ. P. 56(a).
	If the court grants summary judgment in either party's favor, judgment is entered in the prevailing party's favor and litigation at the trial level ends. The case will continue only if the losing party appeals.
Motion in limine	Motions in limine are requests that certain materials be excluded from the trial or be deemed admissible. Usually, a party will request that material be excluded from the trial because the material was improperly obtained, would be overly prejudicial, or irrelevant to the proceedings.
Pre-trial order	Before trial begins, the parties will draft a proposed pre-trial order outlining the case as it will be presented at trial. If the proposed order is acceptable to the judge, the judge signs the pre-trial order and it governs the events at trial. The pre-trial order addresses the issues that remain in dispute, the witnesses that will appear at trial, and the need for further decisions by the court.

B. Trial

Most civil cases settle before the trial begins. In fact, in most jurisdictions, and depending on the type of case, less than five percent of all complaints filed proceed to trial.[2] Those cases that proceed to trial usually unfold as shown in Table A-3.

Table A-3 · Typical stages of a civil trial

Stage	Explanation
Jury selection	In a civil case, a plaintiff or defendant must request a jury for the case to be heard by a jury. If a party does not request a jury trial, the case will be heard and decided by a judge. See Fed. R. Civ. P. 38, 39.
	When a case is to be heard by a jury, individual jurors must be selected from a pool of potential jurors. Selecting jurors begins with a process called "voir dire." During voir dire, attorneys and the judge question potential jurors about any pre-existing beliefs or experiences that may affect the juror's perception of the case. A juror can be dismissed "for cause" when the voir dire establishes that the juror cannot be impartial or will be unable to attend the trial. An attorney can also use one of several "peremptory" challenges or strikes to exclude a person from the panel without providing a reason for the exclusion.

Chart continues on the next page

---

2. *See, e.g.*, U.S. Dept. of Justice, Civil Justice Survey of State Courts, 2005, at 1 (Oct. 2008), http://www.bjs.gov/content/pub/pdf/cbjtsc05.pdf.

Table A-3 • Typical stages of a civil trial, *continued*

Stage	Explanation
Opening statement	The plaintiff's lawyer opens the trial by making an "opening statement." In the opening statement, counsel describes what will be proved during the trial. The defendant's attorney then follows with an opening statement describing, from the defendant's perspective, what the evidence will show.
Plaintiff's case-in-chief	Because the plaintiff has the burden of proof, the plaintiff's case is presented first. Plaintiff's counsel provides evidence witness-by-witness. Each witness's testimony is recorded. Witnesses also can identify and present documentary or other physical evidence, which is then entered into the record. After plaintiff's attorney examines each witness, defendant's attorney has the opportunity to cross-examine that witness.
Motion for judgment as a matter of law	After the plaintiff's case-in-chief, the defendant will often move that the case be dismissed because the evidence presented was insufficient to prove the plaintiff's case. Such a motion is usually made orally and is often ruled upon quickly. In federal courts, such a motion is called a "motion for judgment as a matter of law." However, in state courts, the same motion is often called a "motion for directed verdict" in jury trials, or a "motion to dismiss" in bench trials.
Defendant's case-in-chief	Next, the defendant puts on his case-in-chief by producing witnesses and evidence to respond to the plaintiff's case and to establish any affirmative defenses or counterclaims. Like the process in the plaintiff's case-in-chief, each witness is questioned by the defense attorney and may be cross-examined by plaintiff's counsel.
Rebuttal and sur-rebuttal	At the end of the defendant's evidence, the plaintiff may put on rebuttal witnesses or evidence to refute the evidence presented by the defendant. The defendant then has the opportunity for a sur-rebuttal, essentially a rebuttal to the rebuttal.
Motion for judgment as a matter of law	After defendant's case has been presented, the plaintiff has the opportunity to move for judgment on the ground that plaintiff's case has been proved and the defendant has failed to undermine that case or prove a defense. This motion must be made before the case goes to the jury.
Closing arguments	During closing arguments, also called summation, each attorney recaps the evidence and organizes it for the jury, explaining why the evidence supports a verdict favorable to that attorney's client. Counsel's closing argument must be consistent with the jury instructions that the court will give (see below). Usually, the plaintiff's counsel will present closing argument first, and the defendant will follow. The plaintiff may follow with a short rebuttal.
Jury instructions	After closing arguments, and if the case is being heard by a jury, the judge will instruct the jury regarding the law that the jury will follow to reach a decision. The instructions that will be read to the jury are often the subject of argument, and counsel may have previously submitted arguments to the court about the precise language that should be read to the jury.

Chart continues on the next page

Table A-3 • Typical stages of a civil trial, *continued*

Stage	Explanation
Verdict	After instructions are read, the jury will deliberate and return a verdict. A jury may return a "general" or "special" verdict. A general verdict simply states which side wins. A special verdict lists the jury's findings with respect to each factual issue or with respect to selected issues. In a bench trial, instead of a verdict, the judge will prepare an order with findings of fact and conclusions of law. Usually, attorneys from each side will submit proposed findings of fact and conclusions of law, and the judge will draft a final order based on those submissions.
Entry of judgment	To conclude a trial, the court must enter a judgment into the court's records. The judgment is a document that is separate from either the jury's verdict or the judge's findings of fact and conclusions of law.

C. Post-Trial

After the trial, verdict, and entry of judgment, the losing party may seek relief from the decision by filing one of the motions described in Table A-4.

Table A-4 • Typical civil post-trial motions

Type of Motion	Explanation
Motion for judgment as a matter of law	Within 28 days after a judgment has been entered, a party can move for a judgment as a matter of law. Such a motion is permitted only if the party has also made a motion for a judgment as a matter of law at the close of all of the evidence. Fed. R. Civ. P. 50(b).
Motion for a new trial	Within 28 days after a judgment has been entered, a party may move for a new trial. Fed. R. Civ. P. 59.
Motion to alter or amend judgment	If an attorney believes that the court's judgment needs to be corrected in some way, the attorney can, within 28 days of the entry of judgment, file a motion explaining why that correction is warranted. Fed. R. Civ. P. 59(e).
Motion to set aside judgment	A motion to set aside the judgment asks the court to relieve a party from a final judgment on the ground that it would be unjust or unnecessary for the court to carry out its judgment. A party might argue that fraud, mistake, or newly discovered evidence would make it unjust for the court to exercise its authority. Fed. R. Civ. P. 60(b).
Motion for attorneys' fees	While parties typically pay their own litigation costs, sometimes the winning party may move to recoup attorneys' fees. Attorneys' fees can be awarded by statute, contract, or as a matter of public policy, depending upon the jurisdiction.

D. Appeals

After judgment is entered at the trial level, the losing party has the opportunity to appeal. The appellate process is described briefly in Table A-5. Chapter 9, *Appellate Briefs & Appellate Practice*, describes the world of appeals in more detail.

Table A-5 · Appellate process[3]

Terminology	Explanation
Appeal as of right	After a final judgment is entered, the losing party is generally entitled "as of right" to have an intermediate appellate court review the decision of the lower court. In an appeal as of right, the intermediate court cannot refuse to hear the case.
Notice of appeal	A notice of appeal must be filed within 30 days of entry of judgment. Fed. R. App. P. 4(a)(1)(A). As its name suggests, a notice of appeal notifies the parties and the courts of a party's intention to appeal.
Forwarding the record	After filing a notice of appeal, the party appealing the decision must order from the court reporter a copy of those portions of the trial transcript that will be relevant to the appeal. That record will then be forwarded to the appellate court. Fed. R. App. P. 10(b), 11(b).
Submission of briefs	The party filing the appeal must file an opening brief within 40 days after the record is filed. The party responding to the appeal has an additional 30 days to file its brief in response. The party appealing then has another 14 days to file a reply brief. Fed. R. App. P. 31.
Oral argument	In many cases, the appellate court allows the attorneys to present oral arguments related to the issues on appeal. During the arguments, the judges may interrupt and ask questions about various points of law or fact.
Opinion	A court issues an opinion to announce its decision in the case and to explain its reasoning regarding the legal issues raised on appeal. When an opinion is published, it both resolves that particular controversy and gives guidance to other potential litigants who have similar issues.

Chart continues on the next page

---

3. Table A-5 assumes an intermediate appellate court. Although most jurisdictions in the United States have an intermediate appellate court, the following states either lack an intermediate court or have an atypical structure for their intermediate courts: Delaware, Maine, Montana, New Hampshire, Rhode Island, North Dakota, South Dakota, Vermont, West Virginia, and Wyoming.

Table A-5 • Appellate process, *continued*

Terminology	Explanation
Disposition	A "disposition" is the appellate court's final determination of the matter. Typical dispositions are listed below. Sometimes an appellate court will have different dispositions for the different legal issues raised on appeal, or will combine dispositions, for example, by reversing and remanding the decision of the lower court.
Affirm	The appellate court agrees with the trial court's judgment.
Reverse	The appellate court disagrees with the trial court's judgment and overturns it.
Remand	The appellate court sends the case back to the trial court with instructions for further action.
Vacate	The appellate court makes the trial court's judgment legally void.
Writ of certiorari	To have a decision heard by the highest appellate court, the parties must, in most cases, file a petition for a writ of certiorari to provide reasons why the court should exercise its discretion and review the case.

III. Criminal Litigation

Whereas a civil case begins with a dispute between two private parties, a criminal case begins when the government suspects an individual or organization has engaged or is about to engage in some criminal activity. A police officer may actually see a crime take place, or the police may learn about possible criminal activity. Two steps then follow: an investigation and an arrest. Depending on the circumstances, the investigation may precede the arrest; however, under some circumstances, a person is first arrested and then police investigate the alleged crime to support the prosecution of the arrestee.

During an investigation, officers may question witnesses, ask a witness to identify the suspect in a line-up, or obtain a search warrant to search a particular location for evidence. Prosecutors may also be involved in an investigation by, for example, issuing a subpoena for documents.

An officer will arrest a suspect when the officer or a prosecutor believes the evidence provides "probable cause" to believe that the suspect has committed a crime.[4]

A. Pre-Trial

After the arrest, the state begins its formal prosecution. Table A-6 describes the typical pre-trial proceedings in a criminal case.

---

4. The tables below draw heavily from the work of Wayne R. LaFave, Jerold H. Israel, Nancy J. King & Orin S. Kerr, *Criminal Procedure* (6th ed. 2016), and from

Table A-6 · Typical criminal pre-trial stages

Stage	Explanation
Complaint	After the defendant is arrested, the prosecutor reviews the case to decide whether to file charges and, if so, what charges to file. If the prosecutor decides to prosecute the case, he will prepare a complaint. The complaint describes the crime allegedly committed and the basic facts that, if proved, would establish the crime. The complaint must be filed with the court within 24 to 48 hours after the arrest. Once the complaint is filed, the arrestee becomes a criminal defendant.
Initial appearance	After the complaint is filed, the defendant is brought before a judge for an initial appearance. This appearance must also occur within 24 to 48 hours after the defendant is arrested. During the initial appearance, the defendant is formally notified of the charges contained in the complaint. If the suspect was arrested without an arrest warrant, the court will also determine whether the officer had probable cause to arrest the suspect. If the officer did not have probable cause to arrest the defendant, the complaint is dismissed. If probable cause did exist, the judge will determine whether the defendant will continue to be held in custody. The judge may temporarily release the defendant based on the defendant's promise to return for future proceedings — that is, released "on her own recognizance." Alternatively, the judge may set bail or other conditions of release, such as a curfew, travel restrictions, or wearing a monitoring device, or the defendant may be held in jail until the next proceeding.
Information or indictment	The next step in the criminal process takes place within two or three weeks after the initial appearance; however, this step differs depending on whether the jurisdiction is an "information jurisdiction" or an "indictment jurisdiction." The majority of jurisdictions are information jurisdictions. In an information jurisdiction, the next step in a criminal case is a "preliminary hearing." The purpose of this preliminary hearing is to review whether probable cause exists to proceed with the case. If a judge determines that probable cause supports each of the allegations in the complaint, the prosecutor files the "information" with the trial court that states the charges against the defendant and the essential facts establishing those charges. A minority of jurisdictions are indictment jurisdictions. In an indictment jurisdiction, the grand jury determines whether sufficient probable cause exists for the case to continue. When the grand jury hears the evidence, the grand jury will hear only from the prosecutor. Neither the defendant nor defendant's counsel will be present. If the grand jury determines sufficient evidence exists, the grand jury (through the prosecutor) will issue an indictment, which sets forth the charges against the defendant and the related facts. Each charge and the related facts are listed as one "count." At this point, the information or the indictment replaces the complaint as the official "charging" or "accusatory" instrument in the case.

Chart continues on the next page

Harry I. Subin, Chester L Mirsky & Ian S. Weinstein, *Federal Criminal Practice: Prosecution and Defense* (1992).

Table A-6 • Typical criminal pre-trial stages, *continued*

Stage	Explanation
Arraignment	After an information or indictment is filed, the defendant is arraigned. At an arraignment, the defendant is informed of the charges against her. The defendant can plead "guilty," "not guilty," or if permitted in the jurisdiction, "*nolo contendere*," which means "no contest." The judge then sets a date for trial or for sentencing, depending on the plea.
Motions to dismiss	Like the defendant in a civil case, the criminal defendant may move to dismiss the case. A criminal defendant may move to dismiss a case because the information or indictment fails to allege an essential element; because critical evidence should be suppressed, Fed. R. Crim. P. 8, 14; because the prosecution is constitutionally barred, for example, because of double jeopardy or violation of speedy trial requirements, *id.*; or because of some other affirmative defenses such as self-defense, insanity, or a statute of limitations.
Discovery	The U.S. Constitution requires the government to disclose any exculpatory evidence. In addition, the discovery rules in most jurisdictions require the government to make further discloures. In those jurisdictions that require the government to disclose additional information, the government usually must disclose defendant's oral statements; defendant's written or recorded statements; defendant's prior record; documents and objects that the government plans to rely on at trial or that would be material to a defense; reports of examinations or tests that would be material to the defense; and any summary of expert testimony the government intends to introduce. Fed. R. Crim. P. 16(a). The defendant, however, need disclose only documents, objects, reports, and expert testimony that the defendant intends to use at trial. Fed. R. Crim. P. 16(b). In some states, however, the government is not required to disclose any documents beyond the exculpatory evidence required by the Constitution. Rather, the defense must show why requested materials should be made available.
Motions to suppress	Motions to suppress are requests that certain evidence be excluded from the trial. If a motion to suppress is granted, counsel and witnesses are prohibited from referring to that evidence during the trial.

B. Trial

The time span from arrest to the start of a felony trial usually falls within five to eight months.[5] However, just as most civil cases settle before making it to court, most criminal cases end in settlement—that is, a plea agreement. "Most defendants—more than 90%—plead guilty rather

---

5. LaFave, *supra* note 4, at 20.

than go to trial."[6] If a criminal case does go to trial, that case will most likely conclude in two to three days[7] and result in a conviction.[8] The stages of that trial are described in Table A-7.

Table A-7 • Typical stages of a criminal trial

Stage	Explanation
Jury selection	A defendant facing more than six months of incarceration has a right to a jury trial; however, a criminal defendant may waive that right and have the case tried by a judge instead of a jury. Fed. R. Crim. P. 23(a). When a criminal case is to be heard by a jury, the trial begins (as it does in a civil case) by selecting the jury from a pool of potential jurors. This process is called "voir dire." During voir dire, the judge and the attorneys question potential jurors about any pre-existing beliefs or experiences that may affect the juror's perception of the case. A juror can be dismissed "for cause" when the voir dire establishes the juror cannot be impartial or will be unable to attend the trial. There is no limit to the number of jurors who can be dismissed for cause. An attorney can also use one of a limited number of "peremptory" challenges or strikes to exclude a person from the panel without providing a reason for the exclusion.
Opening statement	The prosecutor opens the trial by making an opening statement. In the opening statement, the prosecutor will identify the charges being brought against the defendant and describe the evidence the government will introduce to prove the charges. The defendant's attorney may present an opening statement or not. In addition, the defense is often given the choice as to whether to follow the prosecutor's opening statement with its own or whether to wait until the beginning of its case.
Government's case-in-chief	Like the plaintiff in a civil action, the government has the burden of proof so the government's case is presented first. The prosecutor presents evidence witness-by-witness. Each witness's testimony is recorded. Witnesses also can identify and present documentary or other physical evidence, which is then entered into the record. Each witness is examined by the prosecutor and, usually, cross-examined by the defendant's attorney. The government may then conduct a redirect examination of the same witness. The government may never call the defendant to the witness stand in its case-in-chief.

Chart continues on the next page

---

6. *How the Federal Courts Work: Criminal Cases*, U.S. Courts, https://www .uscourts.gov/about-federal-courts/types-cases/criminal-cases (last accessed Aug. 10, 2021); *see also Missouri v. Frye*, 566 U.S. 134, 143 (2012) (noting "ninety-seven percent of federal convictions and ninety-four percent of state convictions are the result of guilty pleas").

7. LaFave, *supra* note 4, at 20.

8. There are approximately two convictions for every one acquittal. *Id.*

Table A-7 · Typical stages of a criminal trial, *continued*

Stage	Explanation
Motion for judgment of acquittal	After the government's case-in-chief, the defendant will often move for the case to be dismissed because the evidence presented was insufficient to prove the government's case beyond a reasonable doubt. Such a motion is usually made orally and is often ruled upon quickly.
Defendant's case-in-chief	In a criminal trial, a defendant need not present any evidence to disprove the government's case. If a defendant chooses to present a case-in-chief, the defendant will also produce witnesses and evidence to establish an alternative narrative or present an affirmative defense. The defense attorney will examine each witness. The government will have the opportunity to cross-examine the witness. Then, finally, the defense attorney may choose to conduct a redirect examination.
Rebuttal	If the defendant has presented evidence, the government may put on rebuttal witnesses or evidence to refute the evidence presented by the defendant.
Closing arguments	During closing arguments, the attorneys recap their version of events and organize the evidence for the jury, explaining why the evidence supports a particular verdict. The arguments must be consistent with the jury instructions that the court gives (see below). The government will present its closing argument first, and the defendant will follow. The government may follow with a short rebuttal.
Jury instructions	The judge will instruct the jury regarding the law that the jury will follow to reach a decision. Usually, instructions are given after closing arguments. The instructions that will be read to the jury are often the subject of argument, and counsel may have previously submitted to the court the precise language that should be read to the jury.
Verdict	After instructions are read, the jury will deliberate and return a verdict. A jury may return a "general" or "special" verdict. A general verdict simply states which side wins. A special verdict lists the jury's findings with respect to selected issues. A jury verdict in a criminal case must be unanimous.

C. Post-Trial

If a jury finds a defendant guilty, that verdict is often followed by post-trial motions. If, after those motions, the guilty verdict stands, the court will sentence the defendant and enter judgment.

1. Motions

Common post-trial motions in a criminal case include those set forth in Table A-8.

Table A-8 · Common post-trial motions in criminal cases

Post-verdict proceeding	Explanation
Motion for judgment of acquittal	A defendant may move for a judgment of acquittal (or renew such a motion) within 14 days after a guilty verdict or after the jury has been discharged. Fed. R. Crim. P. 29.
Motion to stay sentence	A defendant may ask the court to stay a sentence while the defendant appeals the judgment. Fed. R. Crim. P. 38.
Motion for a new trial	A motion for a new trial is usually filed when new evidence is discovered that may exonerate the client, or when the attorney has discovered some procedural error or misconduct that casts doubt on the verdict. Fed. R. Crim. P. 33. In some states, the losing party must move for a new trial before filing an appeal.

2. Sentencing

After a guilty plea, a plea of no contest, or a guilty verdict has been entered, the defendant will be sentenced. Sentencing procedures vary at the state and federal levels. However, in most states and at the federal level, the judge determines the sentence for a convicted defendant.[9]

Before sentencing the defendant, judges will often consider facts that did not or were not allowed to come to light at trial, such as a defendant's prior criminal record, family relationships, health, and work record.[10]

Some states and the federal courts have sentencing guidelines that guide judges when they impose a sentence. The guidelines are intended to help judges impose proportionate sentences and to foster uniform sentencing.[11] In jurisdictions where the sentencing judge's discretion is limited by sentencing guidelines, a judge who departs from the "presumptive sentence"

---

9. *See* LaFave, *supra* note 4, at 20. The major exception is death penalty cases. In death penalty cases, a jury determines whether to sentence a convicted defendant to death.

10. So that a judge can determine an appropriate sentence, a probation officer usually submits a presentencing report that includes biographical information about the defendant, major information about his or her living situation, and relevant legal information about the crimes he or she is accused of committing. After addressing any objections, the report is then submitted to the court for consideration as a part of the sentencing. *See* Fed. R. Crim. P. 32(e)-(f); Fed. R. Crim. P. 32(d); *see also* LaFave, *supra* note 4, at 21 (describing the role of a presentence report and the parties' ability to present additional information or challenge information in a report).

11. LaFave, *supra* note 4, at 21.

is usually required to make findings of fact regarding those factors that led to the sentence.[12]

3. Entry of judgment

Finally, the court must enter judgment. The judgment must state the plea or jury verdict and, if the defendant is found guilty, the final sentence imposed.[13] Once the judgment has been entered, the trial concludes.

D. Appeals and Other Post-Conviction Remedies

In criminal cases, usually only the defendant has a right to appeal.[14] The government's ability to appeal is limited by double jeopardy, the constitutional prohibition against a defendant being tried twice for the same crime. When a defendant does appeal, the conviction will usually be affirmed. Convictions are affirmed 90 to 95 percent of the time.[15]

Criminal appeals generally proceed in the same way that civil appeals proceed. That is, the defendant appeals to an appellate court and asks the appellate court to review the record below for some error. Because a criminal appeal generally follows the same process as a civil appeal, you can review Table A-5, *Appellate Process*, for an overview of the criminal appellate process. The one difference between a criminal appeal and a civil appeal is that, in a criminal appeal, the defendant must file a notice of appeal within 14 days of entry of judgment.[16] By contrast, the civil appellant has 30 days to file a notice of appeal.[17]

If a traditional (or direct) appeal fails, defendants can challenge the legality of their conviction or sentence in ways that are unavailable to the civil litigant. Defendants convicted in state courts can seek review of their conviction or sentence under that state's post-conviction review proceedings. If that fails, the defendant may then file a petition for a writ of habeas corpus in federal court. Defendants convicted in a federal court can also seek review of their conviction by filing a petition for a writ of habeas corpus in federal court.

---

12. *See id.*

13. Fed. R. Crim. P. 32(k). In the case of a bench trial, the judgment will state the court's finding of facts and its adjudication. *Id.*

14. *Id.* Some states do allow the state to appeal in limited circumstances, most frequently to clarify aspects of the law. Because of double jeopardy (the federal constitutional prohibition against being tried twice for the same crime), if the state can appeal, it usually must appeal before the trial and not after the verdict.

15. LaFave, *supra* note 4, at 20.

16. Fed. R. App. P. 4(b)(1)(A).

17. Fed. R. App. P. 4(a)(1)(A).

These procedures are called "collateral remedies." A collateral remedy is an attack on the conviction by means other than direct appeals.[18] These processes are briefly explained in Table A-9.

Table A-9 • Additional post-conviction (collateral) remedies

Terminology	Explanation
State post-conviction review	A defendant convicted in state court may challenge the conviction or sentence (or both) in state court on the ground that it violates the state or federal constitutions. How a defendant seeks post-conviction review in state court varies from state to state. In some states, the defendant files a motion or application in the court in which he was convicted. In other states, the defendant files a separate petition for post-conviction review, initiating a new civil action. If a defendant loses a post-conviction review at the trial level, the defendant may then appeal the trial court's decision through the normal appeals process.
Federal writ of habeas corpus	A defendant convicted in federal court who has exhausted all appeals has a collateral remedy in federal court. The defendant can file a petition for a writ of habeas corpus in a federal district court, asserting that his conviction or sentence violates the United States Constitution. 22 U.S.C. §§ 2241–55. Again, if a defendant loses at the district court level, the defendant may appeal the decision through the normal appeals process. In addition, a state court defendant who has exhausted all state court remedies can then file a petition for a writ of habeas corpus in federal court. In essence, state-court defendants get two chances (in addition to direct appeal) to challenge their convictions and sentences; federal court defendants get only one.

---

18. *Collateral attack*, Black's Law Dictionary (11th ed. 2019).

Appendix B

Prakash v. Starr Publishing Corp. **Trial Briefs**

Appendix B provides examples of the central documents in a motion for summary judgment: the motion, the memorandum of law in support of the motion, and the responding memorandum of law in opposition to the motion for summary judgment. Before you jump into the examples, it may help to have some background. This overview begins with a brief summary of the arguments. The summary should make it easier to absorb the legal arguments. Once you have absorbed the legal arguments, then you will be able to look beyond the arguments and examine the skills that the lawyers used to build their arguments. To that end, this overview also lists some of the skills that you should look for as you review these examples.

I. Summary of the Arguments

In this case, two law professors have sued a publishing company for defamation *per se*. The professors argue that they were defamed when the publishing company wrote "by Amit Prakash and Helen Vinocur … and the Publisher's Staff" on a pocket part update, even though Professors Prakash and Vinocur did not participate in the production of that edition of the pocket part.

The publisher now seeks summary judgment on several grounds: (1) the plaintiffs cannot establish that the attribution was defamatory; (2)

the plaintiffs cannot prove they were harmed; (3) the contract permitted the publisher to use the professors' names in connection with the pocket part, even if they did not participate in producing it; and (4) truth is a defense to defamation, and the attribution to the professors was true or substantially true. The professors argue to the contrary on each of these points.

II. Skills and Techniques

In reviewing these examples, you can see many of the techniques discussed in this book. You may want to adopt some of the techniques you see and use them in your own writing. If you do decide to adopt a technique from one of these samples, please keep in mind that no two documents are ever the same. Each client's legal problem is different. Therefore, these samples will be most useful if you go beyond the words on the page. Ask yourself *why* the writer drafted the argument as the writer did. What point was the writer trying to make? How did the writer shape the text to make that particular point? Then, ask yourself whether you can use that same technique in your document. If you think you can use the same technique in your own document, then ask yourself one final question: How will you adjust that technique to suit your client's particular problem?

Please remember, though, that the format for motions and their supporting memoranda vary from jurisdiction to jurisdiction. Thus, be particularly careful about adopting the format of these documents. With respect to the format of your documents, check your local rules and follow those rules. If you are still unsure about how your document should look, ask a trusted colleague for an example of a motion or memorandum of law that has been submitted to the same court.

Fortunately, the skills for writing an effective memorandum of law are the same no matter the jurisdiction. Thus, in the argument section, you might look for these skills and techniques:

- Assertive **point headings** that outline the argument

- Arguments that are **structured in a traditional way**—with a conclusion, an explanation of the law, an application of the law to the facts, and a final conclusion

- **Thesis sentences** that clearly and accurately assert the point that will be established in each paragraph

- Arguments that use **rule-based reasoning**

  - Notice how the lawyers take key language from the rule and integrate that language into the application. The re-integration of key ideas from the rule into the application emphasizes how the lawyer's analysis is consistent with the law.

- Arguments that use **analogical reasoning**
  - Notice how counsel uses parallel structure to draw out the factual similarities between the current case and a prior case.
  - Notice also how counsel always explains the legal conclusion that results from the factual similarity.
- Arguments that **address weaknesses**, without giving undue airtime to that weakness
- **Polished writing**
  - Sentences have a clear subject and verb and use the active voice.
  - Words are simple and easy-to-understand.
  - The writing has no grammatical, punctuation, or citation errors.

More substantively, you might look at the different approaches each party takes to the summary judgment standard and the defamation claim. Ask these questions:

- **Summary judgment standard**
  - How does each party describe the standard for summary judgment?
  - Throughout the argument, how does each party emphasize those aspects of the standard that are favorable to that party?
- **Defamation** *per se*
  - Compare the arguments side by side. For each issue that the party addresses, does one seem more compelling? Why?
  - How does each party deal with weaknesses in its own argument?

Outside of the argument section, you might look for these skills:

- A **preliminary statement** that gives a concise and persuasive overview of each party's arguments
- A **persuasive statement of facts** that
  - Provides context before jumping into the details.
  - Includes all legally relevant facts.
  - Presents the party in a favorable light.
  - Places unfavorable facts in perspective.
  - States legally relevant facts in precise detail.

III. The Documents

The documents that follow include the publisher's motion for summary judgment and the memorandum of law in support of the publisher's motion.[1] In reply, the professors submit a memorandum of law in opposition to the motion for summary judgment.

_____

1. The sample documents were drawn from the arguments presented in *Rudovsky v. West Publishing Corp.*, 2010 WL 2804844 (E.d. Pa. 2010) (No. 09-cv-00727-JF). These documents were chosen for the excellent advocacy demonstrated on both sides.

A. Defendant's Motion for Summary Judgment

**IN THE UNITED STATES DISTRICT COURT
FOR THE EASTERN DISTRICT OF PENNSYLVANIA**

Amit Prakash and Helen Vinocur, 　　　　　Plaintiffs, v. Starr Publishing Corporation, 　　　　　Defendant.	CIVIL ACTION NO. 23-CV-727 **DEFENDANT'S MOTION FOR SUMMARY JUDGMENT**

　　Pursuant to Federal Rule of Civil Procedure 56, defendant Starr Publishing Corporation moves to enter judgment in favor of defendant and to dismiss plaintiff's amended complaint in its entirety with prejudice.

　　As explained in the accompanying memorandum of law in support of defendant's motion for summary judgment, the undisputed facts show that plaintiffs Prakash and Vinocur cannot, as a matter of law, establish their claim for defamation.

This motion, like most motions, states the rule on which the motion is based and cross-references the memorandum of law where the court will find the arguments in support of the motion.

Dated: April 21, 2023　　　　Respectfully submitted,

/s/ _____
James F. Collier, Esq.
Aaron M. Goldstein, Esq.
Donahue Hartgrove LLP
1750 Market Street, 48th Floor
Philadelphia, PA 19103-7599
(215) 617-9200
jcollier@donhart.com
agoldstein@donhart.com

B. Memorandum of Law in Support of Defendant's Motion for Summary Judgment

**IN THE UNITED STATES DISTRICT COURT
FOR THE EASTERN DISTRICT OF PENNSYLVANIA**

Amit Prakash and
Helen Vinocur,
       Plaintiffs,
 	
v.
 	
Starr Publishing Corporation,
       Defendant.
	CIVIL ACTION
	
	NO. 23-CV-727
	
	**MEMORANDUM OF LAW IN
	SUPPORT OF DEFENDANT'S
	MOTION FOR SUMMARY
	JUDGMENT**

Defendant Starr Publishing Corporation submits this memorandum of law in support of its motion seeking summary judgment on the claims of plaintiffs Amit Prakash and Helen Vinocur as set forth in the March 24, 2023 amended complaint.

Preliminary Statement

Discovery has now confirmed that Starr Publishing Corporation should be granted judgment in its favor. Plaintiffs allege that they were defamed when Starr published a pocket part to update "Starr's Pennsylvania Criminal Practice & Procedure" and listed the plaintiffs as authors; however, plaintiffs' claim fails as a matter of law and undisputed fact.

First, plaintiffs cannot establish the essential elements of a defamation claim. Plaintiffs cannot, for example, establish that attributing the authorship to the plaintiffs is a defamatory statement. In addition, plaintiffs cannot establish that they suffered damages. The record includes no evidence that plaintiffs suffered economic damage or that their reputations were harmed.

Plaintiffs' defamation claim also fails because they consented to the use of their names in connection with the 2022–2023 pocket part even if they did not participate in its production. Finally, plaintiffs' defamation claim must fail because the statement that the 2022–2023 pocket part was "by Amit Prakash and Helen Vinocur" and "The Publisher's Staff" is true or substantially true.

For all of these reasons, plaintiffs' claim for defamation fails as a matter of law, and summary judgment in Starr Publishing's favor should be granted.

Statement of Facts

Starr Publishing is engaged in the business of publishing legal casebooks, treatises, and practice guides. Am. Compl. ¶ 6; Carter Decl., ¶ 1. Plaintiffs Amit Prakash and Helen Vinocur are law professors who have had distinguished careers in law. Am. Compl. ¶¶ 1–2. Plaintiffs assert that Starr Publishing made a

The preliminary statement (or introduction) provides an overview of the publisher's argument. This section is the publisher's first opportunity to persuade. Notice how the section asserts the publisher's arguments as indisputable conclusions. By doing so, the section outlines the publisher's arguments and does so persuasively.

The statement of facts opens by providing context. The first paragraph explains who the parties are and the crux of the dispute.

false statement of fact that defamed them when Starr published the cover page to a 2022–2023 pocket part. Am. Compl. ¶ 37. The cover page of the 2022–2023 pocket part provides that it was "by Amit Prakash and Helen Vinocur" and "The Publisher's Staff." Am. Compl. ¶ 37. Although plaintiffs had themselves written "the overwhelming majority" of the 2022–2023 pocket part, they were unsatisfied with the updates made by the publisher's staff. Am. Compl. ¶¶ 24–29; Vinocur Tr. 212:4–11.

In 2014, plaintiffs executed an agreement that allowed Starr Publishing to use the plaintiffs' name on the pocket parts to the treatise *Starr's Pennsylvania Criminal Practice & Procedure*, even if plaintiffs did not participate in the production of the pocket part. Prelim. Inj. Hr'g Tr. 38:14–39:3, 39:22–40:16. The 2014 Agreement defines "Work" as *Starr's Pennsylvania Criminal Practice & Procedure*. 2014 Agmt. §§ 1, 2(b). The 2014 Agreement also provides that references to the "Work" "also apply to such upkeep as well as to the original work." The agreement provides Starr Publishing with the right to use the plaintiffs' names in connection with the Work and upkeep of the Work, and in advertising and promotion, even if plaintiffs did not participate in its upkeep. 2014 Agmt. §§ 3(A)(2), 7(4). Section 3(A)(2) of the agreement states

Use of Authors' Names. Publisher will have the right to use Authors' names in connection with the Work and upkeep of the work. If the Work or upkeep is prepared by a person other than Authors, Publisher may identify that person on the new material and any related advertising and give him or her authorship credit in addition to or in lieu of credit given to Authors.

Under the 2014 Agreement, plaintiffs were required to deliver the first update of the Work to Starr Publishing in 11 months, and plaintiffs agreed that "subsequent upkeep will be due annually thereafter." 2014 Agmt. § 2(B)(1).

Plaintiffs prepared annual pocket parts to update the material each year, until they declined to do so for the 2022–2023 pocket part. Carter Decl. ¶¶ 6–8; Am. Compl. ¶¶ 11, 18. Nevertheless, the pocket part was ultimately published. Am. Compl. ¶ 19. Plaintiffs acknowledge that the plaintiffs authored the "overwhelming majority of the content" of the 2022–2023 pocket part. Vinocur Tr. 212:4–11; *see also* Am. Compl. ¶ 24.

Plaintiffs cannot identify anyone whose opinion of them has changed based on the publication of the pocket part. Ms. Vinocur testified that she could not identify anyone who thought less of her as a result of the 2022–2023 pocket part, and Mr. Prakash testified that he had "received no such complaints." Vinocur Tr. 6:12–18, 7:16–22; Prelim Inj. Hr'g Tr. 49:15–22. Starr Publishing has searched its records and has found no complaints from any customer concerning the sufficiency and quality of the 2022–2023 pocket part. Carter Decl. ¶¶ 3, 6.

Plaintiffs also have not identified any injury. Plaintiffs testified that they suffered no emotional distress or similar damages. Vinocur Tr. 6:12–15, 7:16–19; Prelim. Inj. Hr'g Tr. at 24:16–20. Even the Court questioned Mr. Prakash about his potential emotional distress, and Mr. Prakash could find no such damages:

2

THE COURT: Would you agree then that you suffered emotional distress as a result of this whole thing?

THE WITNESS: I—distress, I—I would say—I—I won't characterize it as emotional distress, Judge, at—at this point.

Prelim. Inj. Hr'g Tr. 24:16–20.

Nevertheless, plaintiffs assert that they have suffered $75,000 each in reputational damages, but they point to no evidence to show how this sum was determined. Vinocur Tr. 196:12–15. Plaintiffs' counsel stipulated that "there will be no specific claim made with respect to any lost opportunity, revenue as a result of lost opportunity, lost jobs, lost teaching assignments, anything like that. There will be no specific evidence offered in that regard. However, [plaintiffs] will be making a claim for presumed injury to reputation . . . ." Vinocur Tr. 123:5–21. Plaintiffs' counsel has similarly agreed that no witnesses will be called to testify as to plaintiffs' loss of reputation—only that plaintiffs enjoy good reputations. Vinocur Tr. 182:20–186:15.

Starr Publishing replaced the allegedly offensive pocket part with a new pocket part in April 2023. Carter Decl. ¶ 5. Nonetheless, a complaint and this lawsuit followed.

Summary Judgment Standard

Summary judgment is appropriate if "there is no genuine issue as to any material fact and that the moving party is entitled to judgment as a matter of law." Fed. R. Civ. P. 56(a). Although the party seeking summary judgment initially bears responsibility for informing the court of the basis for its motion and identifying those portions of the record that it believes demonstrates the absence of a genuine issue of material fact, it is not required to support the motion with affidavits or other materials that negate the opponent's claim. *See Celotex Corp. v. Catrett*, 477 U.S. 317, 322–23 (1986).

Once the moving party has satisfied its initial burden, Rule 56(e) requires the nonmoving party to "go beyond the pleadings and by her own affidavits, or by the 'depositions, answers to interrogatories, and admissions on file,' designate 'specific facts showing that there is a genuine issue for trial.' " *Id.* at 324 (quoting Fed. R. Civ. P. 56(e)); *see also Lujan v. Nat'l Wildlife Fed'n*, 497 U.S. 871, 888 (1990) (holding that the non-moving party must bring forth "specific facts" to support its Complaint and cannot rely on conclusory allegations at the summary judgment stage).

Here, the submitted declarations, deposition testimony, and stipulations establish that there is no genuine issue of material fact for trial and that summary judgment should be granted in favor of Starr Publishing.

Argument

I. Plaintiffs' claim for defamation should be dismissed based on any of the four reasons explained below.

Discovery now confirms that plaintiffs cannot prove their claim of defamation *per se*, and therefore, summary judgment should be granted in

3

Starr Publishing's favor. To succeed in a claim for defamation, plaintiffs must establish seven elements: (1) the defamatory character of the communication, (2) its publication by the defendant, (3) its application to the plaintiff, (4) the understanding by the recipient of its defamatory meaning, (5) the recipient's understanding that the communication is intended to be applied to the plaintiff, (6) special harm resulting to the plaintiff from its publication, and (7) abuse of a conditionally privileged occasion. 42 Pa. Cons. Statutes § 8343(a).

The last paragraph focuses the judge's attention on the particular defamation claim that is at issue and the outcome the publisher seeks.

Notice how the publisher emphasizes that the trial court has four separate grounds on which to grant the motion for summary judgment. That statement lets the trial court know that it does not have to agree with every assertion to grant the motion.

An effective persuasive argument will provide an outline of the argument in both the point headings and the thesis sentences. After you have read through this argument once, try reading just the point headings or just the thesis sentences to see whether they achieve that goal.

Part A presents a short rule-based argument. Notice how the publisher re-uses key language in the application. (The key language is shaded in both the explanation and the application.) Re-using key language in the application helps the judge see how your argument is consistent with the law.

A claim of defamation *per se* requires the plaintiffs to establish all the elements of defamation except the sixth element, special harm. Instead of establishing special harm, plaintiffs must show that the words impute "(1) a criminal offense, (2) a loathsome disease, (3) business misconduct, or (4) serious sexual misconduct." *Synygy, Inc. v. Scott-Levin, Inc.*, 51 F. Supp. 2d 570, 580 (E.D. Pa. 1999). Plaintiffs have the burden of proving each of the seven elements. *Id.*

In this case, plaintiffs allege defamation *per se* on the ground that the words imputed business misconduct. As explained below, the undisputed facts establish that plaintiffs cannot establish their claim of defamation *per se*, and summary judgment should be granted based on any one of the four reasons explained below.

A. Plaintiffs cannot establish the first element of a defamation claim—that the statement was defamatory.

Plaintiffs cannot establish the first element of their defamation claim—the defamatory nature of the communication. Whether the statement at issue is capable of a defamatory meaning is a question for the court, not the jury, to resolve. *Cornell Cos. v. Borough of New Morgan*, 512 F. Supp. 2d 238, 271 (E.D. Pa. 2007). For the court to conclude that a statement imputes business misconduct, "the statement must be more than mere *general disparagement*." *Synygy*, 51 F. Supp. 2d at 580 (emphasis added). The statement must be of the type that would be "particularly harmful to an individual engaged in the plaintiff's business or profession." *Id.* Moreover, the defamatory meaning must be apparent on its face. *See* Robert D. Sack, *Sack on Defamation: Libel, Slander and Related Problems* § 2.8.3 (5th ed. 2017). If extrinsic facts are required to understand the defamatory statement, the statement is not *per se* defamatory. *Id.*

Here, plaintiffs' defamation claim should fail as defamation *per se* because the allegedly defamatory communication does not on its face impute any business misconduct to plaintiffs. The statement at issue is the phrase "by Amit Prakash and Helen Vinocur" and "The Publisher's Staff." On its face, those words impute no business misconduct and make no statement that would be particularly harmful to a lawyer or a law professor. Because plaintiffs cannot prove that the statement at issue has a defamatory character, plaintiffs' claim for defamation must be dismissed.

B. Plaintiffs have suffered no general damages.

Plaintiffs also cannot prove that they suffered any damages. In cases of defamation *per se*, a plaintiff cannot rely on presumed damages but must prove "general damage, *i.e., proof of reputational harm.*" *Synygy*, 51 F. Supp. 2d at 581; *see also Walker v. Grand Cent. Sanitation, Inc.*, 430 Pa. Super. Ct. 236, 634 A.2d 237, 242 (1993). Reputational damages must be "judged by the reaction of other persons in the community, and not by the party's self-estimation." *Pyle v. Meritor Sav. Bank*, No. Civ. A. 92-7361, 1996 WL 115048 at *3 (E.D. Pa. Mar. 13, 1996).

Part B uses both a rule-based and an analogical argument to make its point.

For example, in *McNulty v. Citadel Broad. Co.*, a radio broadcaster's claim for defamation *per se* was dismissed because the broadcaster could not prove that his reputation was actually damaged in anyone's eyes. 58 Fed. Appx. 556, 567 (3d Cir. 2003) (unpublished). Witnesses testified that the defendant's statements about the plaintiff's age and inability to attract a younger audience were the "kiss of death" in the plaintiff's industry. *Id.* After the district court granted summary judgment in the defendant's favor, the Third Circuit affirmed, concluding that plaintiff had not proved "that his reputation was actually damaged in anyone's eyes." *Id.*

Discovery has established that plaintiffs can offer no proof of reputational harm. At deposition, Ms. Vinocur testified that she could not identify anyone in the legal community who reacted negatively to the attribution or who thought less of her as a result of the 2022–2023 pocket part. Similarly, Mr. Prakash testified that he had received "no such complaints." Moreover, although plaintiffs were apparently angry about the publication of the 2022–2023 pocket part, the record demonstrates that plaintiffs suffered no emotional distress or similar damages. Plaintiffs simply assert that they have suffered $75,000 each in reputational damages, without providing any evidence substantiating how that sum was determined. Plaintiffs' self-estimation of their harm is an insufficient basis for a claim of defamation *per se.*

Here, in the rule-based argument, notice again how key language from the rule (shaded) is reused in the application.

Thus, this case is like the *McNulty* case in which the Third Circuit affirmed the district court's grant of summary judgment. Just as the plaintiff in *McNulty* failed to produce any evidence of actual damages, so too have the plaintiffs here failed to produce any evidence of any actual damages. Therefore, based on the undisputed facts, summary judgment should be granted in favor of Starr Publishing, and plaintiffs' claim for defamation should be dismissed.

The rule-based argument is supported by an analogical argument, comparing this case to *McNulty*. Notice how the publisher uses parallel language (underlined) to emphasize the similarity between the prior case and this case.

C. Plaintiffs consented to the use of their names in connection with the 2022–2023 pocket part.

Plaintiffs' claim for defamation should also be dismissed because plaintiffs consented to have their names used in connection with the pocket part whether or not plaintiffs participated in its production. Courts applying Pennsylvania law have long held that a plaintiff's consent to a defendant's communication precludes any liability for defamation. *See Sharman v. C. Schmidt & Sons, Inc.*, 216 F. Supp. 401, 405 (E.D. Pa. 1963) (stating that release signed by plaintiff precluded any liability on behalf of defendant with respect to the communications at issue); *Baker v. Lafayette Coll.*, 504 A.2d 247, 249 (Pa. Super. Ct. 1986) (concluding that professor's consent to publication of performance evaluations gave college absolute privilege against defamation claim with respect to those evaluations).

In this rule-based argument, the publisher uses parenthetical explanations to emphasize the rule. Here, parenthetical explanations of the case help strengthen the rule. However, if the publisher had wanted to create an analogical argument, the publisher would have described the cases in a case illustration.

Here, plaintiffs consented to the use of their names on the pocket part. In the 2014 Agreement, which both Starr Publishing and plaintiffs signed, plaintiffs agreed that Starr Publishing would have the right to use plaintiffs' names in connection with the treatise and its upkeep even if plaintiffs did not participate in its upkeep:

> Publisher will have the right to use Authors' names in connection with the Work and upkeep of the Work. *If the Work or upkeep is prepared by a person other than Authors, Publisher may identify that person on the new material and any related advertising and give him authorship credit in addition to or in lieu of credit given to Authors*.

2014 Agmt. §3(A)(2) (emphasis added). Notably, plaintiffs agreed if "the Work or upkeep is prepared by a person other than Authors," Starr Publishing could identify that new person "in addition to…[the] Authors." Thus, plaintiffs gave Starr Publishing the authority to do exactly what it did. Plaintiffs cannot now complain of an act that they previously agreed to.

Plaintiffs' argument that the 2014 Agreement does not apply is still without merit. The applicability of the parties' 2014 Agreement to plaintiffs' action is a question of law for this court to decide. *Great Am. Ins. Co. v. Norwin Sch. Dist.*, 544 F.3d 229, 243 (3d Cir. 2008). Plaintiffs' argument is predicated on the idea that the 2014 Agreement is superseded by a 2021 Agreement.

That argument misreads the 2021 Agreement. The 2021 agreement includes this integration clause:

> This is the entire agreement of the parties. All prior negotiations and representations are merged into this Agreement. This Agreement supersedes all previous agreements concerning the Work.

The integration clause is limited to the "Work" as defined in the 2021 Agreement. The 2021 Agreement defines the "Work" as *Starr's Pennsylvania Criminal Practice & Procedure 2021 Supplement* and "negotiations, representations, or agreements concerning the 2021 supplement." Thus, the integration clause in the 2021 Agreement is an integration clause as to the 2021 supplement. It does not affect any agreements about any work other than the 2021 supplement.

Accordingly, this Court should reject any argument that the 2014 Agreement is superseded by the 2021 Agreement. Under that 2014 Agreement plaintiffs consented to the use of their names in connection with the upkeep of the Work, including all pocket parts. Their consent is a bar to any defamation claim based on the use of their names in connection with the upkeep of the Work. Plaintiffs' defamation claim must therefore be dismissed.

D. The statement that the 2022–2023 pocket part was "by Amit Prakash and Helen Vinocur" and "The Publisher's Staff" was true or substantially true.

Plaintiffs' claim should also be dismissed because the statements, as a matter of law, are true or substantially true. Under Pennsylvania law, "truth…is

---

**Sidebar notes (left margin):**

Because the contract language is critical to publisher's argument, the publisher provides the contract's exact language.

Here, the publisher addresses the professors' arguments head-on. Because of earlier exchanges—a motion for a preliminary injunction and a motion to dismiss—the publisher has an idea of the arguments the professors will make. The publisher takes this opportunity to explain why summary judgment is still appropriate.

Notice that the publisher emphasizes that this issue is a question for the court to decide. The defendant does not want the case to go to the jury.

Notice, too, that the publisher does not provide a detailed explanation of plaintiffs' argument. The publisher acknowledges that plaintiffs have an argument based on the integration clause, but the publisher focuses on how it believes the integration clause should be understood.

a defense to a defamation claim." *Pierce v. Capital Cities Comm., Inc.*, 576 F.2d 495, 507 n.46 (3d Cir. 1978); *Bobb v.* Kraybill, 511 A.2d 1379, 1380 (Pa. Super. 1986). Moreover, a defendant "need only show substantial rather than complete truth" to establish such a defense. *Pierce v. Capital Cities Comm., Inc.*, 576 F.2d 495, 507 n.46 (3d Cir. 1978); *Bobb v.* Kraybill, 511 A.2d 1379, 1380 (Pa. Super. 1986).

This argument is also a rule-based argument that integrates the key language of the rule into the application.

Here, the statement that the pocket part was by "The Publisher's Staff" and plaintiffs is substantially, if not completely, true because both plaintiffs and staff members contributed to the pocket part. A pocket part, by its nature, is a cumulative work, and plaintiffs have consistently asserted that virtually all of the content in the 2022–2023 pocket part was work they authored. Indeed, Ms. Vinocur admitted at deposition that plaintiffs were *the* authors of "the overwhelming majority of the content" contained in the 2022–2023 pocket part. Vinocur Tr. 212:4–11. Thus, the complained-of statements about the pocket part—that it was "by Amit Prakash and Helen Vinocur" and "The Publisher's Staff"—are true or substantially true, and Starr Publishing should be granted summary judgment.

CONCLUSION

Pursuant to Federal Rule of Civil Procedure 56, defendant respectfully requests that the Court grant its motion for summary judgment and dismiss the amended complaint in its entirety.

As with most supporting memoranda of law, the final conclusion is formulaic.

Dated: April 21, 2023   Respectfully submitted,

/s/ _____
James F. Collier, Esq.
Aaron M. Goldstein, Esq.
Donahue Hartgrove LLP
1750 Market Street, 48th Floor
Philadelphia, PA 19103-7599
(215) 617-9200
jcollier@donhart.com
agoldstein@donhart.com

CERTIFICATE OF SERVICE

I, Aaron Goldstein, hereby certify that the foregoing memorandum of Law in Support of Defendant's Motion for Summary Judgment has been filed electronically and is available for viewing and downloading from the Court's ECF system. I further certify that on this date I served the foregoing upon counsel listed below by hand delivery as follows:

Richard L. Handelman
Handelman Moore & Fields, P.C.
1500 Market Street, Suite 700
Philadelphia, PA 19102-1907
(215) 865-1155
rhandelman@handelman.com

April 21, 2023

/s/ _____
James F. Collier, Esq.
Aaron M. Goldstein, Esq.
Donahue Hartgrove LLP
1750 Market Street, 48th Floor
Philadelphia, PA 19103-7599
(215) 617-9200
jcollier@donhart.com
agoldstein@donhart.com

C. Memorandum of Law in Opposition to Defendant's Motion for Summary Judgment

**IN THE UNITED STATES DISTRICT COURT
FOR THE EASTERN DISTRICT OF PENNSYLVANIA**

Amit Prakash and
Helen Vinocur,
      Plaintiffs,
 	
v.
 	
Starr Publishing Corporation,
      Defendant.
	CIVIL ACTION
	
	NO. 23-CV-727
	
	MEMORANDUM OF LAW IN OPPOSITION TO DEFENDANT'S MOTION FOR SUMMARY JUDGMENT

Preliminary Statement

Summary judgment is inappropriate. Despite defendant's assertion to the contrary, discovery has confirmed both the strength of plaintiffs' claims and the egregiousness of defendant's misconduct. That misconduct provides sufficient evidence for a jury to conclude that Starr Publishing Corporation has defamed the plaintiffs.

In 2023, defendant sold a 2022–2023 pocket part that allegedly updated "Starr's Criminal Practice & Procedure." The pocket part's cover stated that it was "by AMIT PRAKASH and HELEN VINOCUR" even though Mr. Prakash and Ms. Vinocur made absolutely no contributions to the pocket part. Defendant now argues that plaintiffs' defamation claims must be dismissed. None of defendant's arguments has any merit.

First, the record includes sufficient evidence that ascribing the names of plaintiffs to an incomplete and misleading pocket part is defamatory.

Second, the record also has sufficient evidence for a jury to conclude that plaintiffs were damaged. Both plaintiffs have testified that they were angry and outraged by the defamatory statements, and that evidence is more than sufficient to support an award of general damages.

Third, the 2014 agreement does not control this dispute. Nothing in the 2014 agreement between defendant and plaintiffs gave defendant the right to defame plaintiffs. Moreover, the 2014 agreement was superseded by a 2021 agreement between plaintiffs and defendant and, thus, does not apply to the 2022–2023 pocket part at issue in this case. If the conflict between the 2014 and 2021 agreements creates any ambiguity, such ambiguity is a question for the jury, and cannot be resolved on a motion for summary judgment.

Finally, the defendant's only other argument on defamation—that the statements at issue were "true or substantially true"—is frivolous because, as everyone agrees, plaintiffs had nothing to do with the 2022–2023 pocket part.

For all of these reasons, the evidence is sufficient for a jury to conclude that the defendant defamed the plaintiffs, and summary judgment should be denied.

Just like the publisher's preliminary statement (or introduction), the professors provide an overview of their arguments.

Notice how the professors emphasize that "sufficient evidence" exists for the "jury" to find in plaintiffs' favor. At summary judgment, the professors must establish that the evidence is sufficient for a jury to find in their favor.

1

Statement of Facts

The first two paragraphs of the statement of facts provide context. Those paragraphs introduce the parties and the conflict. Notice how the professors take some time to establish their eminent reputations even though, strictly speaking, such facts are not legally relevant.

Plaintiffs in this case, Amit Prakash and Helen Vinocur, are distinguished and long-standing members of the Bar of the Commonwealth of Pennsylvania, each residing in the Eastern District of Pennsylvania. Am. Compl. ¶¶ 1–2. During their careers, they have each practiced law, served as faculty members at law schools, and authored legal books and articles. Am. Compl. ¶¶ 1–2. In each of these roles, their work has focused on criminal, constitutional, and civil rights law. Am. Compl. ¶¶ 1–2. Mr. Prakash and Ms. Vinocur both enjoy excellent reputations in the legal and academic communities. Am. Compl. ¶¶ 1–2.

Defendant is a well-known regional publisher of legal casebooks, treatises, practice guides, and other materials. Am. Compl. ¶ 6; Carter Decl. ¶ 1. This litigation results from Starr's statement that the 2022–2023 pocket part was "by Amit Prakash and Helen Vinocur" when the plaintiffs took no part in its production.

A. The most recent agreement between Starr Publishing and the plaintiffs

The most recent agreement between Starr Publishing and the plaintiffs was signed in 2021. 2021 Agmt. (Ex. D.) Another agreement had been in place between 2014 and 2021. Under that earlier agreement, plaintiffs agreed to produce a second edition of the treatise, "Starr's Pennsylvania Criminal Practice & Procedure." 2014 Agmt. §§ 1–2 (Ex. C.) Plaintiffs also agreed to produce supplements and pocket parts, which they did until 2021. *Id.* In 2021, plaintiffs and Starr Publishing signed another agreement, which governed the publication of the 2020–2021 pocket part. That agreement includes a merger clause. 2021 Agmt. § 25. The merger clause states that the 2021 agreement "is the entire agreement of the parties." *Id.*

> This is the entire agreement of the parties. All prior negotiations and representations are merged into this Agreement. This Agreement supersedes all previous agreements concerning the Work.

Id.

This statement of facts uses point headings to help organize the information. As is appropriate for point headings in a statement of facts, the point headings are descriptive rather than assertive.

B. Starr's decision to assign an inexperienced editor to produce the 2022–2023 pocket part

In early 2022, Starr staff members, including Ms. Melanie Vargas, who was Starr's Attorney Editor for the treatise, and Ms. Roberta Jones, who was the Team Coordinator for Starr's State Practice Group, recommended terminating publication of the treatise. Jones Dep. 31:13–32:2. Rather than terminate the publication, however, Starr offered to pay plaintiffs half of their prior compensation (i.e., to cut their payment from $5,000 each to $2,500 each) to prepare a pocket part for 2022–2023. Vargas Dep. 58:19–59:9. Plaintiffs declined this offer. Vinocur Dep. 45:7–9.

After plaintiffs declined an offer that cut their compensation in half for doing the same amount of work, Starr took no action with respect to the treatise until early November 2022, when a number of Starr employees met to discuss the future of the treatise. Jones Dep. 20:2–20:16. Although all in attendance had agreed that Starr should stop publishing the treatise, the decision was not executed during 2022 because "it was close to the end of the year," and Starr did not have enough time to obtain all the necessary formal approvals to terminate the publication. Jones Dep. 21:17–22:18; 25:6–17. Accordingly, Starr's decision to terminate the treatise would not be implemented until 2023. Jones Dep. 25:24–26:3.

That decision put Ms. Jones between a rock and a hard place: Because the treatise would not be terminated during 2022, their business unit was expected to produce a supplement to the treatise by the end of 2022; however, because the supplement was part of their unit's 2022 "Publishing Plan" for 2022–2023, they had made an internal "commitment" to Starr to publish one by year's end. Jones Dep. 26:8–16. Ms. Jones believed that it was necessary to publish a supplement, even though Starr had decided to terminate the treatise, because the revenue from the sale of the treatise to the paying subscribers was included within her unit's revenue projections for 2022. Jones Dep. 47:1–48:24. Accordingly, if Ms. Jones failed to produce a "2023 Supplement" to be sent to paying subscribers, Ms. Jones's State Practice Unit would not meet its 2022 revenue target. Jones Dep. 49:15–22.

Responsibility for producing the supplement was assigned to Ms. Francesca Quinn, a newly hired Attorney Editor trainee. Vargas Dep. 60:20–61:7. Ms. Quinn had graduated from law school in May 2021 and had been employed as an Attorney Editor at Starr for a little more than a year. Quinn Dep. 8:12–14. She testified that she was trained for that position by "shadowing" Melanie Vargas. Quinn Dep.16:10–17:6. Ms. Vargas, however, testified that Ms. Quinn did not shadow her. Vargas Dep. 37:11–22. Ms. Vargas believed that a woman named Caroline Abbott had trained Ms. Quinn. Vargas Dep. 37:16–22. Ms. Quinn, however, could not remember being trained by Ms. Abbott. Quinn Dep. 20:10–21:4. Given the contradictory testimony of the two Starr witnesses, the record does not elucidate whether anyone at Starr actually trained Ms. Quinn to be an Attorney Editor.

Although Ms. Quinn had not authored any manuscript on her own at that point and had virtually no background in or knowledge of criminal law (much less Pennsylvania criminal law or procedure), Quinn Dep. 66:19–67:13, no one at Starr provided her with any input on how to update a supplement on her own. Quinn Dep. 66:1–18; Jones Dep. 43:2–44:15. Even more incredibly, once Ms. Quinn completed her manuscript, no one at Starr ever reviewed it to determine whether it was worthy of publication. Jones Dep. 49:16–51:4.

Instead, Quinn's manuscript went directly to Starr's production department, where it was packaged as the 2022–2023 supplement to the treatise, and was sent to each of approximately 400 subscribers to the treatise, each of whom was charged $46.50 for it. Quinn Dep.74:1–8.

C. Deficiencies in the 2022–2023 pocket part

Starr's 2022–2023 supplement to the treatise had serious deficiencies. For example, while the prior pocket parts that Prakash and Vinocur had prepared typically included citations to between 100 and 150 cases decided since the

> All of part B of the statement of facts is legally irrelevant. Do you think the professors benefit from including these facts? Or will the judge be frustrated at the time spent on irrelevant facts?

prior version was published, the "2022–2023 Pocket Part" contained only three new cases that had not been cited in the 2020–2021 pocket part. Hr'g Tr. (Prakash) 10:3–12:5.

Moreover, the 2022–2023 pocket part failed to include a number of cases in which the Pennsylvania Supreme Court reversed or vacated lower courts, including at least the following:

- *Commonwealth v. Mallory*, 888 A.2d 854 (Pa. Super. Ct. 2019), vacated by 941 A.2d 686 (Pa. 2020), cert. denied, 129 S. Ct. 257 (2021);
- *Commonwealth v. Brown*, 853 A.2d 1029 (Pa. Super. Ct. 2020), rev'd by 925 A.2d 147 (Pa. 2021);
- *Commonwealth v. West*, 868 A.2d 1267 (Pa. Super. Ct. 2013), rev'd by 938 A.2d 1034 (Pa. 2021);
- *Commonwealth v. Wilson*, 866 A.2d 1131 (Pa. Super. Ct. 2018), rev'd by 934 A.2d 1191 (Pa. 2021);
- *Commonwealth v. Bennett*, 842 A.2d 953 (Pa. Super. Ct. 2018), vacated by 930 A.2d 1264 (Pa. 2021);
- *Commonwealth v. Gravely*, 918 A.2d 761 (Pa. Super. Ct. 2021), allowance of appeal granted, ____ A.2d ____, 2020 WL 878654 (Pa. Apr 02, 2021); and
- *Commonwealth v. Lee*, 935 A.2d 865 (Pa. 2021).

Hr'g Tr. (Prakash) 10:3–12:5.

Finally, the 2022–2023 pocket part also failed to reflect relevant changes to pertinent rules. For example, the 2022–2023 pocket part failed to include any reference to the amendment to Pennsylvania Rule of Appellate Procedure 2111, which added new section (a)(7), providing that an appellant's brief must include a "[s]tatement of the reasons to allow an appeal to challenge the discretionary aspects of a sentence, if applicable." Hr'g Tr. (Prakash) 12:10–15.

D. Starr Publishing's attribution of the deficient 2022–2023 pocket part to Mr. Prakash and Ms. Vinocur

Even though Prakash and Vinocur did not in any way prepare the 2022–2023 pocket part, its cover page identified it as being "by AMIT PRAKASH [and] HELEN VINOCUR," modified only by the innocuous qualifier and, in smaller type, "THE PUBLISHER'S STAFF." *See* Ex. E. Nothing on the supplement, or mailed with the supplement, informed subscribers or readers that Prakash and Vinocur had not prepared the supplement.

E. Prakash and Vinocur shocked by the attribution

Both Prakash and Vinocur testified to the harm they suffered from the publication. When Prakash received the 2022–2023 supplement in the mail sometime after the New Year in January 2023, he was "stunned" that it was a virtual copy of the prior version, and he found it "very upsetting." Hr'g Tr. (Prakash) 12:5, 23:19–21; Vinocur, for her part, "was really, angry…very, very angry" and "pretty upset." Vinocur Dep. 40:16–20, 53:24–54:12. As Mr. Prakash explained,

My understanding…if someone found that we did not include—or you did not include—a case that was highly relevant, I wouldn't expect them to call me and complain. I would expect them to think, Prakash and Vinocur aren't up to snuff.

Hr'g Tr. (Prakash) 24:1–3. Likewise, Ms. Vinocur testified that,

Besides the fact that it is an incompetent effort, there is still a harm to Mr. Prakash and me because many users are not going to know that this wasn't prepared by us when they use this volume and, therefore, we can be associated with this incompetent effort of a pocket part.

Vinocur Dep. 17:12–14.

Plaintiffs filed the complaint in this case on February 19, 2023, along with a motion for preliminary injunction on March 24, 2023. Only after this action was filed did Starr finally agree to send a letter to subscribers informing them that the 2022–2023 supplement was deficient. Exhibit I.

Summary Judgment Standard

Rule 56(a) of the Federal Rules of Civil Procedure provides that summary judgment is appropriate only if "the movant shows that there is no genuine dispute as to any material fact and the movant is entitled to judgment as a matter of law." The party moving for summary judgment bears the burden of demonstrating the basis for its motion and identifying "particular parts of materials in the record" that demonstrate the absence of a genuine issue of material fact. Fed. R. Civ. P. 56(c); *Celotex Corp. v. Catrett*, 477 U.S. 317, 322 (1986).

In determining whether a dispute is genuine, the Court's function is not to weigh the evidence or determine the truth of the matter, but only to determine whether the evidence of record "is such that a reasonable jury could return a verdict for the nonmoving party." *Anderson v. Liberty Lobby Inc.*, 477 U.S. 242, 248–49 (1986). "The evidence of the non-movant is to be believed." *Id.* at 255.

All inferences must be drawn in the light most favorable to the non-moving party. *Am. Eagle Outfitters v. Lyle & Scott Ltd.*, 584 F.3d 575, 581 (3d Cir. 2009). "[W]hen there is a disagreement about the facts or the proper inferences to be drawn from them, a trial is required to resolve the conflicting versions of the parties." *Id.* "Summary judgment may not be granted…if there is a disagreement over what inferences can be reasonably drawn from the facts even if the facts are undisputed." *Ideal Dairy Farms, Inc. v. John Labatt, Ltd.*, 90 F.3d 737, 744 (3d Cir. 1996).

Argument

I. Summary judgment is inappropriate because the record establishes sufficient evidence for a jury to find defamation per se.

This Court should deny defendant's motion for summary judgment because discovery has produced sufficient evidence for a jury to conclude that defendant defamed plaintiffs per se. Defendant correctly explains the seven elements necessary to establish defamation and that the sixth element, special harm, need not be proved in a claim of defamation per se. Def.'s Mem. of Law in Support of Def.'s Mot. Summ. J. 4. Rather, a plaintiff can establish that the

5

defamatory words imputed "business misconduct." *Id*. In that case, the plaintiff need not establish special harm. *Id*.

As explained below, the evidence is sufficient for a jury to conclude that defendant defamed plaintiffs per se. First, the evidence is sufficient for a jury to conclude that the statement was defamatory. Second, the evidence is sufficient for a jury to conclude that the plaintiffs suffered damages. Finally, plaintiffs never consented to the defamation, and the alleged truth of the statements is not a bar to proceeding to trial. For all of these reasons, defendant's motion for summary judgment should be dismissed and a trial date set.

The professors take this opportunity to focus the court's attention on the arguments it will make below.

A. The statements were defamatory.

Part A is a rule-based argument. The first sentence is the conclusion. The rest of the first paragraph and the second paragraph explain the law. Key ideas from the explanation of the law (shaded) are repeated in the application to emphasize how the professors' analysis is consistent with the law.

First, the evidence is sufficient for a jury to conclude that the statement was defamatory. As a general rule, a statement alleges business misconduct when "the particular quality disparaged…is peculiarly valuable in the plaintiff's business and profession." *Id*. (quoting Restatement (Second) of Torts § 573, cmt. e (1977)).

The professors have done a very good job of framing rules that will be helpful to them. No case in Pennsylvania has addressed whether an assertion that a professor produced a deficient pocket part attributes business misconduct to that professor. So, the professors marshal authorities that will lead the judge to conclude that such an assertion would be attributing business misconduct to a professor.

With respect to lawyers, a statement imputes business misconduct when the statement suggests "a total disregard of professional ethics." *Clemente v. Espinosa*, 749 F. Supp. 672, 678 (E.D. Pa. 1990). Professional ethics require lawyers to make a reasonable inquiry into the law before submitting briefs to the court. Part of that reasonable inquiry is "Shepardizing, or otherwise checking the validity of the legal authority for an argument." Georgene M. Vairo, *Rule 11 Sanctions: Case Law, Perspectives, and Preventive Measures* § 6.05[d][6] (3d ed. 2004). In fact, lawyers have been sanctioned for failure to update their legal authority. *Id*. The purpose of a pocket part is to update the law so that lawyers can perform their professional duties. *See Pocket part*, *Black's Law Dictionary* (Bryan A. Garner 11th ed. 2019) (defining a pocket part as a "supplemental pamphlet inserted usu. into the back inside cover of a lawbook…to update the material in the main text"). For these reasons, a legal scholar who asserts that a legal authority is up-to-date when, in fact, the legal authority is not up-to-date would be acting with "total disregard for professional ethics."

Part A is responsive to the publisher's argument that the professors cannot prove that the statements were defamatory. In responding to the publisher's assertion, the professors never outline defendant's argument. Rather, the professors simply assert their own argument as to why the attribution was defamatory.

Based on the evidence in the record, a jury could find that the statement "by Amit Prakash and Helen Vinocur" and "The Publisher's Staff" was defamatory because it imputes a total disregard for professional ethics. A lawyer would expect that a pocket part labeled "2022–2023" would be up-to-date through 2023. This pocket part was not.

The deficiencies of the pocket part include the following:

- It failed to identify relevant rule changes, such as amendments to Pennsylvania Rule of Appellate Procedure 2111, which created a new briefing requirement for criminal appellants.
- It failed to include at least seven cases in which the Pennsylvania Supreme Court had reversed or vacated the lower court.
- It included only three new cases while prior pocket parts authored by plaintiffs have included between 100 and 150 new cases.

A jury could find that the use of the plaintiffs' names on a deficient work product imputed business misconduct to the plaintiffs. As Professor Prakash explained

> My understanding…if someone found that we did not include—or you did not include—a case that was highly relevant, I wouldn't expect them to call me and complain. I would expect them to think, Prakash and Vinocur aren't up to snuff.

Likewise, Ms. Vinocur testified that

> Besides the fact that it is an incompetent effort, there is still a harm to Mr. Prakash and me because many users are not going to know that this wasn't prepared by us when they use this volume and, therefore, we can be associated with this incompetent effort of a pocket part.

Vinocur Dep. 17 (Ex. G). Starr's assertion that the plaintiffs authored the deficient pocket part went to the core of plaintiffs' professional reputations as lawyers, law professors, legal writers, and authorities on Pennsylvania criminal law and procedure. A jury could thus find that the statement "by Amit Prakash and Helen Vinocur" and "The Publisher's Staff" was defamatory, and summary judgment is not appropriate.

B. The evidence in the record allows a jury to find that the plaintiffs suffered harm to their reputations.

The evidence is also sufficient for a jury to conclude that plaintiffs suffered harm to their reputations. When the issue is defamation *per se*, plaintiffs can show harm by establishing harm to their reputation and standing in the community, personal humiliation, or mental pain and suffering. *Clemente*, 749 F. Supp. at 680. "Such harm may be temporary in nature." *Id.*

The suffering need not be great. For example, in *Marcone v. Penthouse Int'l Magazine for Men*, the plaintiff testified that he was "frustrated, distraught, upset, and distressed." 754 F.2d 1072, 1080 (3d Cir. 1985.) The Third Circuit held that the plaintiff's testimony constituted sufficient evidence of harm and entitled the plaintiff to recover for injury to his reputation. *Id.* Similarly, in *Brinich v. Jencka*, a general contractor brought a defamation claim against a homeowner. 757 A.2d 388, 392 (Pa. Super. Ct. 2000). The jury returned a $33,000 verdict in favor of the contractor. *Id.* at 395. The superior court affirmed the verdict, holding that the damages award was supported by the contractor's testimony that he became "so angry" that he confronted the defendant was sufficient evidence to prove damages. *Id.* at 398. Likewise, in *Clemente*, the court awarded general damages after a bench trial on the basis of the plaintiff's testimony that he suffered anxiety, embarrassment, humiliation, and a sense of being shunned. 749 F. Supp. at 680–81.

To establish damages plaintiffs need not show that other peoples' opinions have changed. *Sprague v. American Bar Ass'n*, 276 F. Supp. 2d 365, 370 (E.D. Pa. 2003). In *Sprague*, the defendant moved for summary judgment on the ground that "all of the numerous witnesses presented by plaintiff concede that their

Part B uses analogical arguments.

Throughout, the professors integrate the summary judgment standard into their argument. Here the professors emphasize that "the evidence is sufficient for a jury to conclude" in their favor.

The hook, "[t]he suffering need not be great," states an implicit rule that counsel found in the *Marcone, Brinich,* and *Clemente* cases.

In both this paragraph and the paragraph below, the hooks for the case illustrations do double-duty as thesis sentences, pointing out concepts the plaintiffs want to emphasize.

estimations of plaintiff did not falter as a result of" the defamatory statements. *Id.* The court rejected the defendant's argument, stating that although the witnesses said that their opinion did not change, the witnesses said their opinion did not change because they knew the plaintiff. *Id.* The witnesses did say they were "outraged," which suggests an inference that without personal knowledge of plaintiff, the alleged defamation would result in a reputational loss to the plaintiff. *Id.*

Defendant's assertion that plaintiffs suffered no general damages is unsupported by the evidence. Both plaintiffs testified about the adverse emotional reactions that they suffered as a result of Starr's defamatory statements. Mr. Prakash testified that it was "unsettling" and "very upsetting," that he was "stunned" and "concerned," and that he "couldn't believe it." Likewise, Ms. Vinocur testified at her deposition that she was "angry," "upset," and "outraged." Ms. Vinocur also confirmed that Mr. Prakash was "very upset." Thus, Mr. Prakash's and Ms. Vinocur's reactions were similar to the reactions of the plaintiff in *Marcone*, who was "frustrated, distraught, upset, and distressed"; similar to the plaintiff in *Brinich*, who was "so angry"; and similar to the plaintiff in *Clemente*, who suffered "anxiety, embarrassment, humiliation, and a sense of being shunned." Accordingly, and just as in those prior cases, the evidence is sufficient for a jury to conclude that the plaintiffs suffered damages.

In fact, even in those cases in which the plaintiffs could not prove injury, the court has explained that the result would have been different if, as in this case, the evidence showed that the plaintiffs suffered adverse emotional reactions to the defamation. *See Walker v. Grand Cent. Sanitation, Inc.*, 634 A.2d 237, 245 (Pa. Super. Ct. 1993) (stressing that "Walker did not testify that she suffered any adverse emotional reaction" to the defamation); *Synygy, Inc. v. Scott-Levin, Inc.*, 51 F. Supp. 2d 570, 582 (E.D. Pa. 1999) (stressing that there was "no evidence that plaintiff suffered humiliation").[1] Because the evidence in the record supports a finding that plaintiffs suffered adverse emotional reactions, summary judgment is not appropriate.

For all of these reasons, the evidence of general damages is sufficient to support an award of general damages for defamation.

C. Plaintiffs did not "consent" to defamation.

Plaintiffs never consented to being defamed. Defendant's argument to the contrary rests on the assertion that the 2014 agreement still binds the parties. However, as explained below, the 2014 agreement has been superseded. Moreover, even if the 2014 agreement has not been superseded, the evidence is not sufficient to conclude as a matter of law that plaintiffs consented to being defamed.

*Sidebar (left margin):*

Here, the professors compare the facts in their case to the facts in the prior case to prove that their reactions to the allegedly defamatory publication is sufficient to establish damages.

After comparing the facts, the professors explain the legal consequence of the factual similarity.

Here, the professors introduce new law in the application. Usually, all law is explained in the explanation of the law before the application begins. Here, however, the professors' point is that these cases are inapplicable, and so the choice to delay explaining them is a reasonable one. Some lawyers might, however, introduce these cases in their explanation of the law. As a reader, what is your reaction to new law presented in the application section?

---

1. Defendant also cites *McNulty v. Citadel Broadcasting Co.*, 58 Fed. Appx. 556 (3d Cir. 2003). The *McNulty* court, however, designated that its opinion is "Not for Publication." Under the Third Circuit's Internal Operating Procedures, such opinions have no precedential value. United States Court of Appeals for the Third Circuit, Local Appellate Rules, Appendix I, Internal Operating Procedure 5.7.

First, the 2014 agreement no longer binds the parties; it has been superseded by the 2021 agreement. The 2021 agreement has an integration clause that states the 2021 agreement is the entire agreement between the parties:

> This is the entire agreement of the parties. All prior negotiations and representations are merged into this Agreement. This Agreement supersedes all previous agreements concerning the Work.

The first sentence of this integration clause states that the 2021 agreement is now controlling for all purposes, *i.e.*, that it is the entire agreement of the parties. The second sentence encompasses *all* prior negotiations and representations, regardless of whether those negotiations and representations led to the 2021 agreement or to the 2014 agreement. Finally, "the Work," as defined in the 2021 agreement is the *"Pennsylvania Criminal Practice & Procedure 2021 Supplement."* The 2014 agreement applied to "supplements" and upkeep. Because the 2021 agreement also addresses a supplement, it — by virtue of the integration clause — supplants the 2014 agreement.

Moreover, if the court concludes that the language of the integration clause is ambiguous, resolving that ambiguity is a question for the jury because the interpretation of an ambiguous contract is a question of fact. The question, therefore, cannot be resolved on a motion for summary judgment. When the jury resolves the question, any ambiguity should be resolved against defendant because defendant authored both the 2014 agreement and the 2021 agreement. *See, e.g., Am. Eagle Outfitters*, 584 F.3d at 587; *Dardovitch v. Haltzman*, 190 F.3d 125, 141 (3d Cir. 1999).

Even if the 2014 agreement did apply here, plaintiffs did not consent to the defamation. In defamation actions, Pennsylvania adheres to the Restatement (Second) of Torts. *See Walker*, 634 A.2d at 244. Under the Restatement's definition, a plaintiff "consents" to the publication of a defamatory statement only if the plaintiff "knows the exact language" that the defendant will use in those statements or "has reason to know that" such language "may be defamatory." Restatement (Second) of Torts § 583 (1977).

In this case, not a shred of evidence indicates that plaintiffs knew "the exact language" of the 2022–2023 pocket part before it was published or that plaintiffs had any reason to know that they would be defamed. Accordingly, Starr's consent argument has no basis in fact or law.

D. Defendant is not entitled to summary judgment on the supposed "truth" of the defamatory statements.

Defendant's next argument that, absent a contract, the truth is a defense to its defamation is similarly without merit. Although "truth" can be a defense to a claim of defamation, in this case, the statement was not true. The test for determining the truth or falsity of a defamatory statement is whether the statement "as published would have a different effect on the mind of the reader from that which the pleaded truth would have produced." Whether an alleged defamatory statement is true, substantially true, or false is a question for the jury. *McDowell v. Paiewonsky*, 769 F.2d 942, 947 (3d Cir. 1985); *see also Krochalis*

In part C the professors make two distinct arguments: (1) the 2014 agreement does not apply, and (2) even if the agreement does apply, the jury resolves conflicting contractual interpretations. Either way, summary judgment in favor of the publisher is not appropriate.

The professors are using the summary judgment standard to their advantage.

The arguments in part C are responsive to the publisher's argument that 2014 contract bars the professors' claims. The professors effectively respond to the publisher's arguments without detailing the publisher's arguments for the court.

Another rule-based argument that effectively integrates key language from the rule into the application.

The professors again emphasize the role of the jury. They want this case to go to the jury. With such emphasis, the professors are reminding the court of the role of the jury and the court's limited role in deciding a motion for summary judgment.

v. *Ins. Co. of N. Am.*, 629 F. Supp. 1360, 1366 (E.D. Pa. 1985) (denying defendant's motion for summary judgment in defamation action because "[t]ruth is typically an issue resolved by the jury in a defamation action").

In this case, the statement was not true because Starr represented that plaintiffs authored the 2022–2023 pocket part when, in fact, plaintiffs had nothing to do with the preparation of that publication. The publishers took work that the plaintiffs had done and incorporated it into the 2022–2023 pocket part, but the 2022–2023 pocket part was entirely the work of the defendant. The plaintiffs had nothing to do with it. For most readers, the statement as published would have told them that the plaintiffs had been involved in the production of the 2022–2023 pocket part. The pleaded truth demonstrates that the plaintiffs were not involved. Thus, the statements were not true. Instead, the statements were indisputably false.

Even if a question exists regarding the truth or falsity of the statement, that question is reserved for the jury and is not an appropriate ground on which to grant summary judgment. Accordingly, the Court should deny defendant's motion for summary judgment.

CONCLUSION

A typical perfunctory conclusion

For all the foregoing reasons, defendant's motion for summary judgment should be denied.

Respectfully submitted,

/s/ *Zev Marinoff*
Richard L. Handelman, Esq.
Zev Marinoff, Esq.
Cynthia Maldonado, Esq.
Handelman Moore & Fields, P.C.
1500 Market Street, Suite 700
Philadelphia, OA 19102-1907
(215) 865-1155
zmarinoff@handelman.com

Attorneys for plaintiffs,
Amit Prakash and
Helen Vinocur

Dated: May 12, 2023

Certificate of Service

I hereby certify that on this 12th day of May, 2023, I served a true and correct copy of the foregoing Plaintiffs' Memorandum of Law in Opposition to Defendant's Motion for Summary Judgment upon the following counsel for defendant, as follows:

via the Court's Electronic Case Filing System:
     James F. Collier, Esq.
     Aaron M. Goldstein, Esq.
     Donahue Hartgrove LLP
     1750 Market Street, 48th Floor
     Philadelphia, PA 19103-7599
     (215) 617-9200
     jcollier@donhart.com
     agoldstein@donhart.com

            /s/ *Zev Marinoff*
            Zev Marinoff, Esq.
            (I.D. No. 89012)

Appendix C

State v. Lynwood
Appellate Briefs

Appendix C provides examples of an appellant's and a respondent's appellate brief. As with the examples in Appendix B, you will likely find it helpful if you have some background about the case before you jump into this set of examples. To that end, this overview begins with a brief summary of the arguments. Then, it lists some of the skills that counsel used when drafting each brief. As you write an appellate brief on behalf of a client, consider how these skills can be adapted to your client's context.

I. Summary of the Arguments

In this case, defendant Jeffrey Lynwood was convicted on two counts of endangering the welfare of a minor. On appeal, the issue is whether the evidence was sufficient to support Mr. Lynwood's convictions. The argument breaks down into two sub-arguments.

The first argument is a statutory construction argument. In that argument, the parties focus on the statutory word "permit." Oregon Revised Statutes § 163.575(1)(d) creates criminal liability for anyone who "permits" a minor to enter or remain in a place where unlawful activities involving drugs are maintained or conducted.

Mr. Lynwood argues for a narrow definition of the verb "permit." He argues that a person can be guilty of permitting something only if that person has authority to deny permission. Mr. Lynwood argues that the defendant must engage in some affirmative conduct to "permit."

Need examples of analogical arguments?

If your brief requires you to construct analogical arguments, please look at the trial memoranda in Appendix B.

Analogical arguments are constructed in the same way whether those analogical arguments appear in a trial memorandum or an appellate brief. Thus, you can use these appellate briefs to see how an appellate brief is formatted and how rule-based arguments are structured, but look to the trial memoranda in Appendix B for examples of analogical arguments.

You may also want to return to § 3.2, *Structuring Analogical Arguments*, and § 3.4, *Using Rule-Based and Analogical Arguments Together*, for additional examples of analogical arguments.

By contrast, the state argues that "permit" has a broader definition and that broader definition is more consistent with the legislature's intent. Under that definition, simply "allowing" or "making it possible" for a child to enter or remain in a place where there is unlawful drug activity is sufficient to "permit." That definition would make a defendant guilty of endangering the welfare of a child if that defendant passively permits a child to be present in a place of illegal drug activity.

After arguing for a broader or narrower definition, the parties address whether, given that definition, the evidence was sufficient to convict Mr. Lynwood of endangering the welfare of a minor. Mr. Lynwood was convicted of endangering the welfare of two minors because he maintained an illegal marijuana-grow operation in the children's home and provided them with marijuana. The father and owner of the house knew of and allowed the marijuana-grow operation and permitted Mr. Lynwood to give the children marijuana.

Mr. Lynwood argues that he did not have sufficient authority to exclude the children from the place with the illegal drug activity and therefore he was incapable of "permitting" them to enter or remain. For that reason, Mr. Lynwood argues, the evidence was insufficient to support his conviction.

Addressing an issue of statutory construction, but in a memorandum of law?

If your client's legal problem involves a question of statutory construction, you can use these examples even if you are drafting a memorandum of law. A statutory construction argument is developed in the same way whether that argument appears in a memorandum of law or in an appellate brief.

The state, by contrast, argues that the evidence was sufficient to support the convictions. First, the defendant participated in the illegal grow, knowing that children were present, and he gave them marijuana when they asked. By agreeing to care for the children, he made it possible for the children to remain in the home. Finally, the state points out that even if Mr. Lynwood's authority was limited in his role as babysitter and houseguest, he had sufficient authority to refrain from his own conduct that permitted the children to be in the presence of illegal drug activity.

II. Skills and Techniques

This book provides examples so that you can see how the various techniques discussed in the book are actually put to work. Examples must, however, be used carefully. Although the introduction to Appendix B provided this warning, it bears repeating here: After reading these examples, you may want to adopt some of the techniques you see and use them in your own writing. When you do that, please keep in mind that no two documents are ever the same. Each client's legal problem is different. Therefore, these samples will be most useful if you go beyond the words on the page. Ask yourself *why* the writer drafted the argument as the writer did. What point was the writer trying to make? How did the writer shape the text to make that particular point? Then, ask yourself whether you can use that same technique in your document. If you think you can use the same technique in your own document, then ask yourself one final question: How will you adjust that technique to suit your client's particular problem?

With that in mind, look for these skills and techniques in the argument section:

- Assertive **point headings** outline the argument.
- **Thesis sentences** clearly and accurately assert the point that will be established in each paragraph.
  - Read just the thesis sentences to see how they outline the argument.
  - Note how every sentence in the paragraph supports that point.
  - Note how the paragraphs reassert the thesis at the end of the paragraph.
- Arguments **address weaknesses** without giving undue airtime to that weakness.
  - When addressing an opposing argument, each party explains how that party wants the court to understand the issue. The party does not flesh out the opposing party's argument.
- **Polished writing**, which includes

> **Need more help with a statutory construction argument?**
>
> If you need more help with a statutory construction argument or you would like to see an additional example, return to §3.3, *Structuring Rule-Based Arguments*.

- ◦ Sentences that have a clear subject and verb and use the active voice.
- ◦ Words that are simple and easy to understand.
- ◦ No grammatical, punctuation, or citation errors.

Because the bulk of the argument addresses an issue of statutory construction, the argument section relies heavily on rule-based arguments. Thus, you can use this example to more closely analyze how to construct complex rule-based arguments. Look for two important skills.

First, in a successful rule-based argument, the application will track the stated rule. The arguments in the examples track the rules in two ways.

- The application **repeats or echoes key language** from the rule in the the explanation of the law.
- The application **does what the rule says to do**.
  - ◦ For example, if the rule says that "words of a statute are best understood in the context of surrounding statutes," the application examines the surrounding statutes as the rule suggests.

Second, a successful rule-based argument emphasizes the point of each argument. Therefore, the arguments

- State a **conclusion** at the outset of the argument and at the end of the argument.
  - ◦ The conclusion is the point that counsel wants the court to walk away with after the court reads that argument.
  - ◦ Sometimes a rule-based argument is one paragraph long; sometimes it spans several paragraphs. Each rule-based argument is one building block within the larger argument.

When reading the other sections of the brief, look for these skills and techniques:

- **Tables** are carefully formatted and easy to read.
- The **question presented** selects facts to suggest the outcome each party seeks.
- The **summary of the argument** gives a concise and persuasive overview of each party's arguments.
  - ◦ Notice how each summary simply asserts the conclusions that each party wants the court to reach.
- The **statement of the case**
  - ◦ Provides context before jumping into the facts.
  - ◦ Includes all of the legally relevant facts.
  - ◦ States legally relevant facts in precise detail.
  - ◦ Places unfavorable facts in perspective.

- ° Includes selected facts that are not legally relevant for the impact that those facts will have on the court.

III. The Briefs

Appellant's and respondent's brief follow.[1] For clarity, we refer to the appellant as "defendant" or "Mr. Lynwood," and we refer to the respondent as the state or the State of Oregon.

---

1. The sample briefs were drawn from arguments presented in *State v. McBride*, 256 P.3d 174 (Or. App. 2011), *rev'd*, 281 P.3d 605 (Or. 2012). Some of the statutes that were relied on in these briefs have since been amended.

A. Appellant's Opening Brief

IN THE COURT OF APPEALS OF THE STATE OF OREGON

———————

STATE OF OREGON,	)	Mercer County Circuit Court
Plaintiff-Respondent,	)	No. 15C50799
	)	
v.	)	CA A139020
	)	
JEFFREY SCOTT LYNWOOD,	)	
Defendant-Appellant.	)	
	)	
	)	

———————

APPELLANT'S OPENING BRIEF

———————

An appellate brief cover provides basic information about the litigation: the names of the parties, the appellate court in which the case is being heard, the court from which the appeal is taken, and the names and contact information for counsel.

Appeal from the Judgment of the Circuit Court
For Mercer County
Honorable Charity A. Beckah Judge

KEN NAKANO #842314
  Chief Defender
VIJAY GREWAL #952421
  Deputy Public Defender

VIVIAN L. KEARA #707902
  Attorney General
ANIYA P. LINDSIE #761699
  Solicitor General
JENNIFER SCHWARZ #500187
  Assistant Attorney General

Office of Public Defense Services
18 Polo Street NE, Suite 412
Salem, Oregon 97231
(513) 341-6439

Oregon Department of Justice
129 Gavel Ave. NE
Salem, Oregon 92123-9301
(514) 321-5938

Attorneys for Defendant-Appellant

Attorneys for Plaintiff-Respondent

Table of Contents

The table of contents provides the first overview of the argument.

Read through the point headings listed in the table of contents. Can you understand the gist of the defendant's argument?

Notice also the formatting. All point headings are evenly spaced, and they line up in a consistent format. A crisp table of contents projects the impression that the brief was written by a professional who cares about the details.

Table of Authorities

Cases

Statutes

The table of authorities is a resource to the court. It explains where in the brief the court can find counsel's discussion of different authorities.

As with the table of contents, a crisp, accurate, consistently-formatted table of authorities will reinforce the impression that the brief was written by a professional who cares about the details.

"Passim" is a latin word meaning "throughout" or frequently. A table of authorities may use "passim" when an authority is used so frequently that listing every instance would not be helpful to the court.

In this statutory construction argument Oregon Revised Statutes § 163.575(1) (2015) is the statutory section being construed. Thus, that statutory section appears on most pages. "Passim" is used to avoid an unwieldy and unhelpful list of pages.

In general, a specific page reference is helpful, so use "passim" rarely.

Other Authorities

Question Presented

Under Oregon Revised Statutes § 163.575(1)(b) (2015), which prohibits a person from "permitting" a child to enter or remain in a home in which illegal drug activity is occurring, does a person "permit" a child to enter or remain when that person is a babysitter with no authority to exclude that child from the home?

Statement of Jurisdiction

The trial court entered a judgment of conviction on September 15, 2016. Defendant filed his Notice of Appeal on October 12, 2016, within the 30 days allowed by Oregon Revised Statutes § 138.071(1) (2015). This court has jurisdiction pursuant to Oregon Revised Statutes § 138.035 (2015).

Statement of the Case

Defendant Jeffrey Lynwood was a houseguest in the home of Wesley Brenton when police executed a search warrant at Mr. Brenton's home. (R. at 119.) When the police executed the search warrant, Mr. Lynwood, Mr. Brenton's daughter Q., and her friend H., were all inside Mr. Brenton's home. (R. at 119.) Mr. Lynwood was subsequently charged with two counts of endangering the welfare of a minor. (R. at 190.) Both after the state rested its case and after the close of all evidence, Mr. Lynwood moved for a judgment of acquittal on the two counts of endangering the welfare of a child, arguing that the state had failed to prove its case. (R. at 190.) The trial court denied both motions. (R. at 191–93.) Mr. Lynwood now appeals those decisions.

Mr. Lynwood became a houseguest in Mr. Brenton's home in 2015. (R. at 37.) Mr. Brenton was a medical-marijuana cardholder, who started growing marijuana in his home in 2014. (R. at 38–40, 42–46.) Mr. Brenton later decided to move the operation outdoors into a greenhouse, and he asked Mr. Lynwood to build a greenhouse for him, which Mr. Lynwood did. (R. at 41.) In June 2015, Mr. Lynwood planted marijuana in the greenhouse. (R. at 38–40, 42–46.) Three months later, in September 2015, they harvested the marijuana and brought the cuttings inside the house to dry. (R. at 52–54, 86, 119–20.) Mr. Lynwood did not have a medical-marijuana card. (R. at 55–56, 82–83.)

Throughout the time of the foregoing events, Mr. Brenton's 15-year-old daughter, Q., lived in the house with him. Around July 2015, Mr. Brenton allowed Q.'s 16-year-old friend, H., to move into the house. (R. at 52, 70.)

In early October 2015, Mr. Brenton asked Mr. Lynwood to move into the house in order to "keep an eye on the house and help [him] with the kids and the marijuana," which he did. (R. at 37.) Mr. Brenton explained that he had asked Mr. Lynwood to keep an eye on the house because he wanted additional adults in the home to help prevent people from stealing the marijuana. (R. at 74, 77.)

Furthermore, Mr. Brenton was concerned about Q.'s use of methamphetamines. (R. at 73–74.) On one occasion, Mr. Lynwood confiscated a substance he believed was methamphetamine from the girls' belongings. (R. at 75.) Mr. Lynwood gave the substance to Mr. Brenton to destroy. (R. at 75.) Consequently, Mr. Brenton worried that some of Q.'s friends would try to bring more methamphetamines into his home.

The question presented both identifies the issue before the court and tries to persuade. Read the question presented. Does it suggest the outcome that the defendant seeks?

This question presented is written as a single sentence, whereas state's question presented is written using multiple sentences. Is one easier to read than the other?

The statement of facts provides all the facts that the court will need to reach its decision.

The opening paragraph provides context by introducing the main players—the defendant, the children who he was accused of endangering, and the decision from which the defendant is appealing.

Here, counsel acknowledges a negative fact: that his client did not have a medical marijuana card. That fact is not relevant to the legal issue, but helps explain one aspect of his prosecution. Notice that counsel does not avoid the negative fact but acknowledges it forthrightly.

This statement of facts is organized both chronologically and topically. At the outset, when it explains how the defendant came to live with the minor children, the statement of facts is chronological.

Beginning with the fourth paragraph of the statement of facts, the organizational structure changes. Counsel wants to emphasize the degree of authority that the defendant had. Thus, in the paragraphs that follow, counsel addresses that issue topic-by-topic.

At trial, defense counsel questioned Mr. Brenton further about "the purpose of [having Mr. Lynwood] at the house with regards to [his daughter]," which produced the following colloquy:

[Mr. Brenton]:   [Mr. Lynwood] was helping me with my daughter—keep[ing] an eye on her. I was, again, at work most of the day and I was concerned for her activities that she may have been involved in while I was gone.

[Defense Counsel]:   . . . And what was the purpose of [Mr. Lynwood] being in the house with regards to those children?

[Mr. Brenton]:   To help, again, make sure that there wasn't anybody coming to the house that we didn't want there or didn't trust there.

[Defense Counsel]:   Were there other people coming by the house—your ex-wife or her friends—that you were asking [Mr. Lynwood] to protect your children from?

[Mr. Brenton]:   Yes. There were a couple of—I don't know who they were specifically. They were driving by the house a couple of times. My daughter noticed them and she told me they were some people that she had met, through her mom, in Salem.

[Defense Counsel]:   Now, hadn't [Mr. Lynwood] actually found what he was fearful of was methamphetamine in some of the girls' stuff, and hadn't he presented that to you to destroy?

[Mr. Brenton]:   Yes.

[Defense Counsel]:   So he was trying to protect your daughter?

[Mr. Brenton]:   Yes. I believe that.

(R. at 76–77.)

In addition, Mr. Brenton testified he had given Mr. Lynwood permission to give Q. and H. marijuana if they asked. (R. at 93.) Mr. Brenton also testified that, subsequently, Mr. Lynwood reported to Mr. Brenton that Mr. Lynwood had given the girls marijuana on a few occasions. (R. at 93–94.)

In late October 2015, police officers executed a search warrant at Mr. Brenton's home and arrested Mr. Lynwood. At the time, Q. and H. were in the house. (R. at 119.) Mr. Lynwood was subsequently tried and convicted of several crimes, including two counts of endangering the welfare of a minor. (R. at 190, 223–24, 226.) The trial court denied Mr. Lynwood's motions for a judgment of acquittal on the two counts of endangering the welfare of a minor, which Mr. Lynwood contends constitutes reversible error. (R. at 191–93.)

Summary of the Argument

In this case, the evidence was insufficient to convict Jeffrey Lynwood of endangering the welfare of a minor. The endangering statute imposes criminal liability on a person who knowingly "[p]ermits a person under 18 years of age

Counsel acknowledges additional negative facts—that the defendant had given marijuana to the girls and smoked it in their presence. Those facts are coupled with a fact that is positive for the defendant—that the father had given him permission to do just that.

The final paragraph of the statement of facts returns to the chronology of events.

to enter or remain in a place where unlawful activity involving a controlled substance is maintained or conducted." Or. Rev. Stat. § 163.575(1)(b) (2015). This case poses the following question: When the legislature enacted the child endangerment statute, upon whom did the legislature intend to impose liability? To answer that question, this Court must construe the phrase "permits a person under 18 years of age to enter or remain."

The text, its context, and the legislative history all point to the conclusion that to "permit" something, one must have authority to forbid it. By hinging liability on the affirmative act of "permitting," the legislature indicated its intent to impose liability on persons in positions of authority vis-à-vis a minor's presence in a drug location. A person who lacks the authority to forbid the minor's entry or remaining is not in a position to permit it.

The authority to "permit" a minor to be in a drug location logically flows from two sources: (1) legal authority over the premises, or (2) authority or control over the minor. Thus, homeowners and parents typically have sufficient authority over their homes or children, respectively, to be liable for "permitting" under the statute. Whether others have the requisite authority depends on the authority or control they possess.

Here, the evidence that Mr. Lynwood was a houseguest or babysitter for the children was insufficient to establish that he "permitted" the homeowner's child and her roommate to enter or remain in the homeowner's home. The homeowner gave Mr. Lynwood the authority to exclude third parties from entering the home during his absence. However, the record contains no evidence that the homeowner gave Mr. Lynwood the authority to prohibit the daughter or roommate from entering into the home. For those reasons, the evidence was insufficient to convict the Mr. Lynwood of violating Oregon Revised Statutes § 163.575(1)(b), Oregon's child endangerment statute. Accordingly, Mr. Lynwood's convictions for endangering the welfare of a minor should be reversed.

This summary of the argument provides an overview of the main points that the brief will establish. The summary of the argument is another way to provide context for the court before it begins reading the detailed argument.

Argument

I. The evidence at trial was insufficient to convict Mr. Lynwood of endangering the welfare of a child.

Defendant Jeffrey Lynwood's motions for judgment of acquittal should have been granted because the evidence at trial was insufficient to establish that Mr. Lynwood violated Oregon's child endangerment statute. Oregon's child endangerment statute provides that

> a person commits the crime of endangering the welfare of a minor if the person knowingly permits a person under 18 years of age to enter or remain in a place where unlawful activity involving controlled substances is maintained or conducted.

Or. Rev. Stat. § 163.575(1)(b) (2015). As explained below, a person can "permit" something only if that person has authority to deny permission. Because Mr. Lynwood did not have the authority to deny the minors the right to enter or remain in their own home, the evidence was insufficient to convict Mr. Lynwood of child endangerment.

This appellate brief addresses a single issue: whether the evidence was sufficient for the jury to convict the defendant. Accordingly, the appellate brief starts with a Roman numeral I, but has no Roman numeral II.

That one issue will be broken down into two sub-issues: (1) how to construe the statutory language, and (2) the application of that construction to this case.

This first paragraph of the argument is a roadmap section. It begins with a conclusion (the first sentence), states the governing rule (block quote), and then provides a roadmap to the argument to follow.

A. The child endangerment statute applies only to those who have authority over the minor or the premises.

The first sub-issue (part A) addresses an issue of statutory construction. A statutory construction argument is a series of nested, rule-based arguments.

The first issue in this case is the meaning of the word "permit." This issue of statutory construction is subject to this Court's plenary review. *See, e.g., State v. Gaines*, 206 P.3d 1042, 1050–51 (Or. 2009) (interpreting Oregon Revised Statutes § 174.020 anew). Using Oregon's traditional methodology, this Court first considers the plain meaning of the word "permit." *Portland Gen. Elec. Co. v. Bureau of Labor & Indus.*, 859 P.2d 1143, 1146 (Or. 1993). Because the meaning of a word is best understood in context, this Court also considers the word in its context. *Id.* at 1146; *Lane Cnty. v. Land Conservation & Dev. Comm'n*, 942 P.2d 278, 283 (Or. 1997). "Context" includes other provisions of the statute and other related statutes. *Portland Gen. Elec. Co.*, 859 P.2d at 1146. Finally, this Court considers the statute's legislative history. Or. Rev. Stat. § 174.020 (2015); *Gaines*, 206 P.3d at 1050–51. As explained below, the statutory phrase "permits a [minor] to enter or remain in a place" makes culpable only one who (1) has legal authority over the place or sufficient authority over a minor to exclude the minor from a place, and (2) consents to, gives leave for, or authorizes the child's entry or remaining in the place.

This paragraph provides a roadmap section for the statutory construction argument. The roadmap section, among other things, explains the governing rule, which is the jurisdiction's methodology for construing a statute. Those rules are then applied in sections 1, 2, and 3, below.

1. The plain meaning of the statute creates liability only for people who have authority over the place or the minor.

A rule-based argument begins with a conclusion. Here, counsel asserts how the court should interpret the verb "permit."

The plain meaning of the verb "to permit" presupposes the authority to permit or to deny permission. When construing statutory text, this Court "presumes that the legislature intended terms to have their plain, natural, and ordinary meaning." *Portland Gen. Elec. Co.*, 859 P.2d at 1146. To determine the plain, natural, and ordinary meaning of a word, this Court turns to the dictionary. *Dowell v. Or. Mut. Ins. Co.*, 343 P.3d 283, 286 (Or. Ct. App. 2015). The dictionary supplies several relevant definitions for "permit":

Next, a rule-based argument explains the relevant rule. Here, the rules explain how this jurisdiction construes the plain meaning of the text.

> 1: to consent to expressly or formally; 2: to give leave: AUTHORIZE; 3: to make possible.

Permit, Merriam Webster, https://www.merriam-webster.com/dictionary/permit (last visited Dec. 1 2015).

Counsel also includes a rule derived from the dictionary: the definition of the verb "permit."

Each of these definitions contemplates a transfer of a "privilege." To "permit," according to the definitions, requires a person to "consent," "grant" or "give." In other words, the person who permits must first possess the right to "consent," "grant," or "give" a privilege to another. Accordingly, the plain and ordinary meaning of "permit" requires the guilty person to first have the authority over the minor or the premises such that the person is capable of consenting to, granting or giving a prohibited privilege.

The application begins here. The shaded text identifies key ideas from the rules that are integrated into the application. That integration of key ideas from the rule into the application is the hallmark of an effective rule-based argument.

In fact, this Court has previously construed the verb "permit" to require a pre-existing authority to forbid. In *State v. Pyritz*, this Court analyzed the dictionary definition of "permit" and prior definitions from case law. 752 P.2d 1310, 1312–13 (Or. Ct. App. 1988). This Court then concluded, "Before one can be said to 'permit' something, one must have authority to forbid it." *Id.* at 1313 (discussing *Lemery v. Leonard*, 196 P. 376 (Or. 1921)).

The discussion of the *Pyritz* and *Lemery* cases is a second rule-based argument.

The first paragraph discussing the *Pyritz* & *Lemery* cases states a conclusion and extracts a rule from those cases.

Thus, the plain meaning of "permit" requires a pre-existing authority to deny permission. When this definition is applied to the child endangerment statute, a person can be guilty of endangering a child only if that person has authority to deny the child the ability to enter or remain on the premises. Such authority exists only if the person has authority over the child or the premises.

(a) Babysitters do not have the authority to deny children access to their own home.

A babysitter has limited authority over a minor. Authority or control over a minor begins with the parents or legal custodians of a child. *Troxel v. Granville*, 530 U.S. 57, 65–66 (2000). Parents and the legal guardians of children have the primary right to make decisions regarding care, custody, and control of their children. *Id.* Parents may delegate authority and control over their children to others. For example, parents may transfer temporary control over their children to babysitters. A babysitter is typically tasked with watching over and keeping children from harm during a parent's absence from the home. Consequently, babysitters have sufficient control of the children to be liable for criminal neglect. *See State v. Mills*, 629 P.2d 861, 862 n.1 (Or. Ct. App. 1981) (quoting legislative commentary to child neglect statute, which notes that babysitters may be liable under the statute because they can have sufficient "custody or control" to be responsible for neglect).

The authority of the babysitter, however, is derived from the parent and is, therefore, limited. That limitation is evident in Oregon's statutory code. For example, a babysitter who removes children from their home without parental permission may be guilty of kidnapping. Under Oregon law, a kidnapping occurs when a person takes another person "from one place to another" without consent or legal authority. Or. Rev. Stat. § 163.225 (2015). In the case of a minor child, "without consent" is "without the consent of the lawful custodian." Or. Rev. Stat. § 163.215 (2015). Thus, Oregon law assumes that the authority of other adults, such as a babysitter, is inferior to the authority of a parent.

Because Oregon law assumes that the authority of other adults is inferior to the authority of a parent, it follows that an adult such as a babysitter has no authority to either permit or deny a child's entry into a home when the parent has explicitly authorized that entry.

(b) Houseguests do not have the authority to limit access of residents.

Similarly, a houseguest's control over a house is also limited. A co-inhabitant typically has the authority to permit or deny access to third parties when the owner is not present. *See, e.g., United States v. Matlock*, 415 U.S. 164, 171 n.7 (1974) (holding that co-inhabitants presumably have right to permit entry by police into common areas of home; other co-inhabitants assume the risk that they will do so); *State v. Carsey*, 664 P.2d 1085, 1093 (Or. 1983) (holding that joint occupier presumed to have authority to permit search of common areas). Thus, courts presume that owners transfer to those living in their homes the authority to grant or deny entry to third parties, like police officers. When

The next paragraph applies that rule to the statute at hand.

In this section of the brief, counsel wants to establish that a babysitter's authority is limited by the authority that a parent gives to that babysitter. Oregon case law has never addressed the relationship between a parent's authority and a babysitter's authority. Therefore, counsel proposes a rule that is implicit in existing Oregon law: A babysitter's authority is derived from and limited by the authority that a parent gives to the babysitter.

the owner leaves a guest in the home alone, the owner assumes the risk that the guest may permit officers to enter into the common areas of the home. *Id.*

However, Oregon courts have never held that a houseguest has the authority to exclude residents from a home. If a non-owner's authority over property is based on what he has been given by its owner, the authority is necessarily limited by the terms of the grant. Therefore, when an owner permits two different people to enter and remain in his home, neither person gains the authority to exclude the other. Rather, the guest's authority is subordinate to the owner's and, therefore, cannot override the permission given by the owner to the other guest. In such situations, only the owner can be said to have "permitted" the entry.

Accordingly, the words of the statute require a person to first have authority to deny access to a location before that person can be liable for permitting minors into the location. Neither a babysitter nor a houseguest has the authority to deny children access to their home.

2. Context corroborates Mr. Lynwood's interpretation.

The context of the statute corroborates the above reading. Context includes other provisions of the statute and related statutes. *Portland Gen. Elec. Co.*, 859 P.2d at 1146. When the legislature uses different terms within a statute, those terms are assumed to have different meaning. *State ex rel. Dep't of Transp. v. Stallcup*, 138 P.3d 9, 14 (Or. 2006).

In this case, the context shows that the legislature intended to criminalize the affirmative act of "permitting" and did not intend to criminalize a passive failure to act. The endangering statute includes five other provisions, each of which proscribes a different type of conduct that creates risks for children. It targets a person who

(a) induces, causes or permits a child to witness sexual acts;
(b) permits a child to enter or remain in a drug environment;
(c) induces, causes or permits a child to gamble;
(d) distributes, sells or allows to be sold tobacco to a child; or
(e) sells drug paraphernalia to a child.

Or. Rev. Stat. § 163.575(1) (2015). Subsection (b) creates culpability if a person merely "permits." Paragraphs (a) and (c) create culpability if a person "induces, causes or permits" certain conduct. The verb "to induce" may include "to move by persuasion" or "bring about." *Induce, Merriam Webster* https://www.merriam-webster.com/dictionary/induce (last visited Dec. 1, 2015). "Cause" is defined as "to serve as a cause or occasion of. *Cause, Merriam Webster* https://www.merriam-webster.com/dictionary/cause (last visited Dec. 1, 2015). The verb "permit" cannot be defined as "to make possible" because such an interpretation fails to give the word "permit" a meaning that is different from the meaning of "induce" or "cause." If the verb "permit" is defined as "to make possible," the word "permit" begins to invade the space occupied by "induce," which is defined as "to bring about," and "cause," which is defined as "to bring into existence." Under such an interpretation, the prohibitory language in paragraph (b) has the same scope as the prohibitory language in paragraph (a) and

Conclusion to the plain language argument

Counsel's context argument is composed of two rule-based arguments.

Conclusion

Rules

The application begins here.

Again, in the shaded text, you can see how key ideas from the rules are integrated into the application.

paragraph (c), despite the legislature's choice to use different terms. Such an interpretation would undermine the legislature's choice to use a different term. Thus, the context also suggests that the legislature did not intend "permit" to have its broadest meaning.

Other statutes that protect children demonstrate that when the legislature intends to create liability for failing to act, it says so. The Oregon Supreme Court has previously relied on statutes that share a common purpose to construe a statute currently at issue. *See State v. Bailey*, 213 P.3d 1240, 1245 n.4 (Or. 2009). Here, the endangering statute is one of eight "offenses against family" and was enacted during the 1971 criminal code revision. *See* 1971 Or. Laws ch. 743. The other offenses against family include bigamy, incest, abandonment of a child, buying or selling a child, child neglect (first and second degree), criminal nonsupport, and failing to supervise. Or. Rev. Stat. §§ 163.515, 163.525, 163.535, 163.537, 163.545, 163.547, 163.555, 163.577 (2015). To be guilty of any of the other crimes requires an affirmative act: marrying (to be guilty of bigamy), engaging in sexual activity (incest), deserting (abandonment), buying or selling, and leaving (neglect). By contrast, criminal nonsupport and failing to supervise criminalize the failure to act, and they do so explicitly by including the phrases "fails to provide support" and "failing to supervise." Or. Rev. Stat. §§ 163.555, 163.577. Thus, when the legislature imposes liability for failing to act to protect children, it expressly says so. Here, the legislature did not expressly create liability for the failure to act. Because the legislature chose not to include liability for the failure to act, such liability should not be read into the statute.

Accordingly, the statute's context also supports the conclusion that the legislature was criminalizing affirmative conduct and not the passive failure to act.

3. The legislative history supports Mr. Lynwood's construction.

The legislative history also supports the above construction. In its commentary to § 163.575, the Criminal Law Revision Commission emphasized that the statute was intended to criminalize particularized conduct:

> Throughout the criminal code revision, the Commission has sought to articulate clear and concise statements of the substantive offenses, prohibiting *particularized conduct* and applying defined elements of culpability. Many of the provisions relate to conduct detrimental to the welfare of minors.

Oregon Criminal Law Revision Commission, *Proposed Oregon Criminal Code*, Final Draft and Rep., § 177, at 178 (1970) (emphasis added) (hereinafter Commentary). The commission further explained that § 163.575 was "designed to provide coverage for *specific acts* injurious to the welfare of minors." *Id.* (emphasis added). In other words, the legislature intended to criminalize affirmative actions and not a passive failure to act.

This same conclusion results when considering the statute that preceded the child endangerment statute. The child endangerment statute was intended

---

Conclusion

Conclusion to the next rule-based argument

Rule

The application begins. Here, the application does not integrate key words from the rule. Rather, the application does what the rule says is permissible: It looks at related statutes and makes an argument based on a distinction in those statutes. In that way, the application applies the rule.

Conclusion to this rule-based argument

Conclusion to the context argument

Counsel's legislative history argument is composed of 3 rule-based arguments.

Conclusion to the first legislative history rule-based argument

The explanation of the legislative history acts as the rules to this rule-based argument.

This final sentence is both an application of and a conclusion to this rule-based argument. Although the last sentence does not re-use the identical language from the legislative history, can you see that counsel chose echoing language?

Conclusion to the second legislative history argument

to cover the same conduct as the former delinquency of a minor statute. Oregon Criminal Law Revision Commission, *Subcommittee No. 2 Minutes, Mar. 6, 1970,* at 10 (1970) (explaining that the endangering statute was an attempt "to cover everything the statute on contributing to the delinquency of a minor encompassed that has not been provided for elsewhere in the proposed code"). The contributing to the delinquency of a minor statute, *former* Oregon Revised Statutes §167.210, also required affirmative conduct before it imposed criminal liability. That statute makes criminally liable

> any person responsible for the act of encouraging, causing, or contributing to the delinquency of such child, or any person who . . . endeavors to induce any child to perform any act or follow any course of conduct which would cause it to become a delinquent child . . . .

Former Or. Rev. Stat. § 167.210 (repealed 1971). Thus, the prior act required affirmative conduct — encouraging, causing, contributing, or inducing. It did not criminalize merely permitting something to take place by failing to act. Because the current act was intended to cover the same conduct as the contributing to the delinquency of a minor statute, it should be construed to also require affirmative conduct before liability is imposed.

Finally, at the same time that the legislature passed the child endangerment statute, it explicitly recognized that criminal liability requires affirmative conduct. During the 1971 revision, the legislature also passed Oregon Revised Statutes §§ 161.085 and 161.095 (1971). Oregon Revised Statutes § 161.095 establishes that the "minimal requirement for criminal liability is the performance by a person of conduct which includes a voluntary act or the omission to perform an act which he is capable of performing." Oregon Revised Statutes § 161.085 defines "omission" as a "failure to perform an act the performance of which is required by law." Those provisions reflect an awareness by the legislature of the prevailing view of Anglo-American law preferring criminal liability for affirmative acts, and generally permitting liability based on omission only when there is a pre-existing legal duty to act. *See, e.g.,* Wayne R. LaFave, *Handbook on Criminal Law* § 26, 182–84 (1970). Thus, part of the context of the legislature's enactment of the endangering statute in 1971 was its understanding of those basic principles of criminal law.

Thus, the legislative history, like the text in context, establishes that the legislature intended to require an affirmative act before imposing criminal liability. It did not intend to criminalize the mere failure to prevent a child's presence in her own home by a person with no pre-existing legal duty to the particular child.

B. The evidence was insufficient to establish that Mr. Lynwood knowingly permitted the children to enter or remain in a place in which drug activity was conducted.

Because Mr. Lynwood was not authorized to exclude the children from their own home, the evidence was insufficient to establish that Mr. Lynwood permitted the children to enter or remain in a place where drug activity was

Margin notes (left column):

The rule is, again, an excerpt from the legislative history.

Key language from the rule is integrated into the application.

The last half of this sentence acts as the conclusion to this second rule-based argument.

This paragraph is the last rule-based argument. Again, excerpts from the legislative history are used as a foundation on which counsel builds an argument about the legislature's intent.

This last paragraph provides a final conclusion to the legislative history argument and to the statutory construction argument.

In Part B, counsel argues that, based on the statute as construed above, the evidence was insufficient to convict the defendant.

conducted. Whether the evidence is sufficient to convict a defendant is a question of law subject to this Court's plenary review. *See, e.g., State v. Cunningham*, 880 P.2d 431, 440 (Or. 1994) (exercising plenary review). When exercising plenary review, this Court applies the same standard as the trial court applied. *Id.* Accordingly, this Court must determine whether the evidence, viewed in the light most favorable to the state, was sufficient for a rational fact-finder to find the essential elements of the crime beyond a reasonable doubt. *Id.*; *Jackson v. Virginia*, 443 U.S 307, 318–19 (1979).

This sentence states the standard of review. "Plenary review" is the same standard as "de novo" review. Under either term, no deference is given to the trial court's decision.

As explained above, "permits," as used in Oregon Revised Statutes § 163.575(1)(b), refers to the act of consenting to or granting leave for a child to enter or remain in the prohibited location, and necessarily requires a person to have authority such that they could forbid the child's entry.

Compare how the standard of decision is explained here and in the state's brief. In this argument, counsel provides the rules but does not emphasize them because these rules — which are deferential to the jury's decision — do not help the defendant.

The evidence in this case never established that Mr. Lynwood had authority to exclude the girls from their home. The evidence established the following:

Here, counsel provides the statutory rule as construed above.

(1) the parent of a teenage girl permitted the teenage girl and her friend to live in his home with his marijuana grow operation;

(2) after those circumstances had existed for a time, Mr. Lynwood was asked to assist in building a greenhouse and otherwise to assist with the grow operation;

(3) Mr. Lynwood had no familial relationship to the teenage girls and no ownership interest in the home;

(4) the parent asked Mr. Lynwood to stay in the home while the marijuana was harvested; and

(5) Mr. Lynwood was also asked to keep an eye on the house and girls because the father was concerned that the girls' methamphetamine connections would seek them out.

Thus, Mr. Brenton, the homeowner and father, never gave Mr. Lynwood the authority to exclude the teenagers from their home. While a houseguest may have the authority to exclude strangers who knock on the door of a home while the homeowner is not present, nothing permits a houseguest to prevent a resident from entering her own home. In fact, had Mr. Lynwood locked the teenage girls out of their home he might have faced criminal liability for criminal mischief. Had he tried to remove them, he could have faced additional criminal liability for kidnapping.

Because Mr. Lynwood could not lawfully have excluded the teenagers from their own home, the evidence was insufficient to find that he "permitted" them to enter or remain there.

CONCLUSION

This Court should reverse Mr. Lynwood's convictions for endangering the welfare of a minor.

Respectfully submitted,
KEN NAKANO
CHIEF DEFENDER

OFFICE OF PUBLIC DEFENSE SERVICES

ESigned
By Vijay Grewal at 2:43 pm, Dec 01 2016

VIJAY GREWAL OSB #974573 DEPUTY PUBLIC DEFENDER
Vijay.Grewal @opds.state.or.us
Attorneys for Defendant-Appellant
Jeffrey Scott Lynwood

CERTIFICATE OF COMPLIANCE WITH ORAP 5.05(2)(d)

Brief length

I certify that (1) this brief complies with the word-count limitation in ORAP 5.05(2)(b) and (2) the word-count of this brief is 4,428 words.

Type size

I certify that the size of the type in this brief is not smaller than 14 point for both the text of the brief and footnotes as required by ORAP 5.05(4)(f).

NOTICE OF FILING AND PROOF OF SERVICE

I certify that I directed the original Appellant's Opening Brief to be filed with the Appellate Court Administrator, Appellate Courts Records Section, 1543 Maple Street, Salem, Oregon 97231, on December 1, 2016.

I further certify that, upon receipt of the confirmation email stating that the document has been accepted by the eFiling system, this Appellant's Opening Brief will be eServed pursuant to ORAP 16.45 (regarding electronic service on registered eFilers) on Jennifer Schwarz, #761699, Solicitor General, attorney for Plaintiff- Respondent.

Respectfully submitted,
KEN NAKANO
CHIEF DEFENDER
OFFICE OF PUBLIC DEFENSE SERVICES

ESigned
By Vijay Grewal at 2:44 pm, Dec 01 2016

VIJAY GREWAL OSB #974573
DEPUTY PUBLIC DEFENDER
Vijay.Grewal@opds.state.or.us
Attorneys for Defendant-Appellant
Jeffrey Scott Lynwood

B. Respondent's Answering Brief

IN THE COURT OF APPEALS OF THE STATE OF OREGON

———————————

STATE OF OREGON,	)	Mercer County Circuit Court
Plaintiff-Respondent,	)	No. 15C50799
	)	
v.	)	CA A139020
	)	
JEFFREY SCOTT LYNWOOD,	)	
Defendant-Appellant.	)	
	)	
	)	

———————————

RESPONDENT'S ANSWERING BRIEF

———————————

Appeal from the Judgment of the Circuit Court
For Mercer County
Honorable Charity A. Beckah Judge

KEN NAKANO #842314
Chief Defender

VIJAY GREWAL #952421
Deputy Public Defender

Office of Public Defense Services
18 Polo Street NE, Suite 412
Salem, Oregon 97231
(513) 341-6439

Attorneys for Defendant-Appellant

VIVIAN L. KEARA #707902
Attorney General

ANIYA P. LINDSIE #761699
Solicitor General

JENNIFER SCHWARZ #500187
Assistant Attorney General

Oregon Department of Justice
129 Gavel Ave. NE
Salem, Oregon 92123-9301
(514) 321-5938

Attorneys for Plaintiff-Respondent

The state's brief cover provides the same basic information as the defendant's brief cover: the names of the parties, the appellate court in which the case is being heard, the court from which the appeal is taken, and the names and contact information for counsel.

Table of Contents

The table of contents provides the first overview of the state's argument.

Read through the point headings listed in the table of contents. Can you understand the gist of the state's argument?

Notice also the formatting. All the point headings are evenly spaced and line up consistently. A crisp table of contents projects the impression that the brief was written by a professional who cares about the details.

Table of Authorities

Cases

Page

Statutes

The table of authorities is a resource to the court. It explains where in the brief the court can find counsel's discussion of different authorities.

Again, a crisp, accurate, consistently formatted table of authorities reinforces the impression that the brief was written by a professional who cares about the details.

Other Authorities

Questions Presented

1. Oregon's child endangerment statute provides that a person is guilty of endangering the welfare of a minor if he or she "permits" a child to enter or remain in a place where unlawful activities involving drugs are maintained or conducted. For purposes of that statute, what does the term "permit" encompass?

2. Did defendant permit the children to enter or remain in a place of unlawful activity involving controlled substances when the defendant provided the children with marijuana, smoked marijuana with the children, and sold marijuana from the children's home?

Statement of the Case

Defendant appeals his convictions for endangering the welfare of a minor. In the summer and fall of 2015, defendant was entrusted with the care of two minor children. (R. at 38.) While the children were entrusted in defendant's care, defendant ran his own marijuana selling business from the children's home, gave marijuana to the children several times, and smoked it with them regularly. (R. at 90–92, 121–22, 148–65.) The jury convicted defendant of endangering the welfare of the children. (R. at 223–24.)

Defendant came to be the children's caretaker after his friend Wesley Brenton asked defendant to move into Brenton's house. Brenton, who had a medical marijuana card and another card allowing him to grow marijuana for another person, grew marijuana in his house. (R. at 38–40, 42–46.) Also in the house were Brenton's 15-year-old daughter, Q., and Q.'s 16-year-old friend, H. (R. at 52, 70.) Both Q. and H. lived in the house "full time." (R. at 52, 70.) Brenton worked a full-time job, "wasn't home a lot during the day," and sometimes did not get home until 9:00 or 10:00 p.m. (R. at 35–36, 62.)

Therefore, Brenton asked and defendant agreed to move into the house to help grow and harvest the marijuana, and to "keep an eye on the house and help with the kids and the marijuana." (R. at 37.)

With respect to the grow operation, Brenton agreed to share the marijuana with defendant, and there was an "option" for defendant to sell some of it. (R. at 42–46, 83–84.) Later that fall, defendant helped harvest the marijuana and store it in Brenton's house. (R. at 52–54, 86, 119–20.) Brenton received half of the marijuana, with defendant getting the other half. (R. at 56–57, 84, 89.) Defendant did not have a medical marijuana card. (R. at 55–56, 82–83.)

With respect to the children, Brenton was "concerned for the activities that Q. may have been involved in" while Brenton was at work. (R. at 72, 83.) Brenton wanted defendant to be in the house to "make sure that there wasn't anybody coming to the house that we didn't want there or didn't trust there." (R. at 74.) Brenton did not want some of Q.'s friends coming to the house because he "didn't trust them" and because he believed that one of them had broken into the house and stolen marijuana. (R. at 74, 77.) Brenton also wanted defendant to protect the children from "other people" coming by the house, including Q.'s mother (Brenton's ex-wife) or her friends. (R. at 75.)

The state's question presented addresses the two sub-issues of the argument: how to construe the statute and whether, based on that construction, the evidence was sufficient to convict the defendant. By contrast, the defendant created one question presented, which addressed both issues.

The state's first question presented is a fairly "straight" question presented. It does not suggest a particular outcome. The second question presented, however, uses facts more aggressively to suggest the legal conclusion the state is seeking.

The opening paragraph of the statement of facts provides context by introducing the main players — the defendant, the children whom he was accused of endangering, and the decision from which the defendant is appealing.

What differences do you see when you compare defendant's opening and the state's?

The state acknowledges facts that are helpful to the defendant, namely, that the homeowner and father had given specific instructions to the defendant about his responsibilities with respect to the children.

Brenton gave his daughter marijuana on a regular basis — "maybe every other day" — and he assumed that Q. was sharing it with H. (R. at 57.) Brenton instructed defendant to provide Q. and H. with marijuana "if they asked." (R. at 93.) On "[m]aybe three to five" occasions the girls asked defendant for marijuana, and he gave it to them. (R. at 93–94.) Brenton observed defendant smoking marijuana with Q. and H. (R. at 78.) Brenton was mostly concerned about Q.'s other drug use, particularly her methamphetamine use. (R. at 73–74.) To "protect" the girls, on one occasion defendant examined some of their "stuff" and confiscated a substance he believed to be methamphetamine, giving it to Brenton to destroy. (R. at 75.)

Initially, defendant stayed at Brenton's home only during the daytime when Brenton was at work. Beginning in October 2015, defendant slept there at night, had his own room, and had keys to that room. (R. at 95, 103, 106.) While living in the home, defendant ran his own marijuana business out of the house. (R. at 90.) He sold his portion of the harvest to a number of people and stored the marijuana he was selling in the bedroom he used. (R. at 90–92, 121–22, 148–65.)

In late October 2015, police executed a search warrant at Brenton's home and arrested defendant. Q. and H. were present in the house during the execution of the warrant. Defendant told police that he had been staying there and "was caring for [Q. and] the house." (R. at 119.)

The state charged defendant with two counts of delivery of a controlled substance to a minor, Oregon Revised Statutes § 475.906 (2015); one count of manufacturing marijuana, Oregon Revised Statutes § 475.856 (2015); one count of felon in possession of a firearm, Oregon Revised Statutes § 166.270 (2015); and two counts of endangering the welfare of a minor, Oregon Revised Statutes § 163.575 (2015). At trial, after the state rested its case and, again, after the close of all evidence, defendant moved for a judgment of acquittal on all counts. (R. at 190, 223–24.) The court denied both motions. (R. at 191–93, 226.) The jury then considered the evidence presented against defendant and convicted defendant on all counts except felon in possession of a firearm. (R. at 223–24, 226.) Defendant now appeals his convictions for endangering the welfare of a minor.

These facts are not legally relevant because the only issue on appeal is about the two counts of child endangerment. The state may have included these facts to paint a negative picture of the defendant. Notice how the state provides facts without characterization and allows the court to reach a conclusion about the defendant's character.

Summary of the Argument

The evidence was sufficient for a jury to reasonably find that defendant endangered the welfare of two children. A person endangers the welfare of a minor if he or she knowingly "[p]ermits a person under 18 years of age to enter or remain in a place where unlawful activity involving controlled substances is maintained or conducted[.]" Or. Rev. Stat. § 163.575(1)(b) (2015). The text, context, and legislative history demonstrate that the legislature intended the statute to reach conduct whereby a person allows or makes it possible for a child to remain in the presence of unlawful drug activity.

In this case, defendant's actions easily fall within the ambit of Oregon Revised Statutes § 163.575(1)(b). At the same time that defendant chose to act as a caretaker for two children, defendant also chose to actively participate in a marijuana growing operation in the children's house, run a drug-dealing

This summary of the argument provides an overview of the main points that the brief will establish. The summary of the argument is another way to provide context for the court before it begins reading the detailed argument.

business from the children's house, give the children marijuana, and smoke marijuana with them. By actively engaging in that conduct, defendant violated Oregon Revised Statutes § 163.575(1)(b).

Defendant's argument to the contrary is without merit. According to defendant, to violate Oregon Revised Statutes § 163.575(1)(b) an adult must have been given explicit, specific authority to prevent a child from entering or remaining on the premises and must choose not to exercise that authority. But defendant's narrow reading of Oregon Revised Statutes § 163.575(1)(b) is inconsistent with the statute's text, context, and legislative history. Moreover, incorporating such a requirement into the statute flies in the face of the legislature's intended goal of protecting children from deliberate exposure to harmful activities.

Assuming that defendant's reading of Oregon Revised Statutes § 163.575(1)(b) is correct, the trial court nonetheless correctly denied his motions for judgment of acquittal. Contrary to defendant's claim, the state's evidence did establish that defendant had sufficient authority to prevent the children from remaining in the house and that he failed to exercise that authority. The evidence showed that defendant chose repeatedly to engage in unlawful drug activity in the children's presence and in their home. Whatever authority he had over the children or the house is irrelevant because he possessed the ability to decline to engage in that conduct.

In addition, the evidence established that defendant was acting in the role of the children's babysitter. As such, defendant was authorized, and in fact obligated, to remove them from danger. Finally, even assuming defendant lacked the authority to physically expel or exclude the children, he was certainly authorized to take some step—including, for example, calling the police to prevent the children from remaining in the house. Because he chose not to do so, defendant permitted the children to remain in a place where unlawful drug activity was occurring. Thus, defendant violated Oregon Revised Statutes § 163.575(1)(b), and the jury appropriately found that he had endangered the welfare of two children.

Argument

I. The jury's conclusion that defendant endangered the welfare of two children was supported by the evidence.

The evidence was sufficient for the jury to conclude that defendant was guilty of two counts of endangering the welfare of a minor. A person commits the crime of endangering the welfare of a minor if he knowingly

> permits a person under 18 years of age to enter or remain in a place where unlawful activity involving controlled substances is maintained or conducted.

Or. Rev. Stat. § 163.575(1)(b) (2015). Whether the jury had sufficient evidence to convict defendant requires a two-step analysis. This Court must first determine the scope of the verb "permit." Then, in light of that understanding, this Court must determine whether the evidence was sufficient to support the jury's

---

This argument is an "even if" argument: Even if the court does not accept the state's construction of the statute, the evidence was still sufficient for the jury to convict the defendant.

Lawyers often make "even if" arguments to provide a way for the court to find in their client's favor even if the court does not adopt every argument in the client's favor.

Here, the respondent (the State of Oregon) would like a broad construction for the word "permit" because such a construction would be helpful in future prosecutions. Even if the state does not get its preferred broad construction, it still seeks to have the conviction of this defendant upheld.

The argument begins with a roadmap section that asserts the state's conclusion (in the first sentence), provides the governing rule (in the second sentence), and a map of the arguments to come (in the final three sentences). Compare the map of the arguments in this roadmap section to defendant's map. Here, by explaining that the analysis is a "two-step analysis," the state provides a more explicit map. One is not necessarily better than the other, but you should be aware of the different ways lawyers might map the arguments to come.

finding that defendant did in fact "permit" two minors to enter or remain in a place where marijuana was being unlawfully grown.

A. A person violates Oregon's child endangerment statute if that person allows or makes it possible for a child to enter or remain in a place where unlawful drug activity occurs.

The text, the text in context, and the legislative history all show that the legislature intended the word "permit" to have a broad reach so that children would be shielded from unlawful drug activity. To ascertain the meaning of a statutory text, this Court first examines the text of the statute. *Portland Gen. Elec. Co. v. Bureau of Labor & Indus.*, 859 P.2d 1143, 1146 (Or. 1993). When construing the text of a statute, this Court gives the words of the text their plain and ordinary meaning. *Id.*; *State v. Gaines*, 206 P.3d 1042, 1050 (Or. 2009). If the legislature has not defined the meaning of a word, this Court may look to a dictionary for the word's plain and ordinary meaning. *Dowell v. Or. Mut. Ins. Co.*, 343 P.3d 283, 286 (Or. Ct. App. 2015). This Court does not, however, look at the words of a statute in isolation; rather, it construes each part together with the other parts to produce a harmonious whole. *Portland Gen. Elec. Co.*, 859 P.2d at 1146; *Lane Cnty. v. Land Conservation & Dev. Comm'n*, 942 P.2d 278, 283 (Or. 1997). To that end, this Court determines the meaning of text by considering that text in the context of the statute and related statutes. *See Portland Gen. Elec. Co.*, 859 P.2d at 1146. Finally, a party may proffer legislative history, and after examining the text and context of the statute, the Court will examine the legislative history "where that legislative history appears useful to the court's analysis." *Gaines*, 206 P.3d at 1050–51.

Applying those steps to the child endangerment statute shows that the legislature intended the word "permit" to encompass any conduct that allows or makes it possible for a child to remain in a place where illegal drug activity occurs.

1. By its definition alone, the word "permit" can have a broad or narrow meaning.

Like many words, the verb "permit" does not have just one meaning. Rather, its definition includes a broader and a more narrow construction. "Permit" is defined as

1: to consent to expressly or formally

2: to give (a person) leave: AUTHORIZE

3. to make possible.

Permit, *Merriam Webster*, https://www.merriam-webster.com/dictionary/permit (last visited Dec. 1, 2015).

The narrower meaning of the verb "permit" contemplates a formal consent or grant that authorizes a person to do something. If the legislature intended "permit" in its narrower sense, the child endangerment statute prohibits a person in a position of authority from specifically consenting or authorizing a child to enter or remain in a place where drug activity is ongoing.

But the verb "permit" also has a broader meaning, which includes to "allow" or "make possible." If the legislature intended "permit" in the broader sense, then the child endangerment statute prohibits conduct that allows, tolerates, or makes it possible for a child to enter or remain in a place where drug activity is ongoing.

In this rule-based argument, the state uses a dictionary definition as part of its rule. It then integrates the language of that rule into the application, here.

In asserting that the verb "permit" has only one meaning, defendant misreads both the dictionary definition and prior case law. As explained above, the plain and ordinary meaning of the verb "permit" allows for a narrower or a broader definition. Similarly, prior case law also contemplates a broader and narrower definition. In *Lemery v. Leonard*, the Oregon Supreme Court interpreted the verb "permit." 196 P. 376, 378 (Or. 1921). The statute at issue made it unlawful for any owner to permit sheep "to run at large or go on the lands of another without the permission of such owner[.]" *Id.* at 376–77. The Oregon Supreme Court held that "[t]o 'permit' means to allow by tacit consent by not hindering, taking no steps to prevent, or to grant leave by express consent or authorization." *Id.* at 378. Although defendant focuses on the phrase "by express consent or authorization," the Oregon Supreme Court noted that "to permit" also means "not hindering" and "taking no steps to prevent." In other words, the Oregon Supreme Court defined "permit" as containing definitions both narrow and broad. Nothing in *Lemery* stands for the proposition that the legislature intended "permit" to be interpreted as narrowly as defendant claims.

Here, the state addresses defendant's argument. Notice that the state does not address defendant's argument until after presenting its own argument.

Although the state acknowledges that it is responding to the defendant's argument, notice that the state avoids giving additional airtime to the defendant's argument. The state simply explains why, from its perspective, the defendant's argument is wrong.

In sum, the plain meaning of the verb "permit" allows for both a broad and narrow construction. The context and legislative history show that the legislature intended the broader construction.

This paragraph provides a final conclusion to the plain language argument and a transition to the next argument.

2. The statute's context establishes that the legislature intended the verb "permit" to broadly encompass any action that allows a child to be in the presence of controlled substances.

Although the verb "permit" can be understood narrowly or broadly, an examination of the text in context shows that the legislature intended the verb to be understood more broadly. The context establishes that the legislature intended to protect children, and the broader interpretation fulfills that intent. "Context" includes both the provisions that immediately surround the statute ◄— in question and statutes that share a common purpose. *Portland Gen. Elec. Co.*, 859 P.2d at 1146; *State v. Bailey*, 213 P.3d 1240, 1245 n.4 (Or. 2009). Oregon's ◄— child endangerment statute includes five subsections. A person "endangers the welfare of a minor" if that person does any of the following:

The first sentence is a conclusion to the rule-based argument. The second sentence is a more focused conclusion that asserts what the context will show.

This is the rule that is then applied.

The application begins here. The first part of the application examines the surrounding subsections and argues what those subsections show.

(a) Induces, causes or permits an unmarried person under 18 years of age to witness an act of sexual conduct as defined by Oregon Revised Statutes § 167.060;

(b) Permits a person under 18 years of age to enter or remain in a place where unlawful activity involving controlled substances is maintained or conducted;

5

(c) Induces, causes or permits a person under 18 years of age to participate in gambling as defined by Oregon Revised Statutes § 167.117;

(d) Distributes, sells, or causes to be sold, tobacco in any form to a person under 18 years of age; or

(e) Sells to a person under 18 years of age any device in which tobacco, marijuana, cocaine, or any controlled substances as defined in Oregon Revised Statutess § 475.005 is burned and the principal design and use of which is directly or indirectly to deliver…into the human body.

Or. Rev. Stat. § 163.575(1).

The common thread that underlies all of the subsections is the protection of the children. More specifically, each subsection protects children from an adult's actions that harm the child. Thus, at a minimum, the context demonstrates that the legislature intended to protect children. Consistent with that intent, "permits" should be construed broadly so that the statute protects children from unlawful drug activities and the actions of adults who expose them to or involve them in those activities.

This broader construction of the word "permit" is also consistent with the legislature's stated purpose in revising § 167.060 and other parts of Oregon's criminal code. At the outset of chapter 743, the same chapter in which § 163.575(1)(b) is located, the legislature explained its "purposes" and "principles of construction." Simply put, the legislature intended to protect individuals from harm:

(1) The general purposes of Chapter 743, Oregon Laws 1971, are:…

(b) To forbid and prevent conduct that unjustifiably and inexcusably inflicts or threatens substantial harm to individual or public interests.

Or. Rev. Stat. § 161.025 (2015). That broad goal applies to § 163.575(1)(b). The intent to "forbid or prevent conduct" that "inflicts or threatens substantial harm" on or to an individual supports a broad reading of the word "permit"—one that encompasses any conduct that allows or enables a child to be in the presence of controlled substances.

Examining other statutes on the same subject also supports the conclusion that "permits" should be read broadly and that formal authority over a child or premises is not necessary to "permit." When language is present in one statute, but absent from another, this Court will assume the absence of that language was intentional. *See, e.g., State v. Rodriguez,* 175 P.3d 471, 478 (Or. Ct. App. 2007) ("The legislature knows how to say that when it so intends."); *Karson v. Or. Liquor Control Comm'n,* 74 P.3d 1163, 1167 (Or. Ct. App. 2003) ("When the legislature wants to impose such a duty, it knows how to say so."); *State v. Walker,* 86 P.3d 690, 697 (Or. Ct. App. 2004) ("Numerous statutes demonstrate that the legislature knows how to say 'the Department of Human Services' when that is the agency it intends.").

The Oregon legislature knows how to limit liability to those with formal authority over children; here, it chose not to. Oregon's child endangerment statute is one of eight statutes categorized as "offenses against family." At the

---

The second part of the application compares the stated purpose of the criminal laws and uses that stated purpose to argue that the word "permit" should be understood more broadly.

The final part of the application examines related provisions and argues that a broader definition of the word "permit" would be consistent with the related provisions.

same time that the legislature passed the child endangerment statute in 1971, it also passed statutes that prohibited abandoning a child, Or. Rev. Stat. § 163.535 (2015); second-degree child neglect, Or. Rev. Stat. § 163.545 (2015); and criminal nonsupport, Or. Rev. Stat. § 163.555 (2015). *See* 1971 Or. Laws ch. 743 §§ 173, 174, 175. To be guilty under any of those three statutes, a defendant must have "custody or control" of the child. In contrast, the child endangerment statute does not require custody or control of the child to endanger that child's welfare. The legislature's decision to not use the word "custody or control" at the very time that it used that language elsewhere points to the conclusion that the legislature intended the child endangerment statute to encompass the actions of people who do not have such authority over a child. Thus, in the context of similar statutes, "permits," as used in § 163.575(1)(b), should be construed broadly such that it does not require "authority" over children.

Despite defendant's argument to the contrary, the broader definition of "permit" does not invade the space of "induce" or "cause." "Induce" means to "influence" or "persuade." *Webster's Third New International Dictionary of the English Language*, *supra*, at 1154. "Cause" means "to bring into existence." *Id.* at 356. "Permit" means "to allow" or "make possible." The person who allows or makes an outcome possible acts differently from the person who influences, persuades, or brings into existence. Thus, the definition of "permit" does not overlap with the definitions of "induce" and "cause," even when read broadly. The context of § 163.575(1)(b) does not support a narrow reading of the word "permit."

3. The legislative history confirms that the word "permit" should be given a broad interpretation.

The legislative history further supports the conclusion that the legislature intended the statute to extend to situations in which adults allow or make possible a child's presence among illegal substances. Section 163.575(1)(b) was intended to shield children from unlawful drug activities and the actions of persons who expose them to such activities. In 1971, the legislature enacted § 163.575(1)(b) as part of its revisions to the Oregon Criminal Code. *See* 1971 Or. Laws ch. 743 § 177. The commentary to those revisions reflects that the child endangerment statute was a catchall provision designed to "provide coverage for specific acts injurious to the welfare of minors not specifically prohibited elsewhere in the proposed Code[,]" and that the proposed revisions related to "conduct detrimental to the welfare of minors[.]"Oregon Criminal Law Revision Commission, *Proposed Oregon Criminal Code*, Final Draft and Rep., § 177 (1970) ("hereinafter Commentary"); *see also*, Statement of Roger Wallingford, Research Counsel for the Commission (April 3, 1970) (the endangering the welfare of a minor statute attempted to encompass crimes that had not been provided for elsewhere in the proposed code).

A broader interpretation of the word "permit" allows the statute to reach conduct that the legislature intended it to reach. Conducting an illegal marijuana grow in front of children, providing children with marijuana, smoking marijuana in front of children, and taking no steps to halt such activities are all

Here, the state responds to an argument in the defendant's brief. Again, notice that the state focuses its attention on its view of how the words of the statute should be read. The argument does not give airtime to defendant's argument.

Conclusion to the legislative history argument

Rules derived from the legislative history argument, which are then applied in the remainder of the paragraph

A statutory construction argument should not refer to facts from the client's case; a statutory construction argument should instead focus on what

continued on next page

the statute means. Here, the
state narrowly skirts that issue
by discussing general conduct
and unspecified children. The
text does not mention the
defendant or the specific
children at issue in this case.

"conduct detrimental to the welfare of children." Thus, the legislature intended to reach such conduct, and giving the word "permit" its dictionary definition of "to allow" or "make possible" is consistent with that intent.

Defendant's interpretation of the legislative history either misunderstands the phrase "particularized conduct" or ignores the background of that phrase. The Criminal Law Revision Commission explained that the 1971 revisions to the criminal code were intended to prohibit "particularized conduct":

This paragraph and the next
respond to arguments raised by
the defendant.

> Throughout the criminal code revision, the Commission has sought to articulate clear and concise statements of the substantive offenses, prohibiting particularized conduct and applying defined elements of culpability.

Commentary, at 178. In criminalizing "particularized conduct," the legislature was attempting to rectify the vagueness problem in former Oregon Revised Statutes § 167.210 (1969) (contributing to the delinquency of a minor) that caused this Court to declare that statute unconstitutional in *Hodges. See* Oregon Criminal Law Revision Commission, *Minutes, Apr. 3, 1970,* at 26 (1970). The legislature's efforts to "articulate clear and concise statements of the substantive offenses, prohibiting particularized conduct" were intended to preclude vagueness problems, not straitjacket the child endangerment statute.

Moreover, adopting defendant's proposed narrow reading of "permit" and, concurrently, his conclusion that "permit" must include a transfer of authority over the children or the property, will lead to absurd results. When a statute is still susceptible to two or more plausible meanings, a court will not adopt the meaning "that would lead to an absurd result that is inconsistent with the apparent policy of the legislation as a whole." *See State v. Vasquez-Rubio*, 917

Appellate courts are concerned
about the effect that a ruling in
one case will have on future
cases. Here, the state is pointing
out the negative consequences
of ruling in defendant's favor.

P.2d 494, 497 (Or. 1996). For example, if the defendant began selling marijuana in a public playground, under defendant's proposed reading, he would not be guilty of endangering the welfare of a child, because he did not "permit" the children to enter or remain in the playground. That is so because no one "transferred" to the defendant the "authority" over the playground or over the children who frequent it, and the defendant therefore would have no right to "exclude" the children from the playground. Yet, by conducting the unlawful drug sales there in the first place, the defendant's actions allowed or made possible the children's presence at the illegal activity. In other words, but for defendant's actions, the children would not be entering or remaining where drug dealing was occurring. It would be absurd in such a case to conclude that the defendant did not "permit" the children to enter or remain in the park because he had no legal right to "exclude" them from that location. The defendant would unquestionably be guilty of endangering the welfare of a minor.

Final conclusion to the
statutory construction
argument

In sum, nothing in the text, context, or history of § 163.575(1)(b) supports defendant's narrow reading of the statute. On the contrary, as explained above, the text, context, and legislative history demonstrate that the legislature intended the statute to be understood broadly, and that it would apply to persons who engage in conduct that allows or makes it possible for children to remain in a place where illegal drug activity is occurring. Thus, in enacting the child endangerment statute, the legislature intended to shield children from unlawful drug activities, and the actions of persons who expose them to such activities. "Permits" should be interpreted broadly to accomplish that aim.

B. Defendant violated Oregon Revised Statutes § 163.575(1)(b) because he made it possible for the children for whom he was caring to remain in a place where unlawful drug activity was occurring.

The jury had sufficient evidence to convict defendant of endangering the welfare of both minor children. After a jury has found a defendant guilty of a crime, a court reviews the conviction to determine whether the evidence was sufficient for a rational fact-finder to find the essential elements of the crime beyond a reasonable doubt. *State v. Cunningham*, 880 P.2d 431, 440 (Or. 1994); *see also Jackson v. Virginia*, 443 U.S. 307, 316 (1979). The evidence is viewed in the light most favorable to the state. *Cunningham*, 880 P.2d at 440. In reviewing the evidence, this Court does not determine whether it believes that the defendant was guilty beyond a reasonable doubt; rather, this Court simply considers whether the evidence was sufficient for the jury to so find. *Id.* Given that the legislature intended the term "permit" to encompass activity whereby an individual allows or makes it possible for a child to remain in the presence of unlawful drug activity, defendant's actions easily fall within the statute's prohibitions. As explained below, that is so for either of two independently sufficient reasons.

1. Defendant permitted the children to be in the presence of unlawful drug activity by repeatedly engaging in such activity in the children's presence.

First, a jury could reasonably find that defendant "permitted" children to "enter or remain in a place where unlawful activity involving controlled substances" was conducted because defendant engaged in illegal drug activity in the presence of the children. He actively participated in growing, harvesting, and selling marijuana in the house, knowing that the children were living there. He gave the children marijuana to smoke when they asked for it. He even admitted to smoking marijuana with the children on several occasions. By engaging in that conduct, defendant allowed and made possible—and thus "permitted"—the children to remain in a place where they were continuously exposed to defendant's own illegal activity. As a result, he endangered the welfare of the two children living in the home.

2. Defendant permitted the children to be in the presence of unlawful drug activity by agreeing to perform the role of their caretaker amid a drug operation.

Even if defendant had not participated in the illegal activity, his decision to act as a babysitter in a house in which he knew marijuana was being illegally grown was sufficient for a jury to find him guilty of endangering a child. By agreeing to take on the role of a "babysitter" amid an ongoing drug operation,

Compare the state's explanation of the standard or review with the defendant's. Notice how the state emphasizes the deference the court gives to the jury's decision. Since the state wants the jury decision to stand, it makes sense that the state and not the defendant would emphasize the limited role of the court.

The state wants to emphasize all the evidence that supports the convictions. Notice how the point headings help make that point.

The point headings expand the space allocated to the supporting evidence.

The point headings allow the initial conclusion to be repeated.

The point headings also suggest that the text that follows is substantial enough to be designated by its own point heading. Thus, the point headings add heft to each point made.

defendant allowed and made it possible for the children to remain in the house and be exposed to illegal activity. The reason Brenton asked defendant to "babysit" the children was because he did not want them to remain there unattended. By knowingly enabling the children's presence, defendant thus "permitted" the children to remain in a place where they would be continuously exposed to illegal drug activity. Defendant's behavior was well within the scope of conduct prohibited by § 163.575(1)(b).

C. Even under defendant's reading of the statute, he "permitted" the children to enter or remain in the house with the illegal drug activity.

Even if this Court adopts a narrow reading of the statute, defendant's argument still fails. Regardless of defendant's authority over the house or the children, defendant violated § 163.575(1)(b) because he actively enabled their presence in a place where they were exposed to illegal drug activity. Contrary to defendant's claim, the state's evidence did establish that defendant had sufficient authority to prevent the children from remaining in the house and that defendant failed to exercise that authority. As explained below, that is true for any of three reasons.

First, defendant chose to act as a "babysitter" knowing full well that the marijuana was being illegally grown in the house. Once defendant agreed to be the children's "babysitter," he accepted responsibility to keep them safe. Just as defendant's "babysitter" status provided him with the authority to remove the children from any other dangerous situation such as a house fire or a burglary — it provided him with the necessary minimum authority to remove them from the dangerous illegal drug operation.

Second, even assuming he was not authorized to physically remove the children from the home himself, he certainly had the authority — and given his role has the children's caretaker, the obligation — to take steps to protect the children and prevent their continued presence there. For example, he could have called the police to put a stop to the situation. Instead, he gave the children marijuana to smoke when they asked for it and even joined them in smoking the illegal substance. He had the authority and responsibility to end the situation, and by failing to do so, defendant "permitted" the children to remain amidst the drug activity.

Third, defendant deliberately and repeatedly engaged in illegal drug activity in the children's presence in their home. Defendant grew, harvested, and sold marijuana in a home where the children lived. It is beside the point whether defendant could "exclude" the children. He had the authority to stop his own illegal conduct — the conduct that exposed the children to illicit drugs. Defendant's contention that he lacked the requisite authority to stop his own illegal activities is nonsensical.

In sum, the evidence in this case was sufficient to establish that defendant had the authority to stop the children from remaining in the house and that he failed to exercise that authority. Accordingly, even under defendant's reading of the statute, the evidence was sufficient to establish that defendant violated

The arguments in section C are all rule-based arguments. The state wants to show that even if the court adopts defendant's proposed construction of the statute, the evidence was still sufficient to convict the defendant.

Under defendant's proposed construction of the statute, a person must have authority to deny permission before being guilty of permitting something. The state takes that rule and applies it to the facts of this case. Notice how the state connects the word "authority" to the facts in this case to make its point.

§ 163.575(1)(b). The trial court therefore correctly denied defendant's judgment of acquittal.

CONCLUSION

This Court should affirm the trial court's judgment.

Respectfully submitted,
VIVIAN L. KEARA
Attorney General
ANIYA P. LINDSIE
Solicitor General

ESigned
By Jennifer Schwarz at 3:57 pm, Jan 5 2017

JENNIFER SCHWARZ #500187
Assistant Attorney General
Jen.schwarz@doj.state.or.us

Attorneys for Plaintiff-Respondent
State of Oregon

NOTICE OF FILING AND PROOF OF SERVICE

I certify that on January 5, 2017, I directed the original Respondent's Answering Brief to be electronically filed with the Appellate Court Administrator, Appellate Records Section, by using the court's electronic filing system.

I further certify that, upon receipt of the confirmation email stating that the document has been accepted by the eFiling system, this Respondent's Answering Brief will be eServed pursuant to Oregon Rule of Appellate Procedure 16.45 on Ken Nakano, #870467, and Vijay Grewal, #974573, attorneys for Defendant-Appellant.

ESigned
By Jennifer Schwarz at 3:57 pm, Jan 5 2017

Jennifer Schwarz #500187
Assistant Attorney General
Jen.schwarz@doj.state.or.us

Attorney for Plaintiff-Respondent
State of Oregon

Certificate of Compliance with ORAP 5.05(2)(d)

I certify that (1) this brief complies with the word-count limitation in ORAP 5.05(2)(b) and (2) the word-count of this brief (as described in ORAP 5.05(2)(a)) is 4,899 words. I further certify that the size of the type in this brief is not smaller than 14 point for both the text of the brief and footnotes as required by ORAP 5.05(4)(f).

> ESigned
> By Jennifer Schwarz at 3:57 pm, Jan 5 2017

JENNIFER SCHWARZ #500187
Assistant Attorney General
Jen.schwarz @doj.state.or.us

Attorney for Plaintiff-Respondent
State of Oregon

Appendix D

Moot Court Competitions

Many students have the opportunity to participate in moot court competitions during law school. A moot court competition is a simulated oral argument. Usually, students have prepared a brief for a hypothetical appellate case. Then, local attorneys and judges participate by acting as appellate judges, asking the students about the case.

Some schools require a moot court experience, while others do not. In addition, many schools have intramural competitions, and various organizations sponsor regional, national, or even international competitions. Competing in moot court allows you an opportunity to practice important skills, including how to really get to know your case, how to stand up in front of attorneys and judges and present your case, and how to answer questions when you are on the "hot seat."

Although moot court competitions simulate the appellate oral argument experience and allow you to practice many of the skills you will need if you become a trial or appellate attorney, the competitions differ in important ways from oral arguments in the "real world." This appendix addresses those differences and how they affect your argument in moot court.

The first major difference between appellate court oral arguments and moot court oral arguments is the audience. Although you may have real appellate judges as the "judges" in your moot court competition, more likely than not, at least some of the judges will be non-judge attorneys or even law students. Usually those attorneys, and certainly the law students, are not appellate specialists, so they may not be familiar with oral arguments in real appellate courts. Accordingly, you should not expect the judges to be experts in appellate practice.

A second difference is that the judges, in most cases, are not as well-prepared for argument and are not as familiar with your case. The judges may not have read your brief but, rather, may have been presented with a bench memorandum or bench brief that summarizes your case and the arguments on either side. And, because they are volunteering their time on a weekend or after a busy day at the office, many lawyers and judges will not have had time to carefully review the provided materials.

Accordingly, you will prepare for a moot court competition differently than you would for an actual oral argument. For example, because the judges will not, in most cases, have read your brief, you will not seek to complement the brief you have written. Instead, you should prepare a self-contained oral presentation on the assumption that the judges are not as familiar with your case as real judges would be. Thus, although the discussion in §11.2, *Preparing for Oral Argument*, generally applies in the moot court context, the judges will likely need more background to understand your arguments.

A third difference is that the judges and competitors in a moot court competition have different goals than do the advocates and decision makers in a real case. In a real case, the judges seek to reach the "right" result in a real dispute, and each advocate seeks to persuade the judges to rule in her favor. In a moot court competition, the judges seek to test the competitors' knowledge of the record and the law, the ability to present orally, and the ability to answer questions. In short, the judges are looking for the best performance, not trying to resolve the legal question before them.

Accordingly, performance may become more important than substance, and you should practice presenting the material in as smooth a manner as possible. For example, students who win moot court competitions sometimes bring no notes with them to the lectern. We have seen law students prevail in a moot court round despite a weaker grasp of the law and record simply because they presented like professional actors playing attorneys. Thus, polish counts.

A fourth difference is that, in most moot court competitions, competitors argue both "on-brief" and "off-brief." That is, although they have briefed only one side of the case, they argue both sides in different rounds. While it is always helpful to prepare by carefully considering your opponent's arguments, in real life of course, the attorneys do not actually argue their opponents' side of the case.

Finally, be aware of two moot court conventions. First, in moot court competitions, the convention is to ask the judges, "Would you like a recitation of the facts?" As mentioned in §11.4, *Trial Courts vs. Appellate Courts*, in most appellate courts, the judges have read the briefs and are familiar with the facts. They will ask you if they have questions. Nonetheless, in moot court, participants traditionally ask that question. Check to see whether, in your moot court setting, you should ask the court if it would like such a recitation.

The second convention is that moot court judges often expect you to use all the time allotted and are surprised if you do not. Given the differences between the purpose of a moot court competition and a real appellate argument, that difference may make sense. Because the judges in a moot court competition seek to rate you on your performance, they expect you to use every last second to show them what a good performer you are. Ending early would be like a competitive figure skater ending her routine early because she believed that she had covered all the moves that were necessary. So, in preparing for a moot court competition, plan to use all your time.

In conclusion, although moot courts differ from appellate arguments in the real world, competing in moot court allows you an opportunity to develop and practice important lawyering skills. Consider competing in moot court during your law school career.

Index